Guidelines for MICROSOFT® Office 2016

Anita Verno • Jan Marrelli • Nancy Muir

PARADIGM
EDUCATION SOLUTIONS

St. Paul

Senior Vice President: Linda Hein
Editor in Chief: Christine Hurney
Senior Editor: Cheryl Drivdahl
Assistant Developmental Editors: Mamie Clark, Katie Werdick
Contributing Writer: Janet Blum
Testers: Pat Jarvis, Jeff Johnson, Barbara J. Shapiro
Director of Production: Timothy W. Larson
Production Editor: Elizabeth Mathews
Cover Designer: Jaana Bykonich
Text Designer and Senior Design and Production Specialist: Valerie King
Proofreader: Margaret Trejo
Indexer: Ina Gravitz
Vice President Information Technology: Chuck Bratton
Digital Projects Manager: Tom Modl
Vice President Sales and Marketing: Scott Burns
Director of Marketing: Lara Weber McLellan

Care has been taken to verify the accuracy of information presented in this book. However, the authors, editors, and publisher cannot accept responsibility for Web, e-mail, newsgroup, or chat room subject matter or content, or for consequences from application of the information in this book, and make no warranty, expressed or implied, with respect to its content.

Trademarks: Microsoft is a trademark or registered trademark of Microsoft Corporation in the United States and/or other countries. Some of the product names and company names included in this book have been used for identification purposes only and may be trademarks or registered trade names of their respective manufacturers and sellers. The authors, editors, and publisher disclaim any affiliation, association, or connection with, or sponsorship or endorsement by, such owners.

Photo Credits: Cover Dahabian/Shutterstock.com; **1** aremafoto/Shutterstock.com; **2** Rawpixel.com/Shutterstock.com; **4** ASUSTek Computer Inc.; **5** Courtesy of Samsung (tablet); **5** Thep Urai/Shutterstock.com (router); **6** Courtesy of Samsung (touchscreen); **6** Courtesy of Intel Corporation (operating system); **77** Squaredpixels/istock.com; **195** Andriy Popov/123RF.com; **309** kadmy/Shutterstock; **369** VladKol/Shutterstock.com; **407** US Food and Drug Administration (video); **407** Cinnamon Vogue (cinnamon sticks); screen caps of Microsoft products are used with permission from Microsoft.

We have made every effort to trace the ownership of all copyrighted material and to secure permission from copyright holders. In the event of any question arising as to the use of any material, we will be pleased to make the necessary corrections in future printings. Thanks are due to the aforementioned authors, publishers, and agents for permission to use the materials indicated.

ISBN 978-0-76386-748-5 (print)
ISBN 978-0-76386-749-2 (digital)

© 2017 by Paradigm Publishing, Inc.
875 Montreal Way
St. Paul, MN 55102
Email: educate@emcp.com
Website: www.ParadigmPublishing.com

Printed in the United States of America

25 24 23 22 21 20 19 18 17 16   1 2 3 4 5 6 7 8 9 10

Contents

Preface

Learning how to use software should be a simple, straightforward, and intuitive experience—right? We think so too, and that's why we developed *Guidelines for Microsoft® Office.*

We listened to what students and instructors were saying about how they wanted to learn and teach the Office suite of applications. What we heard time and again was that people wanted an easy-to-understand book about Office basics that they could use without feeling overwhelmed.

The first edition of this book was the result. In this third edition, *Guidelines for Microsoft® Office 2016*, we apply those basics to the newest version of the Office suite. As in the earlier editions, you will find a step-by-step, visual approach that will help you quickly learn the key features of the Office applications, building knowledge in a logical and easy-to-follow way. For every skill, you will have the opportunity to work through the steps in an interactive tutorial. Structured end-of-chapter and end-of-unit exercises and assessments will help reinforce what you have learned and assess how well you can apply your new skills to realistic work and school situations. As you work through the skills, exercises, and assessments in each chapter, you will gain confidence and proficiency.

Clear and Simple Learning

Guidelines 2016 offers a simple path to mastering the basics of Office 2016. This path is designed with you in mind and created to support you in a number of ways. First, you prepare to succeed in the course by learning essential computer hardware and software concepts, downloading the student data files and setting up working folders for this course, and exploring how to use Outlook to manage your time. Next, you learn how to use important Office features that you will encounter frequently when working in the major Office applications.

In the Word, Excel, Access, and PowerPoint units, you focus on completing tasks using the ribbon, which displays tools and commands organized into tabs and groups based on common tasks. In addition, you find out about keyboard shortcuts and other ways to get things done. A new element for this edition is Use Your Touchscreen, which gives suggestions for accomplishing certain steps using a touch device. By the time you complete this book, you will be familiar with all the basic tools the ribbon offers and understand the advantages of shortcuts and other alternative methods of accomplishing tasks.

Throughout the book, you will find helpful information that expands on the basic background and steps provided for each skill. Tips in the margin offer a variety of support, ranging from explanations of how your screen might differ from the ones shown in the book, to how you might use related commands to accomplish additional tasks. Taking It Further boxes introduce related Office features and encourage you to explore them on your own.

Each chapter begins with an overview of the features presented in the chapter. Read the list of skills to preview what you will accomplish as you work through the chapter. Also read the list of student data files you will need, and look at the images of the final files you will produce.

Before you begin each skill, read the introductory paragraphs to gain an understanding of the features highlighted in that skill. Each skill is presented in a two- or four-page layout with steps on the left page and screenshots on the right page. In the screenshots, callouts showing you where to click are numbered to match the steps. By reading the steps and studying the screenshots, you can easily complete every task covered in this book. When you have finished a skill, compare your file against the Completed Skill Preview image showing you what the file should look like.

Interesting Step-by-Step Application

The units of this book that address the main Office programs (Word, Excel, Access, and PowerPoint) follow an engaging scenario involving an online periodical called *Guidelines for Healthy Living Magazine*. This scenario offers you the opportunity to complete tasks related to writing feature articles, preparing fact sheets, creating budgets, planning advertising campaigns, and more.

Each file created in this scenario has a goal—to communicate, to educate, to manage, or to entertain. When you reach the end of a chapter, you will have created useful materials and learned Office features and skills along the way.

Course Features

The following guide shows how this textbook and its digital resources use a guided, step-by-step, competency-based approach to teach the basic skills you need to use Microsoft Office 2016 successfully in business, home, and academic settings.

 SNAP Resources
SNAP icons in the margins of the textbook are accompanied by blue text listing exercises and assessments that are available in SNAP. If you are a SNAP user, go to your SNAP Assignments page to complete the activities.

Interactive Student Resources
Violet icons in the margins of the textbook indicate interactive resources that are available through the links menu in your ebook and, in some cases, in SNAP.

Precheck quizzes test your knowledge of the chapter content before you study the material. Use the results to help focus your study on the skills you need to learn. *SNAP users should go to their SNAP Assignments page to complete these quizzes.*

Tutorials guide you through the steps for the skills and then allow you to practice on your own. These interactive tutorials include simple instructions and optional help. *SNAP users should go to their SNAP Assignments page to complete these tutorials.*

 Student data files are needed to complete many of the skills, activities, and assessments in this book. In Unit 1, Chapter 2, you will learn how to download these files to a storage medium, create working folders, and use the files and folders with the course assignments. In the *Workbook* ebook, you can download individual data files for each exercise that requires them.

Preview images show how your file should look when you have completed each chapter, skill, review exercise, or assessment. You may preview, download, or print these images from your ebook.

 Recheck quizzes at the end of each chapter enable you to recheck your understanding of the chapter content. You may recheck your understanding at any time and as many times as you wish. *SNAP users should go to their SNAP Assignments page to complete these quizzes.*

 The ***Workbook*** ebook provides study resources (such as presentations with audio support, Study Notes, and Tips & Hints), review exercises, and assessments to help reinforce your understanding of the concepts, features, and skills covered in the textbook.

Textbook Elements

Clear and concise text and screen captures teach essential concepts, features, and skills in an easy-to-understand format.

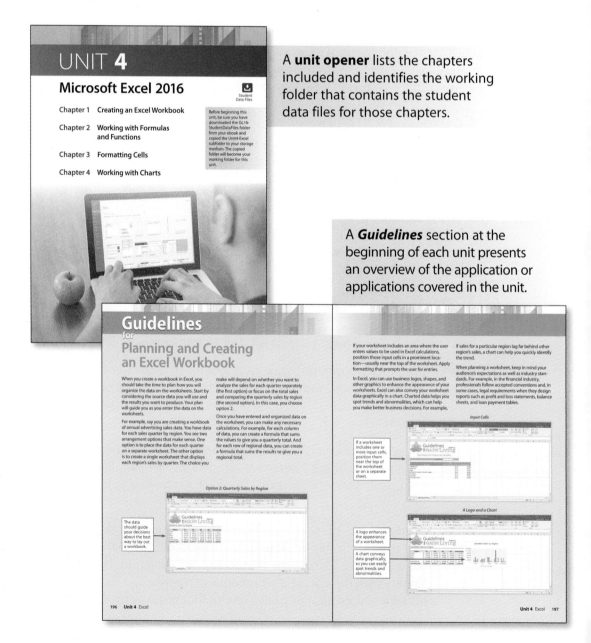

A **unit opener** lists the chapters included and identifies the working folder that contains the student data files for those chapters.

A ***Guidelines*** section at the beginning of each unit presents an overview of the application or applications covered in the unit.

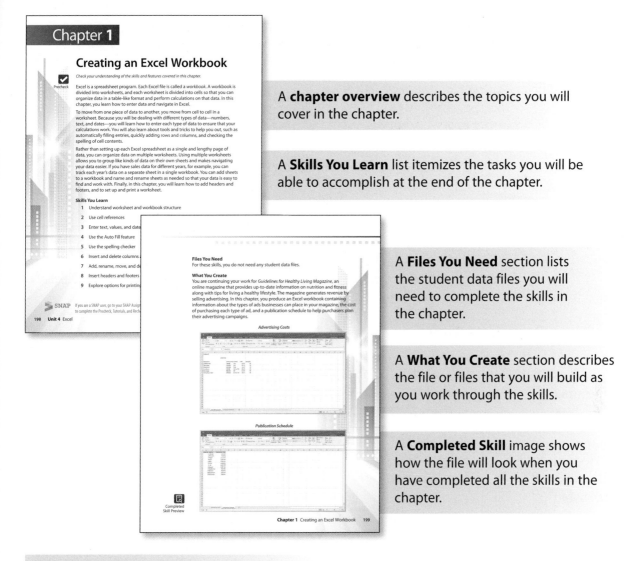

A **chapter overview** describes the topics you will cover in the chapter.

A **Skills You Learn** list itemizes the tasks you will be able to accomplish at the end of the chapter.

A **Files You Need** section lists the student data files you will need to complete the skills in the chapter.

A **What You Create** section describes the file or files that you will build as you work through the skills.

A **Completed Skill** image shows how the file will look when you have completed all the skills in the chapter.

Use Your Touchscreen features describe how to accomplish certain steps using a touch device.

Numbered steps and screen captures provide instant reinforcement to help you learn each skill quickly and easily.

A **skill introduction** describes the features and tasks you will explore in the skill.

Tips offer hints and troubleshooting advice.

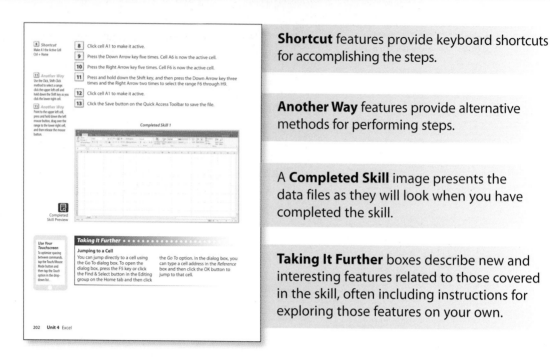

Shortcut features provide keyboard shortcuts for accomplishing the steps.

Another Way features provide alternative methods for performing steps.

A **Completed Skill** image presents the data files as they will look when you have completed the skill.

Taking It Further boxes describe new and interesting features related to those covered in the skill, often including instructions for exploring those features on your own.

A **Tasks Summary** lists the key tasks covered in the chapter, along with the ribbon commands used to initiate them as well as shortcuts and alternative ways to perform them.

Workbook eBook Elements

You can access the *Workbook* ebook through the links menu in your ebook. The *Workbook* ebook provides a variety of materials you can use to check your understanding of the concepts and features covered in the textbook. Complete the *Workbook* activities to demonstrate your ability to apply the skills taught. The following elements are offered in the *Workbook* ebook and, in some cases, in SNAP.

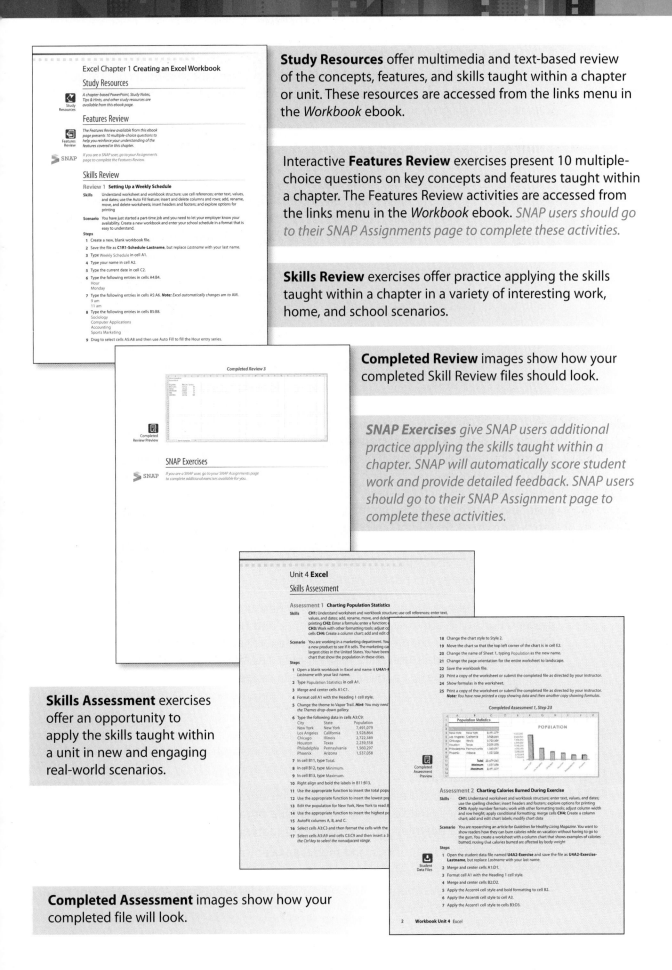

Study Resources offer multimedia and text-based review of the concepts, features, and skills taught within a chapter or unit. These resources are accessed from the links menu in the *Workbook* ebook.

Interactive **Features Review** exercises present 10 multiple-choice questions on key concepts and features taught within a chapter. The Features Review activities are accessed from the links menu in the *Workbook* ebook. *SNAP users should go to their SNAP Assignments page to complete these activities.*

Skills Review exercises offer practice applying the skills taught within a chapter in a variety of interesting work, home, and school scenarios.

Completed Review images show how your completed Skill Review files should look.

SNAP Exercises give SNAP users additional practice applying the skills taught within a chapter. SNAP will automatically score student work and provide detailed feedback. SNAP users should go to their SNAP Assignment page to complete these activities.

Skills Assessment exercises offer an opportunity to apply the skills taught within a unit in new and engaging real-world scenarios.

Completed Assessment images show how your completed file will look.

Course Components

The *Guidelines for Microsoft© Office 2016* textbook contains the essential content you will need to master the features and skills covered. Additional resources are provided by the following digital components.

SNAP Web-Based Training and Assessment for Microsoft® Office 2016

SNAP is a web-based training and assessment program and learning management system (LMS) for Microsoft Office 2016. SNAP offers rich content, a sophisticated grade book, and robust scheduling and analytics tools. SNAP courseware supports the Guidelines 2016 content and delivers live-in-the-application exercises and projects for students to demonstrate their mastery of skills. Interactive tutorials increase skills-focused moments with guided training and measured practice. SNAP includes a quiz and exam for each chapter, plus an item bank that can be used to create custom assessments. SNAP provides automatic scoring and detailed feedback on the program's many exercises and assessments to help identify areas where additional support is needed, evaluating student performance at both the individual level and the course level. The Guidelines 2016 SNAP course content is also available to export into any LMS system that supports LTI tools.

Paradigm Education Solutions provides technical support for SNAP through 24-7 chat at ParadigmCollege.com. In addition, an online user guide and other training tools for SNAP are available.

Student eBook and *Workbook* eBook

The student ebook and *Workbook* ebook provide access to the *Guidelines 2016* content from any type of computing device (desktop, tablet, or smartphone), anywhere, through a live Internet connection. The versatile ebook platform features dynamic navigation tools including a linked table of contents and the ability to jump to specific pages, search for terms, bookmark, highlight, and take notes. The ebooks offer live links to the interactive content and resources that support the printed textbook, including the student data files. The student ebook includes links to the interactive Precheck and Recheck quizzes, interactive tutorials, and related *Workbook* pages.

The *Workbook* ebook includes access to Study Resources such as chapter-based presentations with audio support, Study Notes, and Tips & Hints. It also provides access to interactive end-of-chapter Features Review exercises, to end-of-chapter Skills Review exercises, and to end-of-unit Skills Assessments. The *Workbook* ebook is accessed through the links menu on the last page of each chapter in the student ebook. It may also be accessed online at Paradigm.bookshelf.emcp.com or from your SNAP course.

SNAP users should go to their SNAP Assignments page to complete the interactive quizzes, tutorials, and exercises.

Instructor eResources

All instructor resources are available digitally through a web-based ebook online at Paradigm.bookshelf.emcp.com. The materials are organized by type and can be previewed from the ebook or downloaded. The instructor materials include the following items:

- Answer keys, grading rubrics, and model answer for evaluating responses to chapter skills, review exercises, and assessments
- Supplemental assessments that can be assigned for additional work on the four major applications (Word, Excel, Access, and PowerPoint)

- Lesson blueprints with teaching hints
- Discussion questions
- Syllabus suggestions and course planning resources
- Chapter-based PowerPoint presentations with lecture notes
- Chapter-based quizzes and exams

Acknowledgments

Letty Barnes
Lake Washington Institute of Technology
Kirkland, WA

Cheryl Brown
Delgado Community College
New Orleans, LA

Lucy Carroll
Kilgore College
Longview, TX

Geraldlyn Johnson
Delgado Community College
New Orleans, LA

Linda Lambert
Heartland Community College
Normal, IL

Mary McMahon
Heartland Community College
Normal, IL

Annette D. Rakowski
Bergen Community College
Paramus, NJ

June Scott
County College of Morris
Randolph, NJ

Maureen Shockley
Salem Community College
Carney's Point, NJ

Troycia Webb
Albany Technical College
Albany, GA

Tom Willingham
Big Bend Community College
Moses Lake, WA

UNIT **1**

Your Digital Toolkit

In Chapter 2 of this unit, you will learn how to download the GL16-StudentDataFiles folder from your ebook and copy the Unit1-Digital Toolkit subfolder to your storage medium. The copied folder will become your working folder for Chapter 2. You will not need any data files for Chapters 1 and 3.

Chapter 1

Computing Essentials

Precheck

Check your understanding of the skills and features covered in this chapter.

This chapter provides a brief overview of fundamental computing concepts, including the components of a computer system, the methods computers use to process data, the elements of a computer network, and the two major types of software. It also explains how to adapt the instructions in the textbook if you have a touchscreen.

Step-by-step activities are not included with these concepts. Instead, you are encouraged to explore your own computer system to identify the hardware and software components described in this unit. Doing so will help you understand the amazing capabilities of the computing devices you work with every day.

A computer system is made up of a central processing unit and any attached equipment, or *hardware*. A set of instructions, called *software*, tells the computer what to do. The computer hardware and software work together to turn data into information through a process called the *information processing cycle*. All computing devices including desktop computers, *mobile computers* (smartphones, tablets, laptops, e-readers, gaming devices), and microcontrollers (computers embedded inside consumer products such as microwaves) use a basic information processing cycle, which follows these steps:

1. The user enters data using an *input device* such as a keyboard or touchscreen.

2. The *central processing unit (CPU)* processes the data into information and stores it in the internal memory.

3. Information is sent to the computer screen or another *output device* such as a printer.

4. Information is stored on a storage medium such as a OneDrive account or other account on a cloud server, a USB flash drive, or a hard disk.

Computer System Hardware

The illustration below shows a typical laptop computer system with the hardware responsible for carrying out the four parts of the information processing cycle.

Input devices. You use hardware items, such as a keyboard, mouse, touchscreen, microphone, and web cam, to enter commands and data into your computer.

Processing component. The CPU performs the mathematical operations and coordinates the functions of the computer system. In a desktop or mobile computer, the CPU is typically a microprocessor. It is located on the motherboard, the main circuit board of the computer. The CPU consists of the *arithmetic control unit (ALU)*, which performs arithmetic and logic operations, and the *control unit (CU)*, which directs the operations of the processor.

Output devices. The job of output devices is to convert information from your computer into a usable form including visual (printout, monitor), sound (speakers), and digital (hard drive, CD/DVD drive) forms.

Storage devices. You use a *storage device* for saving data that you want to use again. Storage media, ranging from your computer hard drive to removable storage such as a USB flash drive, vary in the amount of data they can store. *Cloud storage*, such as OneDrive, has become a popular option because you can access the data from any device with an active Internet connection.

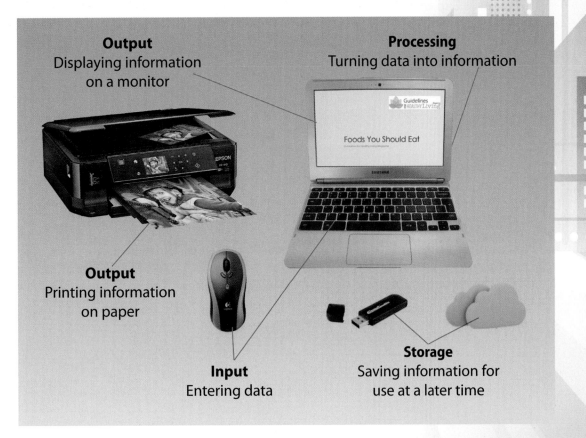

Output
Displaying information
on a monitor

Processing
Turning data into information

Output
Printing information
on paper

Input
Entering data

Storage
Saving information for
use at a later time

The Motherboard

The main circuit board in a computer is called the *motherboard* and its importance in the system deserves special attention. The motherboard is a thin sheet of fiberglass or other material with electrical pathways that connect these key components of the information processing cycle:

- microprocessor/CPU
- memory chips
- expansion slots for holding expansion cards

The illustration below shows these motherboard components, along with other necessary elements, including a power supply and ports for "plugging in" external hardware, such as a keyboard, mouse, and USB flash drive.

Microprocessor. The CPU of your computer is a *microprocessor* or *processor* located on the motherboard. It is a thin wafer or chip containing an integrated circuit that processes your requests. Today, most processors are dual-core or multi-core, containing two or more independent processing units or cores.

Memory. Your computer has two kinds of *memory*, which are located on tiny silicon chips etched with electrical circuits: (1) permanent memory, called *read only memory (ROM),* which contains start-up instructions and other permanent instructions; (2) temporary memory, called *random access memory (RAM)*, which holds data while your computer is on. When you close a program, restart, or turn off your computer, the RAM content is erased.

Expansion slots. You can use an *expansion slot* to add expansion cards to your motherboard to add capabilities such as increased processing power and enhanced video and audio.

memory module (RAM slots)   CPU slots

ports

expansion slots

A Computer Network

Computers can be linked together in a network. A *network* allows the computers to share files, software, and resources, such as a printer. Two key types of networks are local area networks (LANs), which connect nearby computers within a home or business, and wide area networks (WANs), which connect distant computers, such as those among a company's branch offices around the country. The Internet is the largest of all WANs. Devices that make up a basic network include the following:

Individual computing devices. You can connect various computing devices to each other and to the Internet via a network. Networks require a communications medium, such as a wireless signal or a cable.

Modem. A *modem* is the hardware that sends and receives data to or from a transmission source, such as a phone or cable line. Types of modems typically used in homes and small offices include cable, DSL, and satellite.

Network adapter. A *network adapter* enables your computer to connect to a wired or wireless network. Wired computers typically support Ethernet standards, and wireless computers support Wi-Fi standards. A network interface card (NIC) is one type of network adapter your computer can contain.

Wireless access point. *Wireless access points* and routers relay data among devices on a network. A wireless access point may be connected to a router or be part of the router.

Bluetooth. Your computing devices may use *Bluetooth* technology to communicate short distances without wires. Bluetooth can connect a hands-free headset, a wireless keyboard, and sync devices, such as your smartphone, with your computer.

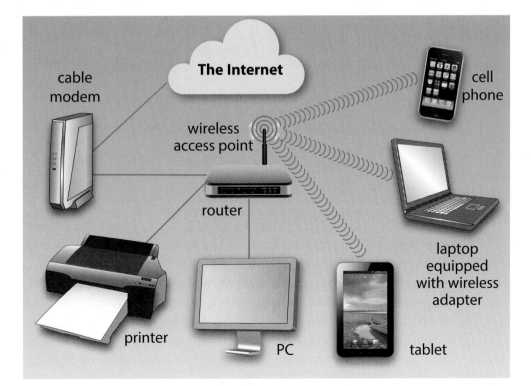

Software

Software is the set of instructions that tells your computer what to do. Your computer has two basic types of software: operating system and application software. Microsoft Windows, Apple OS X, and Linux are examples of operating systems. Word, Excel, PowerPoint, and the other programs in the Microsoft Office suite are examples of applications.

The most important piece of software used on a computer system is its *operating system (OS)*. When you turn on the computer, it performs a power-on self-test (POST) to check that the hardware is working properly. Then it loads the OS into memory. The OS performs several key functions:

- Manages the operations of the CPU and the computer's hardware devices
- Provides a user interface that allows a person to interact with the computer
- Supports operations initiated from within application programs, such as opening and closing programs and saving and printing documents

Operating System Software

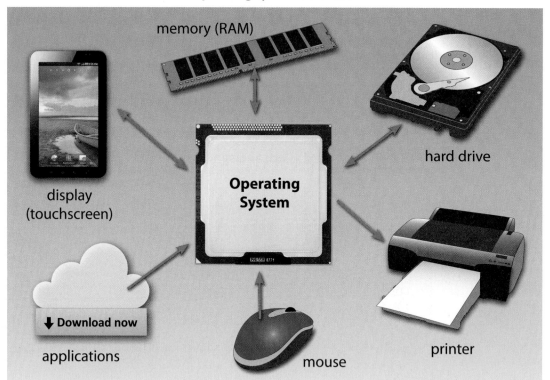

Application software is the name for the group of programs you use to get your computer-based projects done. Applications include spreadsheets that perform numeric calculations, word processors that create text-based documents, presentation software that creates slide shows, and database software that sorts and organizes huge amounts of data. Other types of computer applications include games, tax preparation, web design, desktop publishing, graphic editing, and audio and video applications. All of these applications enhance your experience using the computer and provide many tools for completing personal, academic, and work projects.

Application software can be purchased and downloaded from a manufacturer's website. Costs vary from free (freeware), to a limited evaluation period followed by a small fee (shareware), to a commercial license fee. Cloud-based subscription software, such as Microsoft Office 365, has become popular. Users pay a rental fee (typically monthly or annually) to use the software. This type of software is advantageous because users access the application from the cloud, making the application accessible from any computing device and reducing the demand on computer resources, such as hard drive space.

Some applications are designed to run on a particular computing device, such as a gaming device. Other applications are designed to run on a specific operating system. For example, Microsoft Office for Mac is a version of the Office suite that runs on the Mac OS.

Application Software

There are also an endless number of small applications called *apps* available for a variety of computing devices. An app is typically written to perform a specific single task, such as to display current headlines, find directions, or play a game. Many apps can be downloaded for free. The app below displays the weather for a particular city:

Touchscreen Gestures

The instructions in this textbook use the mouse-based interface to select commands. If you have a *touchscreen* (a screen that can be manipulated using your fingers or a stylus), you can easily adapt those instructions by becoming familiar with touchscreen terminology and understanding which touch gestures execute parallel mouse-based actions. Touch gestures include the following:

Tap. Tap the screen once. A *tap* is similar to a click with a mouse. It is used to select a command or button on the ribbon, such as the Copy button.

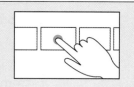

Press and hold. Press on the screen until a complete circle appears. Lifting the finger displays a shortcut menu. A *press and hold* is similar to a right-click with a mouse. It is used to select a shortcut menu.

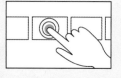

Pinch. Touch the screen with two or more fingers spread apart and move them toward one another. A *pinch* is similar to a zoom in with a mouse. It makes the text or image smaller.

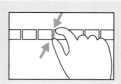

Stretch. Touch the screen with two or more fingers close together and then move the fingers apart. A *stretch* is similar to a zoom out with a mouse. It makes the text or image larger.

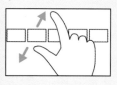

Rotate. Touch the screen with two or more fingers and then turn your hand. A *rotate* turns the text or image in the direction of your hand movement. It is used to turn a picture or other object on the screen in a clockwise or counterclockwise direction. Note: Not all items can be rotated.

Slide. Touch the screen and drag to the left, right, up, or down. A *slide* is like a scroll with a mouse.

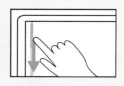

Move. Press an image or a text area and drag it from one part of the screen to another. A *move* positions an object in another location on the screen.

Swipe. Use a quick, short movement to swipe in from the edge of the screen. A *swipe* does different things on different areas of the screen, depending on the application you are in.

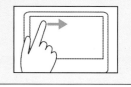

 Recheck your understanding of the skills and features covered in this chapter.
Recheck

 Chapter study resources are available in the Workbook *ebook.*
Workbook

Working with Student Data Files

Precheck

Check your understanding of the skills and features covered in this chapter.

To complete the skills in this book and the Skills Review exercises and Skills Assessments in the workbook (accessed from your ebook), you will need to download the student data files to a storage medium such as your OneDrive account or a USB flash drive.

OneDrive is a cloud storage system that is provided by Microsoft as part of the Windows 10 operating system. When you sign in to your computer with a Microsoft account, Windows automatically connects with the OneDrive server. This allows you to access your OneDrive files via File Explorer just like you access all your other files. The OneDrive folder in the Navigation pane of the File Explorer window makes it easy to access files you have saved to the cloud from your computer, and OneDrive can automatically *sync* your files so you always access to the most up-to-date version. However, the real advantage to using OneDrive is being able to access your files from any computing device that has Internet access. For example, if you save a file to OneDrive from your school computer, you can access that file from your home computer without having to email the file or use a portable storage device, such as a flash drive. You can also access your OneDrive files from the OneDrive website at https://onedrive.live.com.

Before starting this chapter, decide whether you will download the student data files to your OneDrive account or a USB flash drive. If you would like to use a different storage medium and need help, check with your instructor.

Skills You Learn

1   Download the student data files to your storage medium

2   Set up working folders for this course

3   Use the student data files with this course

Files You Need

For these skills, you need the following student data file:

   C2S3-GettingStarted

What You Create

In this chapter, you download the student data files for this course to your OneDrive account, USB flash drive, or other storage medium. You learn to use either OneDrive or a USB flash drive as a storage medium, and you create working folders that will be used to save the answer files you create as you work through the assignments in your textbook and workbook.

Skill 1 ## Download the Student Data Files to Your Storage Medium

To complete the assignments in your textbook and workbook, you must download the student data files from your ebook. All the student data files are bundled into one compressed file often referred to as a ZIP file. A *ZIP* file format compresses and then stores multiple files in a single container file with a .zip extension. When you extract the ZIP file, you will have all the files you need to complete the skills in the textbook and the review exercises and assessments in your workbook.

In this skill, you will use File Explorer to download the student data files, *navigate* (move) through a hierarchy of folders, and then extract the files to a folder on your storage medium.

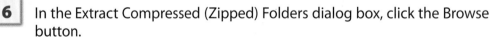

Tutorial

Student
Data Files

1 Open Microsoft Edge and go to your *Guidelines for Microsoft® Office 2016* ebook.

2 Navigate to this page in your ebook and then click the Student Data Files link in the links menu.

3 At the OneDrive page that opens, verify that the GL16-StudentDataFiles ZIP file is selected and the GL16-StudentDataFiles.zip button appears at the bottom of the page. If the button does not appear, click the Download button in the bar at the top of the page.

4 Click the GL16-StudentDataFile.zip button when the file has finished downloading, and then click the *Open* option in the pop-up list.

5 In File Explorer, click the Compressed Folder Tools Extract tab if necessary to make it active, and then click the Extract all button.

6 In the Extract Compressed (Zipped) Folders dialog box, click the Browse button.

7 In the Navigation pane of the Select a destination dialog box, click your storage medium.

8 Click the Select Folder button to return to the Extract Compressed (Zipped) Folders dialog box.

9 Click the Extract button in the dialog box. The files are extracted and copied to your OneDrive folder in a folder named GL16-StudentDataFiles.

10 Close one File Explorer window and the OneDrive browser window. Leave the remaining File Explorer window open for the next skill.

Taking It Further

Syncing Files with OneDrive

You can set your computer to make sure it is syncing all your files from OneDrive to your computer. On the Windows taskbar, click the Show hidden icons button and then right-click the OneDrive icon (📁).

Click the *Settings* option in the pop-up list, click the Choose folders button, click the *Sync all files and folders in my OneDrive* check box to insert a check mark, and then click the OK button.

Skill 2 Set Up Working Folders for This Course

You will be creating files and modifying student data files throughout this course. As you work, you will want to keep your files organized in folders on your storage medium. In Skill 1, you extracted the student data files to a folder named GL16-StudentDataFiles. Inside that folder you will find seven folders, one for each unit in the text-book. Each unit folder contains the student data files you will need to complete the assignments for that unit. In this skill, you will open each unit folder and create a new working folder within it. As you complete the assignments, you will save your answer files to the working folders.

Tutorial

▶**Tip** After Step 2, if necessary, browse to the location of the GL16-StudentDataFiles folder.

1 On the Windows taskbar, click the File Explorer button.

2 In the Navigation pane, double-click your storage medium.

3 In the file list pane, double-click the *GL16-StudentDataFiles* folder to display its contents.

4 In the file list pane, double-click the *Unit1-Toolkit* folder to display its contents.

5 On the Home tab, click the New folder button in the New group to create a new folder.

6 Type Unit1-Toolkit-Completed and then press Enter to replace the *New folder* highlighted folder name.

7 Click the Back button.

Taking It Further •

Understanding Sync Status

File Explorer displays symbols that let you know the sync status of the files and folders between your local computer and OneDrive. The symbol indicates the file or folder is in sync with the online version. The symbol indicates the file or folder is in the process of syncing. The symbol indicates the file or folder on your local computer is out of sync. To find out why files or folders are out of sync, you can click the OneDrive icon on the Windows taskbar and then click *View sync problems*.

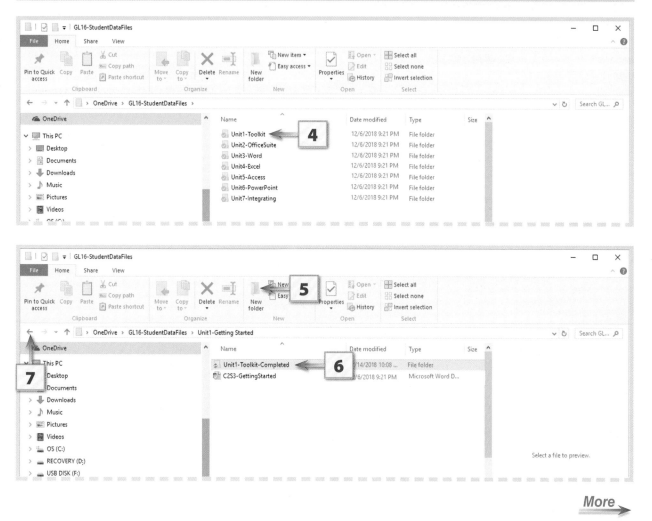

More

Chapter 2 Working with Student Data Files **13**

8 In the file list pane, double-click the *Unit2-OfficeSuite* folder to display its contents.

 9 *Another Way*
Right-click a blank area of the file list pane, click the *New* option in the pop-up list, and then click the *Folder* option in the second pop-up list.

9 Click the New Folder button.

10 Type Unit2-OfficeSuite-Completed and then press Enter to replace the highlighted folder name.

11 Repeat Steps 7–10 to open each of the five remaining unit folders and create five more working folders with the following names:
Unit3-Word-Completed
Unit4-Excel-Completed
Unit5-Access-Completed
Unit6-PowerPoint-Completed
Unit7-Integrating-Completed

12 Click the Close button to close the File Explorer window.

Completed Skill 2

▶**Tip** To expand a list item in the Navigation pane, point to the item and then click the right-pointing arrow that appears in front of it.

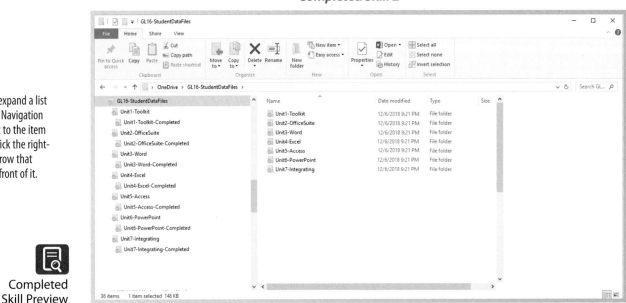

Completed
Skill Preview

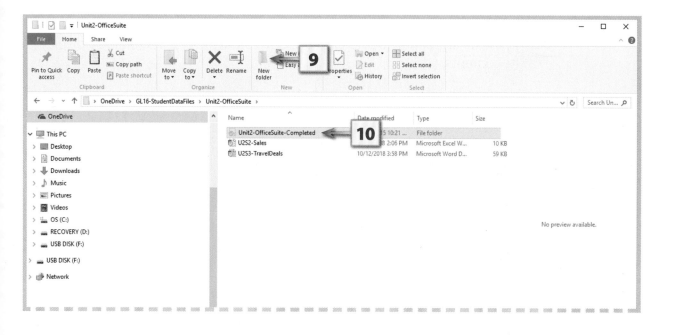

Taking It Further •

Navigating in File Explorer

The *Address bar* in File Explorer displays a bread-crumb trail or path to the current folder location. In the screen capture above, the path in the Address bar is *OneDrive > GL16StudentDataFiles > Unit2-OfficeSuite*. To move up a level (to *OneDrive* > *GL16StudentDataFile*), click the Up arrow. You can also navigate to another location by clicking that location in the Navigation pane; for example, in the screen capture above, click *USB DISK (F:)* to view the contents of the USB flash drive.

Skill 3   Use the Student Data Files with This Course

When you use your Microsoft account to sign in to Windows 10 on a computer connected to the Internet, Windows automatically connects to the OneDrive server so you can access your OneDrive files via File Explorer. File Explorer displays links to all available storage media, such as your OneDrive folder or USB flash drive.

In this skill, you will learn how to use File Explorer to access the student data files and working folders for this course on your storage medium. You will learn how to save files to your OneDrive account or other storage medium from the backstage area in the Office 2016 applications.

Tutorial

1   On the Windows taskbar, click the File Explorer button.

2   In the Navigation pane, click your storage medium to display its contents.

3   In the file list pane, double-click the *GL16-StudentDataFiles* folder to display its contents.

4   In the file list pane, double-click the *Unit1-Toolkit* folder to display its contents.

5   In the file list pane, double-click the *C2S3-GettingStarted* file to open it in Word. Read the file contents.

Taking It Further ●

Using the Preview and Details Views

In File Explorer, you are able to see a preview or details of a folder or file without actually opening it. On the View tab, click the Preview pane button in the Panes group and then click a file or folder to see its contents. Click the Details pane button to see a thumbnail plus key properties of the file. To hide the Preview or Details pane, click the View tab (the View ribbon collapses each time you click a button) and then click the Preview or Details button again.

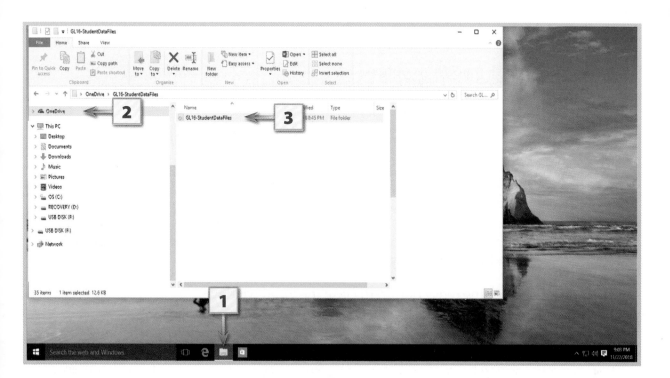

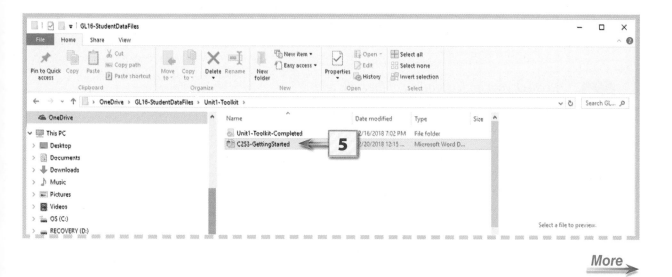

More →

6 Click the File tab.

7 Click the *Save As* option.

8 Click the *Browse* option.

▶ **Tip** In Step 7, you click the *Save As* option to save an open file under a different file name. Alternatively, you would click the *Save* option to save changes to an open file without changing its file name.

9 In the file list pane, double-click the *Unit1-Toolkit-Completed* folder.

10 In the Save As dialog box, click at the end of the text in the File name box to deselect the text and place the insertion point, and then type -Lastname, but replace Lastname with your last name.

11 Click the Save button to save the file as **C2S3-GettingStarted-Lastname** in your Unit 1 working folder and close the dialog box.

12 Click the Close button to close the Word window.

13 Click the Close button to close the File Explorer window.

Completed Skill 3

Completed
Skill Preview

Recheck your understanding of the skills and features covered in this chapter.

Recheck

Chapter study resources are available in the Workbook ebook.

Workbook

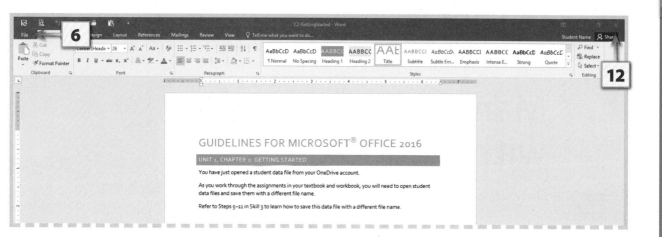

GUIDELINES FOR MICROSOFT® OFFICE 2016

UNIT 1, CHAPTER 2: GETTING STARTED

You have just opened a student data file from your OneDrive account.

As you work through the assignments in your textbook and workbook, you will need to open student data files and save them with a different file name.

Refer to Steps 5–11 in Skill 3 to learn how to save this data file with a different file name.

Chapter 3

Managing Your Time with Outlook

Precheck

Check your understanding of the skills and features covered in this chapter.

Developing good organizational and time management skills can help you succeed in both school and your career. *Personal information management software*, such as *Outlook*, can simplify the organization of personal and business activities and help you stay on top of things. Outlook contains tools for organizing appointments, managing email, and keeping track of people.

One aspect of managing time involves keeping an organized schedule. *Calendar* is an Outlook scheduling tool you can use to keep track of appointments, create reminders about events, and schedule meetings.

Knowing where to quickly find email addresses or phone numbers for personal and business contacts is also an essential organizational and time management skill. *People* is an Outlook tool for creating an electronic address book that stores contact information for the people and businesses with which you communicate. People is linked to your Outlook email address book, so you do not have enter contact information in more than one location.

You may have noticed that a Calendar app and a People app are installed with Windows 10. These apps are also designed to help you manage your time. However, the focus of this chapter is Outlook, which is part of the Microsoft Office 2016 suite.

Skills You Learn

1. Open Outlook and use Peeks
2. Display the Calendar
3. Schedule an appointment
4. Schedule a meeting
5. Add people
6. Search for people and appointments

Files You Need

For these skills, you do not need any student data files.

 SNAP *If you are a SNAP user, go to your SNAP Assignments page to complete the Precheck, Tutorials, and Recheck.*

What You Create

In this chapter, you use Outlook to organize personal, school, and career activities. You schedule an appointment and a meeting in the Outlook digital Calendar. You then send an electronic invitation asking others to attend a scheduled meeting. You also add personal and business contacts to the Outlook People list. Finally, you search Outlook to find schedule and contact information that is always at your fingertips.

A Scheduled Appointment

A Scheduled Meeting

A Business Card

Completed
Skill Preview

Skill 1 — Open Outlook and Use Peeks

Outlook contains four main views— Mail, Calendar, People, and Tasks. When you start Outlook, *Mail view* displays by default. Use the *Navigation bar* in the bottom left of the screen to switch to Calendar view. You can also use a feature called *Peeks* to view your Calendar, People, or Tasks without having to switch views.

Tutorial

▶**Tip** To open Outlook, type *outlook* in the search box on the Windows taskbar and then click *Outlook 2016 Desktop app* in the search results list.

▶**Tip** In Step 1, if you do not have an Outlook account, you will be prompted to set one up. If you are working on a public computer, such as the computer in your school lab, select the option to open Outlook without an email address.

▶**Tip** To pin Outlook 2016 to your Windows taskbar, with the Outlook 2016 desktop app open, right-click the Outlook icon on the taskbar and then click *Pin this program to taskbar*.

▶**Tip** When a peek is pinned within a view, it only displays in that view. For example, if you want to see the Calendar peek in both the Mail view and the People view, you will need to pin it in both views.

1 Open Outlook.

2 Hover over the Calendar button on the Navigation bar to peek at the Calendar.

3 Move the mouse pointer off the Calendar button to make the Calendar peek disappear.

4 Hover over the Calendar button again to reopen the Calendar peek.

5 Click the Dock the peek button to pin the Calendar peek to the right edge of the Outlook window.

6 Click the Remove the peek button to remove the Calendar peek.

7 Keep the Outlook Calendar open. You continue to work in Outlook in the next skill.

Taking It Further

Customizing the Look of Your Navigation Bar

By default, the Navigation bar displays buttons for four views: Mail, Calendar, People, and Tasks. The number of view buttons displayed and the order in which the buttons appear can be changed by clicking the ellipsis on the Navigation bar and then clicking *Navigation Options* in the pop-up list. In the Navigation Options dialog box, you can change how many buttons appear by changing the maximum number of visible items. To change the order in which the buttons appear, click the name of a button in the *Display in this order* box and then click the Move Up or Move Down button.

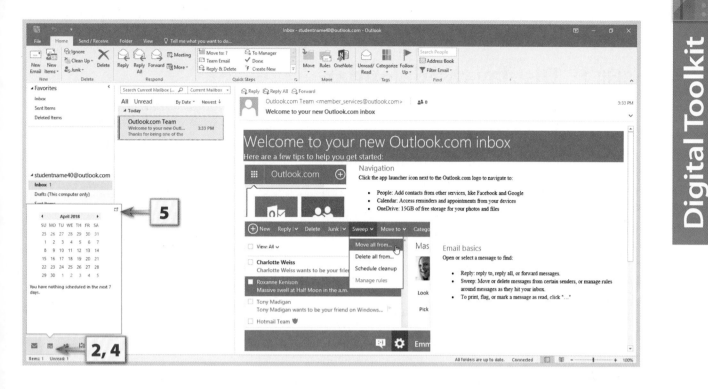

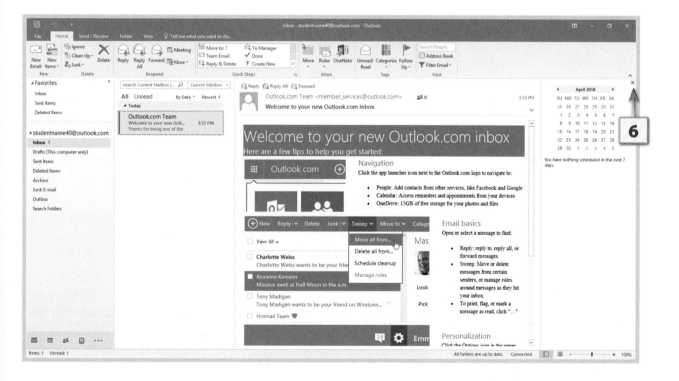

Your Digital Toolkit

Skill 2 Display the Calendar

You can display your calendar in a daily, weekly, or monthly view. You can navigate to different days using buttons on the Home tab or using the *Date Navigator*. While you are viewing your calendar, you are also able to view your local weather forecast on the *Weather bar*.

Tutorial

1 *Shortcut*

Display Calendar
Ctrl + 2

▶**Tip** To move forward or backward a day in Day view, or to move to the next or previous month in Month view, you can use the Forward and Back navigation buttons.

▶**Tip** If you do not see the Date Navigator in Step 5, click the Folder Pane Minimize/Maximize button.

▶**Tip** To add another city to the Weather bar, click the city name arrow (the *Washington, D.C.* arrow in the example shown), click the *Add Location* option in the drop-down list, type the name of the city, and then press Enter.

▶**Tip** Depending on the size of your monitor screen, you may need to minimize the Folder pane to see *Tomorrow* on the Weather bar.

1 With the Outlook open, click the Calendar button on the Navigation bar to display Calendar view.

2 On the Home tab, click the Day button in the Arrange group.

3 Click the Month button.

4 Click the Next 7 Days button in the Go To group.

5 In the Folder pane, click tomorrow's date in the Date Navigator.

6 Click the Today button in the Go To group to display your calendar for today.

7 Hover over *Today* on the Weather bar to display additional weather details.

8 Hover over *Tomorrow* on the Weather bar to display additional weather details.

9 Keep the Outlook Calendar open. You continue to work in Outlook in the next skill.

Taking It Further

Customizing the Look of Your Calendar

The View tab contains many options for customizing the look of your calendar. To change the background color, click the Color button in the Color group and then click a background color. You can change the time intervals shown in the Calendar by clicking the Time Scale button in the Arrangement group and clicking an interval in the drop-down list. You can also use the Time Scale button to change the time zone.

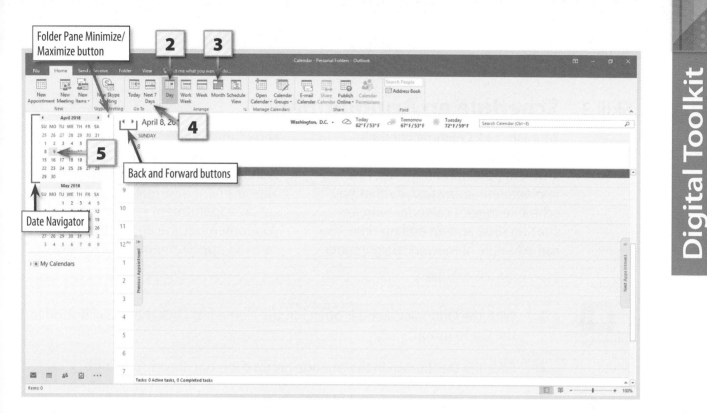

Digital Toolkit

Skill 3 Schedule an Appointment

Your Outlook Calendar can help keep you organized when you use it to schedule appointments. An *appointment* is any activity that you schedule in your calendar with a starting time and an ending time. You can schedule homework assignments and exams as appointments. If you specify an appointment location, it is shown in parentheses next to the appointment information. You can also set an appointment reminder to help you remember the appointment. You can add appointments in any view.

Tutorial

3 Shortcut
Create New Appointment
Ctrl + N

1 With the Outlook Calendar open, on the Home tab, click the Today button in the Go To group.

2 Click the Day button in the Arrange group if it is not already selected.

3 Click the New Appointment button in the New group.

4 Type Nutrition Seminar in the *Subject* box and then press the Tab key.

5 Type Board Room in the *Location* box.

▶**Tip** Click the *All day event* check box to insert a check mark if the activity lasts the entire day and does not have a start or end time, such as a vacation day.

6 Click the *Start time* arrow and then click the *9:00 AM* option in the drop-down list. (You may need to scroll to locate *9:00 AM* in the list.)

7 Click the *End time* arrow and then click the *10:30 AM (1.5 hours)* option in the drop-down list.

▶**Tip** Choose another date for *End time* in order to schedule a multiple-day appointment, such as a conference.

8 Click the *Reminder* arrow in the Options group.

9 Click the *1 day* option in the drop-down list.

10 Click the Save & Close button in the Actions group.

▶**Tip** In the Options group, use the Recurrence button to enter an appointment that occurs on a regular basis, such as daily, weekly, monthly, or yearly.

11 Keep the Outlook Calendar open. You continue to work in Outlook in the next skill.

Completed Skill 3

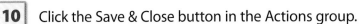

Completed Skill Preview

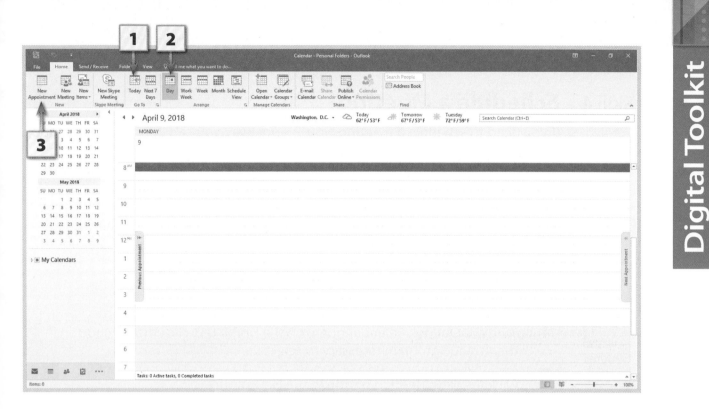

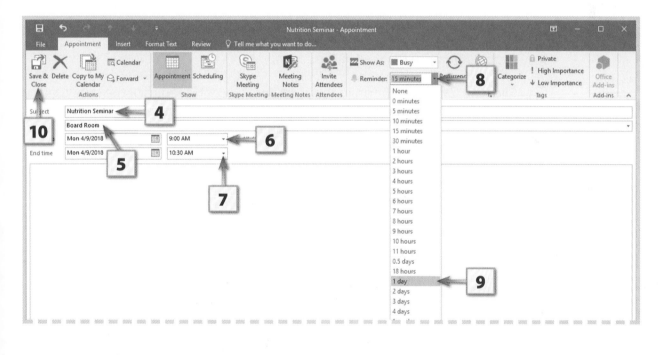

Taking It Further

Organizing Your Calendar

To help organize your school schedule, you can create appointments for project due dates and homework assignments. You may want to add reminders to these appointments to help you get your work finished on time. You can plan your course work by creating a multiple-day appointment to show which days you plan to work on a particular chapter, naming the appointment with the unit and chapter number—for example, *Unit 1, Chapter 2*.

Your Digital Toolkit

Skill 4   Schedule a Meeting

If you need to schedule a meeting, you can use Outlook Calendar to send out a meeting request. A *meeting request* is an appointment that is sent to other people and can include the location and other important information about the meeting, such as its topic and goals. Sending a meeting request is one way you can integrate the Outlook Calendar and Mail tools. Responses to your meeting requests appear in your email Inbox folder. Recipients can respond to a meeting request by adding the meeting to their Outlook Calendars or by declining the request.

Tutorial

Use Your Touchscreen

In Step 3, instead of pressing the Tab key, tap the Location box to place the insertion point.

1   With the Outlook Calendar open, on the Home tab, click the Day button in the Arrange group if necessary to select it.

2   Click the New Meeting button in the New group.

3   Press the Tab key, type May Issue Planning Meeting in the *Subject* box, and then press the Tab key again.

4   Type Conference Room A in the *Location* box.

5   Click the Calendar button in the *Start time* box and then click the date that is one week from today in the drop-down calendar. Notice that the date displayed in the *End time* box also changes.

6   Click the *Start time* arrow and then click the *1:00 PM* option in the drop-down list.

7   Click the *End time* arrow and then click the *3:00 PM (2 hours)* option in the drop-down list.

Taking It Further

Using Tasks

In Outlook, you can use the *Tasks* tool to create a To-Do list to keep track of tasks you need to complete. Your To-Do list can be set to remind you to complete the task and track your progress. You can also prioritize your tasks. To start creating a To-Do list, click the Tasks button in the Navigation bar and then, on the Home tab, click the New Task button in the New group. Type a name for the task in the *Subject* box, and set the start and due dates. You can also set the priority and a reminder. To always have your To-Do list visible, click the View tab, click the To-Do Bar button in the Layout group, and then click the *Tasks* option in the drop-down list.

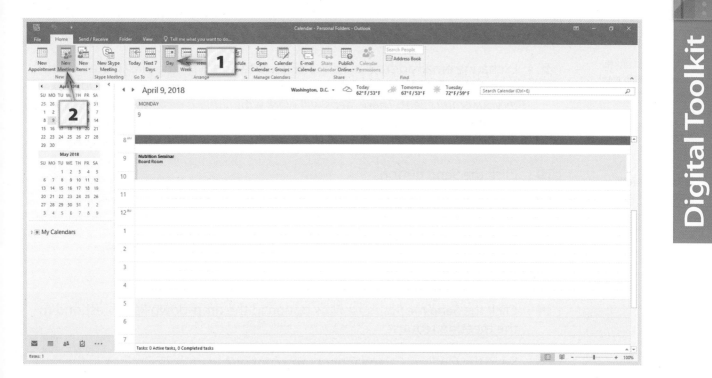

Tip You can click the *To* button to select email addresses from your Address Book.

Tip Separate email addresses with a comma (,) or semicolon (;) if you are inviting more than one person to the meeting.

8 Type Please bring your research notes. in the body of the meeting request.

9 Exchange email addresses with a classmate and type the classmate's email address in the *To* text box. **Note:** *For Steps 9–14, you must be using Outlook as your email client. These steps will work with either a desktop or web-based version of Outlook that has been configured for your personal use. If you are working in a classroom lab, ask the instructor how to proceed.*

10 Click the Send button.

11 Click the Mail button on the Navigation bar to check your email.

12 Double-click the new email you received from your classmate.

13 Click the Accept button arrow.

14 Click the *Send the Response Now* option in the drop-down list to respond to the meeting request.

15 Keep the Outlook Calendar open. You continue to work in Outlook in the next skill.

Completed Skill 4

Completed
Skill Preview

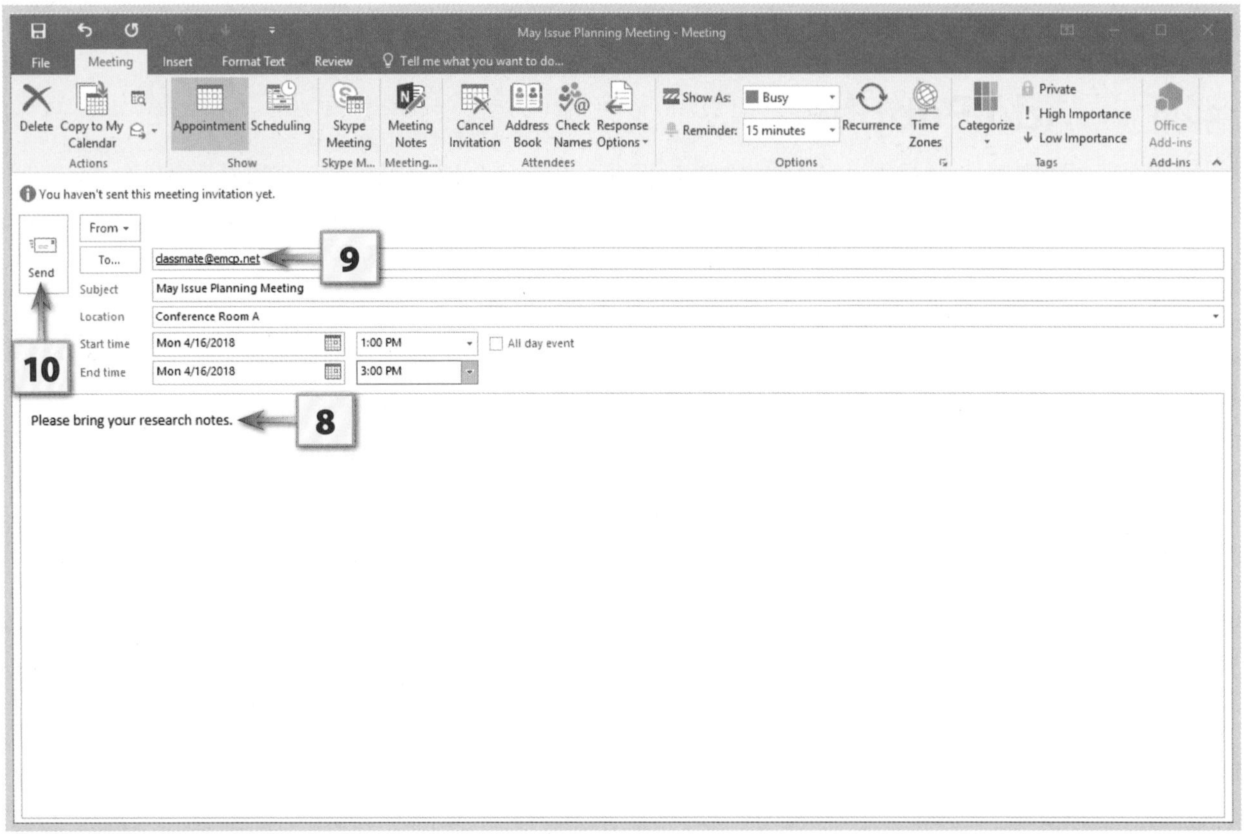
May Issue Planning Meeting - Meeting
File
Meeting
Insert
Format Text
Review
Tell me what you want to do...
Delete
Copy to My Calendar
Actions
Appointment
Scheduling
Show
Skype Meeting
Skype M...
Meeting Notes
Meeting...
Cancel Invitation
Address Book
Check Names
Response Options
Attendees
Show As:
Busy
Reminder:
15 minutes
Recurrence
Time Zones
Options
Categorize
Private
High Importance
Low Importance
Tags
Office Add-ins
Add-ins
You haven't sent this meeting invitation yet.
Send
From
To...
classmate@emcp.net
9
Subject
May Issue Planning Meeting
Location
Conference Room A
Start time
Mon 4/16/2018
1:00 PM
All day event
10
End time
Mon 4/16/2018
3:00 PM
Please bring your research notes.
8

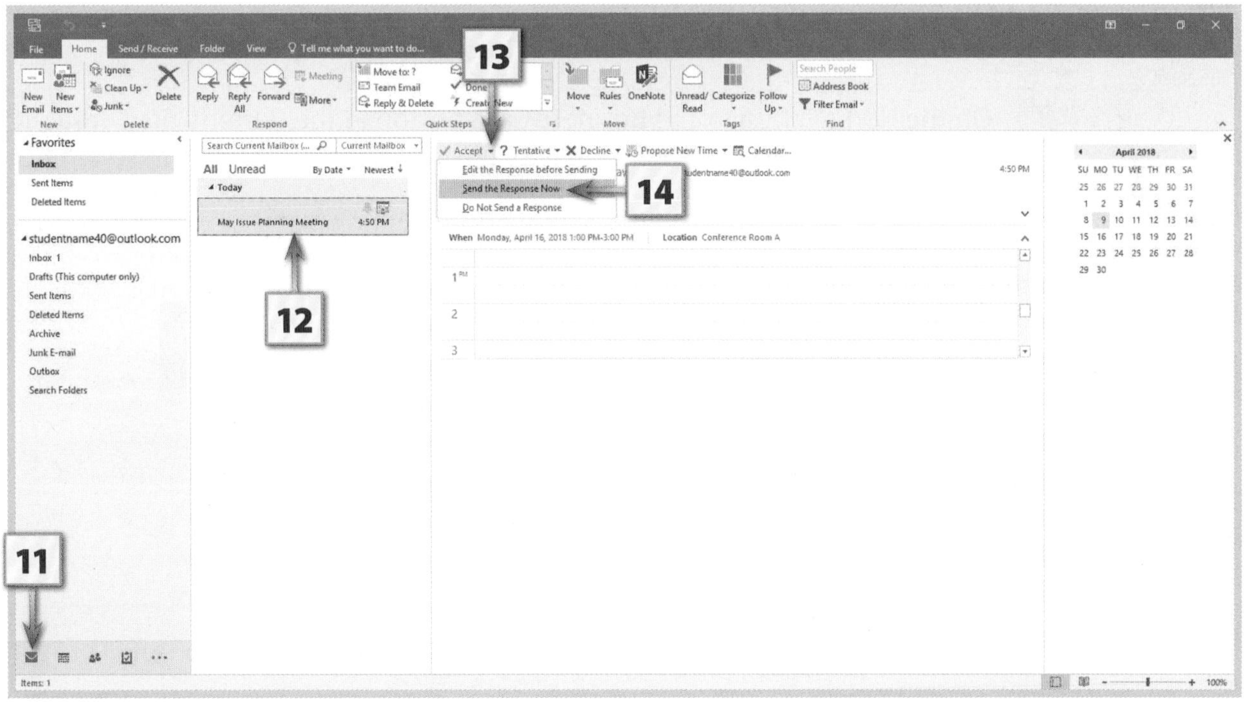
File
Home
Send / Receive
Folder
View
Tell me what you want to do...
13
Ignore
Clean Up
Junk
New Email
New Items
Delete
Reply
Reply All
Forward
Meeting
More
Move to: ?
Team Email
Reply & Delete
Done
Create New
Move
Rules
OneNote
Unread/ Read
Categorize
Follow Up
Search People
Address Book
Filter Email
New
Delete
Respond
Quick Steps
Move
Tags
Find
Favorites
Inbox
Sent Items
Deleted Items
Search Current Mailbox
Current Mailbox
All
Unread
By Date
Newest
Today
May Issue Planning Meeting
4:50 PM
Accept
Tentative
Decline
Propose New Time
Calendar...
Edit the Response before Sending
Send the Response Now
Do Not Send a Response
14
studentname40@outlook.com
When Monday, April 16, 2018 1:00 PM-3:00 PM
Location Conference Room A
studentname40@outlook.com
Inbox 1
Drafts (This computer only)
Sent Items
Deleted Items
Archive
Junk E-mail
Outbox
Search Folders
12
April 2018
SU MO TU WE TH FR SA
11
Items: 1
100%

Your Digital Toolkit

Skill 5 Add People

People is an Outlook tool that you can use to organize and save information about the people and businesses with which you communicate. The information you enter about a person or business can include just the name and email address, or it can include additional information, such as the physical address and cell phone number. Once an address has been entered for the contact, you can click the Map It button to open a browser that automatically displays the address in Bing Maps.

Tutorial

1 **Shortcut**
Display People
Ctrl + 3

▶**Tip** The *File as* box is completed automatically after you type the full name. This entry is used to organize the People list in alphabetical order.

▶**Tip** The *Display as* box is completed automatically after you enter the email address.

▶**Tip** When you receive an email message in Outlook, you can add the sender as a new contact by right-clicking the person's name at the top of the message and then clicking the *Add to Outlook Contacts* option in the pop-up list.

1 With Outlook open, click the People button on the Navigation bar to display People view.

2 On the Home tab, click the New Contact button in the New group.

3 In the new Contact window, type Michaela Williams in the *Full Name* box.

4 Type Align Computers in the *Company* box.

5 Type williamsm@ParadigmCollege.net in the *E-mail* box.

6 Type (561) 555-2322 in the *Business* box.

7 On the Contact tab, click the Save & Close button in the Actions group.

8 On the Home tab, click the Business Card button in the Current View group to change to Business Card view.

9 Keep Outlook open. You continue to work in Outlook in the next skill.

Completed Skill 5

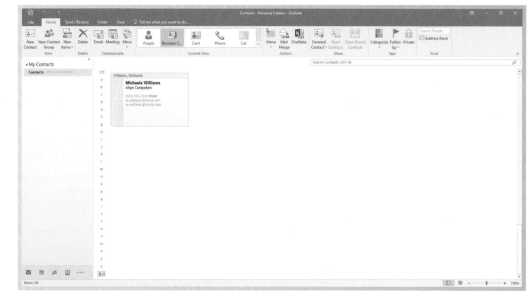

Completed
Skill Preview

Taking It Further ●

Adding a Picture

You can add a picture of your contact to help you quickly connect a face to a name or a logo to a business contact. If both the sender and the recipient use Microsoft Outlook 2016, 2013, 2010, or 2007, the person's picture will appear in the email message header. To add a picture, click the image icon in the New Contact window, browse to locate the picture you want to add, and then double-click the file name.

Skill 6 Search for People and Appointments

Being organized means having information at your fingertips and knowing how best to manage it. With Outlook, you can easily find people and appointments using the *Search Contacts* and *Search Calendar* boxes. You only need to type in the information you are looking for—and you can even search using partial information. For example, you can type part of a name or phone number. As you type, Outlook will suggest keywords and people based on your mailbox content.

Tutorial

2 *Shortcut*
Open *Search Calendar* Box
Ctrl + E

▶**Tip** You can refine a search by using the buttons on the Search Tools Search tab.

8 *Shortcut*
Open *Search Contacts* Box
Ctrl + E

1 With Outlook open, click the Calendar button on the Navigation bar.

2 Click in the *Search Calendar* box and then type Nutrition. Outlook displays the appointment you created in Skill 3.

3 Double-click the appointment.

4 In the appointment window, change the start time to *2:30 PM*.

5 Change the end time to *4:00 PM*.

6 Click the Save & Close button in the Actions group.

7 Click the People button on the Navigation bar.

8 Click in the *Search Contacts* box and type (561. Outlook displays the Michaela Williams contact.

9 On the Search Tools Search tab, click the Close Search button in the Close group.

10 Click the Close button to close Outlook.

Taking It Further • • • • • • • • • • •

Exploring the Search Tools Search Tab

When you click in the *Search Contacts* box or *Search Calendar* box, the Search Tools Search tab appears, enabling you to refine your search. Commands in the Scope group specify which Outlook folders are included in your search. Use commands in the Refine group to narrow your search. Commands in the Options group allow you to reuse previous searches, saving you the time and effort of retyping search criteria. For example, click the Recent Searches button and you will find the search you conducted in this skill in the drop-down list.

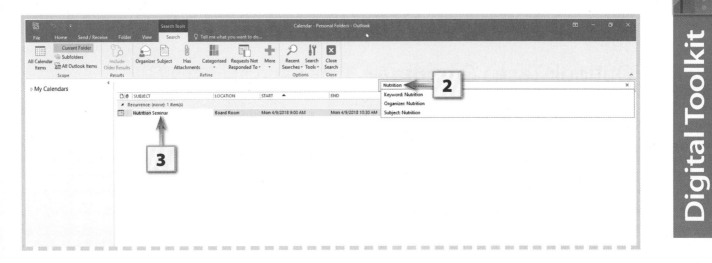

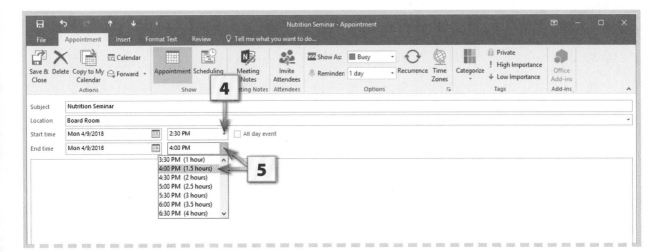

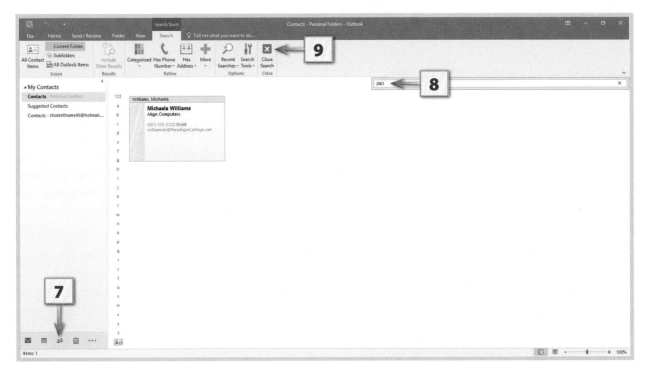

Outlook **Tasks Summary**

Task	Ribbon Tab, Group	Button, Option	Shortcut, Alternative
Display Calendar in Day view	Home, Arrange	Day	
Display Calendar in Month view	Home, Arrange	Month	
Display Calendar in Next 7 Days view	Home, Go To	Next 7 Days	
Display Calendar in Today view	Home, Go To	Today	
Change Calendar background color	View, Color	Color	
Change the time intervals on the Calendar	View, Arrangement	Time Scale	
Change the time zone on the Calendar	View, Arrangement	Time Scale, *Change Time Zone*	
Create a Calendar appointment	Home, New	New Appointment	
Save and close a Calendar appointment	Appointment, Actions	Save & Close	
Send a Calendar meeting request		Send	
Accept a Calendar meeting request		Accept	
Create a Calendar meeting	Home, New	New Meeting	

Task	Ribbon Tab, Group	Button, Option	Shortcut, Alternative
Create a task	Home, New	New Task	
Create a contact	Home, New	New Contact	
View People in Business Card view	Home, Current View	Business C...	

Recheck your understanding of the skills and features covered in this chapter.

Recheck

Chapter study resources are available in the Workbook *ebook*.

Workbook

UNIT **2**

Office Suite

Student
Data Files

Precheck

Check your understanding of the skills and features covered in this unit.

Before beginning this unit, be sure you have downloaded the GL16-StudentDataFiles folder from your ebook and copied the Unit2-OfficeSuite subfolder to your storage medium. The copied folder will become your working folder for this unit.

Skills You Learn

1. Open the application, create a file, and display the backstage area
2. Open and save a file
3. Use the ribbon
4. Navigate within a file
5. Use Find and Replace
6. Use Undo and Redo
7. Change views and zoom percentage
8. Check spelling and grammar
9. Use formatting tools
10. Print a file
11. Use Help

Files You Need

For these skills, you need the following student data files:

U2S2-Sales

U2S3-TravelDeals

What You Create

The Microsoft Office applications share many features and commands. In this unit, you learn to create, open, and save Office files using Excel workbooks. You then edit, format, and print a travel agency flyer in Word using features that are common across several applications. Finally, you explore the Help options using the Excel 2016 Help feature.

Travel Deals Flyer

Completed
Skill Preview

 SNAP   *If you are a SNAP user, go to your SNAP Assignments page to complete the Precheck, Tutorials, and Recheck.*

Guidelines

for

Understanding Office Suite Basics

The Microsoft Office 2016 suite is made up of several applications. Earlier in this book, you learned to use Outlook to manage your schedule and people. Other applications in the Office suite include these:

Word 2016   Use the *Word* document application to produce professional-looking documents, including letters, resumes, reports, and much more.

Excel 2016   Use the *Excel* spreadsheet application to enter numbers or other data into a grid of rows and columns. Once data is entered, Excel can perform automatic calculations, such as adding numbers to get a total. Excel can also create graphs from the data. Organizations and individuals use spreadsheets to track inventory, manage budgets, balance checkbooks, and create income statements.

Access 2016   Use the *Access* database application to store and organize large amounts of data. For example, all the bits of information a company gathers about its customers and suppliers can be stored in a database. You can query a database to find specific information, such as all customers who live in a certain city. You can also produce reports from the data.

PowerPoint 2016
Use the *PowerPoint* presentation application to create slides that support a presentation. The slides help the audience follow and understand the key points of the presentation. Photos and charts in the slides can add visual interest.

Even though each application in the Office suite is designed to perform a specific task, all applications have some common interface elements and commands. Learning about the shared features of the applications—their common "look and feel"—reduces the time you need to master the entire Office suite.

Shared Interface Elements
Each Office application interface includes the *Quick Access Toolbar* and the ribbon. The Quick Access Toolbar allows you to add icons for the actions you use often, such as undoing a change and saving a file. You can place your own choices on this toolbar for most-often-used commands.

The *ribbon* is the main interface feature. The File tab on the ribbon displays the backstage area, which includes file management options, such as opening, printing, and saving. The ribbon offers other tabs and groups of commands that are related to each other—for example, the View tab allows you to change the zoom and decide how to view multiple windows. Some common interface elements are shown in the image below.

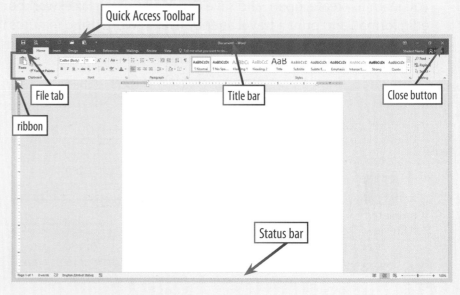

Your ribbon may look different depending on your screen resolution and monitor size. For example, some groups change to a button with the name of the Group when there isn't enough room to display all the commands on the ribbon.

Other features common to Office application interfaces include the Title bar, Status bar, and Close button. The *Title bar* displays the file and program name. The *Status bar* displays status messages, such as the page number. The *Close button* is used to close an open file.

Shared Commands

In the Print backstage area, many of the commands are the same for Excel, Word, and PowerPoint. Compare the screens below for similarities.

Becoming familiar with common interface elements and commands now, before starting the skills in the Word, Excel, Access, and PowerPoint units, will speed up your learning in each application.

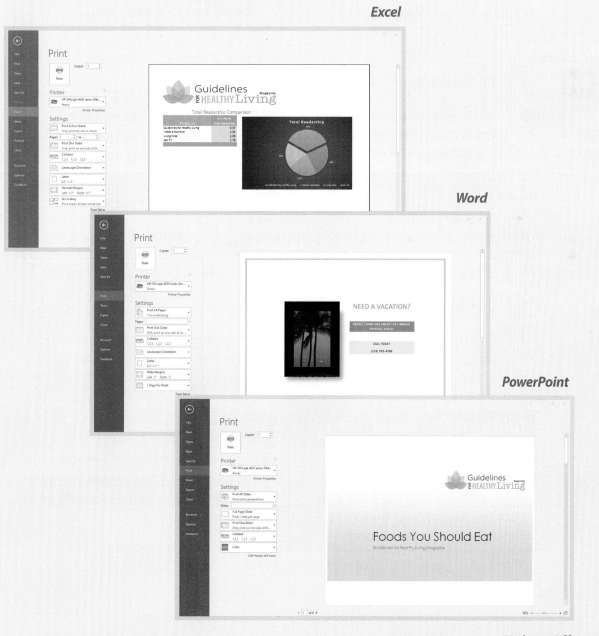

Excel

Word

PowerPoint

Skill 1 — Open the Application, Create a File, and Display the Backstage Area

When you open an Office application, such as Excel, PowerPoint, or Word, you have various templates to choose from. Templates are predesigned files that contain basic content and layout information for specific types of files, such as brochures, newsletters, budgets, and presentations. Using a template is a quick way to create a professional-looking file. In the template list, you will also find options for creating a file from a blank slate, such as a blank workbook in Excel and a blank document in Word.

When you are working in an application, you will use the *backstage area* to manage your files and perform file tasks such as saving or printing. In all the programs, the backstage area displays the same list of options: *Info, New, Open, Save, Save As, Print, Share, Export, Account,* and *Options.*

Tutorial

1–2 *Another Way*
Click the Start button, click *All apps,* and then scroll and click *Excel 2016.*

▶**Tip** The Title bar displays the file and program name.

▶**Tip** Each application in the Office suite has a different colored backstage area. The Excel color is green.

7 *Shortcut*
Create New File
Ctrl + N

1 On the Windows taskbar, type excel in the search box.

2 In the search results list, click *Excel 2016 Desktop app* to open the Excel application on your computer and view the options for creating a blank workbook or a workbook based on a template.

3 Click the *Blank workbook template* to create a new, blank workbook in the Excel window.

4 Notice that *Book1 - Excel* displays in the Title bar of the workbook.

5 Click the File tab to display the backstage area.

6 Click the *New* option.

7 Click the *Blank workbook* template to create another new, blank workbook in the Excel window. Notice that *Book2 - Excel* displays in the Title bar.

Taking It Further

Using the History Feature

A new feature for Office 2016 applications is the History feature. Click the File tab and then click the *History* option to see a complete list of changes that have been made to your document and to access earlier versions.

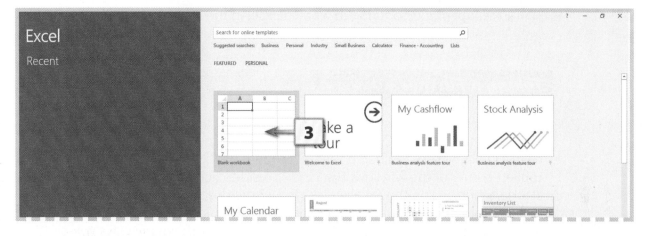

More ➔

8 Click the Close button to close the unsaved Book2 workbook and redisplay Book1.

9 Click the File tab to display the backstage area.

10 Click the Back button to redisplay the blank Book1 Excel workbook.

11 Click the File tab.

12 Click the *Close* option to close the unsaved Book1 workbook while keeping Excel open. You continue to work in Excel in the next skill.

Use Your Touchscreen

In Steps 9 and 11, instead of clicking the mouse, tap the tab. Similarly, in Step 10, tap the Back button and in Step 12, tap the *Close* option.

Taking It Further •

Customizing the Quick Access Toolbar

The applications in the Office suite have a Quick Access Toolbar in the top left corner of the window. The standard buttons on the Excel Quick Access Toolbar include Save, Undo, and Redo. You can customize the toolbar by clicking the Customize Quick Access Toolbar button and selecting from the options in the drop-down list. If you want to see more commands organized by the tab of the ribbon on which they reside, click the *More Commands* option in the drop-down list. Adding buttons to the Quick Access Toolbar is just one example of the many ways you can customize the Office applications to help you work more efficiently.

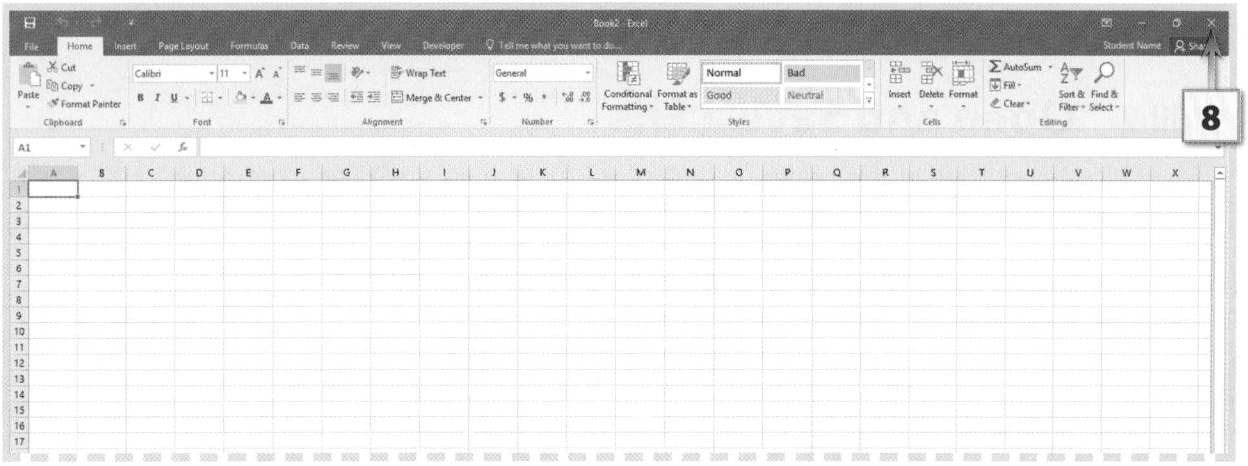
Book2 - Excel
8

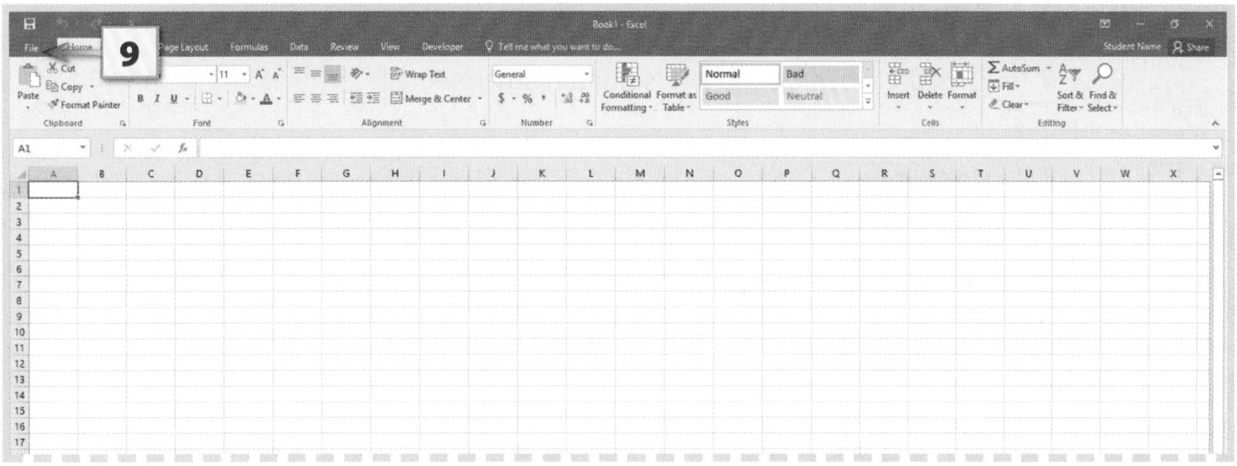
Book1 - Excel
9

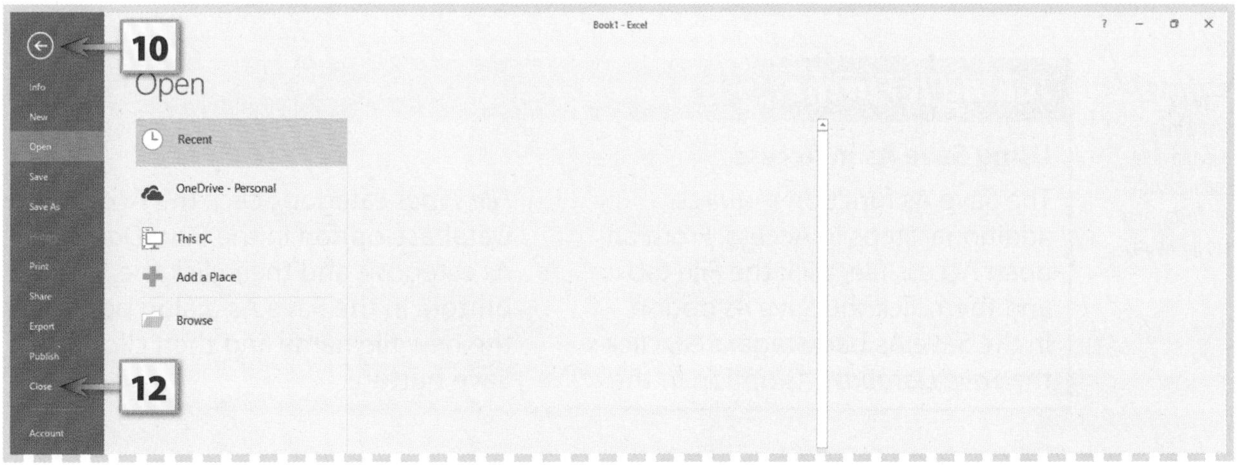
Book1 - Excel
10
Open
Info
New
Open
Save
Save As
Print
Share
Export
Publish
Close
12
Account
Recent
OneDrive - Personal
This PC
Add a Place
Browse

Office Suite

Skill 2 Open and Save a File

As you saw in the previous skill, files can be created by selecting a template in the backstage area. You can also find the commands for saving a file and opening an existing file in the backstage area. When you save a file, save it to the storage medium you have been instructed to use, such as your OneDrive account or a USB flash drive. File names should be descriptive of the file contents so you can easily find the file you need. A valid file name cannot contain certain characters. Colons (:), asterisks (*), and question marks (?) are examples of unacceptable characters.

Tutorial

▶**Tip** In Step 1, if Excel is not already open, start Excel and then click the File tab.

 Shortcut
Open Existing File
Ctrl + O

▶**Tip** In the Open backstage area, you may have files listed in the right panel under headings such as *Today* and *Older* if files were previously saved in Excel.

 Shortcut
Save As
F12

▶**Tip** In the Save As backstage area, you may have files listed in the right panel under headings such as *Current Folder*, *Today*, and *Older* if files were previously saved in Excel.

1 With the Excel window active, click the File tab.

2 Click the *Open* option if it is not already selected.

3 In the Open backstage area, navigate to the student data file named **U2S2-Sales** saved on your storage medium. In the Open dialog box, click the file to select it.

4 Click the Open button to display the selected file in the Excel window.

5 Click the File tab.

6 Click the *Save As* option.

7 Click the *Browse* option.

Taking It Further

Using Save As in Access

The Save As function requires additional steps in Access. From an open Access file, click the File tab and then click the *Save As* option. In the Save As backstage area, click the *Save Database As* option in the *File Types* category, click the Access Database option in the *Save Database As* category, and then click the Save As button. In the Save As dialog box, enter the new file name and then click the Save button.

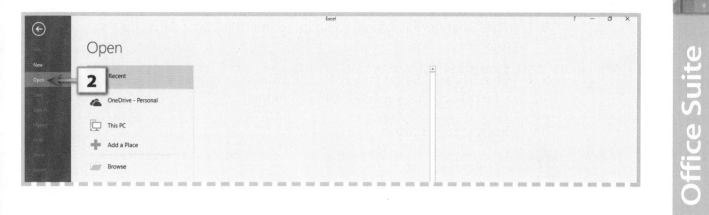

8 In the Save As dialog box, navigate to the Unit 2 working folder on your storage medium.

9 In the Save As dialog box, type U2S2-Sales-Lastname in the *File name* box, but replace *Lastname* with your last name.

10 Click the Save button.

11 Click the File tab.

12 Click the *Close* option to close the file.

13 Click the Close button to close Excel.

Taking It Further ● ● ● ● ● ● ● ● ● ● ● ● ● ● ● ● ● ● ●

Saving Files in Alternative Formats

By default, documents, workbooks, presentations, and databases are saved as files in their native format: *DOCX* in Word, *XLSX* in Excel, *PPTX* in PowerPoint, and *ACCDB* in Access. However, you can save files in an alternative format, such as PDF, by selecting that format from the *Save as type* drop-down list in the Save As dialog box. (PDF is the format used by a document reader program called Adobe Reader, which can be downloaded free from www.adobe. com and which allows users without the original software to view a file with formatting intact.) You can also save files in an alternative format by clicking the File tab, clicking the *Export* option, and then selecting one of the options listed in the backstage area.

Completed Skill 2

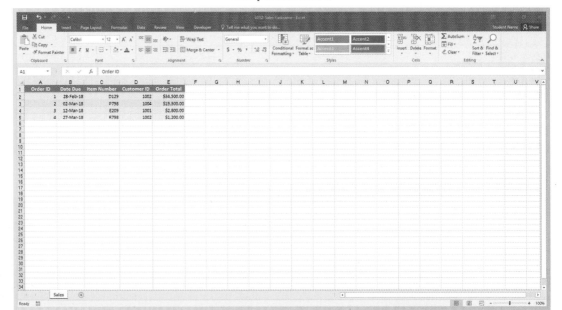

Completed
Skill Preview

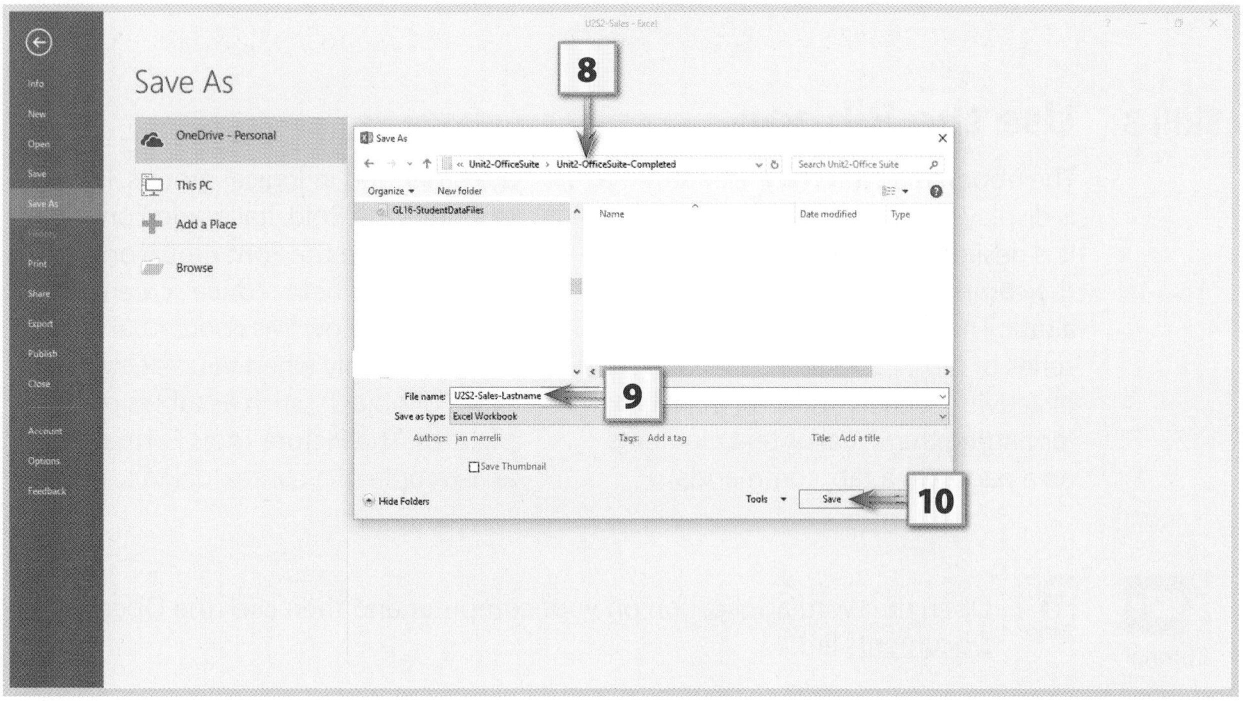

U2S2-Sales - Excel
Save As
8
OneDrive - Personal
This PC
Add a Place
Browse
Save As
Unit2-OfficeSuite > Unit2-OfficeSuite-Completed
Search Unit2-Office Suite
Organize
New folder
GL16-StudentDataFiles
Name
Date modified
Type
File name: U2S2-Sales-Lastname
9
Save as type: Excel Workbook
Authors: jan marrelli
Tags: Add a tag
Title: Add a title
Save Thumbnail
Hide Folders
Tools
Save
10
Info
New
Open
Save
Save As
Print
Share
Export
Publish
Close
Account
Options
Feedback

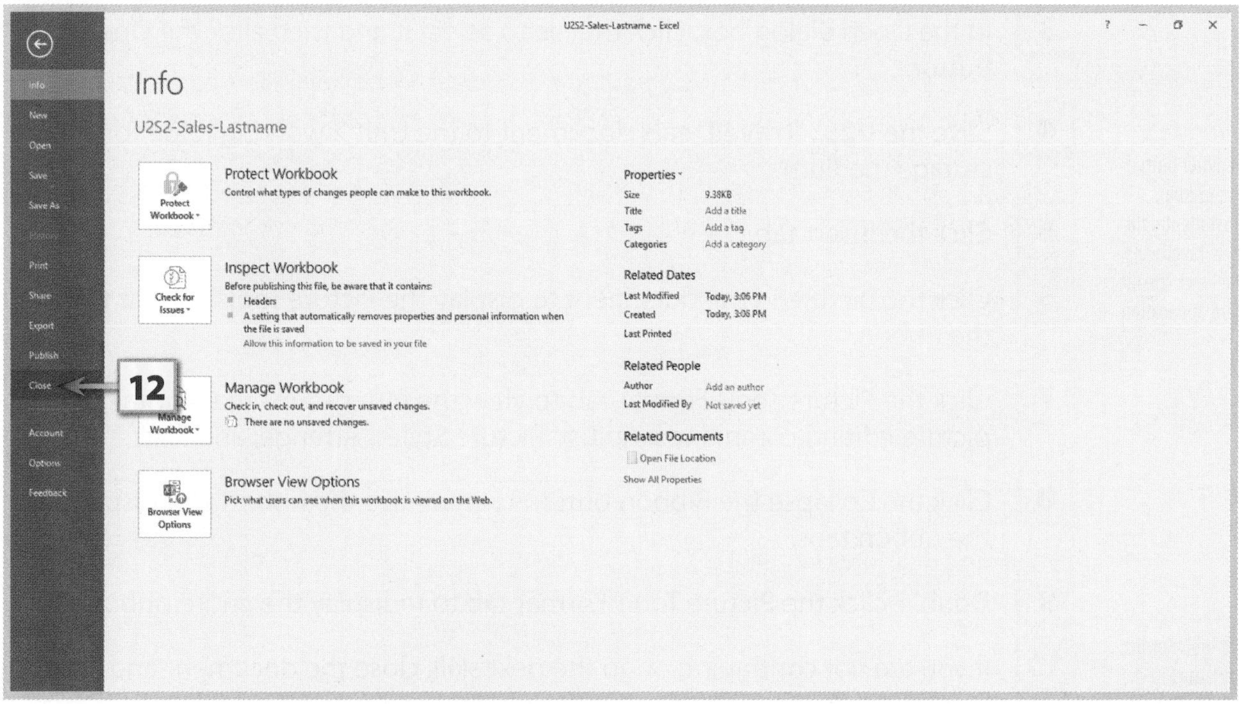

U2S2-Sales-Lastname - Excel
Info
U2S2-Sales-Lastname
Protect Workbook
Control what types of changes people can make to this workbook.
Inspect Workbook
Before publishing this file, be aware that it contains:
Headers
A setting that automatically removes properties and personal information when the file is saved
Allow this information to be saved in your file
Check for Issues
Manage Workbook
Check in, check out, and recover unsaved changes.
There are no unsaved changes.
Browser View Options
Pick what users can see when this workbook is viewed on the Web.
Properties
Size 9.38KB
Title Add a title
Tags Add a tag
Categories Add a category
Related Dates
Last Modified Today, 3:06 PM
Created Today, 3:06 PM
Last Printed
Related People
Author Add an author
Last Modified By Not saved yet
Related Documents
Open File Location
Show All Properties
12
Close

Excel
File
Home
Insert
Page Layout
Formulas
Data
Review
View
Developer
Tell me what you want to do...
Clipboard
Font
Alignment
Number
Styles
Cells
Editing
13

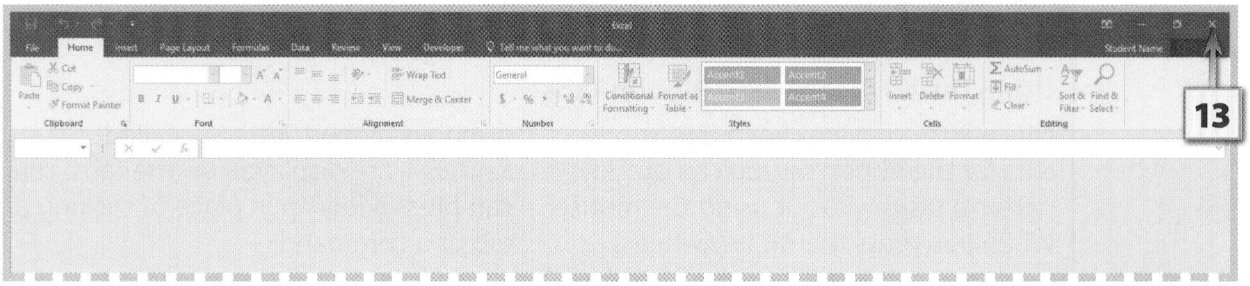

Skill 3 Use the Ribbon

The ribbon is an interface element that is displayed in the application window. It is designed to help you quickly find the commands you need to complete a task. The ribbon is organized into a series of tabs. Each tab relates to a type of activity, such as inserting objects or formatting the visual or text elements on a page. On a tab, commands are organized in logical groups. For example, the Bold, Italic, and Font Color buttons are in the Font group on the Home tab. To help reduce screen clutter, some tabs, known as contextual tabs, are shown only when you select certain types of objects, such as tables or pictures. The Picture Tools Format tab is an example of a contextual tab.

Tutorial

> **Tip** To open Word, type *word* in the search box on the Windows taskbar and then click *Word 2016 Desktop app* in the search results list.

1–3 *Another Way*
Click the File Explorer button on the Windows taskbar, navigate to the student data file named U2S3-TravelDeals, and then double-click the file to open the Word application and the file.

1 Open the Word application on your computer and then click the Open Other Documents link.

2 In the Open backstage area, navigate to the student data file named **U2S3-TravelDeals** saved on your storage medium.

3 In the Open dialog box, click the file to select it and then click the Open button.

4 Save the **U2S3-TravelDeals** document to the Unit 2 working folder on your storage medium.

5 Click the Insert tab.

6 Click the picture in the document to display the Picture Tools Format tab on the ribbon.

7 Click the Picture Tools Format tab to view the four groups that contain the picture editing commands: Adjust, Picture Styles, Arrange, and Size.

8 *Shortcut*
Collapse Ribbon
Ctrl + F1

8 Click the Collapse the Ribbon button to minimize the ribbon and display only the ribbon tabs.

9 *Another Way*
Click the Picture Tools Format tab and then click the Pin the ribbon button (looks like a pushpin).

9 Double-click the Picture Tools Format tab to redisplay the entire ribbon.

10 *Shortcut*
Close Application
Alt + F4

10 If you are not continuing on to the next skill, close the document and Word by clicking the Close button.

Taking It Further

Using the Keyboard with Ribbon Tabs

Office 2016 provides keyboard shortcuts for the ribbon so you can quickly perform tasks without using the mouse. When you press the Alt key while a ribbon is pinned, letters—called *KeyTips*—are displayed on the tabs. You can press a KeyTip in place of clicking a tab or a command.

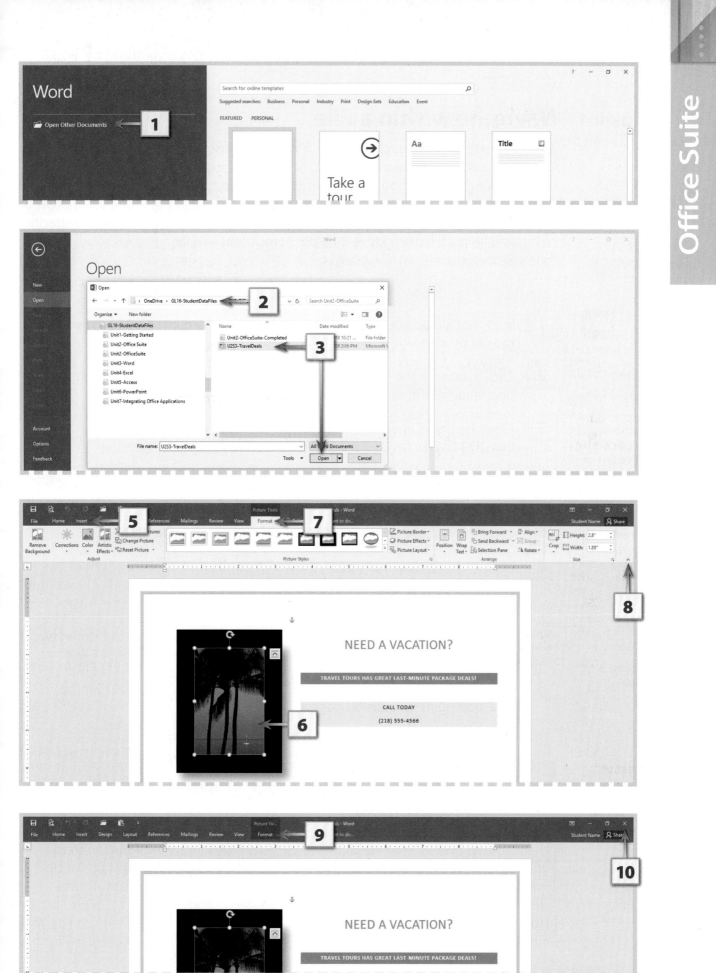

Skill 4 Navigate within a File

Many files you create in each of the Office applications will be more than one page long. Your monitor is a fixed size and may not be able to display the contents of the entire file at once. To navigate within a file or window, it helps to know how to *scroll*. Scrolling helps you quickly find information or reach a specific location in the file so that you can then make edits or apply formatting. You can use the keyboard, the mouse, or your touchscreen to navigate to specific locations in a file.

Use Your Touchscreen
In Step 2, tap the appropriate location to place the insertion point.

Tutorial

2 Shortcut
Go to Beginning
Ctrl + Home

▶**Tip** When you open a Word document, the insertion point is automatically at the beginning of the document.

Use Your Touchscreen
To scroll in a file, touch the screen and then slide the file up and down with your finger.

▶**Tip** Scrolling moves the portion of the file that you see, not the insertion point.

5 Shortcut
Go to End
Ctrl + End

▶**Tip** Your keyboard may not look exactly the same as the keyboard shown. For example, some keys may be in different locations.

8 Another Way
If your mouse has a scroll wheel, you can roll the wheel to scroll through the document.

1 If it is not already open, open the student data file named **U2S3-TravelDeals**, the file used in Skill 3.

2 Click in front of the title *NEED A VACATION?* to place the insertion point at the beginning of the document.

3 Press the Page Down key to move the insertion point to display within the title *TOP TRAVEL DEALS AND CHEAP FLIGHTS* on page 2.

4 Press the Home key to move the insertion point to the beginning of the title on page 2.

5 Press the End key to move the insertion point to the end of the title.

6 Position the mouse pointer on the down scroll arrow at the bottom of the vertical scroll bar. Click the down scroll arrow several times, until you see the top few lines of page 2.

7 Press the Down Arrow key two times to move the insertion point down two lines.

8 Drag the scroll box upward to display the top of page 1. Notice that the insertion point remains on page 2.

Taking It Further

Navigating on a Touchscreen

If you have a touchscreen, you may want to turn on Touch mode to make the ribbon roomier. To turn on Touch mode, click the Customize Quick Access Toolbar button on the Quick Access Toolbar and then click the *Touch/Mouse Mode* option in the drop-down list. This adds the Touch Mode button to the Quick Access Toolbar, and the button can then be clicked to turn Touch mode on and off.

Skill 5 # Use Find and Replace

The *Find* feature enables you to search for specific characters or formatting. When the Find feature locates items that match your search terms, the results are displayed in the Navigation pane. Similarly, the *Find and Replace* feature allows you to search for specific characters or formatting and replace them with other characters or formatting.

Tutorial

1 If it is not already open, open the student data file named **U2S3-TravelDeals** and save it as **U2S5-TravelDeals**. Be sure to save it in your Unit 2 working folder on your storage medium.

Shortcut
Find
Ctrl + F

2 On the Home tab, click the Find button in the Editing group.

3 In the Navigation pane search box, type September. Matches are highlighted in the document and listed in the Navigation pane.

4 Click the Navigation pane Close button.

5 Scroll to the top of the document and click in front of the title *NEED A VACATION?* to place the insertion point at the beginning of the document, if it is not already there. You decide to update the flyer by replacing all occurrences of *September* with *December*.

Shortcut
Replace
Ctrl + H

6 Click the Replace button in the Editing group.

7 In the Find and Replace box, confirm that *September* appears in the *Find what* box and then type December in the *Replace with* box.

Taking It Further ●●●●●●●●●●●●●●●●●●●●●●●●●

Using Smart Lookup

If you need to find a definition or more information about the word you are using in a Word document, you can select the word and then right-click to display a pop-up list. Click *Smart Lookup* in the pop-up list to open the SmartLookup pane with information about the word you are looking up. Using the Smart Lookup feature is similar to using a search engine to look up information. The advantage is you don't have to leave Word to search for information.

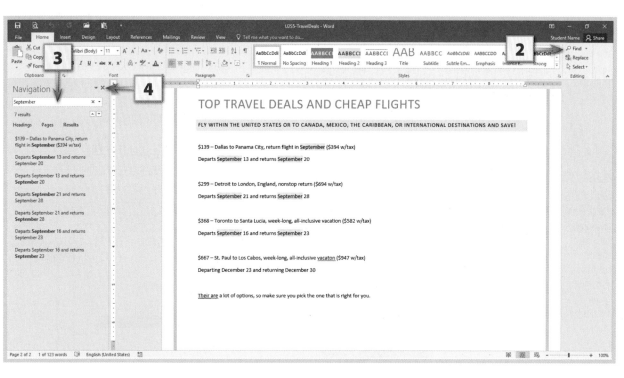

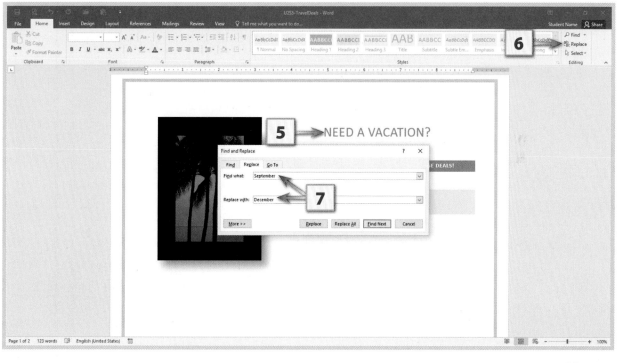

More

▶**Tip** In the Find and Replace dialog box, clicking the Replace button will make one change at a time. Clicking the Replace All button changes all occurrences.

 8 Click the Replace All button.

9 Click the OK button to close the message box indicating that seven replacements have been made.

10 Click the Close button to close the Find and Replace dialog box.

11 Click the Save button on the Quick Access Toolbar to save the file.

Use Your Touchscreen

On touchscreen devices, the Quick Access Toolbar displays the Touch/Mouse mode button by default. If you don't see this button, you can add it by pressing and holding the Customize Quick Access Toolbar button and then tapping the *Touch/Mouse mode* option.

Completed Skill 5

NEED A VACATION?

TRAVEL TOURS HAS GREAT LAST-MINUTE PACKAGE DEALS!

CALL TODAY

(218) 555-4566

TOP TRAVEL DEALS AND CHEAP FLIGHTS

FLY WITHIN THE UNITED STATES OR TO CANADA, MEXICO, THE CARIBBEAN, OR INTERNATIONAL DESTINATIONS AND SAVE!

$139 – Dallas to Panama City, return flight in December ($394 w/tax)
Departs December 13 and returns December 20

$299 – Detroit to London, England, nonstop return ($694 w/tax)
Departs December 21 and returns December 28

$368 – Toronto to Santa Lucia, week-long, all-inclusive vacation ($582 w/tax)
Departs December 16 and returns December 23

$667 – St. Paul to Los Cabos, week-long, all-inclusive vacaton ($947 w/tax)
Departing December 23 and returning December 30

Their are a lot of options, so make sure you pick the one that is right for you.

Completed
Skill Preview

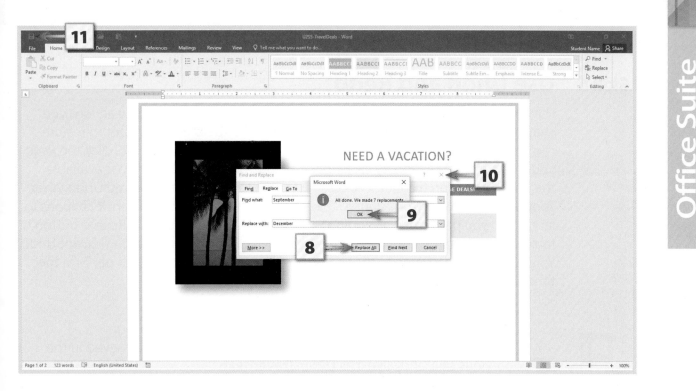

Taking It Further •

Finding with Narrower Limits

Click the More button in the Find and Replace dialog box to display additional search options. Click the *Match case* check box to insert a check mark if you want to locate text with the same capitalization as that of the search text. For example, if the *Match case* option is selected, a search for *January* will not find *JANUARY*. Click the *Find whole words only* check box to insert a check mark if you want to locate text that entirely matches the search text. For example, if this option is selected, a search for *every* will not find *everyone*. Click the Format button in the Find and Replace dialog box to display options for locating text with specific formatting, such as a specific font.

Skill 6 Use Undo and Redo

Have you ever deleted text and then changed your mind? Fortunately, you can restore text you deleted during your current work session by clicking the *Undo* button on the Quick Access Toolbar. The Undo button reverses the last action you performed, including formatting, deletions, and insertions. You can even undo several actions at a time by clicking the arrow on the Undo button and selecting the actions you want to delete. If you want to restore the last Undo performed, click the *Redo* button. The Redo button is available only after you have clicked Undo. After you click the Redo button, it changes to the Repeat button. The Repeat button is available after every action except Undo. Use the *Repeat* button to perform the same action again.

Tutorial

1 If it is not already open, open **U2S5-TravelDeals**, the file you saved in the previous skill, and save it as **U2S6-TravelDeals**.

2 On the first page of the document, double-click in the word *Need* in the document title.

 Shortcut
Cut
Ctrl + X

3 On the Home tab, click the Cut button in the Clipboard group to remove the word *Need*.

 Shortcut
Undo
Ctrl + Z

4 Click the Undo button on the Quick Access Toolbar to reverse the last action so that *Need* reappears in the title.

▶**Tip** When you click the Undo button in Step 4, the Repeat button changes to the Redo button. Clicking the Redo button reverses the last change you made.

5 Press the End key to move the insertion point to the end of the title.

6 Type ?. (Do not type the period.)

Taking It Further ● ● ● ● ● ● ● ● ● ● ● ● ● ● ● ● ● ● ●

Using the Repeat Button

The Repeat button is displayed on the Quick Access Toolbar when the Redo button has no actions to undo. You can use the Repeat button to perform repetitive tasks such as applying a format such as bold or typing text. For example, if you press the Delete key to delete a letter and then move the insertion point to a different location in the document and press the Repeat key, a letter would be deleted because that was the last action performed.

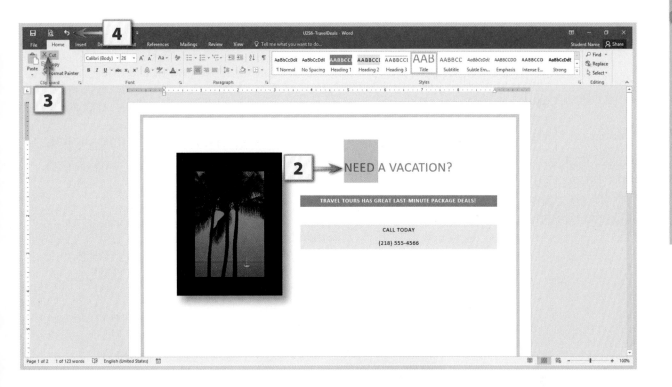

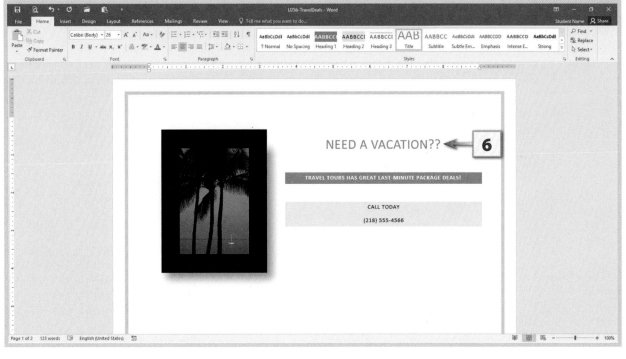

More

Office Suite

Shortcut

Repeat

Ctrl + Y

▶**Tip** You can undo two actions at once by selecting the second item in the Undo drop-down list, three actions by selecting the third, and so on.

7 Click the Repeat button to insert a third *?* at the end of the title.

8 Click the Undo button to remove the third *?* at the end of the title.

9 Click the Undo arrow.

10 Click the option *Typing "?"* in the drop-down list to leave just one *?* in the document.

11 Save the file.

Completed Skill 6

NEED A VACATION??

TRAVEL TOURS HAS GREAT LAST-MINUTE PACKAGE DEALS!

CALL TODAY

(218) 555-4566

TOP TRAVEL DEALS AND CHEAP FLIGHTS

FLY WITHIN THE UNITED STATES OR TO CANADA, MEXICO, THE CARIBBEAN, OR INTERNATIONAL DESTINATIONS AND SAVE!

$139 – Dallas to Panama City, return flight in December ($394 w/tax)
Departs December 13 and returns December 20

$299 – Detroit to London, England, nonstop return ($694 w/tax)
Departs December 21 and returns December 28

$368 – Toronto to Santa Lucia, week-long, all-inclusive vacation ($582 w/tax)
Departs December 16 and returns December 23

$667 – St. Paul to Los Cabos, week-long, all-inclusive vacaton ($947 w/tax)
Departing December 23 and returning December 30

Their are a lot of options, so make sure you pick the one that is right for you.

Completed
Skill Preview

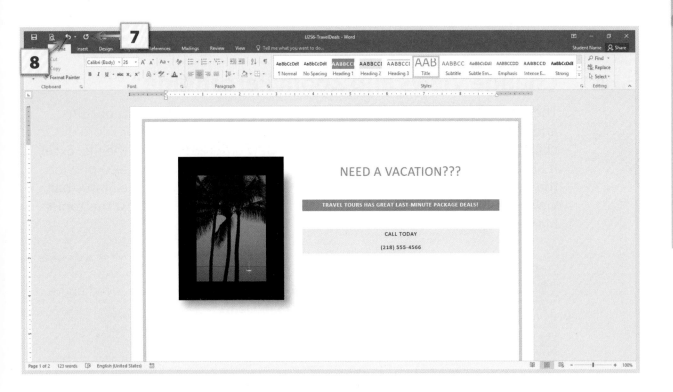

Skill 7 Change Views and Zoom Percentage

The View tab in Excel, PowerPoint, and Word contains buttons for changing the view of the open file. It also includes buttons for changing the zoom percentage while you are viewing a file. By default, a new, blank file opens at 100% of its normal size. However, the zoom buttons allow you to zoom in or zoom out to view different parts of the file. Excel, PowerPoint, and Word also provide a *Zoom slider bar* on the Status bar that allows you to adjust the zoom percentage.

1 If it is not already open, open **U2S6-TravelDeals**, the file you saved in the previous skill, and save it as **U2S7-TravelDeals**.

2 Click the View tab.

3 Click the Multiple Pages button in the Zoom group.

4 Click the One Page button.

5 Click the Zoom button.

6 In the Zoom dialog box, click the *75%* option in the *Zoom to* section.

7 Click the OK button.

8 Drag the Zoom slider bar on the Status bar to *100%*.

> **Use Your Touchscreen**
> Zoom in by touching the screen with two or more fingers and then moving the fingers away from each other (stretch). Zoom out by moving the fingers together (pinch).

Taking It Further

Experimenting with Views

Additional information about views is presented later in the book, but you can experiment now by clicking the various view options on the View tab. For example, in Word, click the Web Layout button in the Views group to view the document as a web page. In Word, you can also click the Read Mode button to view the document in a full screen, which maximizes the screen space available and makes a document easier to read. In Excel, click the Page Layout button in the Workbook Views group to view the worksheet as a printed page, in *Page Layout view*. In PowerPoint, click the Notes Page button in the Presentation Views group to view and edit the speaker notes.

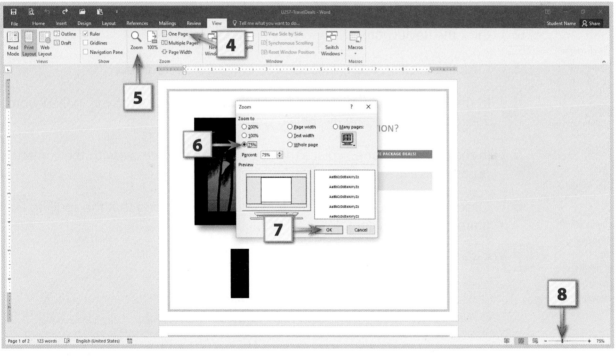

Taking It Further •••••••••••••••••••••••••••

Working with Multiple Documents

You may need to create two documents that are very similar. An easy way to do this is to make a copy of the current document and then modify it. You can do this by clicking the New Window button in the Window group on the View tab. This makes a copy of the current document and opens it in a new window. When you have more than one Word document open, you can click the Switch Windows button in the Window group on the View tab to display a drop-down list of open documents. Click a document name to switch to its active window.

Skill 8 Check Spelling and Grammar

The Office applications include a spelling checker that verifies that words are correctly spelled by comparing them to a built-in dictionary. In Word and PowerPoint, both spelling and grammar are checked and the checker runs automatically. If a word is spelled incorrectly or is not in the dictionary file, a red wavy line appears below it. A blue wavy line indicates a possible grammatical error. In Excel and Access, only spelling is checked, and the checker does not run automatically. You can start the spelling checker by clicking the Spelling button, which is in the Proofing group on the Review tab in Excel and in the Records group on the Home tab in Access. The spelling and grammar checkers are helpful but cannot identify all errors, so you should always carefully proofread your files.

Tutorial

2–6 *Another Way*
You can manually check the spelling and grammar by right-clicking a word or phrase that has a red or blue wavy line and then clicking the correct option or command in the pop-up list.

3 *Shortcut*
Check Spelling & Grammar
F7

▶ *Tip* When the spelling checker presents several suggestions, select the correct choice in the list box in the Spelling pane before clicking the Change button.

1 If it is not already open, open **U2S7-TravelDeals**, the file you saved in the previous skill and save it as **U2S8-TravelDeals**.

2 Click the Review tab.

3 Click the Spelling & Grammar button in the Proofing group.

4 In the Spelling pane, click the Change button to replace the misspelled word *vacaton* with the correctly spelled word, *vacation*.

5 In the Grammar pane, replace the incorrect use of *Their are* with the correct phrase *There are*.

6 Click the OK button to close the message box indicating that the spelling and grammar check is complete.

7 Save the file.

Completed Skill 8

Completed Skill Preview

NEED A VACATION?

TRAVEL TOURS HAS GREAT LAST-MINUTE PACKAGE DEALS!

CALL TODAY
(218) 555-4566

TOP TRAVEL DEALS AND CHEAP FLIGHTS

FLY WITHIN THE UNITED STATES OR TO CANADA, MEXICO, THE CARIBBEAN, OR INTERNATIONAL DESTINATIONS AND SAVE!

$139 – Dallas to Panama City, return flight in December ($394 w/tax)
Departs December 13 and returns December 20

$299 – Detroit to London, England, nonstop return ($694 w/tax)
Departs December 21 and returns December 28

$368 – Toronto to Santa Lucia, week-long, all-inclusive vacation ($582 w/tax)
Departs December 16 and returns December 23

$667 – St. Paul to Los Cabos, week-long, all-inclusive vacation ($947 w/tax)
Departing December 23 and returning December 30

There are a lot of options, so make sure you pick the one that is right for you.

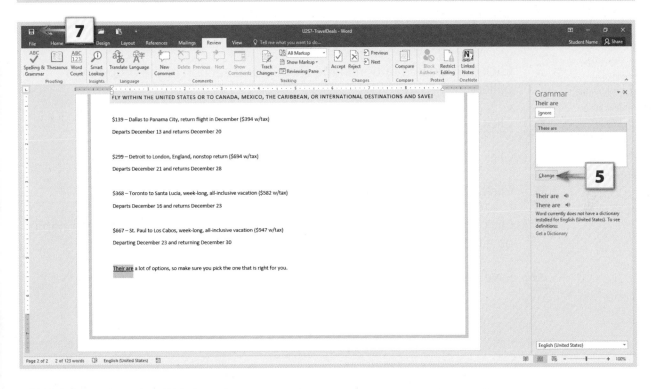

Taking It Further •

Changing the Proofing Language

If you are creating a document in a different language such as Spanish, you can change the proofing language to check the spelling in the language that you are creating the document in. To change the proofing language, click the Language button in the Language group on the Review tab and then click *Set Proofing Language* in the drop-down list. Click the language you are using in the Language dialog box and then click the OK button.

Skill 9 Use Formatting Tools

The way text appears on a page is called its *format*. The Font group on the Home tab in Excel, PowerPoint, and Word and the Text Formatting group in Access contain many of the same formatting buttons, such as Bold, Italic, Underline, Font, and Font Size. These buttons can all be used to apply character formatting. To apply formatting to existing text, you need to select the text first. You can also select formatting options and then enter new text that will automatically be formatted based on the selections.

Tutorial

1 If is not already open, open **U2S8-TravelDeals**, the file you saved in the previous skill, and save it as **U2S9-TravelDeals**.

2 At the bottom of page 2, triple-click the paragraph that begins *There are a*.

3 Click the Home tab.

4 *Shortcut*
Bold
Ctrl + B

4 Click the Font arrow in the Font group.

▶ **Tip** The default font used by all the Office applications is Calibri.

5 Click the *Cambria* option in the *Theme Fonts* section of the drop-down gallery.

6 Click the Bold button.

7–8 *Another Way*
Click in the *Font Size* box and then type *14*.

7 Click the Font Size arrow.

8 Click the *14* option in the drop-down gallery.

9 Click at the end of the last line of text, press Enter, and then type your name on a new line.

10 Save the file.

Completed Skill 9

**Completed
Skill Preview**

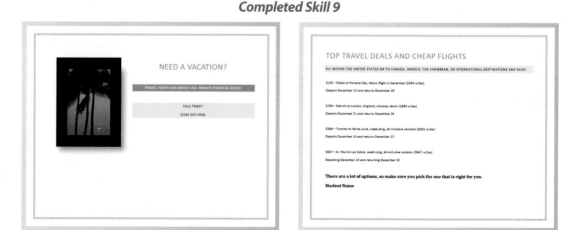

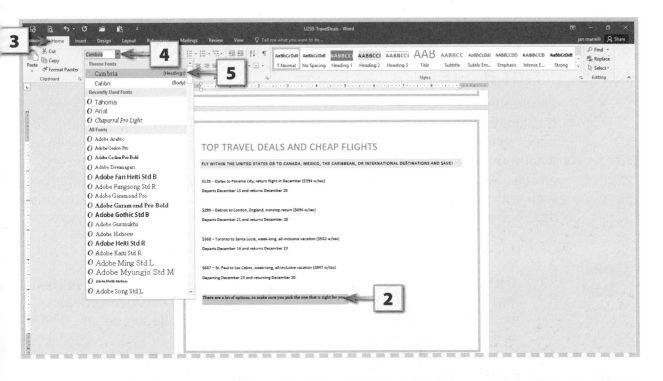

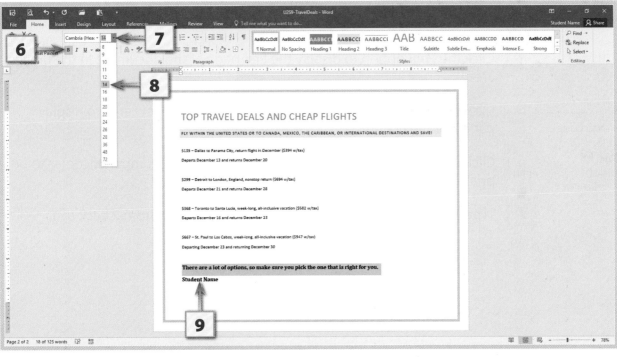

Taking It Further

Using Other Formatting Buttons

The Font group contains other buttons, such as the *Increase Font Size* and *Decrease Font Size* buttons, with which you can quickly increase or decrease the text size. You can change the color of your text with the Font Color button. The Italic button applies italic formatting and the Underline button applies underlining to the selected text. If you apply formatting and then decide to remove it, click the Clear Formatting button.

Office Suite

Skill 10   **Print a File**

Print settings are accessed from the Print backstage area. The Print backstage area displays a preview of what your printed file will look like and also lets you change print options, such as the number of copies to print, *page orientation*, (whether the longer side of the page runs along the top or side) page size, and page margins. You can zoom in on the preview image to make sure all settings are correct prior to printing a copy. *Previewing a file* carefully and printing only the final copy saves you time, money, and paper.

Tutorial

1   If it is not already open, open the student data file named **U2S9-TravelDeals**, the file you saved in the previous skill, and save it as **U2S10-TravelDeals-Lastname**, but replace *Lastname* with your last name. Be sure to save the file in the Unit 2 working folder on your storage medium.

2   Place the insertion point at the beginning of the document.

3   Click the File tab.

 Shortcut
Print
Ctrl + P

▶**Tip** To go back to your file and make changes before you print it, click the Back button in the upper left corner of the window.

4   Click the *Print* option to display the first page of the document in the preview area.

5   Click the Next Page button at the bottom of the preview area to display page 2 of the document.

6   Click the *Copies* increment (up) arrow to change the number of copies to be printed from *1* to *2*.

7   Type 1 to change the number of copies to be printed from *2* back to *1*.

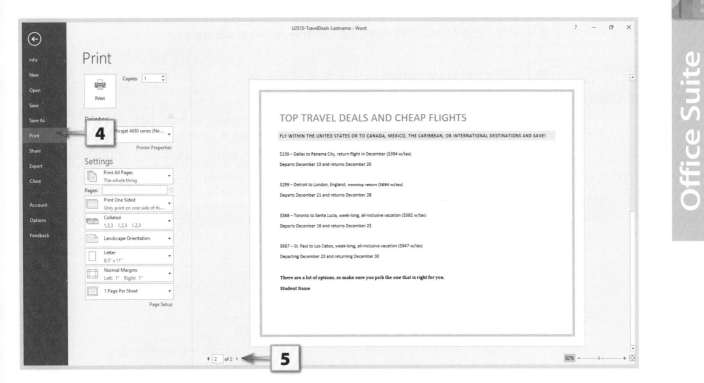

8 Click the *Normal Margins* box in the *Settings* category.

▶**Tip** The preview image may change when you change the print settings.

9 Click the *Wide* option in the drop-down list.

10 Verify that your instructor would like you to submit a printed copy of the document. Click the Print button if you need a printout. ***Note:*** *If you do not need a printed copy and do not click the Print button, skip Step 11 and go directly to Step 12.*

11 Click the File tab to return to the Print backstage area.

12 Click the *Save* option.

13 Click the Close button.

Completed Skill 10

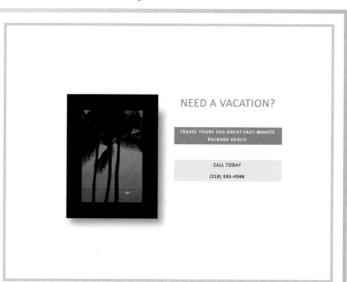

Completed
Skill Preview

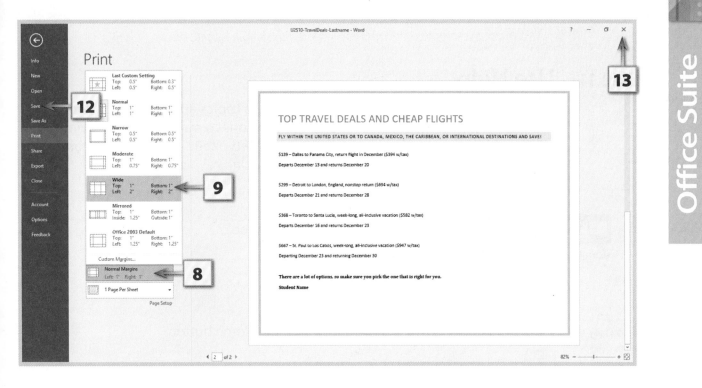

Taking It Further ●

Experimenting with Print Settings

When you change a print setting in the Print backstage area, the preview adjusts to show you what impact the change will have on the printed file. Try changing the paper size, the page orientation (portrait versus landscape), and the margins. Click the *Print All Pages* box to explore options for printing selected pages when you don't need to print the entire document.

Click the *Print One Sided* box to see an option for printing on both sides of the paper manually if your printer cannot perform that function automatically. You can also click the <u>Printer Properties</u> link to display printer options, such as the type of paper (e.g., plain paper or photo paper), print quality (e.g., draft or high), and color options (e.g., sepia or grayscale).

Skill 11 Use Help

Each Microsoft Office application has its own Help window. The *Help* window functions similarly to a web browser. You can click links to view Help topics and use Navigation buttons to move among previously visited pages. You can also search for specific keywords.

Tutorial

2–3 *Shortcut*

Help
F1

▶**Tip** You can print Help topics by clicking the Print button on the Help window toolbar.

1 Start Excel and create a new, blank workbook.

2 Click the File tab.

3 Click the Microsoft Excel Help button.

4 In the Excel 2016 Help window, click the Home button.

5 Click the Get started link.

6 Click the Basic tasks in Excel 2016 link and then read about basic tasks in Excel.

7 Click the Back button to return to the previous page.

8 Click in the search box, type conditional formatting, and then press Enter.

9 Click a link to read information about conditional formatting.

10 Click the Close button to close the Help window.

11 Close Excel.

Taking It Further

Using the Tell Me Feature

Another way to access help and actually get the Office application to execute commands for you is to use the *Tell Me* feature. For example, type print in the *Tell me what you want to do* box on the ribbon to display options associated with printing in the drop-down list. Clicking *Print Preview and Print* in the drop-down list automatically displays the document in Print Preview or clicking *Print* in the drop-down list automatically prints the document.

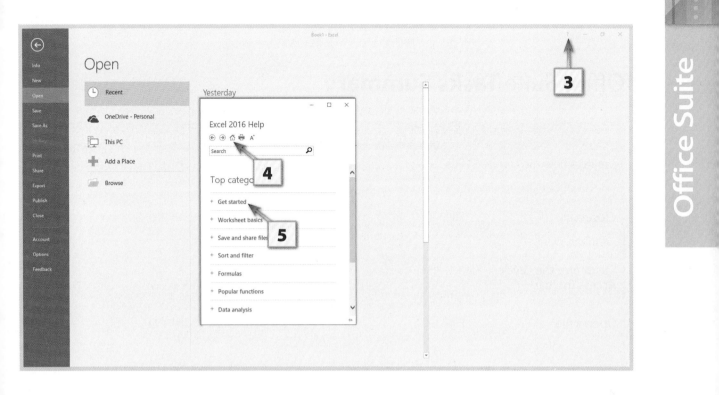

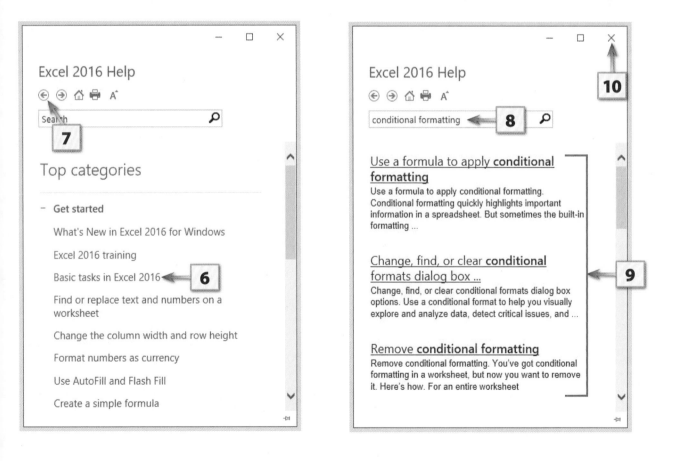

Office Suite **Tasks Summary**

Task	Ribbon Tab, Group	Button, Option	Shortcut, Alternative
Create a new file	File	*New*	Ctrl + N
Close a file	File	✕ , *Close*	
Customize the Quick Access Toolbar		▾	
Open a file	File	*Open*	Ctrl + O
Save a file with a new file name	File	*Save As*	F12
Save a file	File	*Save*	Ctrl + S, 💾
Collapse Ribbon		︿	Ctrl + F1
Go to beginning			Ctrl + Home
Go to end			Ctrl + End
Find text or formatting	Home, Editing	🔍 Find ▾	Ctrl + F
Replace text or formatting	Home, Editing	ab/ac Replace	Ctrl + H
Undo an action	Quick Access Toolbar	↶ ▾	Ctrl + Z
Redo an action	Quick Access Toolbar	↷	Ctrl + Y
Repeat an action	Quick Access Toolbar	↻	

Task	Ribbon Tab, Group	Button, Option	Shortcut, Alternative
Change the view	View, Views		
Change the zoom	View, Zoom	Zoom	Status bar, — ▮ +
Check spelling and grammar	Review, Proofing	ABC ✓ Spelling & Grammar	F7
Change the font	Home, Font	Calibri (Body) ▾	
Change the font size	Home, Font	11 ▾	
Apply bold formatting	Home, Font	B	Ctrl + B
Print a file	File	*Print,* Print	Ctrl + P
Open the Help window	File	?	F1

Recheck

Recheck your understanding of the skills and features covered in this chapter.

Workbook

Chapter study resources are available in the Workbook *ebook.*

UNIT 3

Word

Student
Data Files

Before beginning this unit, be sure you have downloaded the GL16-StudentDataFiles folder from your ebook and copied the Unit3-Word subfolder to your storage medium. The copied folder will become your working folder for this unit.

Guidelines
for
Planning and Creating Word Documents

Using Word, you can create a variety of documents, such as business letters, reports, and recipe cards, as shown in these examples.

You can also use predesigned documents called *templates* to create common marketing and business documents such as agendas, brochures, expense reports, and flyers.

Business Letter

Article

Recipe Card

Templates in the Backstage Area

Whatever type of document you create, taking the time to plan your message will help ensure clear and effective communication. Planning involves deciding on a purpose, identifying your audience, selecting the topic, and choosing a format that gives your document the best possible appearance.

Your purpose, or reason for writing, might be to make a point, to inform, to convince others to believe as you do, or to entertain. Making sure you know your goal helps you decide what to say as you begin to write.

Your audience is the person or group of people you expect to read what you write. The more you know about your audience, the better you can target your message.

Often, the type of document you are creating and the features available in Word help shape your decisions about how much to write and how to present your message. For example, if you are writing a memo about schedule changes that you will send to a group of editors, you are likely to keep the memo short and visually attractive while making sure the information can be read quickly and easily. Word offers features to help you achieve that goal, as shown below.

Insert graphics to add visual interest or to create a professional look.

Format and align text to get your message across.

Use features such as tables and bulleted or numbered lists to organize data.

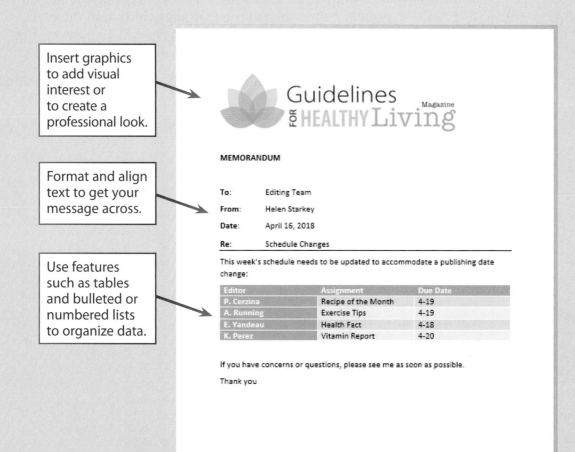

Guidelines
FOR HEALTHY Living Magazine

MEMORANDUM

To: Editing Team
From: Helen Starkey
Date: April 16, 2018
Re: Schedule Changes

This week's schedule needs to be updated to accommodate a publishing date change:

Editor	Assignment	Due Date
P. Cerzina	Recipe of the Month	4-19
A. Running	Exercise Tips	4-19
E. Yandeau	Health Fact	4-18
K. Perez	Vitamin Report	4-20

If you have concerns or questions, please see me as soon as possible.

Thank you

Chapter 1

Creating Documents

Precheck

Check your understanding of the skills and features covered in this chapter.

In Word, you can start from scratch with a blank document, open existing documents, or open documents based on templates (predesigned documents). In this chapter, you practice a combination of these three methods.

With a document open, the next logical step is to enter and edit text. (These actions are the digital equivalent of scribbling text on a piece of paper, crossing out what you do not like, and adding more words as needed.) Word offers tools that help you enter text, select text and make changes to it, and move or copy text from one place to another in that document.

If you are not a spelling expert, you will appreciate the spelling checker feature, which can spell *Mississippi* even if you can't. Word also allows you to change various properties of your document pages, such as the margins (which determine the width of the white space bordering your text) and breaks between one page and another (for example, between the title page and the first page of a report).

Other skills you will learn include setting tabs to align columns of text and adding a header and a footer to a document.

Skills You Learn

1 Enter and edit text

2 Use the Show/Hide ¶ feature

3 Use cut, copy, and paste

4 Perform a spelling and grammar check

5 Create a document based on a template

6 Indent and add tabs using the ruler

7 Set margins

8 Insert a page break

9 Insert headers and footers

 If you are a SNAP user, go to your SNAP Assignments page to complete the Precheck, Tutorials, and Recheck.

Files You Need

For these skills, you need the following student data file:

C1S6-Subscription

What You Create

You work for *Guidelines for Healthy Living Magazine*, an online magazine that provides readers with up-to-date information on nutrition and fitness along with tips for living a healthy lifestyle. The magazine provides a limited amount of free content, and readers must purchase a subscription for full access to the magazine content. Through this and the next several units of this book, you create and edit a variety of files to help the magazine manage subscriptions, sales and advertising, content, staff and publication schedules, and other aspects of its business operation.

In this chapter, you create a letter addressed to existing subscribers with details of a special offer for renewing their subscription.

Subscription Letter

Completed
Skill Preview

Skill 1 Enter and Edit Text

In Unit 2, you learned how to create and save new documents in any Office application. In this skill, you open Word and begin to type text into a new, blank Word document. Once you enter text, you can then perform basic edits to it, such as adding new text, deleting text you no longer need, and correcting errors. In this skill, you learn to use both soft returns and hard returns. A *soft return* moves the insertion point to the next line without creating a new paragraph and maintains the line spacing that appears within the paragraph. A *hard return* moves the insertion point to the next line and at the same time creates a new paragraph.

Tutorial

▶**Tip** To open Word, type *word* in the search box on the Windows taskbar and then click *Word 2016 Desktop app* in the search results list.

▶**Tip** In Step 3, click *OneDrive* in the Save As menu if your working folder is saved in your OneDrive account.

▶**Tip** Pressing Shift + Enter inserts a soft return. Pressing Enter inserts a hard return.

▶**Tip** You only need to press the Enter key at the end of a paragraph or after an entry in a list. Within paragraphs, Word wraps your text to a new line automatically.

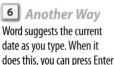 **Another Way**

Word suggests the current date as you type. When it does this, you can press Enter to insert the date rather than typing the rest of it.

 **Another Way**

Click the Date & Time button in the Text group on the Insert tab.

1 Open Word and then click the *Blank document* template to create a new, blank document in the Word window.

2 Click the File tab and then click the *Save* option to display the backstage area.

3 Click *Browse* in the Save As menu and then navigate to the Unit 3 working folder you created on your storage medium.

4 In the Save As dialog box, type C1S1-Subscription in the *File name* box and then click the Save button to close the dialog box.

5 In the open Word document, type the following text:
Guidelines For Healthy Living Magazine [**Shift + Enter**]
2551 Jardine Drive [**Shift + Enter**]
Boston, MA 02115 [**Shift + Enter**]
(617) 555-9890 [**Enter**]

6 Type the current date and then press Enter.

7 Type the text at the top of the next page. (Type it exactly as written, pressing Shift + Enter only where specified—if there are mistakes, you will correct them later!)

8 Click at the end of the line *2551 Jardine Drive*, to the right of the word *Drive*. A blinking insertion point indicates the place where you are currently working in the document.

Mrs. Agatha Kimbell [**Shift + Enter**]
22 Oak Lane [**Shift + Enter**]
Watertown, MA 02118 [**Enter twice**]

Dear Mrs. Kimbell: [**Enter**]

Thank you for your dedicated readership over the past year. We hope you have enjoyed the enhanced digital subscription service that gave you unlimited access to all of our online content. As a thank-you, we are enclosing our annual calendar with tips for healthy living. [**Enter**]

To renew your membership, just visit our website and select the *Renewal* option on the home page. We will continue to deliver quality content And and look forward to being a part of your healthy lifestyle in the ftur. [**Enter**]

This month we are offering our digital subscription customers a chance to renew their membership at a reduced cost. If you renew your subscription in the next 30 days, you will get unlimited access to all of our online content at a cost of just $2.99 a mnth. [**Enter**]

Sincerely yours, [**Enter twice**]

[Your name] [**Shift + Enter**]
Editor

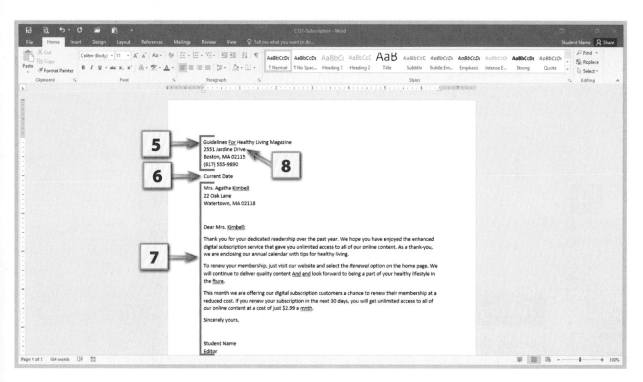

More →

9 Press the Backspace key five times, noticing that the letters to the left of the insertion point are being deleted one at a time.

10 Type the word Street.

11 You made a mistake in the street number (*2551*). To fix it, click between the two 5s in that number and then type 4. Press the Delete key to delete the number 5 to the right of the insertion point. The address should now read *2541*.

12 Click the Save button on the Quick Access Toolbar to save the file.

Completed Skill 1

Guidelines For Healthy Living Magazine
2541 Jardine Street
Boston, MA 02115
(617) 555-9890

Current Date

Mrs. Agatha Kimbell
22 Oak Lane
Watertown, MA 02118

Dear Mrs. Kimbell:

Thank you for your dedicated readership over the past year. We hope you have enjoyed the enhanced digital subscription service that gave you unlimited access to all of our online content. As a thank-you, we are enclosing our annual calendar with tips for healthy living.

To renew your membership, just visit our website and select the *Renewal* option on the home page. We will continue to deliver quality content And and look forward to being a part of your healthy lifestyle in the future.

This month we are offering our digital subscription customers a chance to renew their membership at a reduced cost. If you renew your subscription in the next 30 days, you will get unlimited access to all of our online content at a cost of just $2.99 a month.

Sincerely yours,

Student Name
Editor

Completed
Skill Preview

Use Your Touchscreen
Use your finger or a touch stylus to write and then edit math equations.

Taking It Further ●

Using the Ink Equation Feature

Including math equations has gotten much easier with Word 2016. Now you can click the Ink Equation button in the Equation group on the Insert tab any time you want to include a complex math equation in your document. Use your mouse to write your equation, and Word will convert it to text. Also use your mouse to erase, select, and correct what you have written.

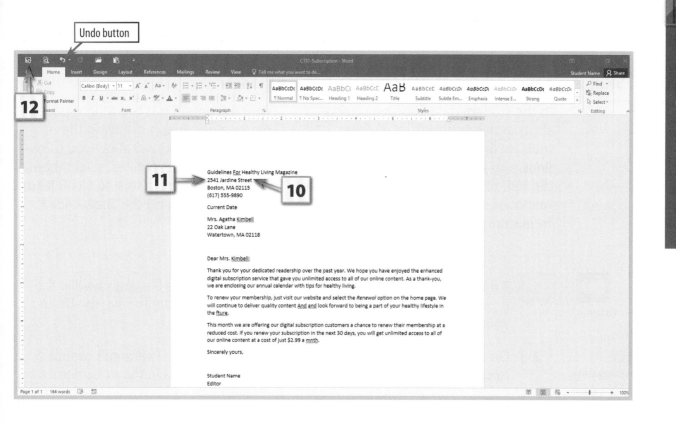

Undo button

Taking It Further

Interpreting Those Wavy Underlines

The wavy underlining in Word calls your attention to potentially misspelled words or possible errors in grammar or formatting. Red wavy lines under text, as under the last name *Kimbell* you enter in Skill 1, flag spelling problems. Blue wavy lines note possible formatting inconsistencies or grammar errors. Because the spelling feature is based on a stored dictionary of words, proper names or names of streets or cities may be flagged as incorrect. *Kimbell* is the correct last name of the letter recipient in this case, so you can ignore the red wavy line. To find and resolve all possible problems and learn how to add words like *Kimbell* to the dictionary, check out Skill 4.

Using the Word Thesaurus

Word has a built-in thesaurus. A *thesaurus* is a collection of synonyms, which are words with similar meanings. For example, *happy* is a synonym for *cheerful*. To replace a word with a synonym from the Word thesaurus, place the insertion point in the word and then click the Thesaurus button in the Proofing group on the Review tab. In the Thesaurus pane, point to the desired synonym, click the arrow to the right of the word, and then click the *Insert* option in the drop-down list.

Skill 2 Use the Show/Hide ¶ Feature

In the student data files and screen-shots in this textbook, marks that indicate formatting such as paragraphs, lines, and spaces are turned off, or hidden. You may want to turn on these marks, or show them, to help you fix formatting problems. For example, if your document has too much space below a paragraph, showing the formatting marks will allow you to see extra paragraphs or lines, select them, and delete them. In this skill, you learn the basics for using the *Show/Hide ¶* feature in Word.

Tutorial

1 If it is not already open, open **C1S1-Subscription**, the file you saved in the previous skill, and save it as **C1S2-Subscription**. Be sure to save the file in your Unit 3 working folder on your storage medium.

 Shortcut
Show/Hide Formatting Marks
Ctrl + Shift + *

2 On the Home tab, click the Show/Hide ¶ button in the Paragraph group. Notice that this turns on (shows) the formatting marks in the document.

▶ **Tip** The Show/Hide button ¶ is a toggle switch. Clicking it when it is not selected turns the Show/Hide ¶ feature on. Clicking it when it is selected turns the feature off.

3 Click just to the left of your first name in the complimentary closing at the end of the letter and then press Enter. Notice that a paragraph mark appears, indicating that you have inserted a new, blank paragraph above your name.

4 Select the line break mark at the end of the line containing the text *Guidelines For Healthy Living Magazine* in the sender's block.

▶ **Tip** The blank lines between *Sincerely* and your name provide space for you to sign the letter.

5 Press Enter to change the line break mark to a paragraph mark. Notice that there is now more space below *Guidelines For Healthy Living Magazine*.

6 Press the Backspace key to remove the paragraph mark you inserted in Step 5, and then press Shift + Enter to restore the line break mark.

▶ **Tip** Standard practice in word processing is to insert only one space between sentences. Be careful not to double-space between sentences in your documents.

7 Click just to the left of the *W* in the sentence beginning *We hope you* in the body of the letter. Press the spacebar to add an extra space between the sentences.

Completed Skill 2

8 Backspace to remove the space you inserted in Step 7.

9 Click the Show/Hide ¶ button again to see how your document looks without the formatting marks displayed.

10 Save the file.

Completed
Skill Preview

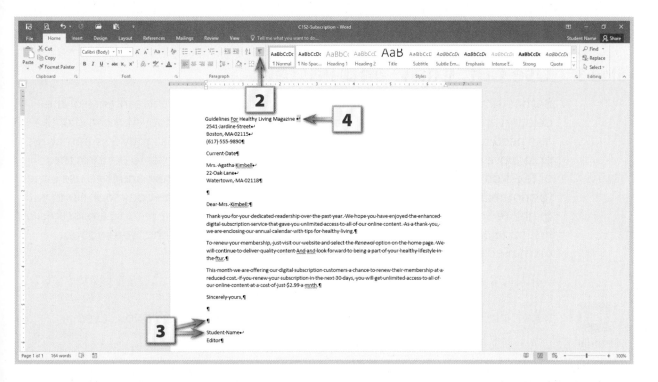

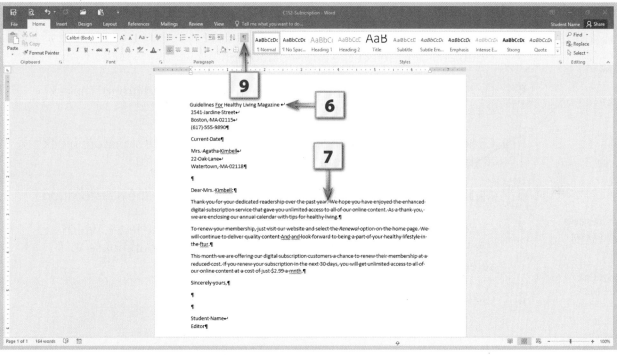

Taking It Further •

Saving Paper

Have you ever printed a document and ended up with an unexpected blank page at the end? This happens when the document contains extra paragraphs or lines at the end of the last page. Use the Show/Hide ¶ feature to look for blank paragraphs and lines at the end of your document—and then delete them to save paper! The Show/Hide feature can also be used to figure out why spacing might be off within a document.

Skill 3 **Use Cut, Copy, and Paste**

Beyond simple text editing such as deleting and adding text, you might also need to *cut* text from the document or to *move* or *copy* a sentence or block of text from one place in a document to another location. For example, you might decide that a paragraph on the first page of a letter really works better on the second page. Or you might want to copy the opening sentence of the letter, place the copy at the end of the letter, and edit it slightly to summarize the letter's purpose. To perform these tasks, select the text and then use either the Cut tool or the Copy tool, along with the Paste tool. These tools are located on the Home tab of the Word ribbon.

Tutorial

▶**Tip** Single-clicking in the selection area at the left of a Word document selects a single line of text, and triple-clicking in the same area selects all the text in the document.

 Shortcut
Cut
Ctrl + X

6 Shortcut
Paste
Ctrl + V

▶**Tip** In Step 6, be sure to click the Paste button, not the Paste arrow.

▶**Tip** To quickly select a word, hover the mouse pointer over the word and then double-click. To select a paragraph, hover the mouse pointer anywhere over the paragraph and then triple-click.

8 Shortcut
Copy
Ctrl + C

1 If it is not already open, open **C1S2-Subscription**, the file you saved in the previous skill, and save it as **C1S3-Subscription**.

2 Hover your mouse pointer over the margin to the left of the second paragraph, which begins with the words *To renew your*. The pointer is in the selection area and it changes from an I-beam to an arrow.

3 Double-click to select the entire paragraph.

4 On the Home tab, click the Cut button in the Clipboard group. The text is cut from the document.

5 Click just to the left of the *S* in the word *Sincerely* in the signature block at the end of the document (but do not select the word).

6 Click the Paste button. The paragraph now appears at the new location.

7 Click at the start of the first sentence in the body of the letter, which begins with the words *Thank you for*, and then drag your mouse to select the sentence.

8 Click the Copy button.

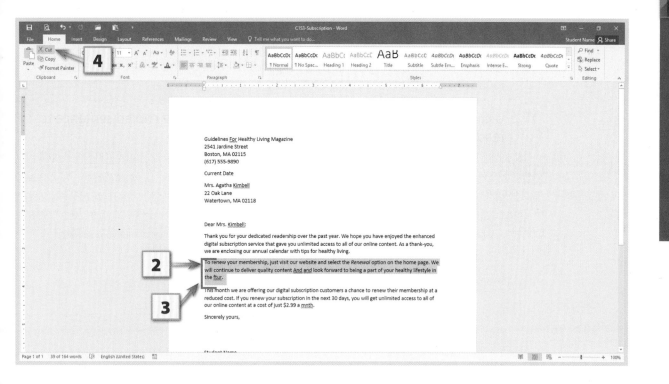

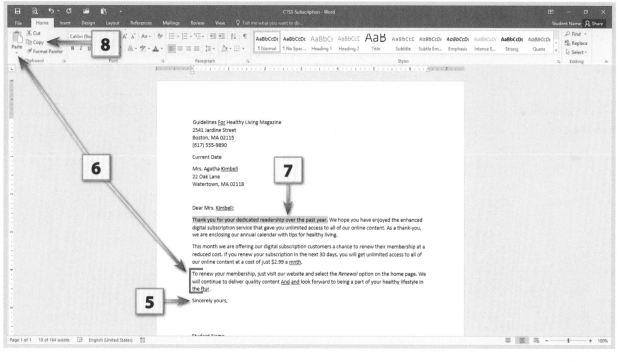

More

Word

9 Click to the left of the word *Sincerely.*

 10 Click the Paste button to copy the first sentence of the letter to the new location, and then press the Enter key.

11 Using any of the editing methods from Skill 2, edit the copied sentence to read *Thank you again for your dedicated readership.*

12 *Shortcut*
Save
Ctrl + S

12 Save the file.

Completed Skill 3

Guidelines For Healthy Living Magazine
2541 Jardine Street
Boston, MA 02115
(617) 555-9890

Current Date

Mrs. Agatha Kimbell
22 Oak Lane
Watertown, MA 02118

Dear Mrs. Kimbell:

Thank you for your dedicated readership over the past year. We hope you have enjoyed the enhanced digital subscription service that gave you unlimited access to all of our online content. As a thank-you, we are enclosing our annual calendar with tips for healthy living.

This month we are offering our digital subscription customers a chance to renew their membership at a reduced cost. If you renew your subscription in the next 30 days, you will get unlimited access to all of our online content at a cost of just $2.99 a mnth.

To renew your membership, just visit our website and select the *Renewal* option on the home page. We will continue to deliver quality content And and look forward to being a part of your healthy lifestyle in the ftur.

Thank you again for your dedicated readership.

Sincerely yours,

Student Name
Editor

Completed
Skill Preview

Taking It Further ●

Using the Clipboard

When you cut or copy text or an object such as a picture, it is placed on the *Clipboard*, a holding area. Immediately after cutting or copying an item, you can click in any document and use the Paste tool to insert the item from the Clipboard. You can use the Paste button to *paste* that item as many times as you want, until you cut or copy another item to the Clipboard. If you want to paste an item that was previously copied to the Clipboard, click the dialog box launcher in the Clipboard group on the Home tab to display the Clipboard pane. Note that the Clipboard is cleared when you save your document and exit Word.

Skill 4 Perform a Spelling and Grammar Check

Even if you are a good speller, the spelling and grammar checker in Word can help you catch typos and other spelling mistakes, as well as common grammar errors. Knowing how to use this important tool can help you ensure that your documents are correct and polished to create the best impression. You can choose to make the suggested corrections or ignore them.

Be aware that this helpful feature isn't foolproof. For example, the spelling checker might flag a correctly spelled company name, such as Asus, as incorrect, and the grammar checker might flag a bullet point phrase as a sentence fragment even though it reads just as you want it to. The spelling and grammar checker may also miss mistakes with sound-alike words, such as using the word fair when you meant fare. To be sure your content is correct, you should always proofread your document carefully. In this skill, you learn how to use the spelling and grammar checker and how to make appropriate choices for changes.

Tutorial

1 If it is not already open, open **C1S3-Subscription**, the file you saved in the previous skill, and save it as **C1S4-Subscription**.

2 Click in front of the first line of text (*Guidelines For Healthy…*) to place the insertion point at the start of the document, and then click the Review tab.

 Shortcut
Open Spelling Pane
F7

3 Click the Spelling & Grammar button in the Proofing group to open the Spelling pane.

▶**Tip** When should you click Ignore and when should you click Ignore All? If you use a term, such as a company name, several times in a document, choose Ignore All. If there is only one instance of a misspelling or misuse—say you are quoting someone who said *ain't*, but you do not want that word anywhere else in your document—choose Ignore.

4 The grammar checker highlights the sender's block and suggests that the word *For* in the title *Guidelines For Healthy Living Magazine* not be capitalized. Click the Change button to change *For* to *for*.

5 The spelling checker identifies *Kimbell* as a possible misspelled word. *Kimbell* is spelled correctly, so click the Ignore All button.

6 Click the Change button to change *mnth* to *month*.

7 The next flagged error is a repeated word error: you have an extra *and* in your sentence. Click the Delete button to correct the error.

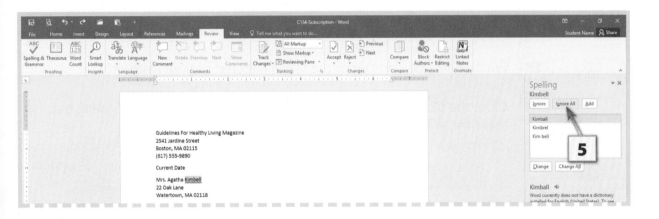

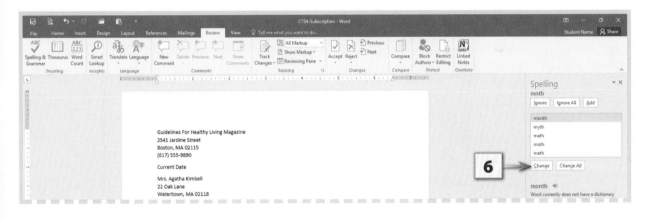

More

8 Click *future* and then click the Change button to change *ftur* to *future*.

9 The checker now highlights the sentence that begins *We will continue* and suggests changing *And* to *and*. Click the Change button to accept the recommended change.

10 If the checker suggests a change in the spelling of your name in the document, confirm that you have spelled your name correctly and then click the Ignore All button.

11 When the checker is finished, you will see a message stating that the spelling and grammar check is complete. Click the OK button to close it.

12 Save the file.

▶ **Tip** Printing files is covered in Unit 2, Skill 10.

13 Print a hard copy or submit the file as directed by your instructor.

14 Close the file. If you have any other Word files open, also close them, but leave the Word application open.

Completed Skill 4

Guidelines for Healthy Living Magazine
2541 Jardine Street
Boston, MA 02115
(617) 555-9890

Current Date

Mrs. Agatha Kimbell
22 Oak Lane
Watertown, MA 02118

Dear Mrs. Kimbell:

Thank you for your dedicated readership over the past year. We hope you have enjoyed the enhanced digital subscription service that gave you unlimited access to all of our online content. As a thank-you, we are enclosing our annual calendar with tips for healthy living.

This month we are offering our digital subscription customers a chance to renew their membership at a reduced cost. If you renew your subscription in the next 30 days, you will get unlimited access to all of our online content at a cost of just $2.99 a month.

To renew your membership, just visit our website and select the *Renewal* option on the home page. We will continue to deliver quality content And look forward to being a part of your healthy lifestyle in the future.

Thank you again for your dedicated readership.

Sincerely yours,

Student Name
Editor

Completed
Skill Preview

94 **Unit 3** Word

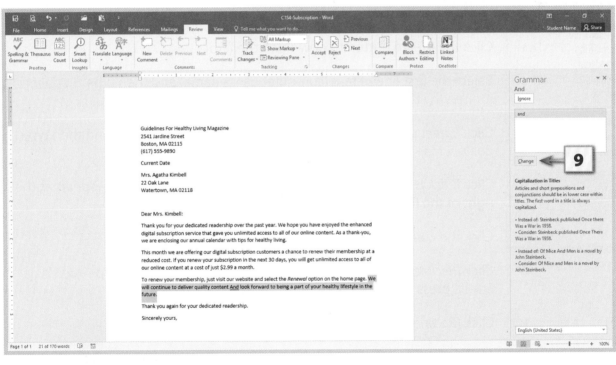

Taking It Further ●

Adding a Word to Your Dictionary

While performing a spelling check, you may encounter a word that you know is correct, but that keeps getting flagged by Word because it is not in the *spelling checker dictionary*. In that situation, you can save yourself the time spent checking the word again and again in each spelling check by adding it to your dictionary. While performing a spelling check, simply click the Add button in the Spelling pane when the word is challenged, and you will never have to verify it again.

Word

Skill 5 Create a Document Based on a Template

You can begin a document in a blank document and then apply formatting and add graphical elements to make it look more appealing. However, a handy shortcut to achieve a more professional-looking document is to open a predesigned document based on a *template*. Several such templates come built into Office 2016, and in this skill, you learn how to locate one and use it to create a professional-looking business letter.

Tutorial

1 With Word open, click the File tab and then click the *New* option. In the backstage area, notice the gallery of available templates and suggested template search categories.

2 Type Business letter (Sales Stripes design) in the search box and then press Enter to locate this specific template.

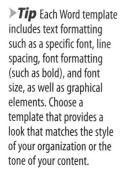
▶ **Tip** Each Word template includes text formatting such as a specific font, line spacing, font formatting (such as bold), and font size, as well as graphical elements. Choose a template that provides a look that matches the style of your organization or the tone of your content.

3 Click the *Business letter (Sales Stripes design)* template.

4 Click the Create button to download the template.

5 Select the first line of text (computer user's name) and then type Guidelines for Healthy Living Magazine.

6 Click *[Street address…]*, type 2541 Jardine Street, press Enter, and then type Boston, MA 02115.

7 Click *[Click Here to Select a Date]* and then click the arrow that appears at the right of the field.

8 *Another Way*
Click the Today button in the drop-down calendar.

8 Click the current date in the drop-down calendar.

9 Click *[Recipient Name]*, type Mr. Arthur Renfrew, press Enter, type 98 Elm Street, press Enter, and then type Brookline, MA 02116.

10 Click *[Recipient]* and then type Mr. Renfrew.

11 Open **C1S4-Subscription**, the file you saved in the previous skill. Select the body of the letter, beginning with the line that starts *Thank you for* and ending with the line that reads *Editor*, and then click the Copy button in the Clipboard group on the Home tab, and then close the file.

12 Click *[Click here to type your letter.]* in the template-based letter.

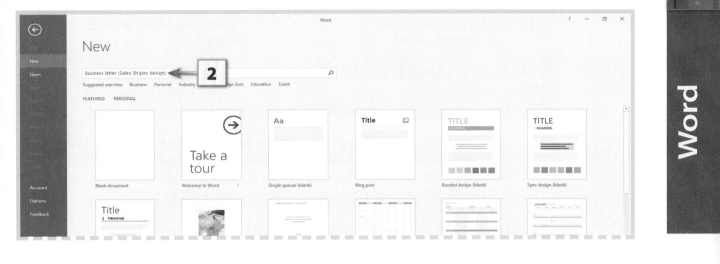

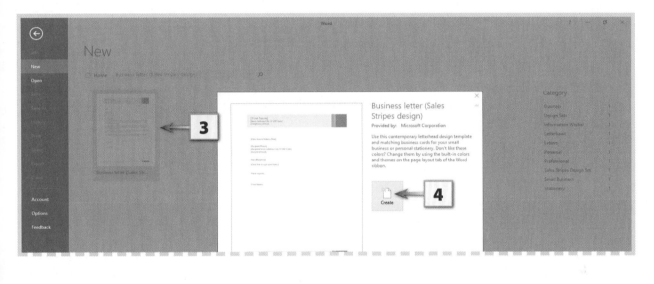

13 Click the Paste button to insert the body and closing block of your subscription letter into the template-based letter.

14 Select all the blank lines and lines of text below the pasted text.

15 Press the Delete key to delete the text selected in Step 14.

▶**Tip** When you upgrade a document to the newest file format, some minor format changes may appear. After you upgrade a document, check the formatting to be sure it looks the way you want it to.

16 Save the file as **C1S5-Template-Lastname**, but replace *Lastname* with your last name. If you see a message that your document will be upgraded to the newest file format, click the OK button. Be sure to save the file in your Unit 3 working folder on your storage medium.

17 Print a hard copy or submit the file as directed by your instructor.

18 Close **C1S5-Template-Lastname**.

Completed Skill 5

Guidelines for Healthy Living Magazine
2541 Jardine Street
Boston, MA 02115

April 25, 2018

Mr. Arthur Renfrew
98 Elm Street
Brookline, MA 02116

Dear Mr. Renfrew,

Thank you for your dedicated readership over the past year. We hope you have enjoyed the enhanced digital subscription service that gave you unlimited access to all of our online content. As a thank-you, we are enclosing our annual calendar with tips for healthy living.

This month we are offering our digital subscription customers a chance to renew their membership at a reduced cost. If you renew your subscription in the next 90 days, you will get unlimited access to all of our online content at a cost of just $2.99 a month.

To renew your membership, just visit our website and select the *Renewal* option on the home page. We will continue to deliver quality content and look forward to being a part of your healthy lifestyle in the future.

Thank you again for your dedicated readership.

Sincerely yours,

Student Name
Editor

Completed
Skill Preview

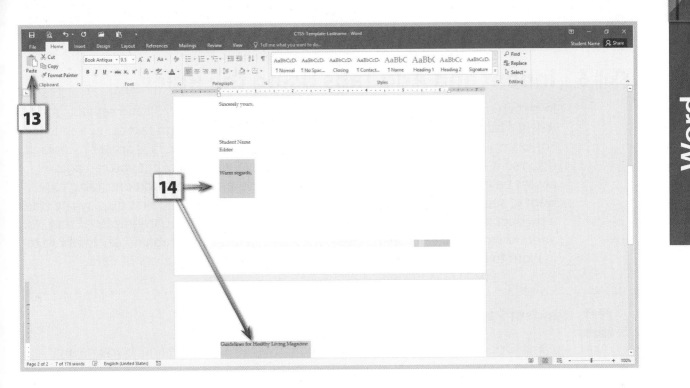

Taking It Further ●

Creating Your Own Template

If you have created a document that you consider a good starting point for other documents of the same type, why not create your own template? You can do this by saving your original file using *Word Template* as the *Save as type* option in the Save As dialog box. When starting a new document, click the File tab, the *New* option, and then the <u>Personal</u> link in the *Suggested searches* section. Locate your template file and click it. A new file opens, based on the template layout and ready for your changes. The file can be saved in the same manner as any other Word document. Using this method, you can reuse the text, formatting, and graphics that you applied to the template. You will save time and add consistency to your documents.

Skill 6 # Indent and Add Tabs Using the Ruler

In certain situations, you may want to *indent* a block of text in a document. For example, according to standard document style, a long quote should always be indented. Or you might want to set off a block of text, such as a product guarantee in a flyer, to call attention to it. You can use the *ruler* in Word to indent text, set margins (discussed in Skill 7), and set tabs. A *Tab* allows you to align text using a specific spot on the ruler. Tabs are set by default at every half inch, but you can adjust these tabs or set additional tabs.

In this skill, you first display the ruler and indent two paragraphs of text. You then add a left tab and decimal tab to create two short lists of data.

Indent Paragraphs of Text

Tutorial

1 Open the student data file named **C1S6-Subscription** and, if you have not already done so, save it in your Unit 3 working folder on your storage medium.

> **Tip** To see how items on your page line up, display gridlines by clicking the View tab and then clicking the *Gridlines* check box in the Show group to insert a check mark.

2 If the ruler is displayed, skip to Step 4. If the ruler is not displayed, click the View tab.

3 In the Show group, click the *Ruler* check box to insert a check mark.

4 Select the fourth paragraph of the body of the letter, beginning with *Good nutrition is* and ending with *and premature death.* **Hint:** *You may need to scroll down to get to this paragraph.*

5 *Another Way* Click the Increase Indent button in the Paragraph group on the Home tab.

5 On the ruler, drag the Left Indent indicator one-half inch to the right so that it rests at the 0.5-inch mark on the ruler.

6 On the ruler, drag the Right Indent indicator one-half inch to the left so that it rests at the 6-inch mark on the ruler.

Set a Left Tab and a Decimal Tab

Tutorial

7 Click at the end of the second paragraph, after *$2.99 a month.*, and then press Enter.

8 Type You can save even more by renewing for a longer period of time: and then press Enter.

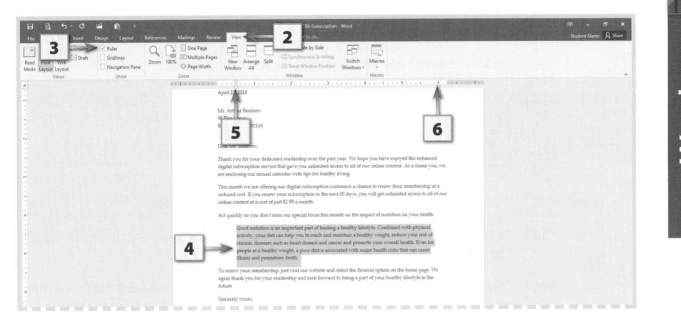

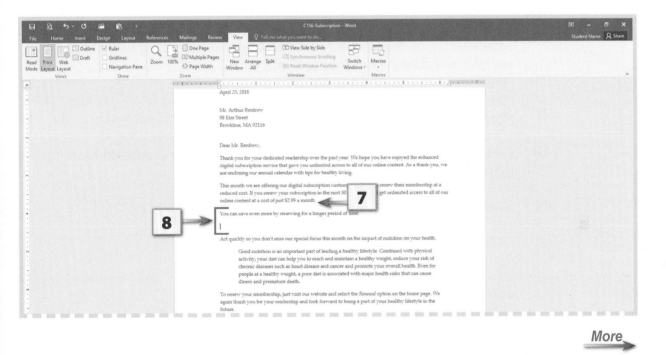

More →

Taking It Further ●

Indenting the First Line in Paragraphs

In the letter example used in this chapter, you use a block style, which does not require the first line of each paragraph to be indented. Other document formats may require you to indent the first line of each paragraph. To do so, click in the paragraph (or drag to select multiple paragraphs) and then drag the First Line Indent marker on the ruler. Alternatively, open the Paragraph dialog box by clicking the dialog box launcher in the Paragraph group on the Home tab. Adjust the measurement for the left indentation, click *First Line* in the *Special* drop-down list, and then click the OK button to save the changes.

▶ **Tip** Left, right, and center tabs tell Word to place the left edge, right edge, or center of the text you enter at the tab location. Decimal tabs are used for columns of numbers—they tell Word to place the decimal point at the specified tab location, thereby vertically aligning those numbers.

9 Click the Home tab.

10 Click the Show/Hide ¶ button in the Paragraph group.

11 Click the 2-inch mark and the 3.5-inch mark on the ruler. These actions place two left tabs and remove any default tabs to the left of them on the ruler for the currently selected line.

12 Press the Tab key and then type Term.

13 Press Tab again, type Monthly Cost, and then press Enter.

14 Remove the left tab symbol at the 3.5-inch mark by dragging it down and off the ruler.

15 Click the tab selector at the left side of the ruler three times until the ScreenTip reads *Decimal Tab* when you hover your mouse pointer over the tab selector.

16 Click the 4-inch mark on the ruler to place a decimal tab at that point.

17 Type the following three lines, pressing Tab and Enter as indicated. Do not press Enter after typing the third line. Notice the tab mark (right arrow) that displays in your document each time you press Tab.
[Tab]　　1 year [Tab]　　$2.99 [Enter]
[Tab]　　2 years [Tab]　　$1.99 [Enter]
[Tab]　　3 years [Tab]　　$1.49

18 Click the Show/Hide ¶ button to hide the tab marks and other formatting marks.

19 Save the file.

Completed Skill 6

Completed
Skill Preview

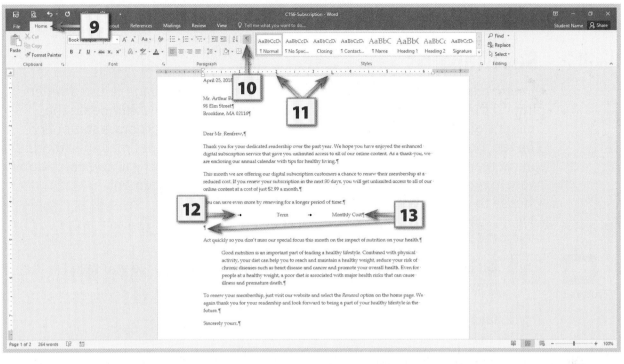

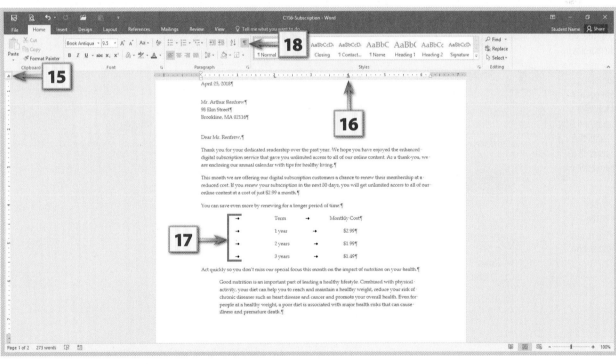

Taking It Further

Adding Tabs to Existing Text

If you have already typed a list using existing tabs and decide you would like to change those tabs—for example, because your columns of text seem too close together to be easily read—you can. Select all the text whose tab settings you wish to change. To move a tab, drag the tab symbol to the new location on the ruler. To remove a tab, drag the tab marker off the ruler. To insert a new tab, follow the method outlined in this skill.

Word

Skill 7 Set Margins

A *margin* is an area of white space around the text on your page. The margins of a document are located at the top, bottom, left, and right. The preset margins for Word documents work in most cases, but you might choose to use narrower margins to fit more text on a page or use a wider top margin to accommodate the letterhead on corporate stationery, for example. Preset margin settings are available, and you can easily apply them to any document.

Tutorial

1 If it is not already open, open **C1S6-Subscription**, the file you saved in the previous skill, and save the file as **C1S7-Subscription**.

2 Click the Layout tab.

3 Click the Margins button in the Page Setup group.

4 *Another Way*
You can also adjust the top, bottom, and side margins in your document by using the vertical or horizontal ruler. Hover your mouse pointer over the area of the ruler where the dark gray and light gray areas meet, until the margin label appears. Drag to adjust the margin size on the ruler.

4 Click the *Moderate* option in the drop-down list to create narrower margins on the left and right of the letter.

5 Save the file.

▶**Tip** In Step 4, the options you see in the drop-down list might vary slightly from those shown in the figure.

Completed
Skill Preview

Completed Skill 7

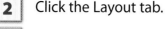

Taking It Further

Creating Custom Margins

You can create custom margins to accommodate any document. Click the Layout tab, click the Margins button in the Page Setup group, and then click the *Custom Margins* option. The Page Setup dialog box appears with the Margins tab selected. Use the arrows in the measurement boxes (*Top*, *Bottom*, *Left*, and *Right*) to set a custom number for each margin. The gutter options are used to set space in a bound document, such as a book. In most books, there is a wider margin on the right side of the left pages and on the left side of the right pages to accommodate the fold, or binding, of the book.

Skill 8 **Insert a Page Break**

When you are working in a document, you may find that an automatic *page break* that Word inserts does not work for you. For example, you might find that a paragraph breaks across a page so that a single line of text or a single row in a list is left dangling. Or you might want a new section of a report or new chapter of a book to start on a new page. In your subscription letter, for example, the page breaks directly below the closing line, leaving the signature block on a page by itself. You can solve this by inserting a manual page break at a better location.

Tutorial

1 If it is not already open, open **C1S7-Subscription**, the file you saved in the previous skill, and save it as **C1S8-Subscription.**

2 On the Home tab, click the Show/Hide ¶ button in the Paragraph group to show formatting marks.

3 Click at the start of the paragraph that begins *To renew your*.

4 Click the Insert tab.

4–5 *Shortcut*
Insert Page Break
Ctrl + Enter

5 Click the Page Break button in the Pages group to insert a page break.

6 Notice the page break mark that appears where you inserted the page break.

▶ **Tip** If you insert a page break in the wrong place, you can delete it by using either the Backspace key (with the insertion point placed just after the page break) or the Delete key (with the insertion point placed just before the page break).

7 Click the Home tab and then click the Show/Hide ¶ button to hide formatting marks.

8 Save the file.

Completed Skill 8

Completed
Skill Preview

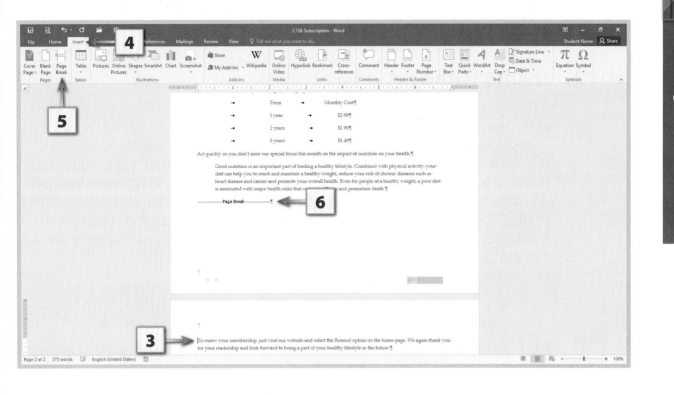

Taking It Further ●●●●●●●●●●●●●●●●●●●●●●●●●●●●

Using Page Breaks Effectively

Page breaks should be used sparingly. If you place breaks throughout a long document, and then edit it by deleting or adding text, the page breaks may not make sense anymore. Say you are working on a 20-page report instead of the 2-page letter in this skill. If you place a page break at the end of each page, and then add a large block of text to page 1, you may need to adjust the page breaks on each of the 20 pages in the report.

While you are writing and revising a document, use page breaks where you truly have to start a new page—for example, to separate the cover page of a report from the first page, the end of a chapter from the start of the next chapter, or the last page of your report from the first page of the index. When you know your document is essentially final, use page breaks to adjust awkward breaks between pages¶ or to avoid splitting tables or lists.

Skill 9 Insert Headers and Footers

If you want text or graphics to appear at the top or bottom of most of the pages in a document, you can add them in either the *header* (top) or *footer* (bottom) area. Word makes it easy to add text—such as your company name or logo, document identifier, page number, or date—to a document. You can also choose not to have your header or footer appear on the first page of your document—for example, on the cover sheet of a report. You can place different header or footer content on odd and even pages. You can also place the page numbers in different locations on odd and even pages, as is often done in books, where page numbers appear opposite each other in the left and right corners.

Tutorial

1 If it is not already open, open **C1S8-Subscription**, the file you saved in the previous skill, and save it as **C1S9-Subscription-Lastname**, but replace *Lastname* with your last name. Be sure to save the file in your Unit 3 working folder on your storage medium.

2 Scroll to page 2, click anywhere on the page, and then click the Insert tab.

3 Click the Header button in the Header & Footer group and then click the *Blank (Three Columns)* option in the drop-down list.

4 Click the *[Type here]* placeholder at the left margin of the header and then type Mr. Arthur Renfrew.

5 Click the *[Type here]* placeholder in the center of the header and then press the Delete key to remove it.

6 Click the *[Type here]* placeholder at the right margin of the header and then type Page followed by a space.

7 Click the Page Number button in the Header & Footer group on the Header & Footer Tools Design tab.

8 Point to the *Current Position* option in the drop-down list and then click the *Plain Number* option in the second drop-down list. A page number is inserted on the right side of the header after the word *Page*.

> **Tip** The advantage of using buttons such as Page Number and Date & Time to insert text in your header or footer is that they automatically update. This means that whenever you print the letter, the current date appears, and however many pages you add to your document, each is numbered correctly.

More →

9 Verify that there is a check mark in the *Different First Page* check box in the Options group on the Header & Footer Tools Design tab. This ensures that the header you just created does not appear on the first page of the document. (The first page of the letter already has a different header.)

10 *Another Way*
Instead of scrolling to see the footer, click the Go to Footer button in the Navigation group on the Header & Footer Tools Design tab.

11 *Shortcut*
Center
Ctrl + E

12 *Another Way*
Double-click in the body of the document.

10 Click in the footer area of the page (you may need to scroll down to locate it) and then type Guidelines for Healthy Living Magazine.

11 Click the Home tab and then click the Center button in the Alignment group.

12 Click the Header & Footer Tools Design tab and then click the Close Header and Footer button.

13 Save the file.

14 Print a hard copy or submit the file as directed by your instructor.

15 Close the file.

Completed Skill 9

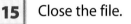

Completed
Skill Preview

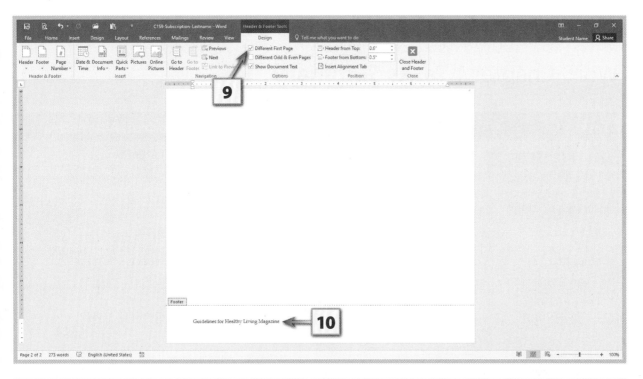

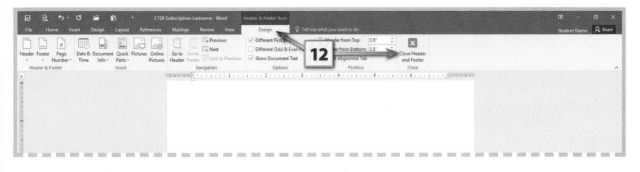

Taking It Further ●

Inserting Document Properties in a Header or Footer

If you click the Quick Parts button in the Insert group on the Header & Footer Tools Design tab and then click *Document Property*, a drop-down list of possible properties appears. This list gives you a handy way to quickly insert fields for information, such as the author or company, drawn from the document properties. You can review the document properties by clicking the File tab, verifying that the *Info* option is selected, and then looking under the *Properties* heading in the right panel of the backstage area. You can edit some of these properties, but others (such as the date last modified) are automatically generated.

Word Chapter 1 **Tasks Summary**

Task	Ribbon Tab, Group	Button, Option	Shortcut, Alternative
Insert a soft return			Shift + Enter
Insert a hard return			Enter
Delete text			Backspace or Delete
Select a word			Double-click word
Select a sentence			Click at start of sentence and then drag to select sentence
Select a paragraph			Triple-click paragraph *or* point to paragraph from left margin and then double-click
Cut text	Home, Clipboard	✂ Cut	Ctrl + X
Paste text	Home, Clipboard	Paste	Ctrl + V
Copy text	Home, Clipboard	Copy	Ctrl + C
Perform a spelling and grammar check	Review, Proofing	ABC ✓ Spelling & Grammar	F7
Show or hide formatting marks	Home, Paragraph	¶	Ctrl + Shift + *
Display the ruler	View, Show	☑ Ruler	
Indent a block of text	Home, Paragraph		Drag indent indicator on ruler
Set tabs	Home, Paragraph	L	Select type in tab selector and click location on ruler

Task	Ribbon Tab, Group	Button, Option	Shortcut, Alternative
	Layout, Page Setup	Margins	Drag margin label on ruler
Insert a page break	Insert, Pages	Page Break	Ctrl + Enter
Insert a headers and footers	Insert, Header & Footer	Header Footer	Double-click top or bottom margin
Edit headers and footers	Insert, Header & Footer	Header Footer	Double-click top or bottom margin
Insert a page number in a header or footer	Header & Footer Tools Design, Header & Footer	# Page Number	Click Page Number button in Header & Footer group on Insert tab
Insert a different header and footer on the first page	Header & Footer Tools Design, Options	☐ Different First Page	
Center text	Home, Format		Ctrl + E

Recheck

Recheck your understanding of the skills and features covered in this chapter.

Workbook

Chapter study resources, exercises, and assessments are available in the Workbook *ebook.*

Chapter 2

Formatting Documents and Citing Sources

Precheck

Check your understanding of the skills and features covered in this chapter.

In Chapter 1 you learned about creating documents, entering and editing text, and working with page layout in Word. In this chapter, you will learn how to modify the *format*, or appearance, of text so that it is attractive and easy to read. Formatting involves working with fonts and effects, such as bold, italic, and color. Word offers some nice shortcuts in the form of styles, which are formatting settings grouped together so that you can apply a group of settings with a single step. World also includes the Format Painter, which allows you to copy formats from one section of text to another. These tools are all accessible on the Home tab. On the Design tab, Word groups some formatting tools together in themes. Themes use unique sets of colors, fonts, and effects to make it even easier for you to give your documents a consistent look and feel.

Formatting tools enable you to organize text by aligning it on the page or putting it into bulleted or numbered lists. You can call attention to the elements of your text and help your readers find their way through the document when you organize and arrange your text and add useful spaces within it.

When writing reports or research papers, you will need to include appropriate citations for the sources you used. Word offers tools to help you cite sources properly, using accepted, professional styles for endnotes, citations, and works cited pages.

Skills You Learn

1 Change font and font size

2 Use formatting tools

3 Apply styles

4 Align text

5 Format paragraph and line spacing

6 Create bulleted and numbered lists

7 Format text in columns

8 Copy formatting with Format Painter

9 Insert a footnote

10 Insert citations using professional styles

11 Create a works cited page

 SNAP

If you are a SNAP user, go to your SNAP Assignments page to complete the Precheck, Tutorials, and Recheck.

Files You Need

For these skills, you need the following student data files:

C2S1-Benefits

What You Create

Guidelines for Healthy Living Magazine regularly publishes research-based articles written to educate their readers about how they can live a healthy lifestyle. A writer has given you a draft copy of an article on the benefits of healthy eating. This article will be published in next month's edition and also posted as a Word document that readers can download. As an editor for the magazine, you have been asked to format the Word document appropriately. You also need to make sure all sources used to write the article are appropriately cited before the Word document is posted.

In this chapter, you work with Word formatting tools to refine the appearance of the article and with references tools to make sure all sources are accurately credited.

Article on Benefits of Healthy Eating

Completed Skill Preview

Word

Skill 1   Change Font and Font Size

combination of a typeface (such as Calibri) and other characteristics, including size and style, that defines the appearance of text. Using fonts effectively can add visual appeal to your documents. Word comes with many built-in fonts that you can apply to some or to all of the text in your document. A *font family* may include several variations. For instance, the Arial font family includes Arial, Arial Bold, and Arial Narrow. You can also modify the *font size* to add emphasis or increase readability.

Tutorial

1 Open the student data file named **C2S1-Benefits**, and if you have not already done so, save it in your Unit 3 working folder on your storage medium.

2 Select the document heading, *Benefits of Healthy Eating*.

3 On the Home tab, click the Font arrow in the Font group and then click the *Arial* option in the *All Fonts* section of the drop-down list.

4 *Another Way*
Click in the *Font Size* box and then type the number of the font size you want.

▶**Tip** A font is typically measured in points (pts). There are approximately 72 points in one inch.

▶**Tip** From the Font dialog box, you can make multiple changes to font formatting (including font style, font size, and font effects). Open the Font dialog box by clicking the dialog box launcher in the bottom right corner of the Font group on the Home tab.

4 With *Benefits of Healthy Eating* still selected, click the Font Size arrow and then click *14* in the drop-down list.

5 Scroll down to the last page of the document and then select the text *Figure 1.1* below the photo.

6 Click the Font arrow and then click the *Arial* option in the *Recently Used Fonts* section of the drop-down list.

7 Click the Save button on the Quick Access Toolbar to save the file.

Completed Skill Preview

Completed Skill 1

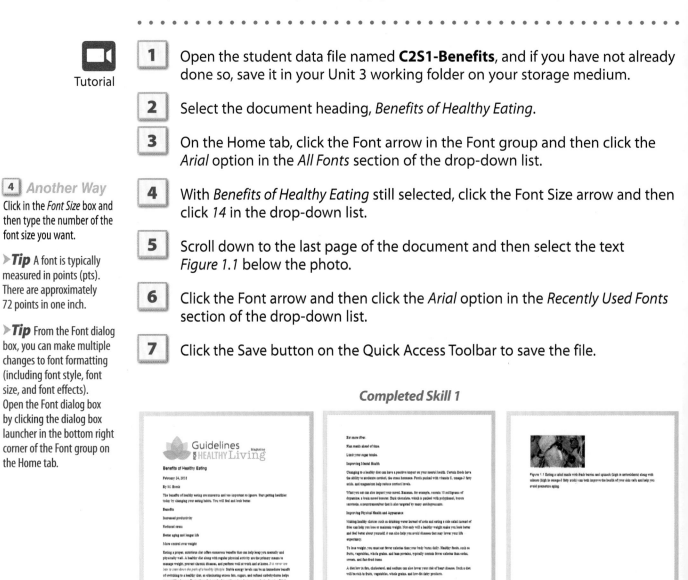

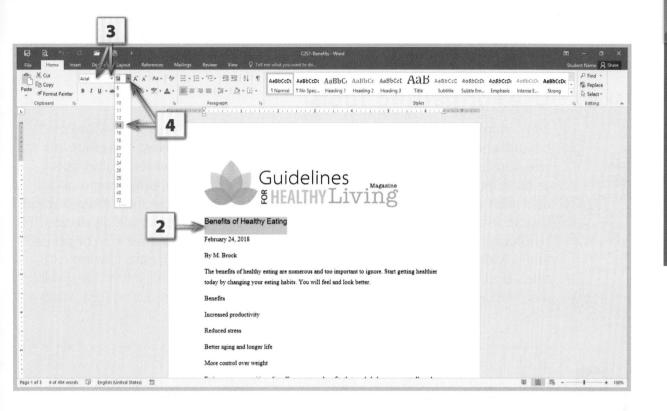

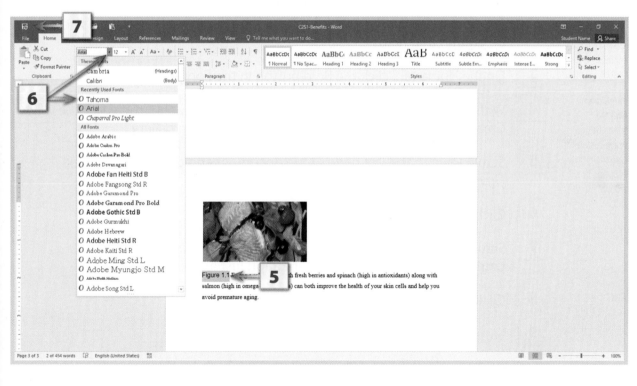

Taking It Further ●

Selecting a Font Size

Your instructor may require that you use a specific font and font size, such as 12-point Times New Roman, when creating a report. If you are not given specific guidelines, for documents that will be printed, use 10–12 points for body text and make the headings slightly larger.

Skill 2 Use Formatting Tools

You can format text in several ways beyond choosing the font and font size. You can apply a *font effect* such as bold, italic, underlining, or color. *Bold* adds emphasis by making the text appear dark and heavy. *Italic* adds emphasis by slanting the characters and is widely used for book and movie titles. Underlining is frequently used to indicate URLs.

You can also change the font color to add visual interest and emphasis. Choose only a few font colors and select colors that either blend or contrast with each other. Keep in mind how your document will be viewed. If it will be presented on-screen or printed on a color printer, emphasizing with color will work well. If it will be printed in black and white, using font colors will not help the look.

Use Your Touchscreen
Scroll by pressing your finger on the screen and then dragging up or down. This action is referred to as swiping. You can also scroll by flicking your finger on the screen.

Tutorial

3 Shortcut
Bold
Ctrl + B

▶**Tip** Access more color options by clicking the Colors button on the Design tab. Create and save custom themes by clicking the *Customize Colors* option in the Colors drop-down list on the Design tab.

1 If it is not already open, open **C2S1-Benefits**, the file you saved in the previous skill, and save it as **C2S2-Benefits**.

2 Scroll up to the first page in the document, if necessary, and then select the paragraph that reads *Benefits*.

3 On the Home tab, click the Bold button in the Font group.

4 With *Benefits* still selected, click the Font Color arrow and then click the *Olive Green, Accent3, Darker 50%* option in the drop-down gallery.

5 Scroll down to the last page of the document and then select the text *Figure 1.1* below the photo.

6 Click the Bold button.

7 Scroll up, if necessary, and then select the text *Figure 1.1* inside the parentheses at the end of the paragraph just above the photo.

8 Shortcut
Italicize
Ctrl + I

8 Click the Italic button.

9 Save the file.

Completed Skill 2

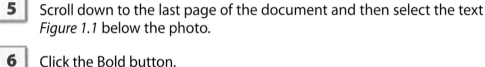

Completed
Skill Preview

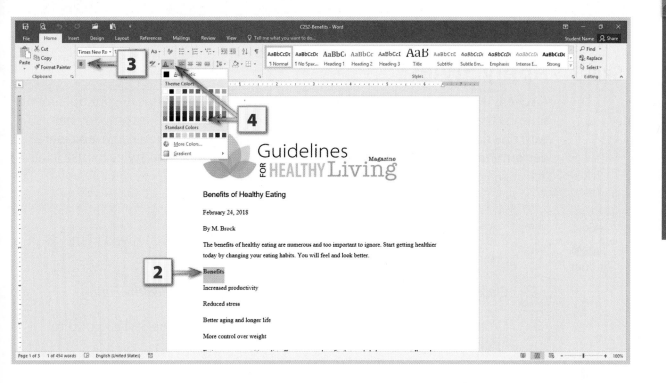

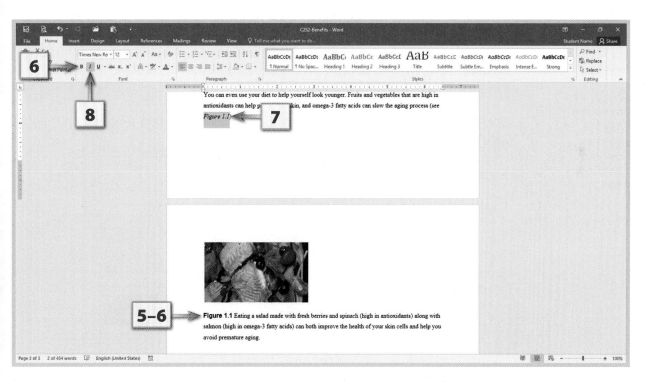

Skill 3 Apply Styles

A *style* is a built-in group of formatting settings that you can apply to text with one action rather than having to perform multiple, separate formatting actions. Styles are useful for tasks such as creating headings in your documents and formatting your company name in a unique way. You can even create and save your own styles for use in all documents.

Tutorial

1 If it is not already open, open **C2S2-Benefits**, the file you saved in the previous skill, and save it as **C2S3-Benefits**.

2 Click anywhere in the document heading, *Benefits of Healthy Eating*.

3 On the Home tab, click the *Heading 1* style option in the Styles group to apply the style.

4 Click anywhere in the date, *February 24, 2018*.

5 Click the *Subtitle* option in the Styles gallery.

6 Scroll to the second page of the document and then apply the Heading 2 style to the following paragraphs: *Improving Mental Health* and *Improving Physical Health and Appearance*.

7 Scroll to the end of the document and then select the last sentence in the article, which begins *Eating a salad*.

8 Apply the Quote style.

9 Save the file.

> **Tip** In Steps 5 and 8, if you don't see the style you are looking for, click the More button in the Styles gallery to display all styles.

> **Tip** To quickly apply a style to several areas of the document, select the first area of text, press and hold down Ctrl while you select the other areas of text, and then click the desired style.

Completed Skill 3

Completed Skill Preview

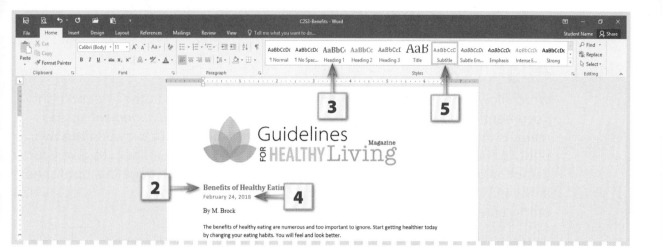

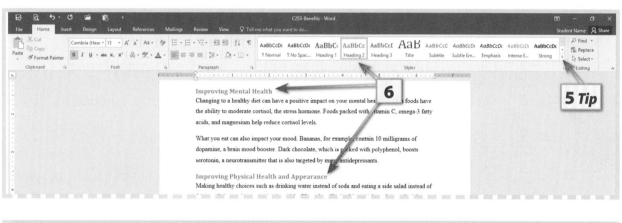

Taking It Further ●

Applying a Theme

You can quickly create a professional-looking document by applying a Theme. A *theme* is a predesigned set of colors, fonts, and effects. Themes are accessible in Word, Excel, Access, and PowerPoint, so files created in all four applications can have a consistent appearance. To apply a theme, click the Themes button in the Document Formatting group on the Design tab and then click a theme in the drop-down gallery.

Word

Skill 4 Align Text

Word allows you to *align* text in your document in four ways relative to the margins that are set: at the left, at the right, in the center, or justified. The default alignment for a document is at the left margin. Document titles are often *center aligned*, or placed at the midpoint between the left and right margins. *Justified alignment* spreads the document out between the two margins, which can help to give your text the look of a page in a published book or magazine.

Tutorial

1 If it is not already open, open **C2S3-Benefits**, the file you saved in the previous skill, and save it as **C2S4-Benefits**.

2 Click anywhere in the document heading, *Benefits of Healthy Eating*.

3 *Shortcut*
Center
Ctrl + E

3 On the Home tab, click the Center button in the Paragraph group.

4 Click anywhere in the date, *February 24, 2018*.

5 *Shortcut*
Align Right
Ctrl + R

5 Click the Align Right button.

▶ **Tip** In Step 6, you can triple-click to select a paragraph.

▶ **Tip** In Step 6, you can see both pages of your document at the same time by clicking the View tab and then clicking the Multiple Page button in the Zoom group.

6 On the first page of the document, select the paragraph that begins *Eating a proper*, press and hold down the Ctrl key, and then select the paragraphs that start with the following phrases:

Changing to a	*What you eat*
Making healthy choices	*To lose weight*
A diet low	*You can even*

7 *Shortcut*
Justify
Ctrl + J

7 Click the Justify button.

8 Save the file.

Completed Skill 4

Completed
Skill Preview

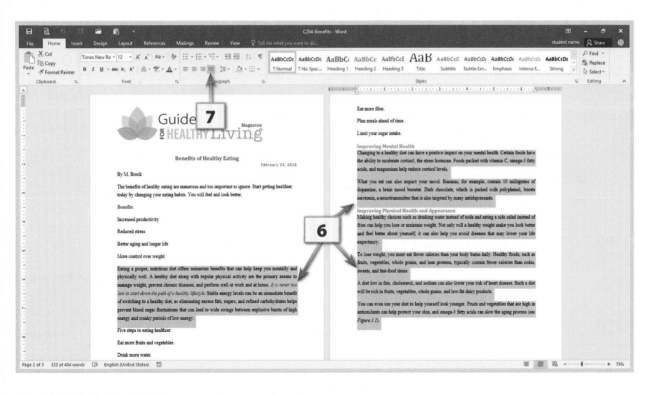

Taking It Further

Formatting with Tabs

You can apply only one alignment setting to a paragraph. For example, if your address and phone number are on the same line at the top of your resume, you cannot align your address at the left and your phone number at the right. To achieve that formatting, you would left align the text and set a right tab at the right margin. You would then type the address, press the Tab key, and type the phone number.

Skill 5   Format Paragraph and Line Spacing

Word enables you to adjust spacing between the lines of a paragraph and between paragraphs. The amount of white space you provide between lines can affect the readability of your document. It can also provide a visual break between the paragraphs in your text. You can apply preset spacing settings to selected text using tools in the Paragraph group on the Home tab.

Tutorial

1   If it is not already open, open **C2S4-Benefits**, the file you saved in the previous skill, and save it as **C2S5-Benefits**.

2   On the first page of the document, select the paragraph that begins *Eating a proper*, press and hold down the Ctrl key, and then select the text paragraphs that start with the following phrases:

Changing to a	*What you eat*
Making healthy choices	*To lose weight*
A diet low	*You can even*

3   **Another Way**
Open the Paragraph dialog box as described in Step 5. In the *Spacing* section, type *1.15* in the *At* box and then click the OK button.

3   With the paragraphs still selected, click the Line and Paragraph Spacing button in the Paragraph group on the Home tab and then click *1.15* in the drop-down list.

4   Select the first two paragraphs of the document (the document heading and date).

5   Click the dialog box launcher () in the bottom right corner of the Paragraph group.

6   **Another Way**
Type *12 pt* in the *After* box.

6   In the *Spacing* section of the Paragraph dialog box, click the *After* increment (up) arrow until *12 pt* displays in the box.

7   Click the OK button to close the dialog box. Extra space has been added after the selected paragraphs.

8   Save the file.

Completed Skill 5

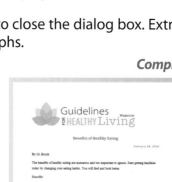

Completed Skill Preview

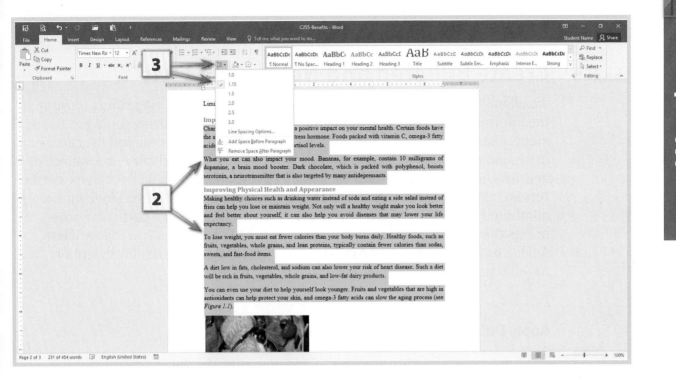

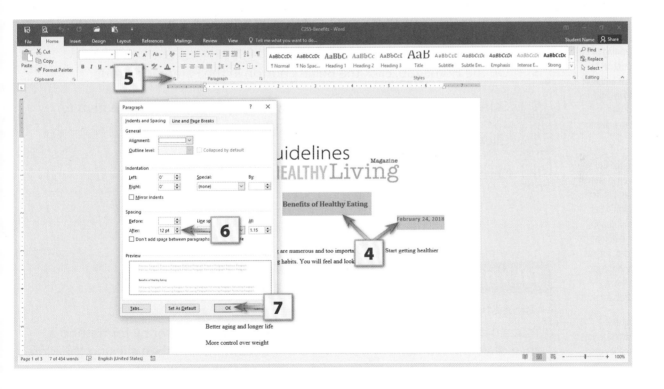

Taking It Further

Formatting Line Spacing

You can set how much space appears before a paragraph by using the *Before* box in the *Spacing* section of the Paragraph dialog box. The Paragraph dialog box can also be used to set paragraph alignment and paragraph indents.

Skill 6 Create Bulleted and Numbered Lists

We all make lists that help us organize the information in our lives. In documents, lists help to set off similar items, indicate steps in a procedure, or draw the reader's attention to certain information. Bulleted lists and numbered lists are two common types of lists that are easy to set up in Word. A *bulleted list* is used for items that have no particular sequence, such as the books or magazines on your bookshelf or movies you want to see. The bullets in a bulleted list can be customized to display as a variety of symbols, such as a check mark symbol. A *numbered list* is used for organizing items that go in a particular order, such as the steps you follow when installing computer hardware or software.

Apply Default Bullet and Number Styles

Tutorial

1 If it is not already open, open **C2S5-Benefits**, the file you saved in the previous skill, and save it as **C2S6-Benefits**.

2 On the first page of the document, select the four paragraphs under the *Benefits* heading.

3 On the Home tab, click the Bullets button in the Paragraph group.

4 Select the five paragraphs after the paragraph that begins *Five steps to*.

5 Click the Numbering button.

6 Save the file.

> **Tip** In Step 2, you can click at the beginning of the first paragraph of text to be selected, press and hold down the Shift key, and then click at the end of the last paragraph to make the selection.

> **Tip** Clicking the Bullets button (as you do in Step 3) applies the default bullet style at the beginning of each selected paragraph. You can choose different bulleted list styles, such as square or diamond shapes rather than circles, by clicking the Bullets arrow.

> **Tip** Clicking the Numbering button (as you do in Step 5) applies the default numbering style at the beginning of each selected paragraph. You can choose different styles for numbered lists by clicking the Numbering arrow. You might prefer using letters or Roman numerals rather than Arabic numerals.

Taking It Further

Using Style Sets

You can quickly change the appearance of your document by applying a style set. A *style set* is a predesigned set of fonts and paragraph properties. To apply a style set, click an option in the Document Formatting group on the Design tab. You can also create your own style set by formatting a document and then clicking the More button in the Document Formatting group. In the list of options at the bottom of the expanded gallery, click *Save as New Style Set*, give the style a name, and then click the OK button.

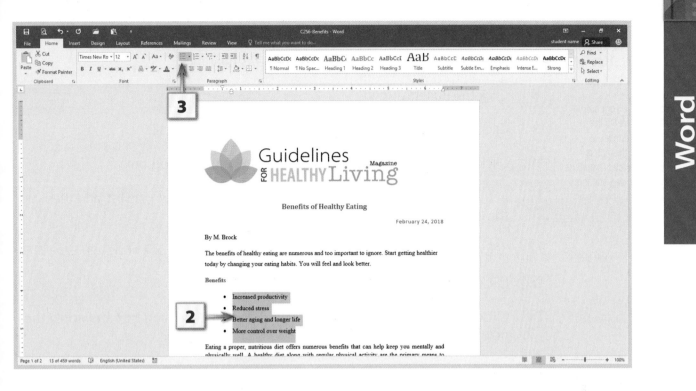

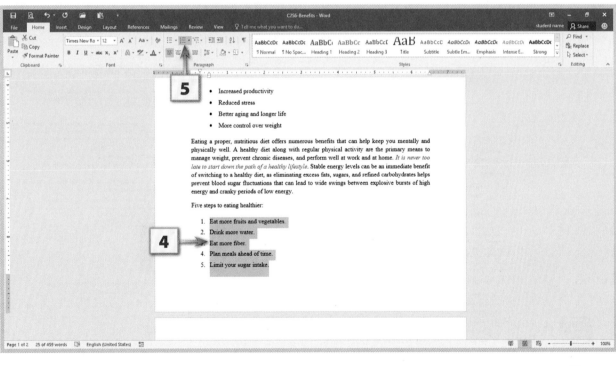

More

Tutorial

Apply a Custom Bullet Style

7 Select the bulleted text under the *Benefits* heading.

8 Click the Bullets arrow.

9 Click the *Define New Bullet* option in the drop-down gallery.

10 Click the Symbol button in the Define New Bullet dialog box.

11 In the Symbol dialog box, click the *Font* arrow, scroll down the list, and then click the *Wingdings* option.

12 Select the number that appears in the *Character code* box and then type 252.

13 Click the OK button to close the Symbol dialog box.

14 Click the OK button to close the Define New Bullet dialog box and apply the new bullet style.

15 Save the file.

▶ **Tip** Click the Font button in the Define New Bullet dialog box to format the appearance of the bullets themselves, such as changing their font, font size, and font color, or applying bold, italic, or underline effects.

11 *Another Way*
Click the *Font* arrow and then type *w*.

12 *Another Way*
Click a symbol in the *Symbol* list box.

Completed Skill 6

Completed
Skill Preview

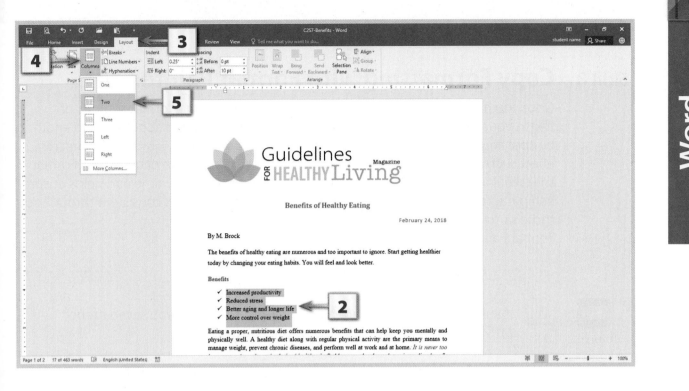

Taking It Further ●

More Options for Formatting Columns

If you wish to have two columns of unequal width, you have two options for creating them. First, when selecting the style of column, you can choose the *Left* or *Right* style options in the *Columns* drop-down list. *Left* makes the left column smaller; *Right* makes the right column larger. If these options do not suit your needs, consider using a table to organize text instead. Tables give you great flexibility in creating columns of varying widths. If you like, you can even remove the border lines around the table and cells within it, which results in a layout that looks more like columns than like a table. See Chapter 3 for more about creating tables.

Skill 8 Copy Formatting with Format Painter

Once you have formatted some of the text in your document—for example, by applying a font style, adding an effect such as bold or italic, modifying the color, or setting the line spacing and paragraph indents—you can apply those same settings to other text using Format Painter. *Format Painter* allows you to copy the format settings of selected text and apply them to another selection, which could be a character, word, or an entire page of text. Format Painter saves you time and helps ensure that formatting is consistent throughout your document.

Tutorial

1 If it is not already open, open **C2S7-Benefits**, the file you saved in the previous skill, and save it as **C2S8-Benefits**.

2 On the first page of the document, click anywhere in the first line of the paragraph that begins *Eating a proper* on page 1.

3, 6 *Shortcut*
Activate Format Painter
Ctrl + Shift + C

3 On the Home tab, click the Format Painter button in the Clipboard group.

4 Click anywhere in the paragraph that begins *The benefits of*. Notice that the formatting is copied to the destination text.

5 Click anywhere in the *Improving Mental Health* heading.

6 Click the Format Painter button.

7 Click anywhere in the *Benefits* heading.

8 Save the file.

Completed Skill 8

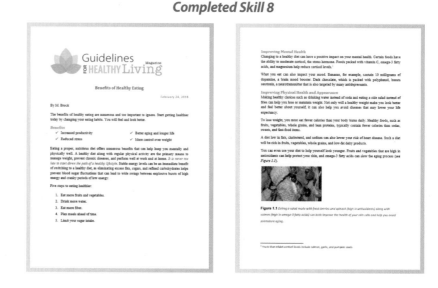

**Completed
Skill Preview**

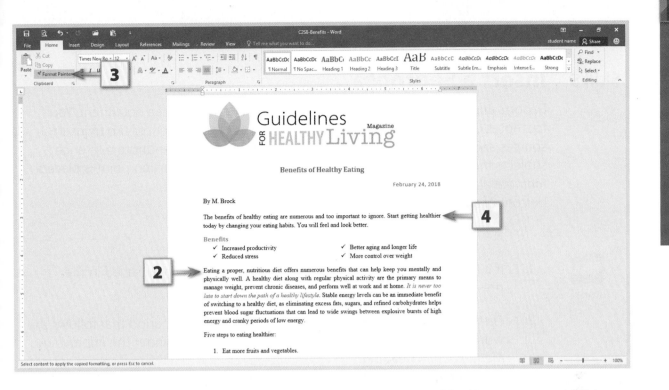

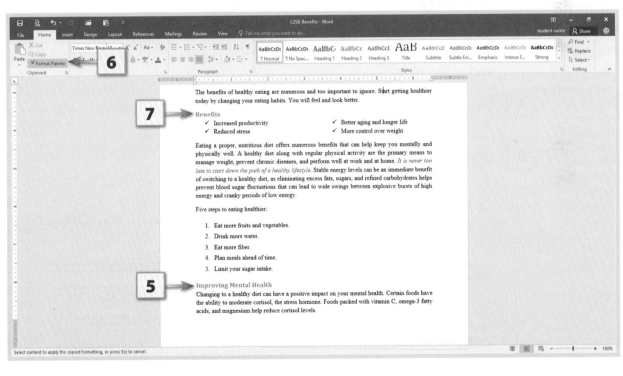

Taking It Further ●

Using Format Painter Multiple Times

You can use Format Painter to copy formatting to more than one place in your document. In Step 3 of this skill, you could double-click the Format Painter button and then apply the format to as many paragraphs, words, or phrases as you like. When you are done, click the Format Painter button again, or press the Esc key on your keyboard, to deactivate Format Painter.

Skill 9 Insert a Footnote

Reports and research papers include footnotes or endnotes to document sources and add information about subjects mentioned in the text. A *footnote* places information at the bottom of a page; an *endnote* places them at the end of a document. You can use the References tab to insert a footnote or an endnote reference wherever the insertion point is placed in your document.

Tutorial

1 If it is not already open, open **C2S8-Benefits**, the file you saved in the previous skill, and save it as **C2S9-Benefits**.

2 On the second page of the document, click after the period that follows the words *cortisol levels* at the end of the first paragraph under the *Improving Mental Health* heading.

3 Click the References tab.

4 *Shortcut*
Insert a Footnote
Alt + Ctrl + F

4 Click the Insert Footnote button in the Footnotes group. A footnote reference number is inserted and the insertion point is moved to a new footnote at the end of the page.

Tip If you prefer to place your notes at the end of the document rather than at the bottom of each page, use endnotes instead of footnotes. Insert an endnote by clicking the Insert Endnote button in the Footnotes group on the References tab or by pressing Alt + Ctrl + D.

5 Type the following footnote text: Foods that inhibit cortisol levels include salmon, garlic, and pumpkin seeds.

6 Save the file.

Completed Skill 9

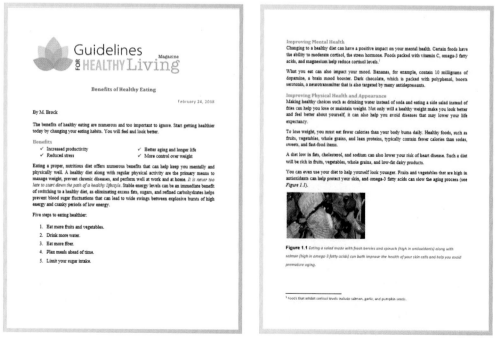

Completed Skill Preview

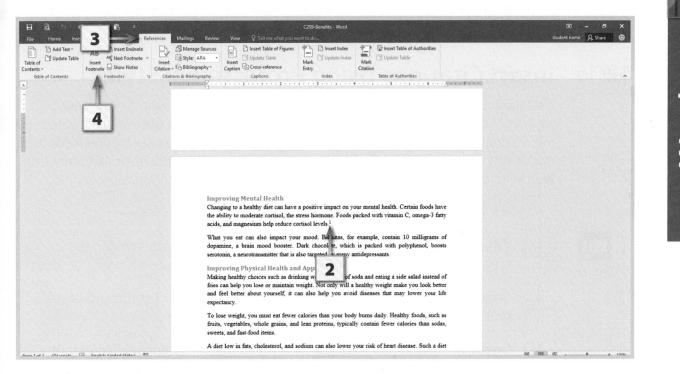

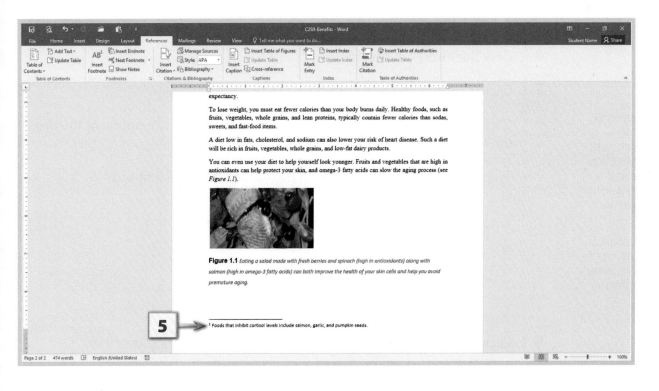

Navigating Footnotes and Endnotes

To locate footnotes or endnotes in a document, you can use the Next Footnote button in the Footnotes group on the References tab. When you click the Next Footnote arrow, you can choose from the options *Next Footnote*, *Previous Footnote*, *Next Endnote*, and *Previous Endnote* to navigate among your footnotes and endnotes.

Skill 10   Insert Citations Using Professional Styles

A *citation* gives appropriate credit to sources you have quoted or taken information from when creating a document. You can use Word's Citation feature to create sources and insert their information within your text according to one of several accepted professional styles, such as *MLA (Modern Language Association)*, or *APA (American Psychological Association)*.

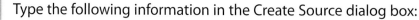

Tutorial

1   If it is not already open, open **C2S9-Benefits**, the file you saved in the previous skill, and save it as **C2S10-Benefits**.

2   On the first page of the document, click after the period at the end of the sentence that begins *Stable energy levels*.

3   On the References tab, click the *Style* arrow in the Citations & Bibliography group and then click the *APA Sixth Edition* option in the drop-down list. This option applies the American Psychological Association professional style for citations.

4   Click the Insert Citation button.

5   Click the *Add New Source* option in the drop-down list.

> ▶ **Tip** Once you enter information about a resource, you can insert it again by choosing it from the drop-down list that appears when you click the Insert Citation button.

6   Click the Type of Source arrow and then click the *Web site* option in the drop-down list.

> ▶ **Tip** When entering a URL, copy the URL from the Address bar of the browser to avoid typing errors.

7   Type the following information in the Create Source dialog box:

Name of Web Page	Eating to boost energy
Name of Web Site	Harvard Health Publications
Year	2011
Month	7
Day	11
URL	http://www.health.harvard.edu

8   Click the OK button to add the source to the document's source list.

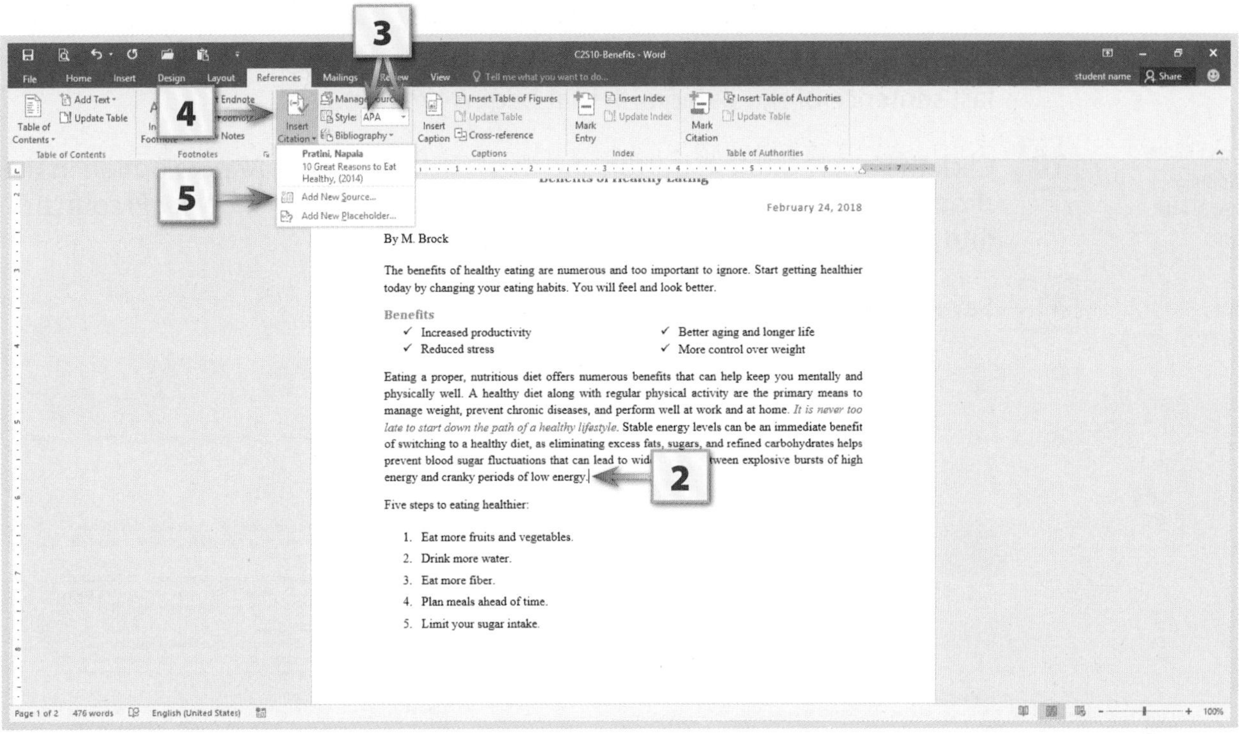
3
4
5
2
C2S10-Benefits - Word
File
Home
Insert
Design
Layout
References
Mailings
Review
View
Tell me what you want to do...
student name
Share
Add Text
Update Table
Table of Contents
Table of Contents
Endnote
Notes
Footnotes
Insert Citation
Style: APA
Bibliography
Pratini, Napala
10 Great Reasons to Eat Healthy, (2014)
Add New Source...
Add New Placeholder...
Insert Table of Figures
Update Table
Insert Caption
Cross-reference
Captions
Mark Entry
Insert Index
Update Index
Index
Mark Citation
Insert Table of Authorities
Update Table
Table of Authorities
February 24, 2018
By M. Brock
The benefits of healthy eating are numerous and too important to ignore. Start getting healthier today by changing your eating habits. You will feel and look better.
Benefits
Increased productivity
Better aging and longer life
Reduced stress
More control over weight
Eating a proper, nutritious diet offers numerous benefits that can help keep you mentally and physically well. A healthy diet along with regular physical activity are the primary means to manage weight, prevent chronic diseases, and perform well at work and at home. It is never too late to start down the path of a healthy lifestyle. Stable energy levels can be an immediate benefit of switching to a healthy diet, as eliminating excess fats, sugars, and refined carbohydrates helps prevent blood sugar fluctuations that can lead to wid tween explosive bursts of high energy and cranky periods of low energy.
Five steps to eating healthier:
1. Eat more fruits and vegetables.
2. Drink more water.
3. Eat more fiber.
4. Plan meals ahead of time.
5. Limit your sugar intake.
Page 1 of 2
476 words
English (United States)
100%

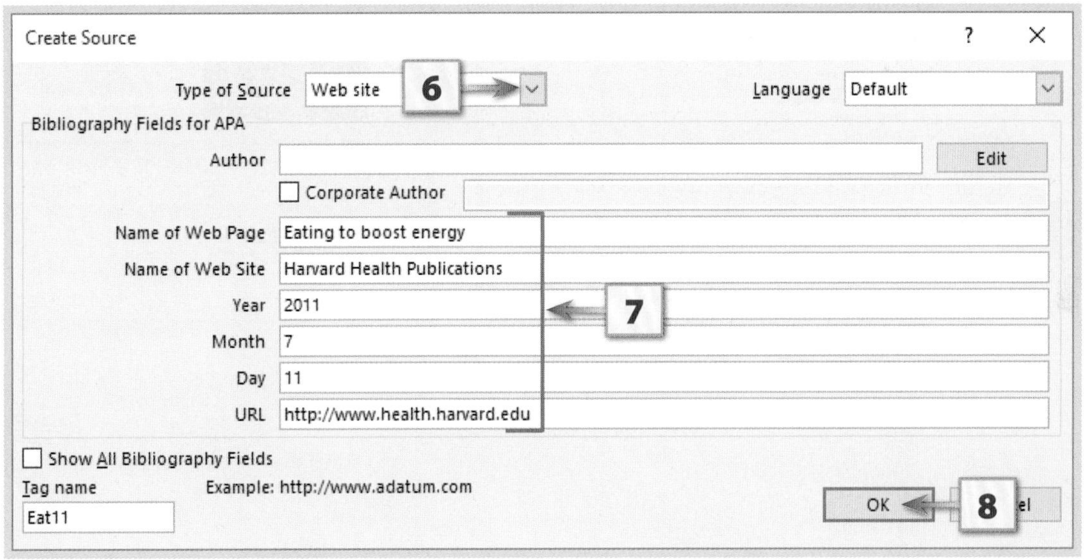
Create Source
6
7
8
Type of Source
Web site
Language
Default
Bibliography Fields for APA
Author
Edit
Corporate Author
Name of Web Page
Eating to boost energy
Name of Web Site
Harvard Health Publications
Year
2011
Month
7
Day
11
URL
http://www.health.harvard.edu
Show All Bibliography Fields
Tag name
Eat11
Example: http://www.adatum.com
OK

More

9 On the second page of the document, click after the period, at the end of the last sentence of the paragraph that begins *What you eat.*

▶ *Tip* The Insert Citation drop-down list displays sources that already exist for the document.

10 Click the Insert Citation button and then click the *Pratini, Napala* option in the drop-down list. This action inserts the citation for the *Pratini, Napala* source into the document.

11 Save the file.

Completed Skill 10

Completed
Skill Preview

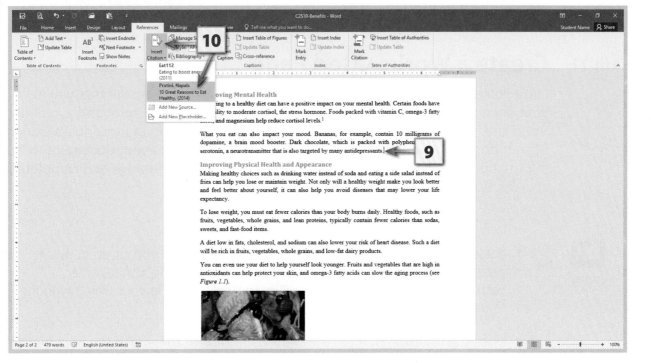

Taking It Further ●

Editing Sources

Once you have entered source information, you may change it by clicking the Manage Sources button in the Citations & Bibliography group on the References tab. Clicking this button opens the Source Manager dialog box. In this dialog box, you can browse for sources you have saved; preview citation styles, such as MLA and APA; and add, edit, or delete sources.

Skill 11 **Create a Works Cited Page**

Once you have inserted citations in your document, you can create a *works cited page* to appear at the end of your document and give detailed information about your quoted sources. Adding citations and a works cited page helps ensure that you have given appropriate credit and avoided plagiarizing another individual's work. This in turn helps your document to be viewed as authoritative and complete.

Tutorial

1 If it is not already open, open **C2S10-Benefits**, the file you saved in the previous skill, and save it as **C2S11-Benefits-Lastname**, but replace *Lastname* with your last name. Be sure to save the file in your Unit 3 working folder on your storage medium.

2 Place the insertion point in the blank paragraph at the end of the document, before the footnote text.

3 Click the References tab.

4 Click the Bibliography button in the Citations & Bibliography group.

5 Click the *Works Cited* option in the drop-down list. This action creates a Works Cited page from the citations in the document.

6 Save the file.

Completed Skill 11

Completed
Skill Preview

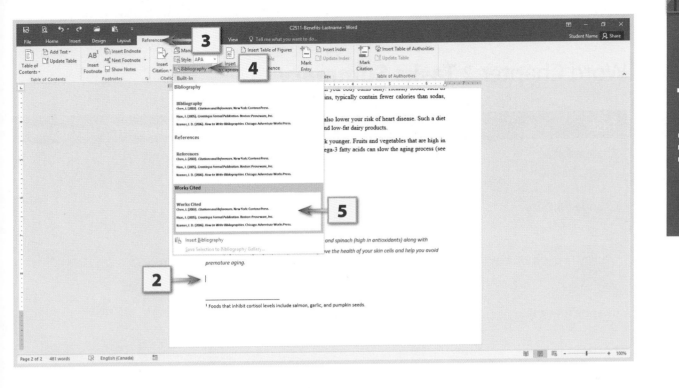

Taking It Further •

Selecting Citation Styles

Citation styles are based on professional standards for publication. Three commonly used standards are MLA (Modern Languages Association), most often used in English and humanities publications; APA (American Psychological Association), usually used in scientific publications; and Chicago, based on *The Chicago Manual of Style*. Ask your instructor which standard he or she prefers.

Word Chapter 2 **Tasks Summary**

Task	Ribbon Tab, Group	Button, Option	Shortcut, Alternative
Change font	Home, Font	Calibri (Body) ▾	
Change font size	Home, Font	11 ▾	
Display Font dialog box	Home, Font	⌐	Ctrl + D
Change font color	Home, Font	**A** ▾	
Apply bold	Home, Font	**B**	Ctrl + B
Apply italics	Home, Font	*I*	Ctrl + I
Apply underlining	Home, Font	U	Ctrl + U
Apply styles	Home, Styles	Styles gallery	
Display more styles	Home, Styles	▾	
Align text right	Home, Paragraph	☰	Ctrl + R
Center text	Home, Paragraph	☰	Ctrl + E
Justify text	Home, Paragraph	☰	Ctrl + J
Change line spacing	Home, Paragraph	↕≡ ▾	Click the dialog box launcher in the bottom right corner of the Paragraph group and then select an option from the *Line Spacing* drop-down list *or* type or select a value in the *At* box

Task	Ribbon Tab, Group	Button, Option	Shortcut, Alternative
Format text as bulleted list	Home, Paragraph		
Format text as numbered list	Home, Paragraph		
Format text in columns	Layout, Page Setup	Columns	
Activate Format Painter	Home, Clipboard	Format Painter	Ctrl + Shift + C
Insert a footnote	References, Footnotes	AB¹ Insert Footnote	Alt + Ctrl + D
Choose a citation style	References, Citations & Bibliography	Style: APA	
Insert a citation	References, Citations & Bibliography	Insert Citation	
Create a works cited page	References, Citations & Bibliography	Bibliography	

Recheck

Recheck your understanding of the skills and features covered in this chapter.

Workbook

Chapter study resources, exercises, and assessments are available in the Workbook *ebook.*

Chapter 3

Working with Tables and Objects

Precheck

Check your understanding of the skills and features covered in this chapter.

Word provides several features that can help you organize information and add visual appeal to your documents. Tables organize information into rows and columns, allowing you to convey a great deal of data in a small, neat space. The data presented in a table can be enhanced visually by changing the page orientation and adding formatting, such as a table style. You can also insert audio and visual media, including photos, SmartArt diagrams, and videos, to better illustrate a point or make your document more attractive. In this chapter you learn how to build and format tables, create SmartArt diagrams, and insert, edit, and format various types of media.

Skills You Learn

1 Create tables
2 Convert text to tables
3 Change page orientation
4 Insert and delete rows and columns in a table
5 Merge rows or columns in a table
6 Format tables
7 Insert SmartArt
8 Insert visual media
9 Resize media
10 Align and format media

Files You Need

For these skills, you need the following student data files:

C3S1-Recipe

C3S8-SalmonBowl

What You Create

Healthy recipes are a regular feature in *Guidelines for Healthy Living Magazine*. The magazine focuses on publishing recipes that not only are delicious but also are easy to make with healthy ingredients that most people have readily available.

 SNAP *If you are a SNAP user, go to your SNAP Assignments page to complete the Precheck, Tutorials, and Recheck.*

This month's recipe is for a salmon bowl. Your boss has asked you to create the page that will feature the recipe, including a table of ingredients, an image of the finished dish, and recipe instructions. You will also create a second page that contains a diagram which represents the magazine's vision for living a healthy lifestyle.

In this chapter, you build the recipe in a Word document using the Word table and column features to organize the recipe contents and then add an image and SmartArt for visual interest.

Salmon Bowl Recipe

Guidelines
FOR HEALTHY Living Magazine

Salmon Bowl

Ingredients

Quantity	Ingredient
4 ounces	Soba noodles
5 ounces	Asparagus, cut into bite-sized pieces
1	Salmon fillet, cut into bite-sized pieces
1 tablespoon	Sesame oil
2	Limes, squeezed for their juice
¼ teaspoon	Salt
¼ teaspoon	Pepper
4 ounces	Cucumber, cut into bite-sized pieces
1	Avocado, cut into bite-sized pieces

Steps

Step 1   Cook the noodles in boiling water until al dente (6–8 minutes). Drain.
Step 2   Cook the asparagus in boiling water until al dente (2 minutes). Drain and rinse under cold water.
Step 3   Cook the salmon in a skillet over medium-high heat until golden brown and firm (about 4–6 minutes). Set aside and keep warm.
Step 4   Prepare the dressing by whisking together the sesame oil, lime juice, salt, and pepper in a small bowl.
Step 5   Combine the noodles, asparagus, and dressing in a medium-sized bowl.
Step 6   Add the cucumber and avocado.
Step 7   Add the cooked salmon.
Step 8   Serve warm or at room temperature.
490 calories per serving

A Recipe from *Guidelines for Healthy Living Magazine*

Eat Healthy ● ● ● ● ➤   Exercise ● ● ● ● ➤   Feel Better ● ● ● ● ➤

Completed
Skill Preview

Word

Skill 1 Create Tables

A *table* uses columns and rows to help organize sets of information and show relationships among separate pieces of information. For example, imagine a table used to compare the nutritional information for types of snacks. The first column of the table lists the name of each snack. The second column lists the number of calories in each snack. The third column lists the number of carbohydrates in each snack. The fourth column lists the quantity of fat in each snack. By reading down the table's columns, you could compare the nutritional ingredients of each type of snack, and you might use that information to help you select which snack to eat. In this skill, you create a table that lists the amount of each recipe ingredient in the first column and the type of ingredient in the second column.

Tutorial

1 Open the student data file named **C3S1-Recipe**, and if you have not already done so, save it in your Unit 3 working folder on your storage medium.

2 Click at the beginning of the blank paragraph between the headings *Ingredients* and *Steps*.

3 Click the Insert tab.

4 Click the Table button in the Tables group.

5 Click the *Insert Table* option in the drop-down list.

6 In the *Table size* section of the Insert Table dialog box, type 2 in the *Number of columns* box and 9 in the *Number of rows* box.

7 Click the OK button.

5 *Another Way*
Drag over the boxes in the *Insert Table* section of the Table drop-down list to select a 2 x 9 table.

6 *Another Way*
Click the increment (up) and decrement (down) arrows to the right of the measurement box to change the number of columns or rows.

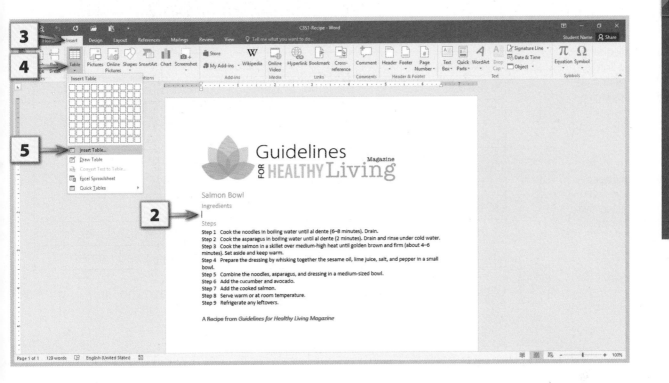

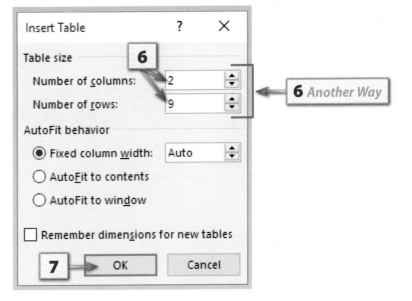

More →

▶ **Tip** Use the Tab key or the Right Arrow key to advance to the next cell in a table. Press the Shift key and Tab key together or use the Left Arrow key to go back to the previous cell.

▶ **Tip** When you type a number, a forward slash, and another number, Word automatically formats it as a fraction.

 8 Click in the cells of the table and type the following text:

4 ounces	Soba noodles
5 ounces	Asparagus, cut into bite-sized pieces
1	Salmon fillet, cut into bite-sized pieces
1 tablespoon	Sesame oil
2	Limes, squeezed for their juice
¼ teaspoon	Salt
¼ teaspoon	Pepper
4 ounces	Cucumber, cut into bite-sized pieces
1	Avocado, cut into bite-sized pieces

9 Click the Save button in the Quick Access Toolbar to save the file.

Completed Skill 1

Salmon Bowl
Ingredients

4 ounces	Soba noodles
5 ounces	Asparagus, cut into bite-sized pieces
1	Salmon fillet, cut into bite-sized pieces
1 tablespoon	Sesame oil
2	Limes, squeezed for their juice
¼ teaspoon	Salt
¼ teaspoon	Pepper
4 ounces	Cucumber, cut into bite-sized pieces
1	Avocado, cut into bite-sized pieces

Steps

Step 1   Cook the noodles in boiling water until al dente (6–8 minutes). Drain.
Step 2   Cook the asparagus in boiling water until al dente (2 minutes). Drain and rinse under cold water.
Step 3   Cook the salmon in a skillet over medium-high heat until golden brown and firm (about 4–6 minutes). Set aside and keep warm.
Step 4   Prepare the dressing by whisking together the sesame oil, lime juice, salt, and pepper in a small bowl.
Step 5   Combine the noodles, asparagus, and dressing in a medium-sized bowl.
Step 6   Add the cucumber and avocado.
Step 7   Add the cooked salmon.
Step 8   Serve warm or at room temperature.
Step 9   Refrigerate any leftovers.

A Recipe from *Guidelines for Healthy Living Magazine*

Completed
Skill Preview

Salmon Bowl

Ingredients

4 ounces	Soba noodles
5 ounces	Asparagus, cut into bite-sized pieces
1	Salmon fillet, cut into bite-sized pieces
1 tablespoon	Sesame oil
2	Limes, squeezed for their juice
¼ teaspoon	Salt
¼ teaspoon	Pepper
4 ounces	Cucumber, cut into bite-sized pieces
1	Avocado, cut into bite-sized pieces

Steps

Step 1 Cook the noodles in boiling water until al dente (6–8 minutes). Drain.
Step 2 Cook the asparagus in boiling water until al dente (2 minutes). Drain and rinse under cold water.
Step 3 Cook the salmon in a skillet over medium-high heat until golden brown and firm (about 4–6 minutes). Set aside and keep warm.
Step 4 Prepare the dressing by whisking together the sesame oil, lime juice, salt, and pepper in a small bowl.
Step 5 Combine the noodles, asparagus, and dressing in a medium-sized bowl.
Step 6 Add the cucumber and avocado.

Taking It Further ●

Formatting Tables

To save yourself formatting time, try the Quick Tables feature. You can access Quick Tables by clicking the Table button in the Tables group on the Insert tab and then clicking the *Quick Tables* option in the drop-down list. Quick Tables includes common table styles that you might find useful, such as two-column lists and calendars.

Word

Skill 2 Convert Text to Tables

If you have entered information in text form, you can convert it to table form. You must provide an indicator, or separator, to mark where each new column of the table should begin. Tabs are commonly used for these indicators, but you can also use commas, paragraphs, or single characters such as hyphens. Hard returns (created by pressing the Enter key) are used to separate your text into rows.

Tutorial

1 If it is not already open, open **C3S1-Recipe**, the file you saved in the previous skill, and save it as **C3S2-Recipe**.

2 On the Home tab, click the Show/Hide ¶ button in the Paragraph group to show the tab arrows and paragraph symbols.

Use Your Touchscreen
To select text, double-tap anywhere in the text and then drag the selection handles.

3 Select the text under the heading *Steps*, from the start of *Step 1* through the end of *Step 9*. (Do not include the paragraph mark at the end of Step 9.) Notice that the step list includes tabs to separate the step numbers from the step descriptions.

4 Click the Insert tab.

5 Click the Table button in the Tables group.

6 Click the *Convert Text to Table* option in the drop-down list.

▶**Tip** Note that the *AutoFit behavior* section of the Convert Text to Table dialog box defaults to *Fixed Column Width*. Another option, *AutoFit to contents*, automatically adjusts the table column widths to fit the text inside them when selected.

7 In the *Separate text at* section of the Convert Text to Table dialog box, be sure that the *Tabs* option is selected.

8 Click the OK button.

9 Click the Home tab and then click the Show/Hide ¶ button in the Paragraph group to hide the tab arrows and paragraph symbols.

10 Save the file.

Completed Skill 2

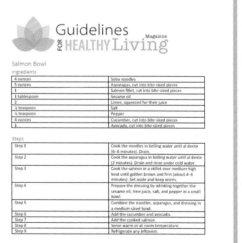

Completed
Skill Preview

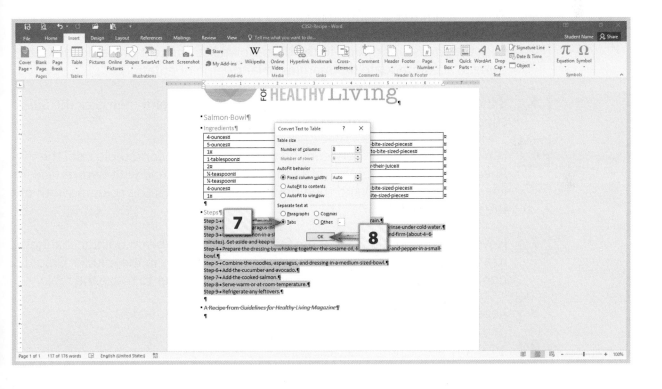

Taking It Further

Converting a Table to Text

You can also convert text in a table into plain text. Do this by selecting the desired section of the table and then clicking the Convert to Text button in the Data group on the Table Tools Layout tab. You then get a choice of what to use as a separator in the text (paragraph marks, tabs, commas, or another symbol you indicate).

Skill 3 Change Page Orientation

To fit more text on a page or improve the design, you may want to change the *page orientation* of a document. By default, Word documents are set up in *portrait* orientation, where the height of a page is greater than the width. You can change the document to *landscape* orientation, where the width of a page is greater than the height. Apply the desired page orientation as early as you can when creating a document. If you decide to change orientation during or after entering content, be sure to check how the text and objects, such as pictures, might have shifted on the page when the new margin settings were applied.

Tutorial

1 If it is not already open, open **C3S2-Recipe**, the file you saved in the previous skill, and save it as **C3S3-Recipe**.

2 Click the Layout tab.

3 Click the Orientation button in the Page Setup group.

4 Click the *Landscape* option in the drop-down list. The text in the document shifts to accommodate the margins of landscape orientation.

5 If the ruler is not already displayed, click the View tab and then click the *Ruler* check box in the Show group to insert a check mark.

6 Hover over the border between the columns of the second table until the I-beam pointer changes to a left-and-right-pointing arrow with two vertical lines in the middle ( ) and then double-click to AutoFit the column width of the first column.

7 Hover over the right border of the first table until the I-beam pointer changes to a left-and-right-pointing arrow with two vertical lines in the middle. Drag the right edge of the table to the 8.5-inch mark on the ruler to resize the table.

8 Repeat Step 7 with the right edge of the second table.

9 Save the file.

Completed Skill 3

**Completed
Skill Preview**

Taking It Further ●

Fitting Text on a Page

The standard page size for most documents is 8.5 inches x 11 inches. If a document in landscape orientation runs slightly longer than a single page, consider printing it on a larger piece of paper, such as legal paper, which is 8.5 inches x 14 inches. You can also fit more text on a page by narrowing the margins in the document. See Chapter 1, Skill 7 for more about adjusting margins in Word.

Skill 4 **Insert and Delete Rows and Columns in a Table**

At times you will need to add more data to an existing table. To accommodate the additional data, you can insert new columns or rows. Rows and columns can also be deleted from a table to remove data. In this skill, you insert a heading row in the first table and insert and delete rows in the second table. Columns are inserted and deleted using similar steps.

Tutorial

2–4 *Another Way*
Right-click anywhere in the first row of the table, click the Insert button on the Mini toolbar, and then click the *Insert Above* option in the drop-down list.

▶*Tip* To insert a column rather than a row, click in a column and then click the Insert Left or Insert Right button in the Rows & Columns group on the Table Tools Layout tab.

7 *Another Way*
Click the Bold button on the Mini toolbar that displays when a row is selected.

1 If it is not already open, open **C3S3-Recipe**, the file you saved in the previous skill, and save it as **C3S4-Recipe**.

2 Click anywhere in the first row of the first table to make it active.

3 Click the Table Tools Layout tab.

4 Click the Insert Above button in the Rows & Columns group. A row is inserted above the active row.

5 Type Quantity in the new top left cell and Ingredient in the new top right cell.

6 Move your mouse pointer to the left of the first row until it turns into a white arrow (⬦) and then click to select the first row.

7 On the Home tab, click the Bold button in the Font group.

Taking It Further ●

Using the Insert Controls to Insert Rows and Columns

When you hover your mouse pointer over the border between two columns or two rows, the Insert Control (looks like a plus sign in a circle) appears between the columns or rows. Click the Insert Control to insert a new column or row at that location. Note that this feature only works with a mouse; it does not work on a touchscreen.

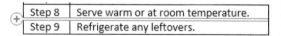

Salmon Bowl

Ingredients

4 ounces	Soba noodles
5 ounces	Asparagus, cut into bite-sized pieces
1	Salmon fillet, cut into bite-sized pieces
1 tablespoon	Sesame oil
2	Limes, squeezed for their juice
¼ teaspoon	Salt
¼ teaspoon	Pepper
4 ounces	Cucumber, cut into bite-sized pieces
1	Avocado, cut into bite-sized pieces

Steps

Step 1	Cook the noodles in boiling water until al dente (6–8 minutes). Drain.
Step 2	Cook the asparagus in boiling water until al dente (2 minutes). Drain and rinse under cold water.
Step 3	Cook the salmon in a skillet over medium-high heat until golden brown and firm (about 4–6 minutes). Set aside and keep warm.
Step 4	Prepare the dressing by whisking together the sesame oil, lime juice, salt, and pepper in a small bowl.
Step 5	Combine the noodles, asparagus, and dressing in a medium-sized bowl.
Step 6	Add the cucumber and avocado.
Step 7	Add the cooked salmon.
Step 8	Serve warm or at room temperature.
Step 9	Refrigerate any leftovers.

Salmon Bowl

Ingredients

Quantity	Ingredient
4 ounces	Soba noodles
5 ounces	Asparagus, cut into bite-sized pieces
1	Salmon fillet, cut into bite-sized pieces
1 tablespoon	Sesame oil
2	Limes, squeezed for their juice
¼ teaspoon	Salt
¼ teaspoon	Pepper
4 ounces	Cucumber, cut into bite-sized pieces
1	Avocado, cut into bite-sized pieces

Steps

Step 1	Cook the noodles in boiling water until al dente (6–8 minutes). Drain.
Step 2	Cook the asparagus in boiling water until al dente (2 minutes). Drain and rinse under cold water.
Step 3	Cook the salmon in a skillet over medium-high heat until golden brown and firm (about 4–6 minutes). Set aside and keep warm.
Step 4	Prepare the dressing by whisking together the sesame oil, lime juice, salt, and pepper in a small bowl.
Step 5	Combine the noodles, asparagus, and dressing in a medium-sized bowl.
Step 6	Add the cucumber and avocado.
Step 7	Add the cooked salmon.
Step 8	Serve warm or at room temperature.
Step 9	Refrigerate any leftovers.

More

8 Click in the last cell of the second table.

9 Click the Table Tools Layout tab.

10 Click the Insert Below button in the Rows & Columns group.

11 Type 490 calories per serving in the new bottom left cell.

12 Click in the cell that contains the text *Step 9*.

13 Click the Delete button.

14 Click the *Delete Rows* option in the drop-down list.

15 Save the file.

Completed Skill 4

Guidelines
FOR HEALTHY Living Magazine

Salmon Bowl

Ingredients

Quantity	Ingredient
4 ounces	Soba noodles
5 ounces	Asparagus, cut into bite-sized pieces
1	Salmon fillet, cut into bite-sized pieces
1 tablespoon	Sesame oil
2	Limes, squeezed for their juice
¼ teaspoon	Salt
¼ teaspoon	Pepper
4 ounces	Cucumber, cut into bite-sized pieces
1	Avocado, cut into bite-sized pieces

Steps

Step 1	Cook the noodles in boiling water until al dente (6–8 minutes). Drain.
Step 2	Cook the asparagus in boiling water until al dente (2 minutes). Drain and rinse under cold water.
Step 3	Cook the salmon in a skillet over medium-high heat until golden brown and firm (about 4–6 minutes). Set aside and keep warm.
Step 4	Prepare the dressing by whisking together the sesame oil, lime juice, salt, and pepper in a small bowl.
Step 5	Combine the noodles, asparagus, and dressing in a medium-sized bowl.
Step 6	Add the cucumber and avocado.
Step 7	Add the cooked salmon.
Step 8	Serve warm or at room temperature.

490 calories per serving	

A Recipe from *Guidelines for Healthy Living Magazine*

Completed
Skill Preview

Taking It Further

Deleting Columns

To select a column you wish to delete, place your mouse pointer at the top of the column until the pointer turns into a solid black down-pointing arrow, click to select the column, and then drag over any additional columns to be deleted. Once you have selected the appropriate columns, right-click and then click the *Delete Columns* option in the pop-up list. You can also use the Delete button in the Rows & Columns group on the Table Tools Layout tab to perform the same action.

Skill 5 Merge Rows or Columns in a Table

The table you have been working with in the previous skills contained consistent sets of rows and columns. However, when organizing information in a table, you may find you need to combine rows and columns. For example, you may want to combine the cells in the top row of a table into a single cell that contains the table title, or you may want to combine several sets of cells to create blocks in a schedule. The process of combining rows or columns is called a *merge*.

Tutorial

1 If it is not already open, open **C3S4-Recipe**, the file you saved in the previous skill, and save it as **C3S5-Recipe**.

2 Select the last row of the second table.

3 Click the Table Tools Layout tab.

▶**Tip** You can merge rows, columns, or rows and columns, depending on the combination of rows and/or columns you select before clicking the Merge Cells button.

4 Click the Merge Cells button in the Merge group to combine the two selected cells.

5 With the last row still selected, click on the Home tab and then click the Bold button in the Font group.

6 Save the file.

Completed Skill 5

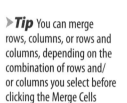

Completed Skill Preview

A Recipe from *Guidelines for Healthy Living Magazine*

Guidelines FOR HEALTHY Living Magazine

Salmon Bowl

Ingredients

Quantity	Ingredient
4 ounces	Soba noodles
5 ounces	Asparagus, cut into bite-sized pieces
1	Salmon fillet, cut into bite-sized pieces
1 tablespoon	Sesame oil
2	Limes, squeezed for their juice
¼ teaspoon	Salt
¼ teaspoon	Pepper
4 ounces	Cucumber, cut into bite-sized pieces
1	Avocado, cut into bite-sized pieces

Steps

Step 1	Cook the noodles in boiling water until al dente (6–8 minutes). Drain.
Step 2	Cook the asparagus in boiling water until al dente (2 minutes). Drain and rinse under cold water.
Step 3	Cook the salmon in a skillet over medium-high heat until golden brown and firm (about 4–6 minutes). Set aside and keep warm.
Step 4	Prepare the dressing by whisking together the sesame oil, lime juice, salt, and pepper in a small bowl.
Step 5	Combine the noodles, asparagus, and dressing in a medium-sized bowl.
Step 6	Add the cucumber and avocado.
Step 7	Add the cooked salmon.
Step 8	Serve warm or at room temperature.
490 calories per serving	

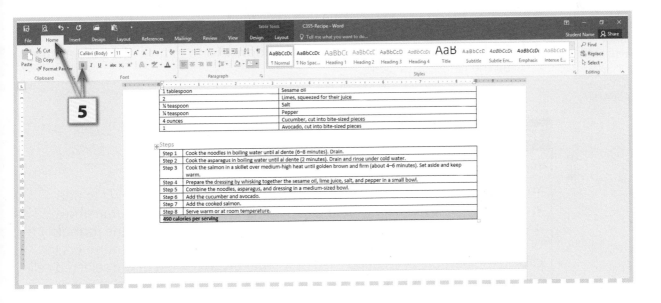

Taking It Further

Formatting with Tables

Use a table and commands (for example, Merge) on the Table Tools Layout tab to build forms or documents such as class schedules. The table to the right is an example of a class schedule. Once the information is organized, you can hide the borders, if you wish.

Spring Semester	English	Monday, Wednesday; 10:00 am
	Biology	Thursday, Friday; 9:00 am
Additional Information	Syllabus will be available to students on the first day of class.	

Word

Skill 6 Format Tables

A table can be formatted in a variety of ways. You can add shading or modify the thickness or color of the lines that define the table cells. You can also specify which border lines should be displayed and which should not. In this skill, you learn how to alter a table so that it has no borders showing at all. A quick way to format a table with borders and shading is to apply a built-in *table style*, which consists of a set of predesigned formats.

1 If it is not already open, open **C3S5-Recipe**, the file you saved in the previous skill, and save it as **C3S6-Recipe**.

2 Click anywhere in the second table.

3 Click the table move handle to select the table.

4 Click the Table Tools Design tab.

5 Click the Borders arrow in the Borders group.

6 Click the *No Border* option in the drop-down list to remove the borders from all the cells in the table.

 Another Way
Drag to select all the cells of the table.

 **Tip** To visually separate cells in your table without using borders, use the Shading button in the Table Styles group on the Table Tools Design tab to apply shading to individual cells.

Taking It Further

Performing Calculations in a Table

You can perform calculations in a Word table. For example, if you have a series of values in a column, add a blank row to the end of the column, click in the new blank cell, and then click the Formula button in the Data group on the Table Tools Layout tab. In the Formula dialog box, type the formula =*SUM(ABOVE)* to add the numbers in the column above the selected cell. Type the formula =*SUM(LEFT)* to add the numbers in the row to the left of the selected cell. To calculate the average of a series of numbers in a column, type the formula =*AVERAGE(ABOVE)*.

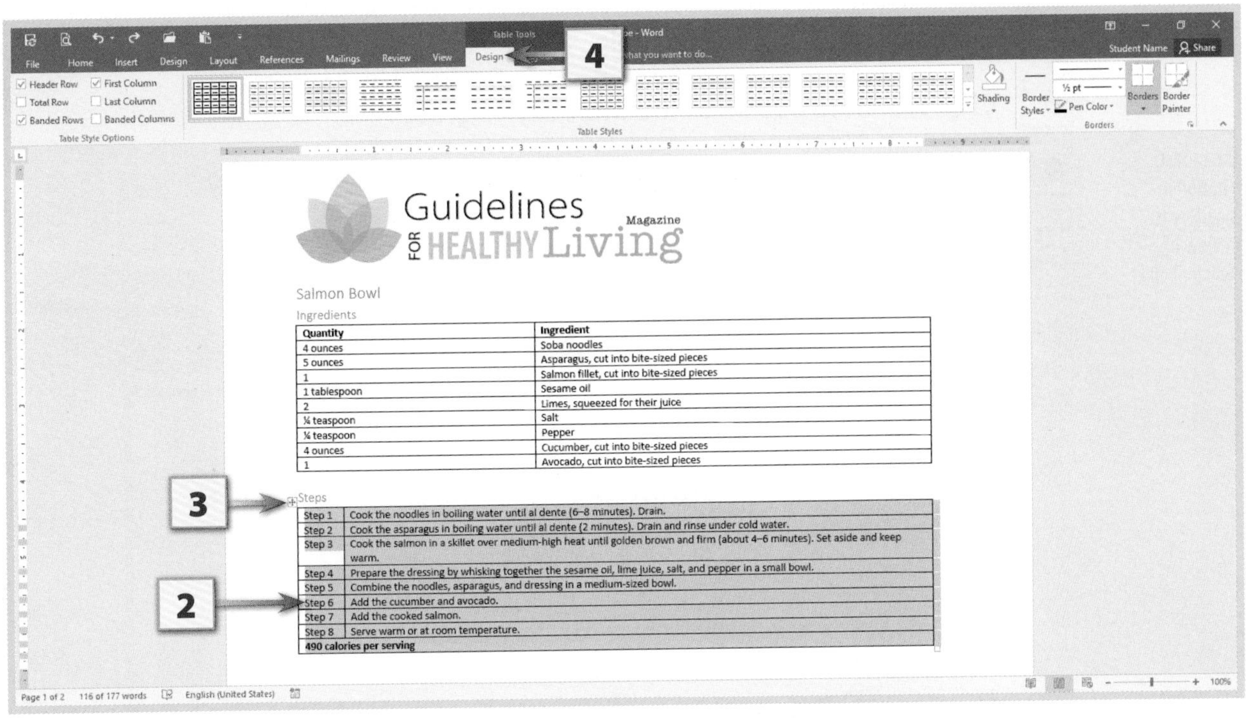

Screenshot 1 (top):

Table Tools

Design **4**

Student Name · Share

Header Row · First Column
Total Row · Last Column
Banded Rows · Banded Columns
Table Style Options

Shading · Border Styles · Pen Color · Borders · Border Painter
Borders

Guidelines
FOR HEALTHY Living
Magazine

Salmon Bowl
Ingredients

Quantity	Ingredient
4 ounces	Soba noodles
5 ounces	Asparagus, cut into bite-sized pieces
1	Salmon fillet, cut into bite-sized pieces
1 tablespoon	Sesame oil
2	Limes, squeezed for their juice
¼ teaspoon	Salt
¼ teaspoon	Pepper
4 ounces	Cucumber, cut into bite-sized pieces
1	Avocado, cut into bite-sized pieces

3 → Steps

Step 1	Cook the noodles in boiling water until al dente (6–8 minutes). Drain.
Step 2	Cook the asparagus in boiling water until al dente (2 minutes). Drain and rinse under cold water.
Step 3	Cook the salmon in a skillet over medium-high heat until golden brown and firm (about 4–6 minutes). Set aside and keep warm.
Step 4	Prepare the dressing by whisking together the sesame oil, lime juice, salt, and pepper in a small bowl.
Step 5	Combine the noodles, asparagus, and dressing in a medium-sized bowl.
Step 6	Add the cucumber and avocado.
Step 7	Add the cooked salmon.
Step 8	Serve warm or at room temperature.
490 calories per serving	

2 →

Page 1 of 2   116 of 177 words   English (United States)   100%

Screenshot 2 (bottom):

Table Tools   C3S6-Recipe - Word

Design   Layout   Tell me what you want to do...   Student Name · Share

Header Row · First Column
Total Row · Last Column
Banded Rows · Banded Columns
Table Style Options

Shading **5** Borders · Border Painter

- Bottom Border
- Top Border
- Left Border
- Right Border
- No Border
- All Borders
- Outside Borders
- Inside Borders
- Insi... **6** ...rder
- Insi... ...er
- Diagonal Down Border
- Diagonal Up Border
- Horizontal Line
- Draw Table
- View Gridlines
- Borders and Shading...

Guidelines
FOR HEALTHY Living
Magazine

Salmon Bowl
Ingredients

Quantity	Ingredient
4 ounces	Soba noodles
5 ounces	Asparagus, cut into bite-sized pieces
1	Salmon fillet, cut into bite-sized pieces
1 tablespoon	Sesame oil
2	Limes, squeezed for their juice
¼ teaspoon	Salt
¼ teaspoon	Pepper
4 ounces	Cucumber, cut into bite-sized pieces
1	Avocado, cut into bite-sized pieces

Steps
Step 1   Cook the noodles in boiling water until al dente (6–8 minutes). Drain.
Step 2   Cook the asparagus in boiling water until al dente (2 minutes). Drain and rinse under cold water.
Step 3   Cook the salmon in a skillet over medium-high heat until golden brown and firm (about 4–6 minutes). Set aside and keep warm.
Step 4   Prepare the dressing by whisking together the sesame oil, lime juice, salt, and pepper in a small bowl.
Step 5   Combine the noodles, asparagus, and dressing in a medium-sized bowl.
Step 6   Add the cucumber and avocado.
Step 7   Add the cooked salmon.
Step 8   Serve warm or at room temperature.
490 calories per serving

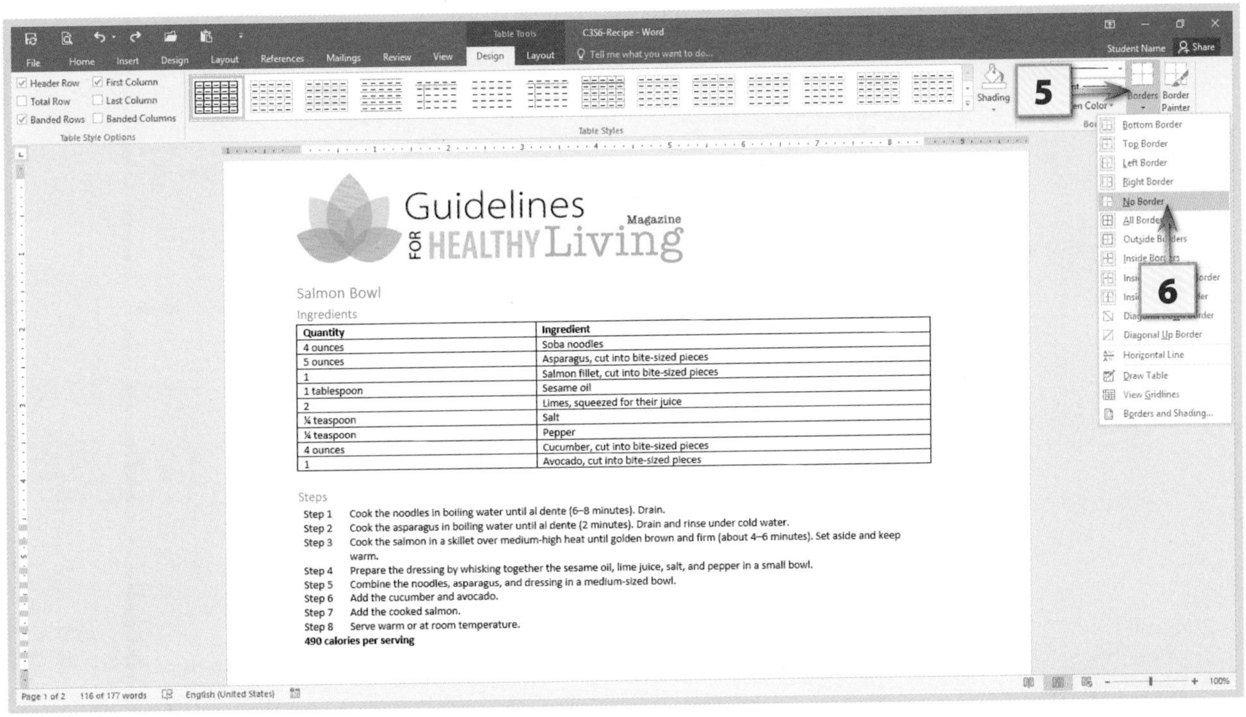

Page 1 of 2   116 of 177 words   English (United States)   100%

More →

7 Click anywhere in the first table.

8 Click the More button in the Table Styles group.

▶**Tip** Hover the mouse pointer over an option in the Table Styles gallery to display a live preview of what the style will look like.

9 Click the *List Table 3 - Accent1* option in the drop-down gallery.

10 Save the file.

Completed Skill 6

Guidelines
FOR HEALTHY Living Magazine

Salmon Bowl

Ingredients

Quantity	Ingredient
4 ounces	Soba noodles
5 ounces	Asparagus, cut into bite-sized pieces
1	Salmon fillet, cut into bite-sized pieces
1 tablespoon	Sesame oil
2	Limes, squeezed for their juice
¼ teaspoon	Salt
¼ teaspoon	Pepper
4 ounces	Cucumber, cut into bite-sized pieces
1	Avocado, cut into bite-sized pieces

Steps

Step 1   Cook the noodles in boiling water until al dente (6–8 minutes). Drain.
Step 2   Cook the asparagus in boiling water until al dente (2 minutes). Drain and rinse under cold water.
Step 3   Cook the salmon in a skillet over medium-high heat until golden brown and firm (about 4–6 minutes). Set aside and keep warm.
Step 4   Prepare the dressing by whisking together the sesame oil, lime juice, salt, and pepper in a small bowl.
Step 5   Combine the noodles, asparagus, and dressing in a medium-sized bowl.
Step 6   Add the cucumber and avocado.
Step 7   Add the cooked salmon.
Step 8   Serve warm or at room temperature.
490 calories per serving

A Recipe from *Guidelines for Healthy Living Magazine*

Completed
Skill Preview

Guidelines
FOR HEALTHY Living
Magazine

Salmon Bowl

Ingredients

Quantity	Ingredient
4 ounces	Soba noodles
5 ounces	Asparagus, cut into bite-sized pieces
	Salmon fillet, cut into bite-sized pieces
1 tablespoon	Sesame oil
2	Limes, squeezed for their juice
¼ teaspoon	Salt
¾ teaspoon	Pepper
4 ounces	Cucumber, cut into bite-sized pieces
1	Avocado, cut into bite-sized pieces

Steps

Step 1   Cook the noodles in boiling water until al dente (6–8 minutes). Drain.
Step 2   Cook the asparagus in boiling water until al dente (2 minutes). Drain and rinse under cold water.
Step 3   Cook the salmon in a skillet over medium-high heat until golden brown and firm (about 4–6 minutes). Set aside and keep warm.
Step 4   Prepare the dressing by whisking together the sesame oil, lime juice, salt, and pepper in a small bowl.
Step 5   Combine the noodles, asparagus, and dressing in a medium-sized bowl.
Step 6   Add the cucumber and avocado.
Step 7   Add the cooked salmon.
Step 8   Serve warm or at room temperature.
490 calories per serving

Word

Skill 7 Insert SmartArt

Word includes a feature called *SmartArt* that lets you easily create a variety of diagrams such as organization charts, cycle, and process diagrams. You can use these diagrams to create illustrations that visually communicate information.

Tutorial

1 If it is not already open, open **C3S6-Recipe**, the file you saved in the previous skill, and save it as **C3S7-Recipe**.

2 Click in the blank paragraph at the end of the document.

3 Click the Insert tab.

4 Click the SmartArt button in the Illustrations group.

5 In the Choose a SmartArt Graphic dialog box, click the *Process* command in the left panel and then click *Basic Process* in the middle panel.

6 Click the OK button.

7 In the text pane that opens to the left of the diagram, type Eat Healthy to the right of the first bullet.

8 Click the *[Text]* placeholder to the right of the second bullet and then type Exercise.

9 Click the *[Text]* placeholder to the right of the third bullet and then type Feel Better.

10 Close the text pane.

11 Click the More button in the Layouts group on the SmartArt Tools Design tab.

> **Tip** Preview a SmartArt layout by hovering over the layout in the Choose a SmartArt Graphic dialog box.

> **Tip** If the text pane does not open automatically in Step 7, click the Text Pane button in the Create Graphic group on the SmartArt Tools Design tab.

Taking It Further

Making a Quick Analysis

When you select a range of cells that contain data, the Quick Analysis button () appears at the bottom right of the selected range. Click the Quick Analysis button to display a gallery where you can select from a variety of tabs to analyze your data. For example, the CHARTS tab lets you display the selected data in a chart. Another tab, FORMATTING, has options that can be used to quickly determine high and low values or highlight values greater than a specified value.

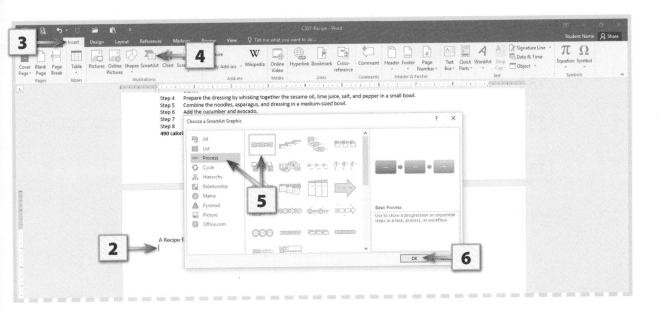

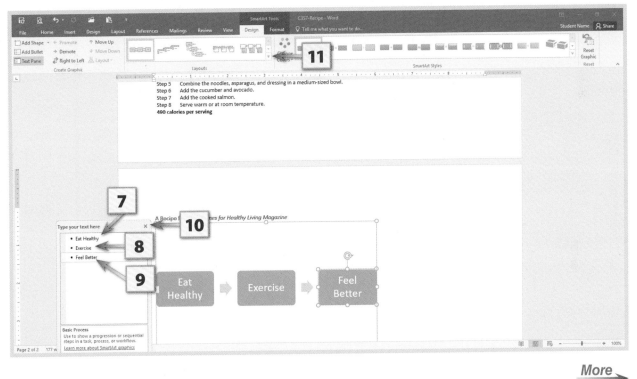

More →

Taking It Further ●

Inserting Shapes

The *Shapes* feature in Word allows you to add a variety of predesigned shapes to your document, including lines, rectangles, basic shapes (circles, squares), and arrows. To add a shape, click the Shapes button in the Illustrations group on the Insert tab, click an option in the drop-down list, and then drag to draw the shape in your document.

Once a shape is drawn, you can size it by selecting the shape and then dragging a *handle* (a small box at the corner or side of a selected object). To add text to a shape, right-click the shape, click the *Add Text* option in the pop-up list, and then type the text inside the shape. Click outside the shape when you are finished.

12 Click the *Converging Text* option in the drop-down gallery to change the SmartArt layout.

13 Click the Change Colors arrow in the SmartArt Styles group.

14 Click the *Colorful Range - Accent Colors 5 to 6* option in the *Colorful* section of the drop-down gallery.

15 Save the file.

Completed Skill 7

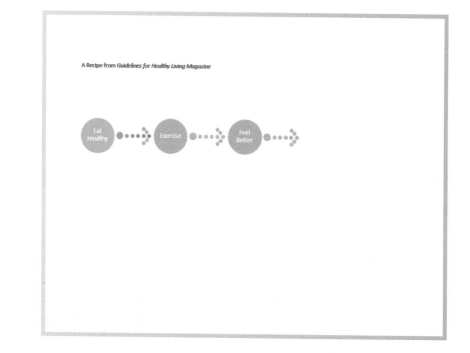

Completed
Skill Preview

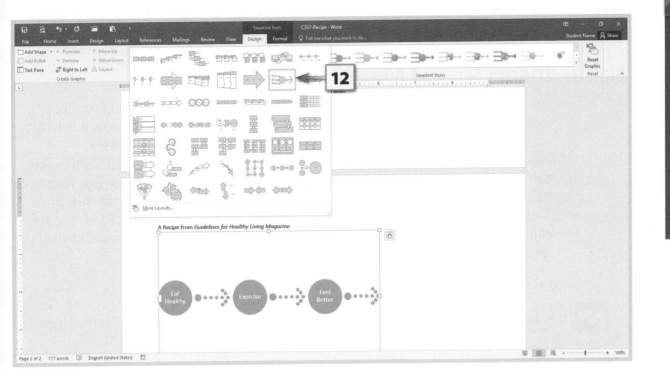

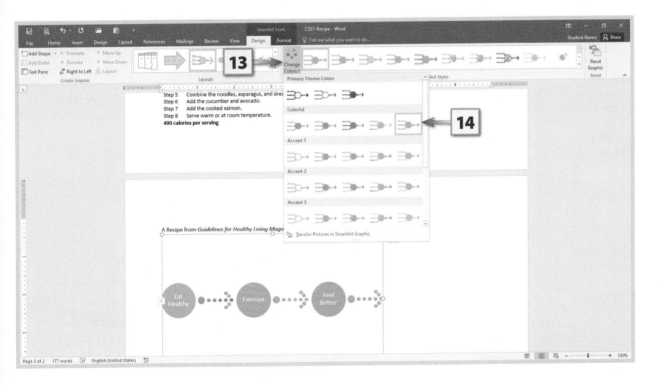

Skill 8   Insert Visual Media

You can insert different types of media, including images and video clips, into your documents to make them more interesting. Without leaving Word, you can use the *Online Pictures* feature to search the web and social media sites such as Facebook for images, or you can use the *Pictures* feature to navigate to picture files stored on your local PC or attached storage medium. Once you have located an image, it is easy to insert it into your document.

Before inserting media from online sources, be sure to review the licensing agreement. You can usually find this information on a page called "Legal," "License Agreement," "Terms of Use," or something similar.

Tutorial

1   If it is not already open, open **C3S7-Recipe**, the file you saved in the previous skill, and save it as **C3S8-Recipe**.

2   Click to the left of the recipe title *Salmon Bowl* to place the insertion point in that location.

3   Click the Insert tab.

▶Tip In Step 4, you are inserting a picture from your computer. If you needed to search for a picture on the web, you would click the Online Pictures button in the Illustrations group instead of the Pictures button.

4   Click the Pictures button in the Illustrations group.

5   Navigate to the student data file **C3S8-SalmonBowl**, which is a picture file showing the finished product.

6   Click the image file to select it.

7   Click the Insert button.

8   Save the file.

Completed Skill 8

Completed Skill Preview

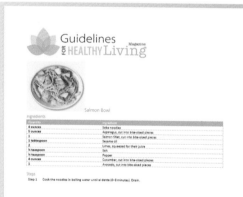

Taking It Further ●

Inserting an Online Video

You can use the *Online Video* feature to insert video from websites such as YouTube into a Word document. To insert an online video, position the insertion point cursor at the desired location in the document and then click the *Online Video* button in the Media group on the Insert tab. You can then search for online videos or paste the embed code from a website if you have that.

Inserting a Screenshot

You can insert a *screenshot* of any open window into a Word document. Start by sizing the open window and positioning the contents so they look exactly the way you want them to. In the Word document, place the insertion point where you wish to insert the screenshot, click the Screenshot button in the Illustrations group on the Picture Tools Format tab, and then click the correct open window in the Available Windows drop-down list. The screenshot is added to the Word document at the insertion point.

Skill 9 Resize Media

You can see from the SmartArt and image inserted in the previous skills that they do not always appear in a size that suits your document. You can easily resize images and other media objects by using the *Height* measurement box in the Size group on the Picture Tools Format tab.

Tutorial

 **Another Way**

Click the object and then drag the bottom right corner handle to size the image proportionally. You can refer to the *Height* and *Width* boxes in the Size group on the Picture Tools Format tab to check the actual size after you release the handle.

1 If it is not already open, open **C3S8-Recipe**, the file you saved in the previous skill, and save it as **C3S9-Recipe**.

2 Click the salmon bowl image on the first page of your document to select it.

3 Click the Picture Tools Format tab.

4 In the Size group, change the value in the *Height* box to *1.5"*. Notice that the value in the *Width* box adjusts to size the image proportionally. Press the Enter key to accept these values.

5 Scroll to the second page of your document and then click the SmartArt diagram.

6 Click the SmartArt Tools Format tab.

7 In the Size group, change the value in the *Height* box to *3"* and change the value in the *Width* box to *8"*. Press the Enter key to accept these values.

8 Save the file.

Completed
Skill Preview

Completed Skill 9

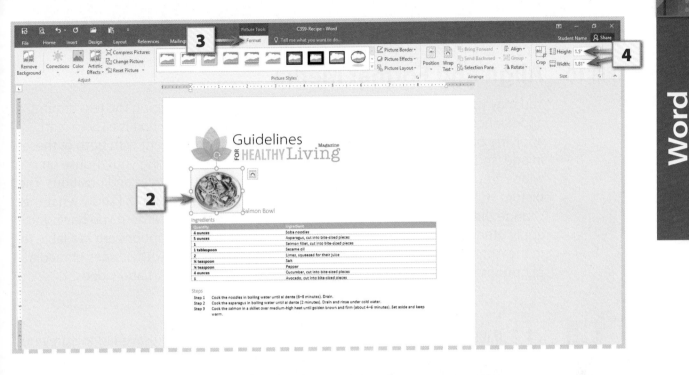

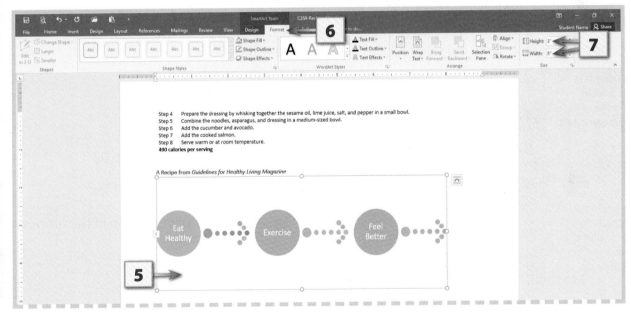

Taking It Further •

Wrapping Styles

When you insert a picture or SmartArt diagram in a document, it is placed in line with the text by default. Thus, you may have text above and below the object, but not next to or behind it. To adjust how the object and text are arranged, select the picture or SmartArt diagram and then click the *Wrap Text* button in the Arrange group on the Picture Tools or SmartArt Tools Format tab. Text wrapping options in the drop-down list include *Square*, *Tight*, *Through*, *Top and Bottom*, *Behind Text*, and *In Front of Text*. These options are also available from the Layout Options button (🖼) that appears beside an object when you select the object.

Skill 10 Align and Format Media

You may want to enhance the appearance of an inserted picture by applying picture styles, moving the image, and modifying the way the text wraps around the image. A variety of picture styles allows you to add frames, change the border edges, rotate, and apply other effects. The Position button in the Arrange group gives a number of options for positioning an image on a page and wrapping the text around the image so the text is easy to read. You can experiment with both of these options by hovering your mouse on various picture styles and positions. The live preview feature will show what the effect looks like without you having to select it. Similar options are available to align and format other types of media including SmartArt and videos.

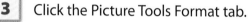

Tutorial

1 If it is not already open, open **C3S9-Recipe**, the file you saved in the previous skill, and save it as **C3S10-Recipe-Lastname**, but replace *Lastname* with your last name. Be sure to save the file in your Unit 3 working folder on your storage medium.

▶**Tip** The Adjust group on the Picture Tools Format tab contains commands for editing images, including correcting the image brightness and changing the image color.

2 Click the salmon bowl image on the first page of the document.

3 Click the Picture Tools Format tab.

4 Click the More button in the Picture Styles group.

5 Click the *Snip Diagonal Corner, White* option in the drop-down gallery.

▶**Tip** You can rotate an image by clicking the Rotate button in the Arrange group on the Picture Tools Format tab or by dragging the *rotation handle* (   )that is displayed just above an image when it is selected.

6 Click the Position button in the Arrange group.

7 Click the *Position in Top Right with Square Text Wrapping* option in the drop-down gallery.

8 Save and close the file.

Completed Skill 10

Completed
Skill Preview

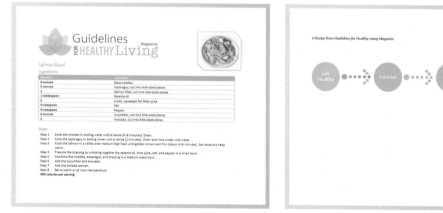

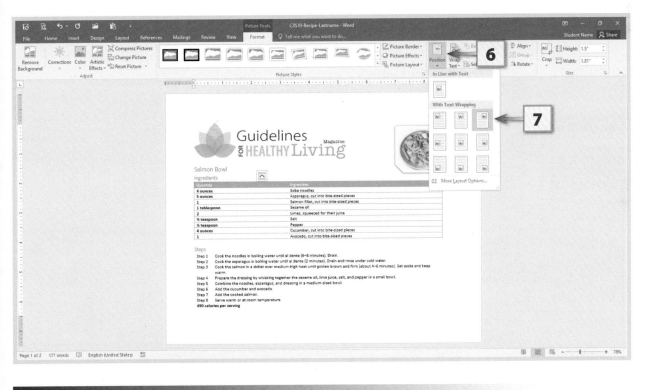

Taking It Further ●

Creating Word Art

You can further enhance Word documents by using *WordArt*. Click the WordArt button in the Text group on the Insert tab and then click an option in the drop-down list to insert a text box with the styled placeholder text *Your text here*. Select the placeholder text and replace it with your own text. Make further formatting changes to the WordArt text by clicking options on the Drawing Tools Format tab, which is available when the WordArt object is active.

Word Chapter 3 **Tasks Summary**

Task	Ribbon Tab, Group	Button, Option	Shortcut, Alternative
Insert table	Insert, Tables	Table , *Insert Table*	
Move to next cell in a table			Tab or Right Arrow
Move to previous cell in a table			Shift + Tab or Left Arrow
Convert selected text to table	Insert, Tables	Table , *Convert Text to Table*	
Change document orientation	Layout, Page Setup	Orientation	
Insert rows	Table Tools Layout, Rows & Columns	Insert Above / Insert Below	
Insert columns	Table Tools Layout, Rows & Columns	Insert Left / Insert Right	
Delete rows	Table Tools Layout, Rows & Columns	Delete , *Delete Rows*	
Delete columns	Table Tools Layout, Rows & Columns	Delete , *Delete Columns*	
Merge cells	Table Tools Layout	Merge Cells	
Format cell borders	Table Tools Design, Table Styles	Borders	
Apply table styles	Table Tools Design, Table Styles		
Insert SmartArt	Insert, Illustrations	SmartArt	

Task	Ribbon Tab, Group	Button, Option	Shortcut, Alternative
Change SmartArt layout	SmartArt Tools Design, Layouts		
Change SmartArt colors	SmartArt Tools Design, SmartArt Styles		
Insert picture from file	Insert, Illustrations		
Insert online picture	Insert, Illustrations		
Resize media	Picture Tools Format or SmartArt Tools Format, Size	*Height* and *Width* boxes	Resizing handles
Change position of media	Picture Tools Format, Arrange		Layout Options button
Wrap Text	Picture Tools Format, Arrange		Layout Options button

Recheck

Recheck your understanding of the skills and features covered in this chapter.

Workbook

Chapter study resources, exercises, and assessments are available in the Workbook *ebook.*

Chapter 4

Finalizing and Sharing Documents

Precheck

Check your understanding of the skills and features covered in this chapter.

Some documents require the input of several people. You might want coworkers to give feedback on a report or project schedule, or you might ask your family to add names to a holiday card list, for example. Word makes it easy to provide that input through tools on the Review tab. These tools allow people to make changes that can be tracked and to insert comments with suggestions or questions. You can then review suggested changes and choose which ones to accept or reject. You can also review comments and questions and decide whether to act on them. When you're done reviewing, you simply delete all comments and accept or reject changes, and your document is final.

Word 2016 offers an option called Simple Mode. Rather than showing you the detailed marked-up changes, this option shows you a cleaner version of the document with edits included. Changes are shown but in a subtle manner. Word also offers an option to lock Track Changes. You might want to use this option to make sure everyone's changes are recorded. With this option, a password is created when you turn Track Changes on and must be provided to turn Track Changes off.

How do you get your document into the hands of other people so they can begin providing feedback, and how do you later distribute the final version to them? Word allows you to share documents by sending them as email attachments or as links to files posted in OneDrive or another cloud storage service. You can also save a Word document in PDF format. This format preserves the formatting and is the format often used to post files to the web. A PDF file can be viewed in the free, easy-to-use Adobe Reader software or opened in Word.

Skills You Learn

1   Turn on and view Track Changes

2   Make changes and add comments

3   Accept or reject changes and review comments

4   Send a document for editing via email

5   Share a file for editing on OneDrive

6   Create a PDF file

SNAP   *If you are a SNAP user, go to your SNAP Assignments page to complete the Precheck, Tutorials, and Recheck.*

What You Need

For these skills, you need the following student data file:

C4S1-HealthFacts

What You Create

Every monthly publication of *Guidelines for Healthy Living Magazine* features a Health Facts article. The article this month focuses on the benefits of drinking water.

You have researched and created a draft article. Before it is published, you will use Track Changes for a final review, and then go through and decide whether to accept or reject your changes and comments before finalizing the draft and sharing it with several editors. They will check the document for errors and make suggestions for improving the article. You will get feedback quickly by sending the document as an email attachment and sharing the document on OneDrive. You will also send the draft to an artist who is creating an illustration for the article. She will not need to edit the draft, so you decide to send her a PDF file.

Health Facts Article

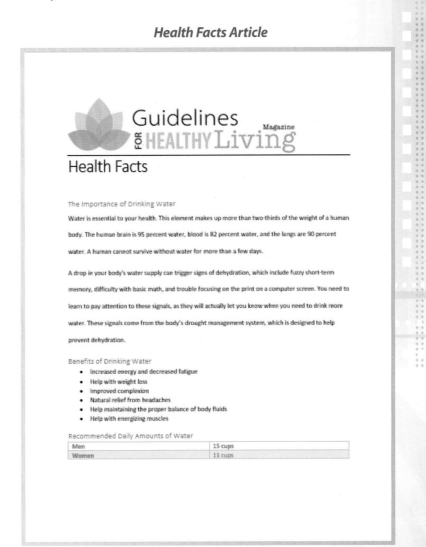

Completed
Skill Preview

Skill 1   Turn On and View Track Changes

When you are working on a document, you may want others to review it. Before you send the document out, you can turn on the *Track Changes* feature in Word to record all changes made by the reviewers. This feature strikes a line through deleted text and applies a font color to added text so you can see what changes each person has suggested. You can lock track changes so that reviewers cannot turn the feature off. When you get the reviewed document back, you can use tools on the Review tab to display various versions of the document. You can also use Track Changes to make your own changes and comments, and then review your edits before finalizing the document. This is what you will do in the first two skills of this chapter.

Tutorial

> **Tip** When Track Changes is locked, reviewers cannot turn off the feature or accept or reject changes unless they have the password.

1 Open the student data file named **C4S1-HealthFacts**, and if you have not already done so, save it in your Unit 3 working folder on your storage medium.

2 Click the Review tab.

3 Click the Track Changes arrow in the Tracking group and then click the *Lock Tracking* option in the drop-down list. Note that if you turn on Lock Tracking, you need to set a password.

4 In the Lock Tracking dialog box, click the Cancel button to close the dialog box without setting a password or turning on Lock Tracking.

5 *Shortcut*
Track Changes
Ctrl + Shift + E

5 Click the Track Changes button.

6 Click the *Display for Review* arrow and then click the *Simple Markup* option in the drop-down list, if necessary.

7 Select and then delete the word *Health* in the document title. Note that the deleted text disappears and a vertical red revision line displays to the left of the line from which it was deleted.

8 *Another Way*
Double-click the red revision line.

8 Click the *Display for Review* arrow and then click the *All Markup* option. Note that the revision line changes color and the deleted text changes color and has a strikethrough mark.

9 *Shortcut*
Undo
Ctrl + Z

9 Click the Undo button on the Quick Access Toolbar to undo the deletion.

**Completed
Skill Preview**

10 Close the file without saving.

Completed Skill 1

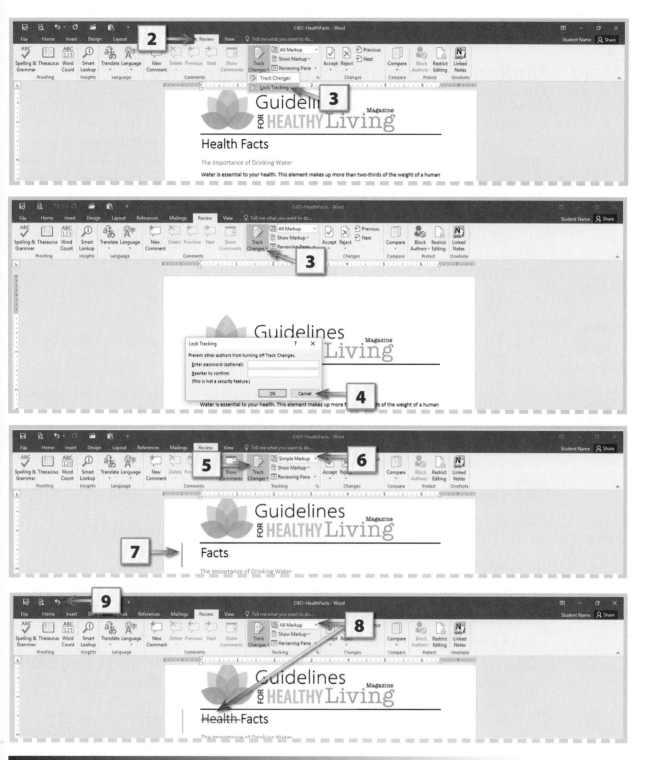

Taking It Further

Displaying Markup

When you click the *Display for Review* button in the Tracking group on the Review tab, you open a drop-down list offering several options for viewing the document. Clicking the *No Markup* setting displays the document as it would look with all changes accepted. The *Original* setting shows the original document with no changes. The *All Markup* setting shows all changes to formatting, as well as all deletions and additions. *Simple Markup* provides a clean view of the document and an indicator in the left margin showing where a change has been made.

Word

Skill 2   Make Changes and Add Comments

When you work in a document that has Track Changes turned on, any changes you make to it are automatically recorded. Any additions or edits you make are indicated in colored text and any deletions you make are indicated with a strike through. Track Changes also records comments and formatting changes. You can choose to display all of these changes, some of them, or none of them, and you can display them in-line, in balloons in the margin, or in the Reviewing pane. The *Comments* feature allows you to suggest changes rather than making them directly in the text, explain your edits, and ask questions. In this skill, you make changes and add comments in the document.

Tutorial

> **Tip** Once selected, the Track Changes features stays on until the Track Changes button is clicked again to turn it off.

> **Tip** In Step 5, note that a user name and a description appear in a balloon connected to the change. See the Taking It Further feature in this skill for information about changing the user name.

1 If it is not already open, open **C4S1-HealthFacts**, the file you saved in Skill 1, and save it as **C4S2-HealthFacts**.

2 Click the Review tab if it is not already active, click the Track Changes button in the Tracking group, and then set the *Display for Review* option to *All Markup*.

3 Select the word *Include* and the space before it in the heading *Benefits of Drinking Water Include*, and then press the Delete key.

4 Select the document title, *Health Facts*.

5 Click the Home tab and then click the Bold button in the Font group.

Taking It Further ●●●●●●●●●●●●●●●●●●●●●●●

Changing the User Name

When Track Changes is activated and *All Markup* is displayed, a reviewer name is displayed in a comment balloon to indicate who made the change. By default, the reviewer name comes from the document properties and is the user name you entered for your computer when you first set up Windows. To change the user name, complete these steps:

1. Click the Review tab and then click the Change Tracking Options dialog box launcher.

2. In the Track Changes Options dialog box, click the Change User Name button.

3. In the *Personalize your copy of Microsoft Office* section of the Word Options dialog box, type a new user name, and then click to insert a check mark in the *Always use these values regardless of sign in to Office* check box.

4. Click the OK button to close the Word Options dialog box and then click the OK button to close the Track Changes Options dialog box.

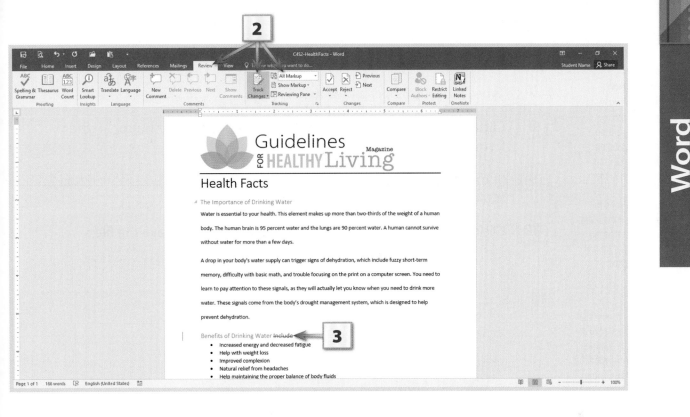

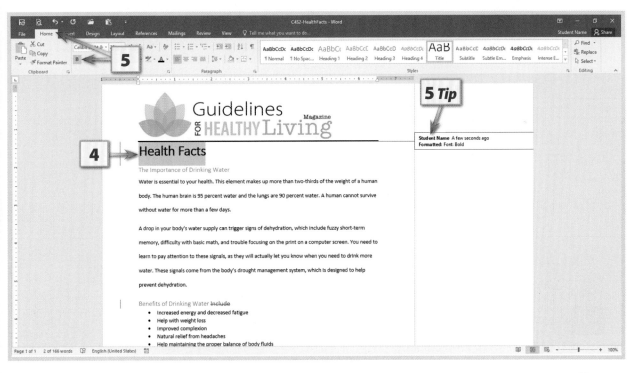

More

6 Click to the right of the words *95 percent water* in the first paragraph of text.

7 Type , blood is 82 percent water,.

8 Click the Review tab and then click the New Comment button in the Comments group.

9 In the comment balloon that appears, type You could add more detail to this sentence.

10 Click the Save button on the Quick Access Toolbar to save the file.

Use Your Touchscreen
To mark up text using digital ink, tap the Start Inking button in the Ink group on the Review tab, tap a pen option in the Pens group, and then start drawing on the screen. The ink is saved as an object that can be moved and rotated within the text.

▶**Tip** In Step 8, note that a user name is added to the beginning of the comment along with the time that has elapsed since the change was made.

Completed Skill 2

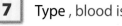

Completed
Skill Preview

Taking It Further

Checking the Word Count

Sometimes a document has to be within a certain word count, such as 500 words. To check the word count of a document, click the Review tab and then click the Word Count button in the Proofing group. This will display a dialog box with a number of statistics associated with the document, including the word, character, and line count.

Comparing Documents

The *Compare* feature on the Review tab is useful if you want to compare two versions of a document but have not turned on Track Changes. Start by clicking the Compare button in the Compare group. You can then select the two documents, review the differences between them as tracked changes, and incorporate or reject those changes. You can also combine revisions from multiple authors into a single document using the Compare feature.

Skill 3 Accept or Reject Changes and Review Comments

Before sending your document out for review, you must take a few more steps to finalize it. In this skill, you review the changes and comments you made in the previous skill and make choices about them. You can use the *Accept* and *Reject* features to either accept or reject the changes one at a time, or make a global decision to accept or reject all document changes at once. After you have acted on the suggested changes, you may have some comments remaining in the margin, because you can make changes without adding a comment and provide comments that are not connected to specific changes. As a last step, you must delete all remaining comments. When you get the document back from reviewers later, you will take similar steps to review all their tracked changes and comments, accepting and rejecting their suggestions to prepare a polished document for publication.

Tutorial

1 If it is not already open, open **C4S2-HealthFacts**, the file you saved in Skill 2, and save it as **C4S3-HealthFacts**. Be sure to save the file in your Unit 3 working folder on your storage medium.

2 If it is not already active, click the Review tab and then set the *Display for Review* option to *All Markup* in the Tracking group.

3 Click the Reviewing Pane button.

4 In the Revisions pane, click anywhere in the change listed under the heading *[Your Name] Deleted*.

> **Tip** In the Revision pane, section headings include the user name for the copy of Microsoft Office. You can change the user name by clicking the File tab, clicking the *General* option if necessary, and then typing a new name in the *Personalize your copy of Microsoft Office* section.

5 Click the Accept button in the Changes group. This accepts the change in the file and removes the *[Your Name] Deleted* change from the Revisions pane.

6 In the Revisions pane, click anywhere in the change listed under the heading *[Your Name] Formatted*.

7 Click the Reject button in the Changes group to reject the change.

5 *Another Way*
Right-click the change in the Revisions pane or within the document and then click the *Accept Deletion* option in the pop-up list.

> **Tip** If you reject a change that has a comment attached, the comment will be removed at the same time that the change is reversed.

Taking It Further

Using Read Mode

If you are simply reading a document, not editing it, you might want to use Read mode. *Read mode* allows you to swipe through pages horizontally as if reading a book. Access Read mode by clicking the View tab and then clicking the Read Mode button in the Views group. Once you are in Read mode, you can customize your experience by clicking the View menu item, pointing to the Column Width, Page Color, and Layout options in the drop-down list, and then clicking options in the secondary drop-down lists.

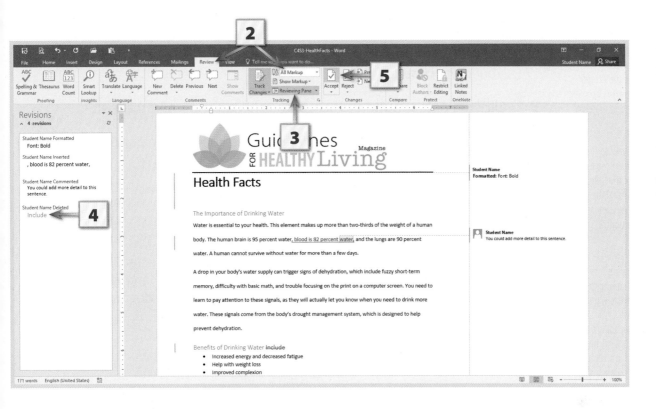

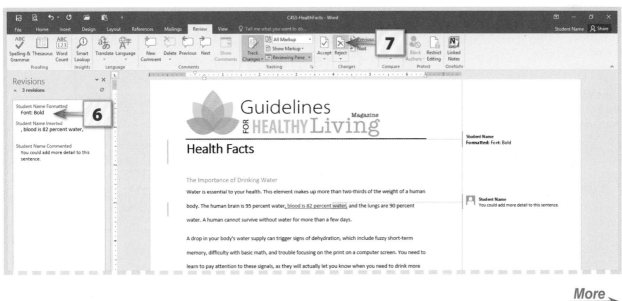

More →

Taking It Further

Protecting Files During the Review Process

The Protect group on the Review tab provides a tool for limiting what reviewers can do when looking over your documents. If you do not want reviewers to directly change your text, but do want them to make comments so that you can decide what changes to make, click the Restrict Editing button. In the *Editing restrictions* section of the Restrict Editing pane, click the *Allow only this type of editing in the document* check box to insert a check mark, click the option box, click *Comments* in the drop-down list, click the Yes, Start Enforcing Protection button, and then set a password if you want to.

8 In the Revisions pane, click anywhere in the change listed under the heading *[Your Name] Inserted*.

9 Click the Accept button to accept the change and insert the text.

10 In the Revisions pane, click anywhere in the change listed under the heading *[Your Name] Commented*.

11 Click the Delete button in the Comments group.

12 Click the Close button to close the Revisions pane.

13 Check to make sure the Track Changes button is still selected. In the next skill, you will email the file for editing, and using the Track Changes feature will allow you to easily see any changes others make to the document.

14 Save the file.

Completed Skill 3

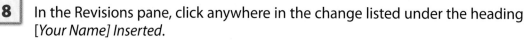

Guidelines FOR HEALTHY Living Magazine

Health Facts

The Importance of Drinking Water

Water is essential to your health. This element makes up more than two-thirds of the weight of a human body. The human brain is 95 percent water, blood is 82 percent water, and the lungs are 90 percent water. A human cannot survive without water for more than a few days.

A drop in your body's water supply can trigger signs of dehydration, which include fuzzy short-term memory, difficulty with basic math, and trouble focusing on the print on a computer screen. You need to learn to pay attention to these signals, as they will actually let you know when you need to drink more water. These signals come from the body's drought management system, which is designed to help prevent dehydration.

Benefits of Drinking Water
- Increased energy and decreased fatigue
- Help with weight loss
- Improved complexion
- Natural relief from headaches
- Help maintaining the proper balance of body fluids
- Help with energizing muscles

Recommended Daily Amounts of Water

Men	15 cups
Women	11 cups

Completed
Skill Preview

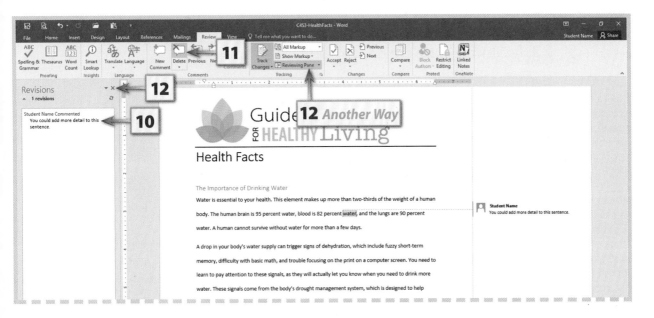

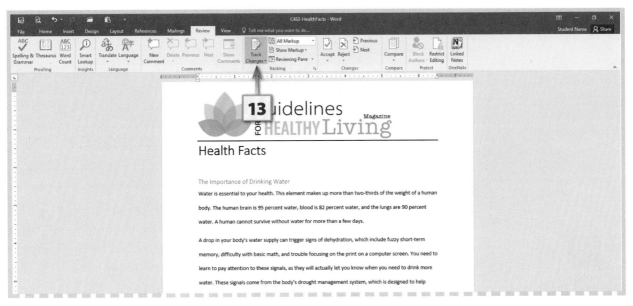

Word

Skill 4 Send a Document for Editing via Email

If you want others to give feedback on your document, you have to get it into their hands. A quick and easy route is to email a copy of the Word file to them and ask them to review and return the marked-up file. You can then accept and reject their changes and review their comments as you did your own in Skill 3, to create a final document. In this skill, you use the simple Send as Attachment button in the *Email* section of the *Share* option in Word to send the file as an attachment in Outlook. If you are unable to use Outlook for this purpose, skip this skill and check with your instructor for alternative tasks.

Tutorial

1 If it is not already open, open **C4S3-HealthFacts**, the file you saved in Skill 3.

2 Click the File tab.

3 Click the *Share* option.

4 Click the *Email* option in the *Share* panel.

5 Click the Send as Attachment button in the *Email* panel. An email form appears.

▶ **Tip** The appearance of the email form that displays in Step 5 will vary depending on the email client you have set as your default.

6 Type your own email address in the *To* box.

7 Edit the Subject line text to read Health Facts Article.

▶ **Tip** Email attachments can contain viruses and therefore should only be opened if they are from a person you know. A descriptive subject line is one way to let the recipient know the email is from a legitimate source.

8 Type the following message in the body of the email: Please review the attached Health Facts document and let me know if you have any edits. [Enter] [Your Name]

9 Click the Send button.

Completed Skill 4

Completed
Skill Preview

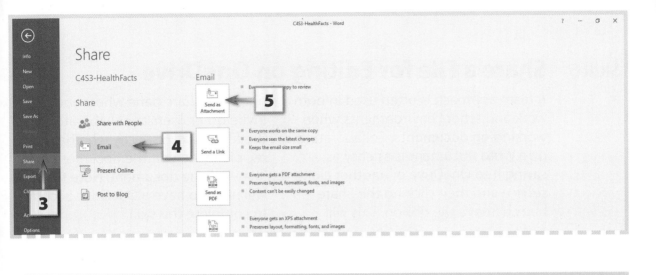

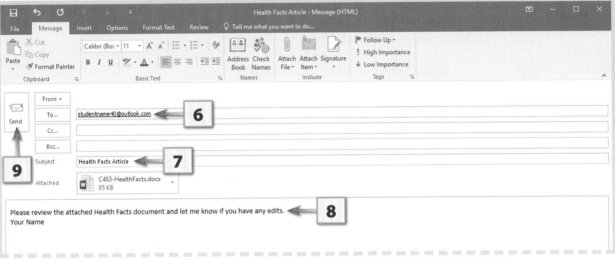

Taking It Further ●

Controlling the Review Process

If you email multiple copies of a document to different people for review, you may find yourself with a "version control" issue when the many responses arrive. You may have to place each copy on your storage medium, separately review each person's changes, and then be careful to integrate all desired changes into a single, master copy of the document. With a short document, such as our health facts article, where each person is likely to change only small bits of content, you may not have a major problem. However, with large documents, such as a 20-page report, filtering through several commented documents to decide upon changes and then implementing those decisions from

multiple documents into the master can be a headache. In such cases, consider routing a single version of the document from person to person with direction to have the last person in the chain return the document to you. Or post one version on an online document-sharing space such as Google Drive or Dropbox. Many sites are free and control access to avoid version-management problems. You can also save the file to your OneDrive account and share the file with each reviewer so that all the reviewers can track their changes in the same document. Skill 5 in this chapter explains how to share files on OneDrive.

Skill 5   Share a File for Editing on OneDrive

A team approach is often used in both work and school environments when working on documents. Collaborating on a Word document is as easy as saving it to OneDrive or another cloud service and then clicking the Share button above the ribbon. This will open the Share pane where you can invite other users to collaborate on the file. You can specify whether the recipient can edit the document or just view the document. Note that you will need to have a OneDrive account to complete this skill.

Tutorial

2–3 *Another Way*
Click the File tab, click the *Share* option, click the *Share with People* option and then click the Save to Cloud button.

▶ **Tip** If the document has already been saved to the cloud, you will skip Steps 3–5.

▶ **Tip** In Step 6, you can click the Search the Address Book for contacts button to find an email address.

▶ **Tip** When sharing with more than one person, separate email addresses with a semicolon (;).

▶ **Tip** When sharing a document, the default is to allow the recipient to edit the document. In Step 6, you can restrict the recipient to just viewing the document by clicking the arrow below the *Invite People* box and then clicking the *Can View* option in the drop-down list.

1 If it is not already open, open **C4S3-HealthFacts**, the file you saved in Skill 3.

2 Click the Share button above the ribbon.

3 In the Share pane, click the Save to Cloud button.

4 In the Save As backstage area, navigate to the appropriate OneDrive location to save the file.

5 In the Save As dialog box, click the Save button.

6 In the *Invite people* box of the Share pane, type your email address.

7 Click in the *Include a message* box and then type Please edit the document posted at this link by the end of the week.

8 Click the Share button.

9 Check your email account for the message you just sent yourself. Click the link in the email to open the shared document in Word online. Close the document and the email.

Completed Skill 5

Completed Skill Preview

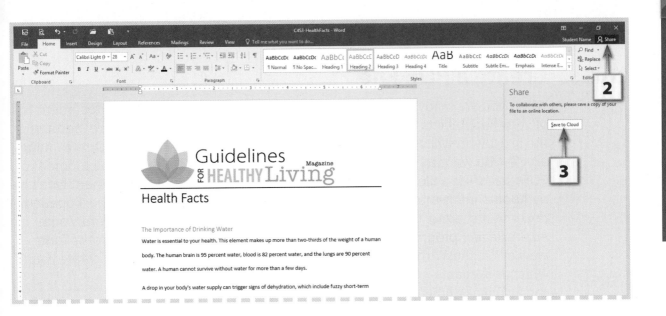

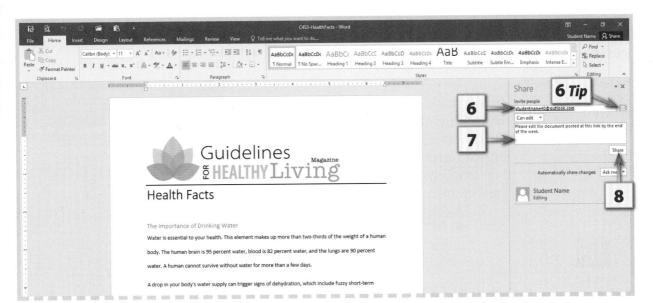

Skill 6 Create a PDF File

When you are ready to share a copy of your health facts document with the artist who will be illustrating the article, you want to save the file as a PDF file. *PDF* is a file format created by Adobe and is the standard for document sharing. Using the free *Adobe Reader* program, anybody can view a PDF file. With *Adobe Acrobat*, which is available for purchase, you can also make edits to PDF files.

A PDF version of your document is in some ways like a picture, because what people see is an accurate image of what you created at the moment of capture. Thus, your document won't be compromised as it might be if opened in different versions of Word, some of which may not support the fonts and features you used to create your document.

Tutorial

1 If it is not already open, open **C4S3-HealthFacts**, the file you saved in Skill 3.

2 Click the File tab.

3 Click the *Save as* option.

4 Click the Browse button and then navigate to your Unit 3 working folder on your storage medium.

5 Change the file name to **C4S6-HealthFacts-Lastname**, but replace *Lastname* with your last name.

6 *Another Way*
Another way to save to the PDF format is to click the File tab and then click the *Export* option. In the Export backstage area, click the *Create PDF/XPS Document* option and then click the Create PDF/XPS button. In the Publish as PDF or XPS dialog box, click the Publish button.

▶ *Tip* To get the free Adobe Reader software used to view PDF files, go to http://www.adobe.com.

6 Click the *Save as type* arrow and then click the *PDF* option in the drop-down list.

7 Click the *Open file after publishing* check box to insert a check mark if necessary.

8 Click the Save button.

9 Review the PDF file and then close the PDF and the student data file. You can now share the PDF as an email attachment or by posting it on OneDrive or another online sharing site.

Completed Skill 6

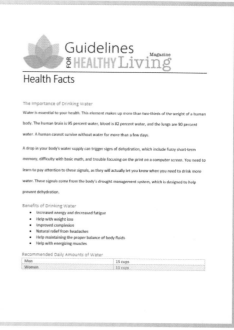

Completed Skill Preview

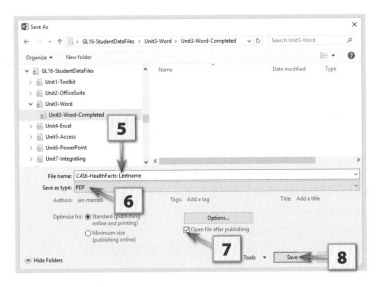

<hr>

Taking It Further ●

Viewing and Editing PDFs

The free Adobe Reader software allows you to read, search, and add annotations and comments to a PDF file. If you need to edit a PDF file, you can use Word 2016. When you open a PDF file in Word, a Word feature called PDF Reflow converts the content of the PDF and displays it in a Word file. After you make your edits, the document can be saved as a Word or PDF file. *Note: When you convert the contents from PDF to Word format, they may not look exactly the same in Word as they did in the PDF. For example, some fonts and art elements may not be supported by PDF Reflow. The conversion works best with files that are mostly text.*

Word Chapter 4 **Tasks Summary**

Task	Ribbon Tab, Group	Button, Option	Shortcut, Alternative
Turn on/off Track Changes	Review, Tracking	Track Changes	Ctrl + Shift + E
Display simple markup	Review, Tracking	Simple Markup	
Display all markup	Review, Tracking	All Markup	
Add a comment	Review, Comments	New Comment	
Open or close the Revisions pane	Review, Tracking	Reviewing Pane	
Accept changes	Review, Changes	Accept	
Reject changes	Review, Changes	Reject	
Limit editing ability	Review, Protect	Restrict Editing	
Restrict who can make changes	Review, Protect	Block Authors	
Share a file online	File, *Share*	*Share with People*	Share
Save in PDF format	FILE, *Save as*	*Save as type PDF*	
Send a document via email	File, *Share*	*Email*	

Recheck

Recheck your understanding of the skills and features covered in this chapter.

Workbook

Chapter study resources, exercises, and assessments are available in the Workbook *ebook.*

Microsoft Excel 2016

Student Data Files

Before beginning this unit, be sure you have downloaded the GL16-StudentDataFiles folder from your ebook and copied the Unit4-Excel subfolder to your storage medium. The copied folder will become your working folder for this unit.

Guidelines

for

Planning and Creating an Excel Workbook

When you create a workbook in Excel, you should take the time to plan how you will organize the data on the worksheets. Start by considering the source data you will use and the results you want to produce. Your plan will guide you as you enter the data on the worksheets.

For example, say you are creating a workbook of annual advertising sales data. You have data for each sales quarter by region. You see two arrangement options that make sense. One option is to place the data for each quarter on a separate worksheet. The other option is to create a single worksheet that displays each region's sales by quarter. The choice you make will depend on whether you want to analyze the sales for each quarter separately (the first option) or focus on the total sales and comparing the quarterly sales by region (the second option). In this case, you choose option 2.

Once you have entered and organized data on the worksheet, you can make any necessary calculations. For example, for each column of data, you can create a formula that sums the values to give you a quarterly total. And for each row of regional data, you can create a formula that sums the results to give you a regional total.

Option 2: Quarterly Sales by Region

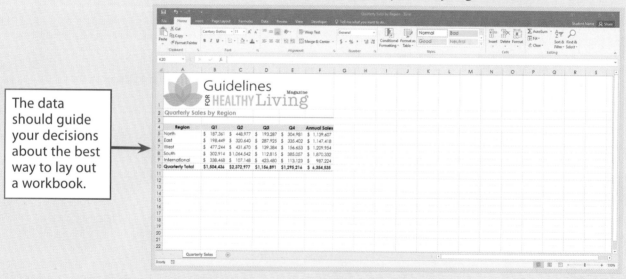

The data should guide your decisions about the best way to lay out a workbook.

If your worksheet includes an area where the user enters values to be used in Excel calculations, position those input cells in a prominent location—usually near the top of the worksheet. Apply formatting that prompts the user for entries.

In Excel, you can use business logos, shapes, and other graphics to enhance the appearance of your worksheets. Excel can also convey your worksheet data graphically in a chart. Charted data helps you spot trends and abnormalities, which can help you make better business decisions. For example,

if sales for a particular region lag far behind other region's sales, a chart can help you quickly identify the trend.

When planning a worksheet, keep in mind your audience's expectations as well as industry standards. For example, in the financial industry, professionals follow accepted conventions and, in some cases, legal requirements when they design reports such as profit and loss statements, balance sheets, and loan payment tables.

Input Cells

If a worksheet includes one or more input cells, position them near the top of the worksheet or on a separate sheet.

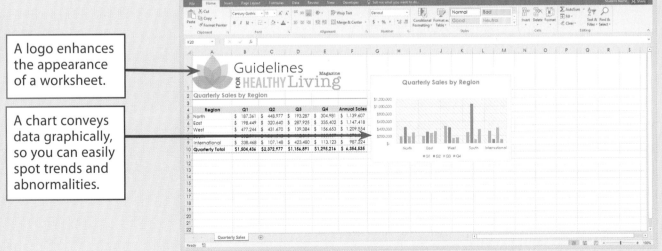

A Logo and a Chart

A logo enhances the appearance of a worksheet.

A chart conveys data graphically, so you can easily spot trends and abnormalities.

Chapter 1

Creating an Excel Workbook

Precheck

Check your understanding of the skills and features covered in this chapter.

Excel is a spreadsheet program. Each Excel file is called a *workbook*. A workbook is divided into worksheets, and each worksheet is divided into cells so that you can organize data in a table-like format and perform calculations on that data. In this chapter, you learn how to enter data and navigate in Excel.

To move from one piece of data to another, you move from cell to cell in a worksheet. Because you will be dealing with different types of data—numbers, text, and dates—you will learn how to enter each type of data to ensure that your calculations work. You will also learn about tools and tricks to help you out, such as automatically filling entries, quickly adding rows and columns, and checking the spelling of cell contents.

Rather than setting up each Excel spreadsheet as a single and lengthy page of data, you can organize data on multiple worksheets. Using multiple worksheets allows you to group like kinds of data on their own sheets and makes navigating your data easier. If you have sales data for different years, for example, you can track each year's data on a separate sheet in a single workbook. You can add sheets to a workbook and name and rename sheets as needed so that your data is easy to find and work with. Finally, in this chapter, you will learn how to add headers and footers, and to set up and print a worksheet.

Skills You Learn

1 Understand worksheet and workbook structure

2 Use cell references

3 Enter text, values, and dates

4 Use the Auto Fill feature

5 Use the spelling checker

6 Insert and delete columns and rows

7 Add, rename, move, and delete worksheets

8 Insert headers and footers

9 Explore options for printing

SNAP *If you are a SNAP user, go to your SNAP Assignments page to complete the Precheck, Tutorials, and Recheck.*

Files You Need

For these skills, you do not need any student data files.

What You Create

You are continuing your work for *Guidelines for Healthy Living Magazine*, an online magazine that provides up-to-date information on nutrition and fitness along with tips for living a healthy lifestyle. The magazine generates revenue by selling advertising. In this chapter, you produce an Excel workbook containing information about the types of ads businesses can place in your magazine, the cost of purchasing each type of ad, and a publication schedule to help purchasers plan their advertising campaigns.

Advertising Costs

Publication Schedule

Completed
Skill Preview

Skill 1   Understand Worksheet and Workbook Structure

An Excel file is called a *workbook*. When you start Excel, you can create a blank workbook or select a workbook template. A blank workbook contains one worksheet. A *worksheet*, or *sheet*, is like a page in a notebook. You can add worksheets to your workbook to keep your data organized.

The capital letters across the top of the worksheet are column headings. Each *column heading* identifies the column below it. The numbers down the left side are row headings. Each *row heading* identifies the row to its right. The intersection of each row and column is a *cell*, into which you can type an entry. An *entry* can be a data value such as name, number, or date, or a *formula* that instructs Excel to perform a calculation. As you work, a heavy green border appears around the *active cell*, which is the cell you have selected by clicking it or navigating to it using the keyboard. The active cell is also sometimes called the current cell. You can only make entries in the active cell.

After you have made cell entries, you can use the *Formula bar*, located above the column headings, to view and work with the entered data and modify individual cells or a range of cells.

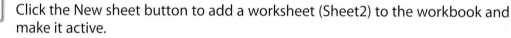

Tutorial

▶Tip To open Excel, type *excel* in the search box on the Windows taskbar and then click *Excel 2016 Desktop app* in the search results list.

▶Tip Only one sheet can be active at any given time. The active sheet is shown with its name underlined in its sheet tab.

▶Tip The active cell is highlighted with a green border.

▶Tip Notice that scrolling does not change which cell is active.

1   Open the Excel application on your computer and then click the *Blank workbook* option in the backstage area. Save the new, blank file as **C1S1-Advertising** in the Unit 4 working folder on your storage medium.

2   Move the mouse pointer over the Formula bar. A ScreenTip that reads *Formula Bar* appears to identify that screen element.

3   Click the New sheet button to add a worksheet (Sheet2) to the workbook and make it active.

4   Click the Sheet1 sheet tab to make Sheet1 active.

5   Click cell B3 (the cell in column B of row 3) to make it active. Notice that the Name box displays *B3*.

6   Click the down arrow button on the vertical scroll bar to move down the worksheet.

7   Click the up arrow button on the vertical scroll bar to move up the worksheet.

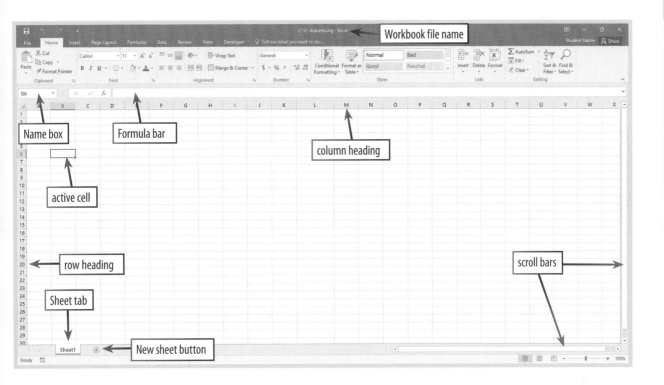

Workbook file name

Name box

Formula bar

column heading

active cell

row heading

scroll bars

Sheet tab

New sheet button

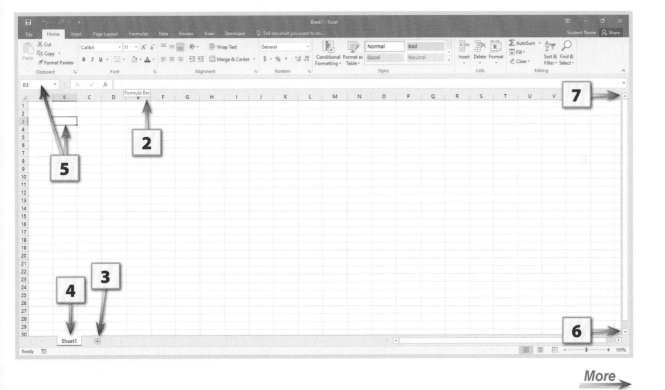

Formula Bar

2

5

7

4

3

6

More

8 Click cell A1 to make it active.

9 Press the Down Arrow key five times. Cell A6 is now the active cell.

10 Press the Right Arrow key five times. Cell F6 is now the active cell.

11 Press and hold down the Shift key, and then press the Down Arrow key three times and the Right Arrow two times to select the range F6 through H9.

12 Click cell A1 to make it active.

13 Click the Save button on the Quick Access Toolbar to save the file.

Completed Skill 1

Completed
Skill Preview

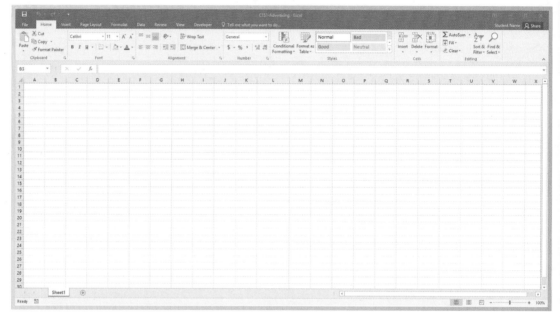

Taking It Further •

Jumping to a Cell

You can jump directly to a cell using the Go To dialog box. To open the dialog box, press the F5 key or click the Find & Select button in the Editing group on the Home tab and then click the *Go To* option. In the dialog box, you can type a cell address in the *Reference* box and then click the OK button to jump to that cell.

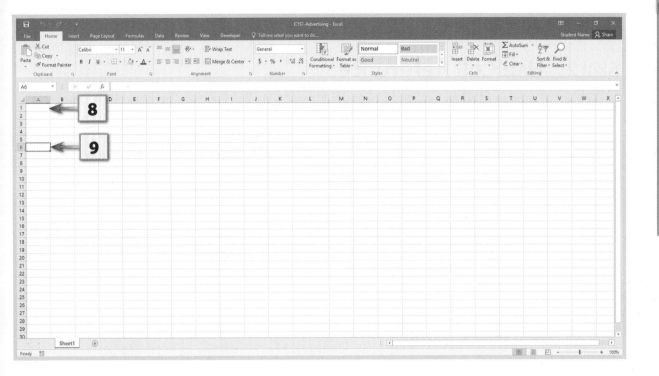

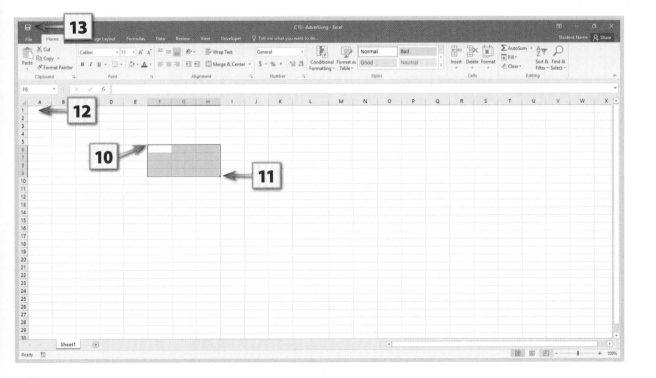

Skill 2 Use Cell References

You can identify each cell by its column letter and row number, a combination that is called its *cell address*, *cell reference*, or *cell name*. For example, the cell in the first column of the first row is cell A1. The cell in the eighth column of the tenth row is cell H10.

A *range* of cells has an address too. Identify a range by the addresses of its upper left and lower right cells, separating the addresses with a colon. For example, D5:J15 is the range that spans from cell D5 at the upper left to cell J15 at the lower right. A range can span a single row, such as when you select several column titles, perhaps A3:F3. A range also can fall within a single column, as in C3:C10.

You can type a cell or range reference in the *Name box* to the left of the Formula bar to go to that location. Understanding cell and range addresses is important when building formulas, a skill you will learn about in Unit 4, Chapter 2.

Tutorial

1 If it is not already open, open **C1S1-Advertising**, the file you saved in the previous skill, and save it as **C1S2-Advertising**.

2 Click the Sheet2 sheet tab to make Sheet2 active.

3 With cell A1 active, type Issue No., and then press the Tab key to make cell B1 active.

4 Type Month and then press the Tab key to make cell C1 active.

5 Type =B1 and then press Ctrl + Enter. This action finishes entering the text and keeps the cell active.

6 Look in the Formula bar and verify that it displays the entry you made in cell C1.

7 With cell C1 still active, type Publication Time and then press Ctrl + Enter to change the cell entry.

8 Click in the Name box to select its contents.

> **Tip** The entire contents of a data cell will display on the worksheet even if it is too long to fit in the cell, as long as the cell immediately to the right is empty. If the cell immediately to the right contains data, the overflow cell content will be hidden.

> **Tip** The entire contents of a cell will always display in the Formula bar.

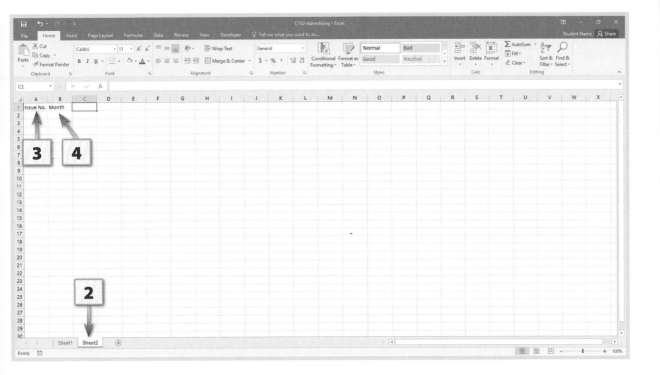

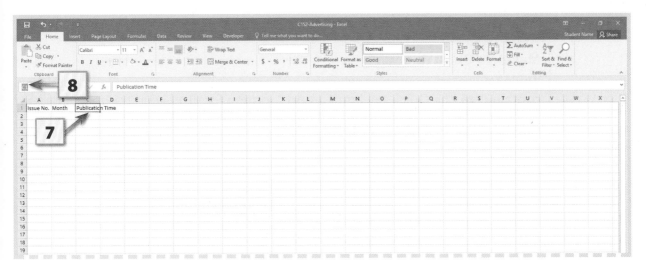

More ▶

9 Type G7 and then press Enter. Cell G7 is selected.

10 Click in the Name box.

11 Type A1:C1 and then press Enter. The range of cells A1 through C1 is selected.

12 On the Home tab, click the Fill Color arrow in the Font group and then click the *Green, Accent 6, Lighter 60%* option in the *Theme Colors* section of the drop-down gallery.

13 Click cell A1 to make it active.

14 Save the file.

Completed Skill 2

Completed
Skill Preview

Taking It Further •

Making a Quick Analysis

When you select a range of cells that contain data, the Quick Analysis button (🖾) appears at the bottom right of the selected range. Click the Quick Analysis button to display a gallery of tabs containing options for analyzing data.

For example, the Charts tab contains an option for displaying the selected data in a chart. The Formatting tab options can be used to quickly determine high and low values or to highlight values greater than a specified value.

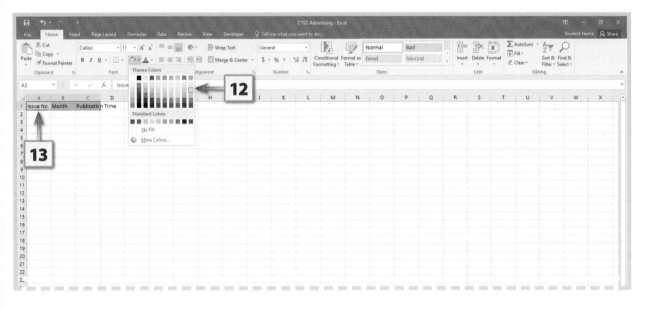

Taking It Further

Exploring a Worksheet

A worksheet contains a fixed number of columns and rows. The number of usable cells depends on the amount of RAM available to your computer. Cells within a worksheet can contain numbers and dates in various formats, text, or formulas using arithmetic operators or functions.

Check to see how many columns your Excel worksheet has by pressing the End key and then pressing the Right Arrow key. Press the End key and then press the Down Arrow key to see the number of rows in your worksheet. Press Ctrl + Home to return cell A1.

Excel

Skill 3 Enter Text, Values, and Dates

Each cell in an Excel worksheet can hold a single entry. That entry can be text, a date, a value, or a formula that calculates a result.

A text entry can contain any combination of letters, numbers, or symbols that you can type on your keyboard. *Qtr 1*, *Sales*, and *Region#* are examples of text entries. By default, Excel aligns text entries at the left side of the cell. This is true even of phone numbers because they usually are entered with hyphens or other characters and are treated as text.

Numeric entries contain numbers, including whole numbers (e.g., 15) and

decimal values (e.g., 2.5). You can enter numbers that have a certain characteristic, such as a currency symbol or a specified number of decimal places. Excel aligns number entries at the right side of the cell.

You enter dates in typical date formats, with hyphens (4-1-18) or slashes (4/1/18). By default, if you enter 4/1/18 or 4-1-18, Excel displays *4/1/2018* in the cell. After you type entries in a column, you may need to resize the column. Double-clicking the divider line between column headings resizes the column on the left to fit its longest entry.

Tutorial

> **Tip** Press Enter to move the active cell down one cell. Press Tab to move the active cell to the right one cell.

 Another Way
Press the Down Arrow key to finish a cell entry and move down one cell, the Right or Left Arrow key to move one cell to the right or left, or the Up Arrow key to move up one cell.

> **Tip** In Step 4, Excel automatically reformats the date to display as *3/26/2018*.

> **Tip** If you type an entry in an incorrect cell, click the cell and then press the Delete key to remove the entry.

> **Tip** If you type an incorrect value in a cell, click the cell, edit the value in the Formula bar, and press Enter.

1 If it is not already open, open **C1S2-Advertising**, the file you saved in the previous skill, and save it as **C1S3-Advertising**.

2 Click the Sheet1 sheet tab to make Sheet1 active.

3 Make cell A1 active, type Media Kit, and then press Enter.

4 Make cell A3 active, type 3-26-18, and then press Enter.

5 Make cell A5 active, type Type of Ad, and then press Enter.

6 Type the following entries exactly as shown in the range A6:A11. You will correct mistakes later!
Leaderboard [Enter]
Skiscraper [Enter]
Lgo [Enter]
Interstitial [Enter]
Pushdonn [Enter]
Interactive Video [Enter]

7 Make cell B5 active, type Dimensions, and then press Enter.

8 Type the following entries in the range B6:B11:
728x90 [Enter]
160x600 [Enter]
100x100 [Enter]
550x480 [Enter]
970x90 [Enter]
639x200 [Enter]

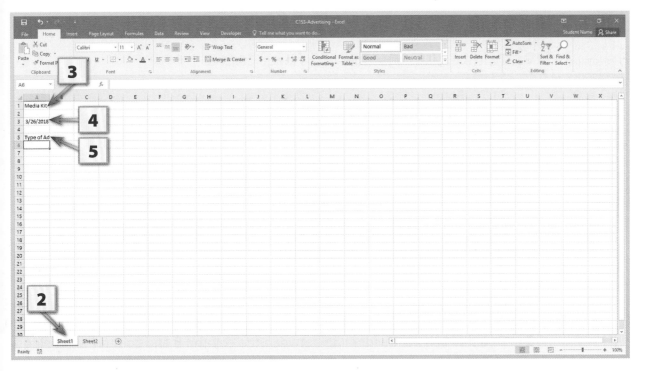

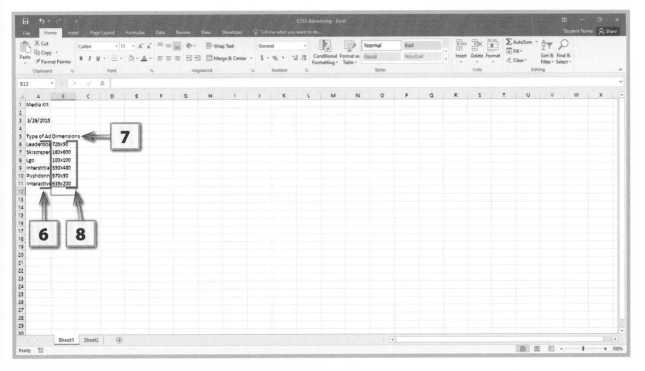

More →

Tip CPM stands for "cost per thousand impressions" and is a measurement of how much money it takes to reach 1,000 readers.

Tip When you type a number with a dollar sign in a cell, Excel automatically applies currency formatting to the cell. In Chapter 3, you will learn to select a cell or cell range and then apply a number format to the selection.

9 Make cell C5 active, type CPM, and then press Enter.

10 Type the following entries in the range C6:C11:
$3.00 [Enter]
$1.25 [Enter]
$1.00 [Enter]
$2.00 [Enter]
$1.50 [Enter]
$3.00 [Enter]

11 Notice that the ad type entries in column A are cut off. You can resize column A to fit the length of its longest entry. Move the mouse pointer over the divider line between the column A and column B headings until it turns into a left-and-right-pointing arrow.

12 Double-click the divider line between the column A and column B headings to resize column A.

13 Double-click the divider line between the column B and column C headings to resize column B.

14 Save the file.

Completed Skill 3

Completed
Skill Preview

Taking It Further ●

Removing ### from a Cell

In certain situations, such as when you enter a very large number in a cell, Excel displays a series of pound signs (###) rather than the entry itself. These signs indicate that the numeric entry is too wide to display in the cell. This feature is designed to keep readers of the data from being mislead by seeing only a portion of a number. Increase the column width for the cell contents to display properly. You will learn more about sizing cells in Chapter 3, Skill 3.

Skill 4 Use the Auto Fill Feature

The Auto Fill and Flash Fill features in Excel 2016 can help you save time when entering data. *Auto Fill* enables you to either copy an entry across a row or down a column or create a series of entries across a row or down a column. For example, if you type *Jan* in a cell and use the Auto Fill feature, Excel enters the following months: *Feb*, *Mar*, *Apr*, and so on. Auto Fill can also be used to fill the days of the week or common business entries such as *Qtr 1*, *Qtr 2*, and so on.

If you use Auto Fill to enter a number or other entry that Excel does not recognize as part of a series, Excel simply copies the entry to the area you are filling. You can create your own series by entering the first two or three values in the series and then using Auto Fill from there.

Flash Fill looks for patterns in your data and then automatically enters the rest of your data based on the pattern.

Tutorial

Tip Pressing Ctrl + Enter finishes an entry without moving the active cell to another cell.

Use Your Touchscreen
To complete Steps 4–5: Tap cell D6 and then press and hold the cell until the Mini toolbar is displayed. Tap the AutoFill button on the Mini toolbar and then drag the AutoFill button that has been added to cell D6 down to cell D8M.

Copy an Entry

1. If it is not already open, open **C1S3-Advertising**, the file you saved in the previous skill, and save it as **C1S4-Advertising**.
2. With Sheet1 active, make cell D5 active, type Size (KB), and then press Enter.
3. Type 40 and then press Ctrl + Enter.
4. Move the mouse pointer over the fill handle (which looks like a small square) in the lower right corner of cell D6. When the mouse pointer changes to a black crosshair, press and hold down the left mouse button and then drag down to cell D8. You will see a ScreenTip that reads *40*.
5. Release the mouse button to Auto Fill the entry from cell D6 to cells D7 and D8.
6. Make cell D9 active, type 60, and then press Ctrl + Enter.
7. Drag over the range D9:D11 to select it.
8. On the Home tab, click the Fill button in the Editing group.
9. Click the *Down* option in the drop-down list. Excel copies the entry *60* down the selected range.

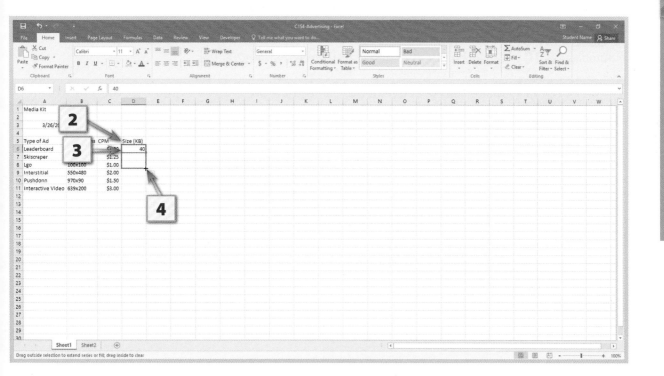

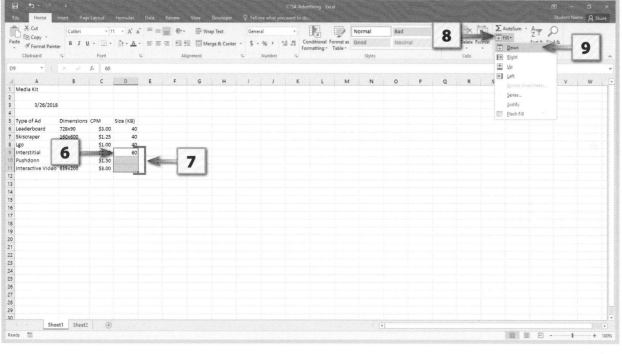

More →

Tutorial

Create a Series of Entries

10 Click the Sheet2 sheet tab to make Sheet2 active.

11 Make cell A2 active, type 1, and then press Ctrl + Enter.

12 Drag the fill handle down to cell A13. Excel copies the value *1* to cells A2:A13.

13 Click the Auto Fill Options button and then click the *Fill Series* option in the drop-down list. Excel fills the series from *1* to *12*.

14 Make cell B2 active, type January, and then press Ctrl + Enter.

15 Double-click the fill handle to fill the series from *January* to *December*.

16 Double-click the divider line between the column B and column C headings to resize column B.

17 Make cell C2 active, type 1:30 AM, and then press Enter.

18 Type 1:00 AM and then press Enter. (The magazine plans to speed up production over the next year, so it is scheduling its publication time to be 30 minutes earlier each month.)

19 Drag over the range C2:C3 to select it.

20 Double-click the fill handle to fill the series from *1:30 AM* to *8:00 PM*.

21 Double-click the divider line between the column C and column D headings to resize column C.

22 Save the file.

> **Tip** To fill a series with an increment other than 1, click the Fill button in the Editing group on the Home tab. Click the *Series* option in the drop-down list and then type an appropriate number in the Step value box.

> **Tip** You may want to remove an entry from a single cell after using Auto Fill. To do this, click the cell and then press the Delete key.

Completed Skill 4

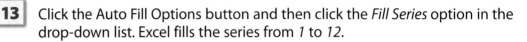

Completed
Skill Preview

214 **Unit 4** Excel

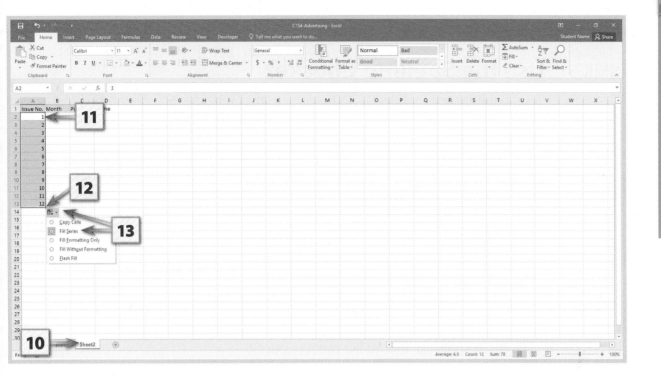

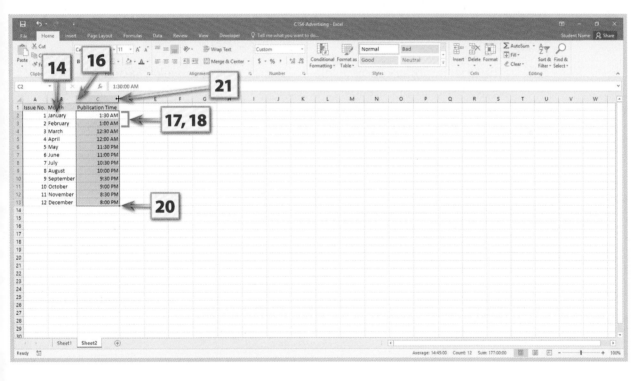

Taking It Further ●

Using Flash Fill

Excel has an automatic feature called *Flash Fill* that will save you time when entering data that is repeated in a pattern. For example, suppose you enter a list of employee email addresses in column A, and each email address contains the employee's last name and first initial. When you start typing employee last names in column B, Excel will recognize the pattern and fill in the remaining last names in column B.

Skill 5 Use the Spelling Checker

Spreadsheets can be filled with typos, requiring an eagle-eyed person to read closely to find and eliminate those pesky misspellings. Excel includes a feature to help you ensure that your worksheets are free of typos. The Excel spelling checker works much like the Word spelling checker, except that it opens in a dialog box instead of a pane. There is one extra caution with using this feature in Excel: the spelling checker only reviews text entries. It cannot ensure that you have entered numbers and dates correctly, so double-check your data thoroughly!

Tutorial

1 If it is not already open, open **C1S4-Advertising**, the file you saved in the previous skill, and save it as **C1S5-Advertising**.

2 With Sheet1 active, make cell A1 active.

 Shortcut
Open the Spelling Checker
F7

3 Click the Review tab.

4 Click the Spelling button in the Proofing group.

▶**Tip** The spelling checker starts from the active cell. When it reaches the last cell on the worksheet, it displays a message asking if you want to continue checking from the beginning of the sheet.

5 The Spelling dialog box displays the first typing mistake, *Skiscraper*. The correct spelling is already selected in the *Suggestions* list box. Click the Change button to replace the misspelled word.

6 Click the correct spelling, *Logo*, and then click the Change button to replace the misspelled word.

7 Click the Change button to replace the next misspelled word with the correct spelling, *Pushdown*.

8 In the message box informing you the spelling check is complete, click the OK button.

9 Save the file.

Completed Skill 5

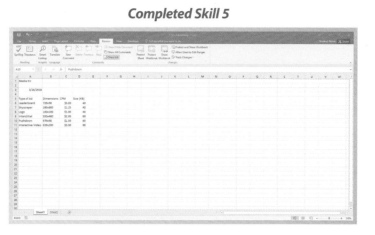

Completed
Skill Preview

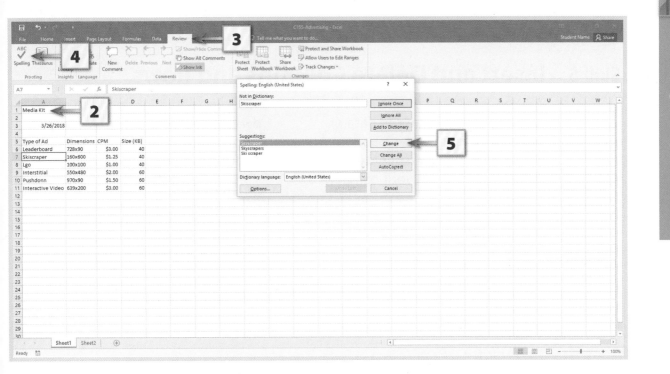

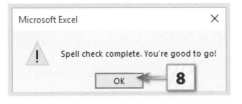

Taking It Further ●

Using AutoCorrect

Excel can correct some misspellings for you as you type. Each of us has our own unique tendency to mistype certain words. For example, perhaps your last name is *Smith*, but you often mistype it as *Simth*. Excel cannot, by default, correct that mistake. However, you can customize the AutoCorrect feature so that the correction will be made. To do so, click the File tab and then click the *Options* option. Click

Proofing at the left side of the Excel Options dialog box and then click the AutoCorrect Options button in the right panel. In the AutoCorrect dialog box, with the AutoCorrect tab selected, type your frequently made typo (such as *Simth*) in the *Replace* box and then type the correction (*Smith* in this instance) in the *With* box. Click the Add button and then click the OK button two times.

Skill 6 Insert and Delete Columns and Rows

You can insert and delete rows and columns to rearrange the data or make room for new data. For example, if you created a worksheet to track the value of products in your company's inventory, you might need to add rows for new products that you add to your catalog or remove rows when products are discontinued.

Tutorial

Insert and Delete Rows

1 If it is not already open, open **C1S5-Advertising**, the file you saved in the previous skill, and save it as **C1S6-Advertising**.

2 On Sheet1, make cell A8 active.

3 Click the Home tab.

3–4 *Another Way*
Right-click a column or row heading and then click the *Delete* command in the pop-up menu.

4 Click the Delete arrow in the Cells group.

5 Click the *Delete Sheet Rows* option in the drop-down list. Excel removes the row immediately without displaying a warning and asking you to confirm the action.

▶**Tip** If you delete a row by accident, click the Undo button on the Quick Access Toolbar (or press Ctrl + Z) to restore the contents of the deleted row.

6 Make cell A10 active.

7 Click the Insert arrow in the Cells group.

7–9 *Another Way*
Right-click a column or row heading and then click the *Insert* command in the pop-up menu.

8 Click the *Insert Sheet Rows* option in the drop-down list.

9 With cell A10 active, type the following entries across the row:
Rectangle [Right Arrow]
300x250 [Right Arrow]
$1.50 [Right Arrow]
60 [Enter]

Taking It Further • • • • • • • • • • • • • • • • • •

Designing Worksheets Using Rows and Columns

Rows and columns can play both functional and design roles in your worksheet. For example, when you perform calculations and certain other activities, such as charting, you will find the actions easiest to perform when all the data is located in adjoining rows and columns.

Insert and Delete Columns

10 Right-click the column C column heading.

11 Click the *Insert* command in the pop-up menu. A new column appears.

12 Make cell C5 active and then type the following entries down the column:
Format [Enter]
JPG [Enter]
JPG [Enter]
PNG [Enter]
FLV or F4V [Enter]
GIF [Enter]
FLV or F4V [Enter]

13 Double-click the divider line between the column C and column D headings to resize column C.

14 Right-click the column D heading.

15 Click the *Delete* command in the pop-up menu. The *CPM* column is deleted and the *Size (KB)* column shifts to the left.

16 Click the Undo button to restore the contents of the deleted column.

17 Save the file.

▶**Tip** Each Excel worksheet always has the same number of rows and columns. When you insert and delete rows and columns, you are simply changing where the blank rows and columns appear in the sheet.

▶**Tip** In Step 12, you will see examples of Flash Fill when you enter data in column C as this feature looks for patterns in your data and then automatically enters the rest of your data based on the pattern. This can save you time as you can press Enter to accept the entry without having to type it in its entirety.

10–11 *Another Way*
Click a cell in column C, click the Insert button in the Cells group on the Review tab, and then click the *Insert Sheet Columns* option in the drop-down list.

14–15 *Another Way*
Click a cell in column D, click the Delete button in the Cells group on the Review tab, and then click the *Delete Sheet Columns* option in the drop-down list.

Completed
Skill Preview

Completed Skill 6

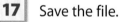

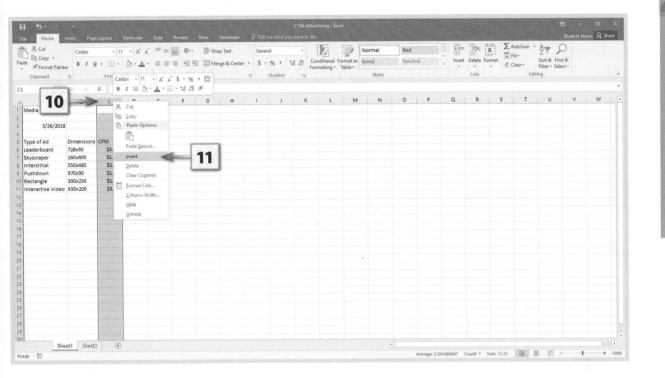

Excel

Skill 7 Add, Rename, Move, and Delete Worksheets

Given the size of each worksheet, it would be possible to arrange a wide variety of different sets of data in ranges spread throughout a single sheet. However, you would have to spend a lot of time scrolling and otherwise navigating to find the data you want to view and use. Dividing data into multiple worksheets is often more efficient. Each Excel workbook enables you to create multiple worksheets. You also can move and delete sheets.

Giving each worksheet a unique name that identifies its contents makes it much easier to determine which sheet tab to click to find the data you need. A sheet name can be up to 31 characters and can contain most characters on the keyboard, including spaces. Only a handful of characters, such as / (slash), \ (backslash), * (asterisk), ' (apostrophe), and : (colon), are not allowed in worksheet names.

Tutorial

▶**Tip** Sheet numbers are not reused in a workbook. If you create Sheet2 and then delete it, the next new sheet will be named Sheet3.

▶**Tip** You can also use commands in the Move or Copy dialog box to copy the current sheet to a new sheet. This feature can be useful, for example, if you need to track the same data for multiple stores. To copy the current sheet, click the *Create a copy* checkbox to insert a check mark. When the checkbox is empty, any option selected in the dialog box will move the current sheet.

1 If it is not already open, open **C1S6-Advertising**, the file you saved in the previous skill, and save it as **C1S7-Advertising**.

2 Click the Sheet2 sheet tab and then click the New sheet button to add Sheet3.

3 Right-click the Sheet1 sheet tab.

4 Click the *Rename* command in the pop-up menu.

5 Type Advertising Costs and then press Enter.

6 Double-click the Sheet2 sheet tab, type Publication Schedule, and then press Enter.

7 Right-click the Sheet3 sheet tab and then click the *Move or Copy* command.

8 In the Move selected sheets dialog box, click the *Publication Schedule* option in the *Before sheet* box.

9 Click the OK button. Sheet3 moves before the Publication Schedule sheet and becomes active.

Taking It Further ● ● ● ● ● ● ● ● ● ● ● ● ● ● ● ● ● ●

Color Coding Sheet Tabs

Color coding worksheet tabs is another way to make it easier to find data in a workbook. For example, if you are tracking store profitability, you could use green sheet tabs for all the stores making a profit and red sheet tabs for all the stores losing money. To change the color of a sheet tab, right-click the sheet tab, point to the *Tab Color* command in the pop-up menu, and then click the color you want in the pop-up palette.

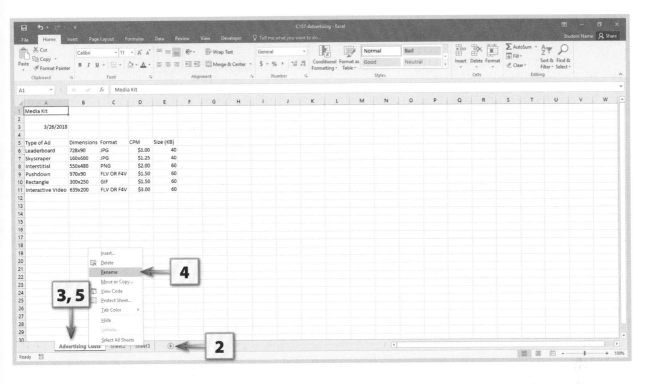

More

Excel

10–11 *Another Way*
Right-click the sheet tab
and then click the *Delete*
command in the pop-up
menu.

▶**Tip** Deleting a sheet
deletes any data the sheet
contains.

10 On the Home tab, click the Delete arrow in the Cells group.

11 Click the *Delete Sheet* option in the drop-down list.

12 Click the Advertising Costs sheet tab.

13 Make cell A1 active.

14 Save the file.

Completed Skill 7

Completed
Skill Preview

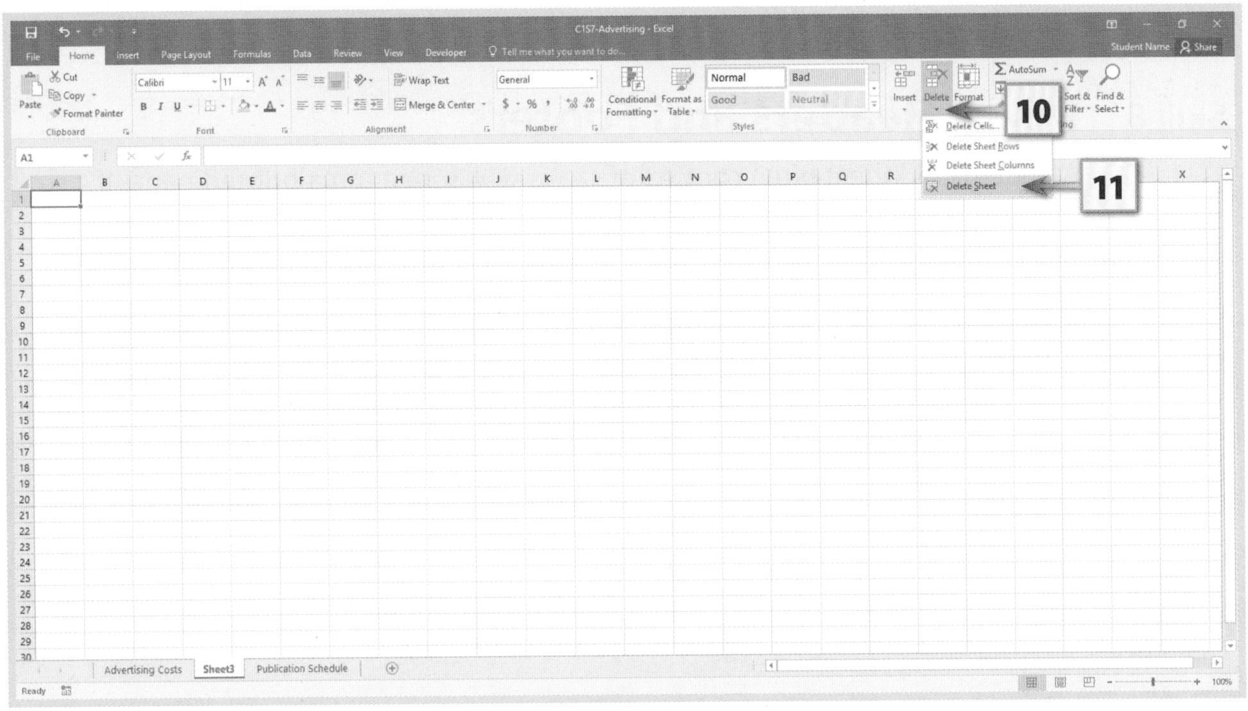

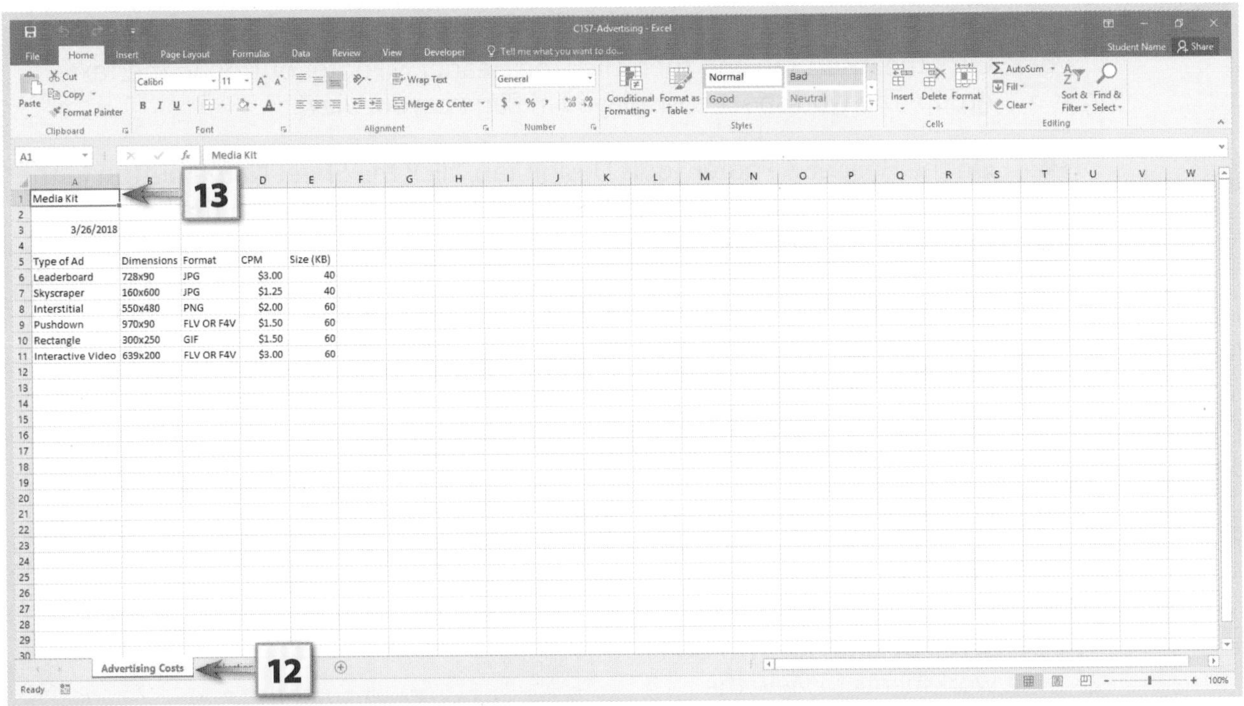

The second screenshot shows a worksheet with the following data:

	A	B	C	D	E
1	Media Kit				
2					
3	3/26/2018				
4					
5	Type of Ad	Dimensions	Format	CPM	Size (KB)
6	Leaderboard	728x90	JPG	$3.00	40
7	Skyscraper	160x600	JPG	$1.25	40
8	Interstitial	550x480	PNG	$2.00	60
9	Pushdown	970x90	FLV OR F4V	$1.50	60
10	Rectangle	300x250	GIF	$1.50	60
11	Interactive Video	639x200	FLV OR F4V	$3.00	60

Taking It Further

Copying Data to Another Workbook

You may have noticed that the Move or Copy dialog box includes a *To book* arrow. If you have another workbook open, you can select it in the *To book* drop-down list to move or copy the specified worksheet to that workbook rather than to another location within the current workbook. This action enables you to transfer data to other workbook files more quickly than you could by copying and pasting.

Skill 8 · Insert Headers and Footers

A printed worksheet often consists of multiple pages. Information such as the date, company logo, and page numbers in the header (top) or footer (bottom) of each page can help identify printouts.

When you insert a header or a footer, the worksheet is automatically displayed in *Page Layout view*. This view displays the worksheet as it will appear on a printed page. If you switch back to Normal view, the headers and footers will not be displayed.

Headers and footers are inserted on individual worksheets. However, you can insert the same header and footer on multiple worksheets by first selecting multiple worksheet tabs.

Tutorial

▶**Tip** You can tell both sheet tabs are selected by the green line under both sheet tabs.

▶**Tip** If you change the sheet name, the header will update automatically.

▶**Tip** To return to Normal view, click a cell in the worksheet outside of the header or footer area, or click the View tab and then click the Normal button in the Workbook Views group.

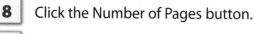

1 If it is not already open, open **C1S7-Advertising**, the file you saved in the previous skill, and save it as **C1S8-Advertising**.

2 Click the Advertising Costs sheet tab, press and hold down the Ctrl key, and then click the Publication Schedule sheet tab to select (or *group*) both sheets.

3 Click the Insert tab and then click the Header & Footer button in the Text group. The worksheet is displayed in Page Layout view.

4 On the Header & Footer Tools Design tab, click the Sheet Name button in the Header & Footer Elements group. A code (*&[Tab]*) appears in the header to represent the sheet name.

5 Click the Go to Footer button in the Navigation group.

6 Click the Page Number button in the Header & Footer Elements group.

7 Press the space bar, type of, and then press the space bar.

8 Click the Number of Pages button.

9 Click a blank cell in the worksheet outside the footer area.

10 Scroll up and down in both worksheets to view the header and the footer.

11 Click the Publication Schedule sheet tab to ungroup the sheets.

12 Save the file.

Completed Skill 8

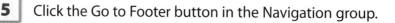

Completed
Skill Preview

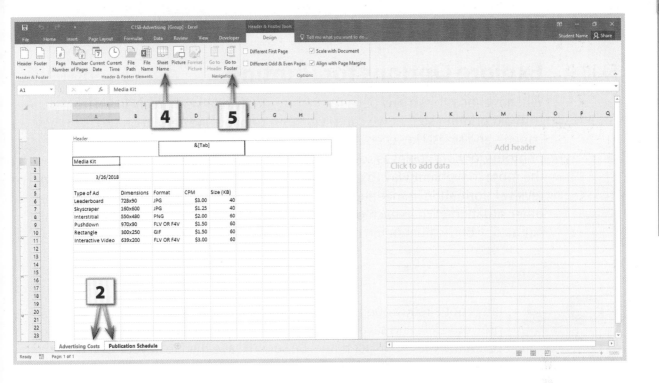

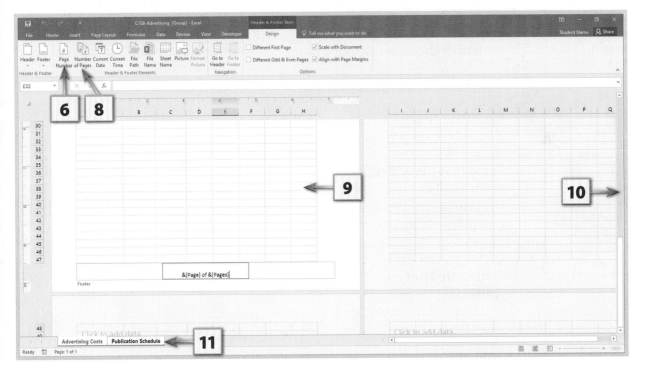

Skill 9 Explore Options for Printing

Whenever possible, many of us try to avoid printing so that we can save paper—and trees! However, distributing printouts, or *hard copies,* is sometimes the most convenient way to collectively review information in meetings and other situations. When each person has a copy of the item being discussed, individuals can freely jump from page to page and zero in on the data they find important.

Excel offers numerous options for setting up and printing a worksheet. For example, gridlines are solid lines that mark off the rows and columns similar to what appears in the Excel window.

Tutorial

>**Tip** The file should still be displayed in Page Layout view. If Normal view is displayed, click the View tab and then click the Page Layout button in the Workbook Views group.

5 *Shortcut*
Print
Ctrl + P

>**Tip** To print only certain data from a worksheet, select the desired range, click the File tab, click the *Print* option, click the *Print Active Sheets* arrow, and then click the *Print Selection* option in the drop-down list.

1 If it is not already open, open **C1S8-Advertising**, the file you saved in the previous skill, and save it as **C1S9-Advertising-Lastname**, but replace *Lastname* with your last name. Be sure to save the file in your Unit 4 working folder on your storage medium.

2 Click the Advertising Costs sheet tab to make it active.

3 Click the Page Layout tab and then click the *Print* check box in the *Gridlines* section of the Sheet Options group to insert a check mark.

4 Click the *Print* check box in the *Headings* section to insert a check mark.

5 Click the File tab, and then click the *Print* option to open the Print backstage area, which displays settings and a preview.

6 Verify that the correct printer is selected in the *Printer* box. Click the *Printer* arrow to display a drop-down list of available options; click the arrow again to close the list without making a selection. Ask your instructor if more than one printer is available and you are not sure which one to choose.

7 Click the *Print Active Sheets* arrow in the *Settings* category, and then click the *Print Entire Workbook* option in the drop-down list to print both sheets in the workbook.

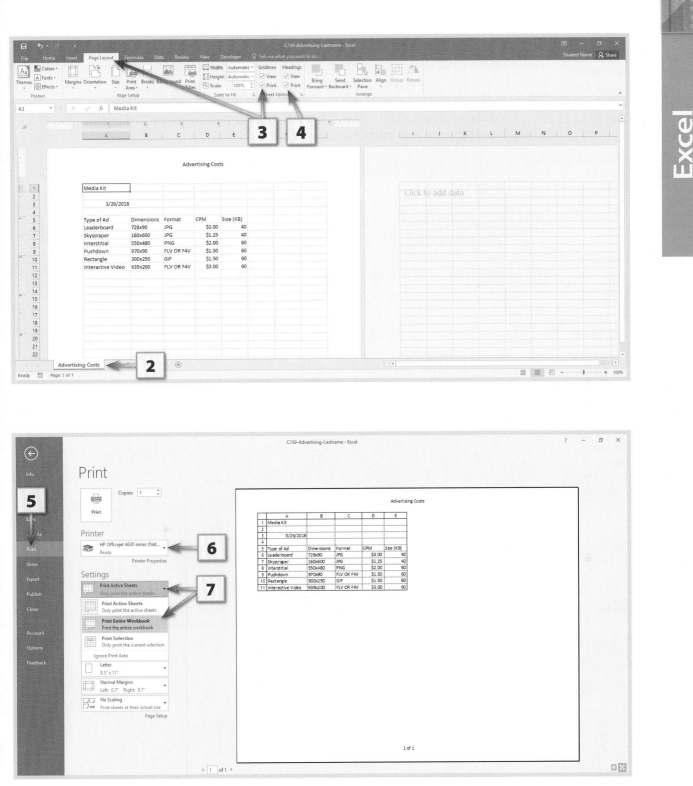

More →

8 *Another Way*

Click the Page Setup link in the Print backstage area and then click the *Landscape* option in the *Orientation* section on the Page tab of the Page Setup dialog box.

▶**Tip** Print settings, such as print orientation, have to be set on individual worksheets.

▶**Tip** The printed appearance of your worksheet can be modified using the Page Layout tab in the worksheet or the Page Setup link in the Print backstage area. In addition to setting page orientation, you can change the paper size, adjust the margins, and add row and column headings to your printout.

▶**Tip** If you want to adjust your printout to have all rows or columns on one page, you can use the scaling options in the last option box in the *Settings* category of the Print backstage area.

8 Click the *Portrait Orientation* arrow and then click the *Landscape Orientation* option in the drop-down list.

9 In the preview panel, click the Next Page arrow to display page 2, the Publication Schedule sheet. Notice the difference when print gridlines and headings are not added to a printout.

10 Click the *Portrait Orientation* arrow and then click the *Landscape Orientation* option.

11 If your instructor asks you to print the document, click the Print button. Otherwise, click the Back button.

12 Save and close the file.

Completed Skill 9

Advertising Costs

	A	B	C	D	E
1	Media Kit				
2					
3	3/26/2018				
4					
5	Type of Ad	Dimensions	Format	CPM	Size (KB)
6	Leaderboard	728x90	JPG	$3.00	40
7	Skyscraper	160x600	JPG	$1.25	40
8	Interstitial	550x480	PNG	$2.00	60
9	Pushdown	970x90	FLV OR F4V	$1.50	60
10	Rectangle	300x250	GIF	$1.50	60
11	Interactive Video	639x200	FLV OR F4V	$3.00	60

1 of 2

Publication Schedule

Issue No.	Month	Publication Time
1	January	1:30 AM
2	February	1:00 AM
3	March	12:30 AM
4	April	12:00 AM
5	May	11:30 PM
6	June	11:00 PM
7	July	10:30 PM
8	August	10:00 PM
9	September	9:30 PM
10	October	9:00 PM
11	November	8:30 PM
12	December	8:00 PM

2 of 2

Completed
Skill Preview

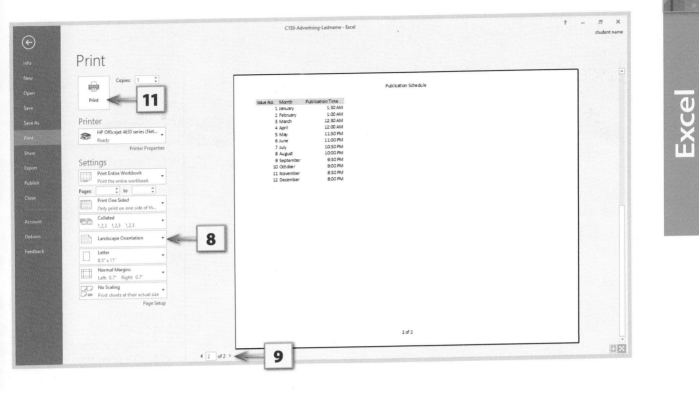

Taking It Further ●

Creating a PDF File

Excel worksheets are often used to organize, calculate, and present financial data. When sharing this data electronically, such as through email, it is important to ensure the data isn't changed by others. One way to preserve the data and also the formatting is to save the sheet as a PDF before it is sent electronically. This also allows individuals to open the file if they do not have access to the Excel software. To save the file as a PDF, click the File tab, click the *Export* option, click the *Create*

PDF/XPS Document option in the *Export* category if necessary to select it, and then click the Create PDF/XPS button in the *Create a PDF/XPS Document* section. In the Publish as PDF or XPS dialog box, you can rename the file and select from a variety of options. Click the Options button to make additional choices, such as which sheets to include in the PDF. Click the OK button to close the Options box and then click the Publish button to create the PDF.

Excel Chapter 1 **Tasks Summary**

Task	Ribbon Tab, Group	Button, Option	Shortcut, Alternative
Make a sheet active			Click sheet tab
Make a cell active			Click cell, use arrow keys to move to cell, or type cell address in Name box and then press Enter; go to cell A1 by pressing Ctrl + Home
Select a cell range	Name box		Drag, click upper left cell, and then Shift + click lower right cell, click upper left cell and then use arrow keys to extend the selection, or type cell range in Name box and then press Enter
Finish a cell entry			Enter, Ctrl + Enter, Tab, or arrow key
Auto Fill cells with a value or series	Home, Editing	⬇ Fill ▾	Drag fill handle
Perform a spelling check	Review, Proofing	ABC ✓ Spelling	F7
Insert a row	Home, Cells	Insert, *Insert Sheet Rows*	Right-click selected row headings and then click *Insert*
Insert a column	Home, Cells	Insert, *Insert Sheet Columns*	Right-click selected column headings and then click *Insert*
Delete a row	Home, Cells	Delete, *Delete Sheet Rows*	Right-click selected row headings and then click *Delete*
Delete a column	Home, Cells	Delete, *Delete Sheet Columns*	Right-click selected column headings and then click *Delete*

Task	Ribbon Tab, Group	Button, Option	Shortcut, Alternative
Insert a blank worksheet	Home, Cells	Insert Sheet	Click New sheet button
Delete a worksheet	Home, Cells	Delete Sheet	Right-click sheet tab and then click *Delete*
Rename a worksheet			Right-click sheet tab, click *Rename*, and then type new name; or double-click sheet name and then type new name
Move a worksheet			Right-click sheet tab, click *Move or Copy*, click *Create a copy* check box to insert check mark, select copy location, and then click OK
Copy a worksheet			Right-click sheet tab, click *Move or Copy*, click location in Move selected sheets dialog box, and then click OK
Insert a header	Insert, *Text*	Header & Footer	
Insert a footer	Insert, *Text*	Header & Footer	
Print	File, *Print*	Print	Ctrl + P

Recheck your understanding of the skills and features covered in this chapter.

Recheck

Chapter study resources, exercises, and assessments are available in the Workbook *ebook.*

Workbook

Chapter 2

Working with Formulas and Functions

Precheck

Check your understanding of the skills and features covered in this chapter.

Excel offers more than the ability to simply organize data in neat rows and columns; it can also perform calculations using that data. You can use calculations to determine the payments on a new car, decide which home would be a better buy, or budget for your next family vacation. In business, Excel can be used for financial tracking, business decision making, trend analysis, and more. Excel recalculates formulas when you change the data in your worksheet. This makes it easier for you to repurpose worksheets you have created for similar projects.

With Excel's help, you can quickly create complicated calculations, even if you are not a math lover. In this chapter, you will learn to use simple mathematical *operators*, such as + for addition, - for subtraction, * for multiplication, and / for division, to create formulas. You will also learn to use parentheses—(and)—to ensure that Excel performs calculations in the correct order. Excel also offers a number of shortcuts for quickly building formulas and for creating complex formulas using the AutoSum button and a calculation feature called functions.

Formulas can be copied from cell to cell, and they will automatically adjust relative to the cell they are copied to. You can override that feature by making a cell reference an absolute reference—so that when the formula is copied, the cell reference remains the same. The contents of a cell can be edited and moved to another location on the worksheet. You can also set the worksheet to show the formulas in the cells themselves.

Skills You Learn

1. Enter a formula
2. Enter a function
3. Insert a function
4. Use AutoSum
5. Use absolute and relative cell references
6. Copy and move cell contents
7. Edit cell contents
8. Use Show Formulas

If you are a SNAP user, go to your SNAP Assignments page to complete the Precheck, Tutorials, and Recheck.

Files You Need
For these skills, you need the following student data file:

C2S1-AdvertisingSales

What You Create
Guidelines for Healthy Living Magazine sells advertising to generate funds to support its annual operating budget. The sales representatives who work at *Guidelines for Healthy Living* earn a commission rate on the amount of sales they make each month. The more they sell, the more money they earn. The magazine tracks this information not only for payroll purposes but also to track the performance of its sales representatives.

In this chapter, you work on the advertising sales worksheet to add the formulas and functions needed to calculate commission earned, net sales, and sales statistics.

January Advertising Sales

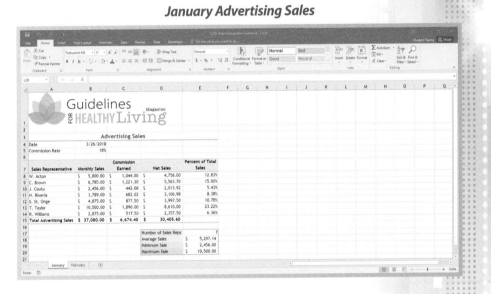

February Advertising Sales

Skill 1 Enter a Formula

In Excel, you can enter a *formula* that performs a calculation. This is one of the most important capabilities offered by Excel. There are rules for creating formulas. If you don't follow the rules, Excel indicates an error.

When you enter a formula, always type an equals sign (=) first, and then enter the rest of the formula. You can enter a number or a cell reference in a formula. For example, if you want to add the number of Leaderboard and Skyscraper ads sold together, you would enter the formula =C1+D1, where C1 and D1 are the cells that contain those values. You can enter a cell reference by typing it or using a point-and-click method. When you finish your entry, the cell displays the calculated result. If you later update the data in any cells referenced in the formula, Excel will automatically recalculate and display the updated result.

Tutorial

1 Open the student data file named **C2S1-AdvertisingSales**, and if you have not already done so, save it in your Unit 4 folder on your storage medium.

2 Click cell B16 to make it active. You will enter a formula to total the monthly sale subtotals here.

3 *Another Way*
When you type a formula in Excel, you may enter letters as either capital or lowercase. The program automatically capitalizes the letters in the cell when you finish the entry.

3 Type =B9+B10+B11+B12+B13+B14+B15.

4 Press Ctrl + Enter. The calculated value *$37,080.00* displays in cell B16 and the formula you entered in Step 3 displays in the Formula bar.

5 Click cell D9 to make it active.

▶ *Tip* All Excel formulas begin with an equals sign, as shown in Step 3.

▶ *Tip* In Step 4, pressing Ctrl + Enter enters the formula without changing the active cell.

▶ *Tip* In Skill 2, you will learn to use functions to simplify formula entries.

Taking It Further

Calculating in Excel

Excel follows the standard mathematical *order of operations* when evaluating formulas. This means that Excel performs multiplication (*) and division (/) before performing addition (+) and subtraction (-). If the operator precedence is the same, Excel calculates from left to right. Adding parentheses enables you to control the calculation order. Parentheses must be used in pairs, and you can use multiple pairs. Excel calculates from the innermost set of parentheses outward. For example, the formula =5+6*3 calculates to 23 because Excel multiplies first. In contrast, =(5+6)*3 calculates to 33 because Excel adds the values in parentheses first.

More

6 Click in the Formula bar and then type =B9-C9, which calculates the net monthly sales for the first sales representative.

Tip In Step 7, click the Formula bar Cancel button (looks like an x) to cancel the cell entry.

7 Click the Formula bar Enter button to finish entering the formula.

8 Click cell E9 to make it active.

9 Type =, click cell D9, type /, and then click cell B16.

10 Press Enter.

11 Save the file.

Completed Skill 1

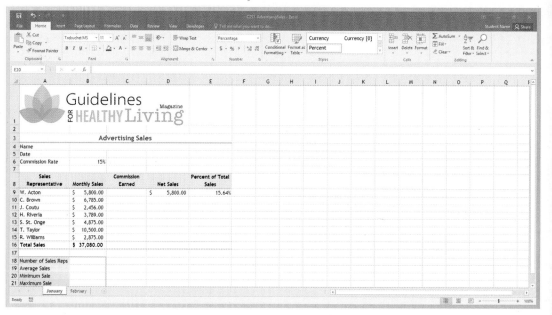

Completed
Skill Preview

Chapter 2 Working with Formulas and Functions   **239**

Skill 2 **Enter a Function**

An Excel *function* simplifies entry of a lengthy and complicated formula. Each function has a name and performs a predefined calculation when you include it in a formula. Excel offers dozens of functions in several different categories, such as *Math & Trig, Financial, Logical, Statistical, Lookup & Reference,* and more.

The function name typically indicates what type of calculation the function performs. For example, the SUM function sums a range of values, the AVERAGE function finds the average of a range of values, and the COUNT function counts the number of cells in a specified range. You can use the MAX and MIN functions to find the maximum and minimum values in a range. Use the TODAY function to enter the current date, which will update each time you open the workbook.

Most functions require one or more arguments surrounded by parentheses. An *argument* is a value on which a function performs its calculations. For example, the SUM function needs to know which values to add.

Tutorial

1 If it is not already open, open **C2S1-AdvertisingSales**, the file you saved in the previous skill, and save it as **C2S2-AdvertisingSales**.

2 Click cell B5 to make it active.

3 Type =TODAY().

> **3 *Another Way***
> Functions are not case-sensitive, so typing them in all lowercase letters also works.

> ▶**Tip** When you are typing a function, a ScreenTip appears to help you type the proper arguments.

4 Press Enter. The current date appears in cell B5.

5 Click cell C16 to make it active.

6 Type =SUM(.

7 Drag to select the range C9:C15 to enter it in the formula.

> **7 *Another Way***
> Type the range address *C9:C15.*

8 Type) to close the function argument list.

> **8 *Another Way***
> This step can be skipped.

9 Press Enter to finish entering the formula. (Cell C16 currently shows $ - because the cells in the selected range do not contain values or formulas. You will enter commission formulas in cells C9 through C15 in Skill 5.)

> **9 *Another Way***
> Click the Formula bar Enter button.

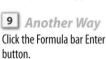

Completed Skill Preview

Completed Skill 2

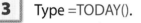

10 Save the file.

Taking It Further ●

Calculating Payments for a Car Loan

The PMT function is used to calculate the equal periodic payments for an installment loan, such as a car loan. The PMT function takes the form =PMT(rate,term,principal). In the function, *rate* is the interest rate per period, *term* is the number of loan payments, and *principal* is the amount borrowed. For example, to calculate the

monthly payments on a 5-year, $20,000 loan with an annual interest rate of 3%, you would have =PMT(3%/12,60,-20000). In the example, the annual interest rate is divided by 12 to calculate the monthly rate and the principal is negative to indicate that the money is owed.

Skill 3 Insert a Function

You can insert a function using buttons in the Function Library group on the Formulas tab. Function buttons organize functions by category, such as *Financial*, *Logical*, and *Math & Trig*. There are additional groupings for *Statistical, Engineering,* and *Compatibility* categories. The groupings help you locate the function you need for your formula.

If you don't know the name of the function you need but do know what you want it to do, you can click the Insert Function button to open the Insert Function dialog box. Here you can type a brief description and view a list of possible function matches. Click an item in the list to view its arguments and a description of what it does. The Insert Function button is located in two places: in the Function Library group on the Formulas tab, and also to the left of the Formula bar.

Excel also has a *Formula AutoComplete* feature that helps you insert a function by displaying a pop-up list of functions as you start to type a formula.

As you will learn in Skill 4, you can also insert common functions such as SUM, AVERAGE, COUNT, MIN, and MAX using the *AutoSum* feature. You begin this skill by entering a function in cell B18 to count the number of sales representatives.

Tutorial

Use the Insert Function Button

1 If it is not already open, open **C2S2-AdvertisingSales**, the file you saved in the previous skill, and save it as **C2S3-AdvertisingSales**.

2 Scroll down if necessary and make cell B18 active.

3 Click the Formula bar Insert Function button to open the Insert Function dialog box.

 Another Way
Click the Insert Function button in the Function Library group on the Formulas tab.

4 Type count to replace the contents of the *Search for a function* box.

▶ **Tip** In Step 4, instead of searching, you could select a category from the *Or select a category* drop-down list.

5 Click the Go button.

6 Confirm that *COUNT* is selected in the *Select a function* box.

7 Click the OK button to close the Insert Function dialog box. The Function Arguments dialog box appears, with the contents of the *Value1* box selected. (Each value box represents an argument.)

 **Another Way**
Press Enter.

▶ **Tip** If the dialog box is covering the cell range in Step 8, either drag the title bar to move the dialog box out of the way, or click the Collapse Dialog box button to the right of the value box to collapse the dialog box.

8 Drag over the range B9:B15 on the January worksheet to enter this range in the *Value1* box.

9 Click the OK button. The counted result *7* appears in cell B18.

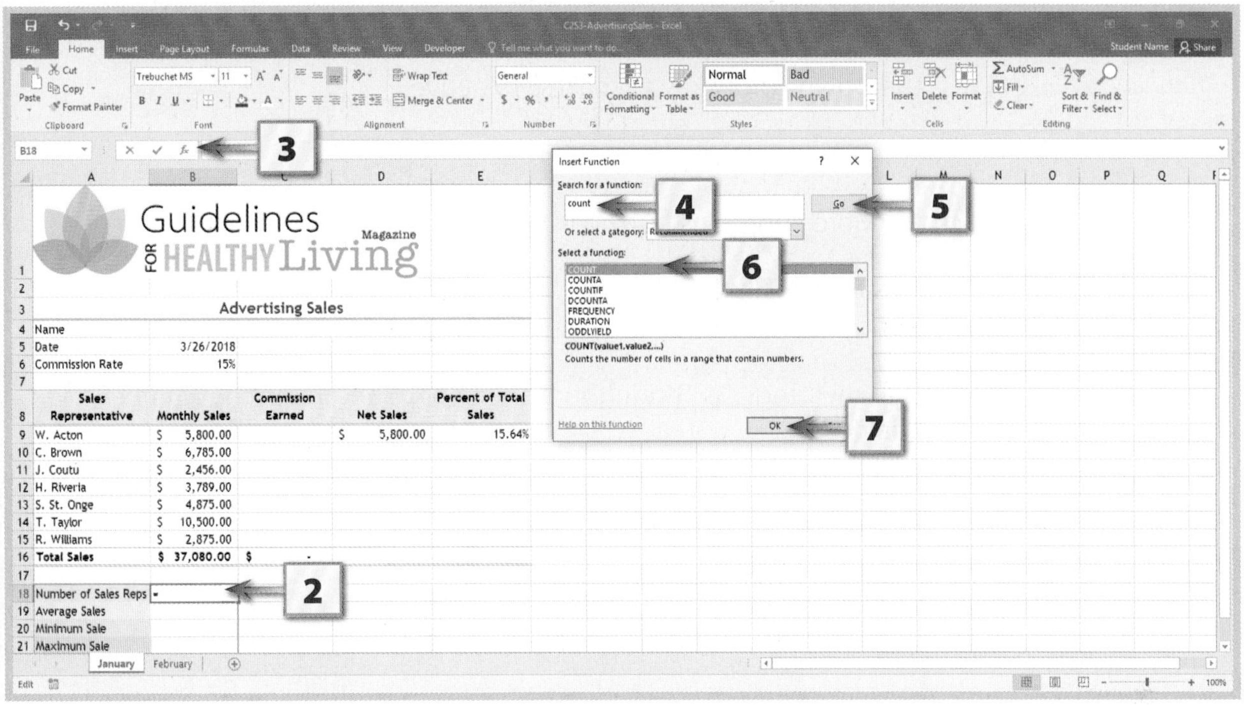

Insert Function
Search for a function:
count
Go
Or select a category:
Select a function:
COUNT
COUNTA
COUNTIF
DCOUNTA
FREQUENCY
DURATION
ODDLYIELD
COUNT(value1,value2,...)
Counts the number of cells in a range that contain numbers.
Help on this function
OK
2
3
4
5
6
7
Guidelines
FOR HEALTHY Living
Magazine
Advertising Sales
Name
Date 3/26/2018
Commission Rate 15%
Sales Representative
Monthly Sales
Commission Earned
Net Sales
Percent of Total Sales
W. Acton $ 5,800.00
C. Brown $ 6,785.00
J. Coutu $ 2,456.00
H. Riveria $ 3,789.00
S. St. Onge $ 4,875.00
T. Taylor $ 10,500.00
R. Williams $ 2,875.00
Total Sales $ 37,080.00
Number of Sales Reps
Average Sales
Minimum Sale
Maximum Sale
January
February

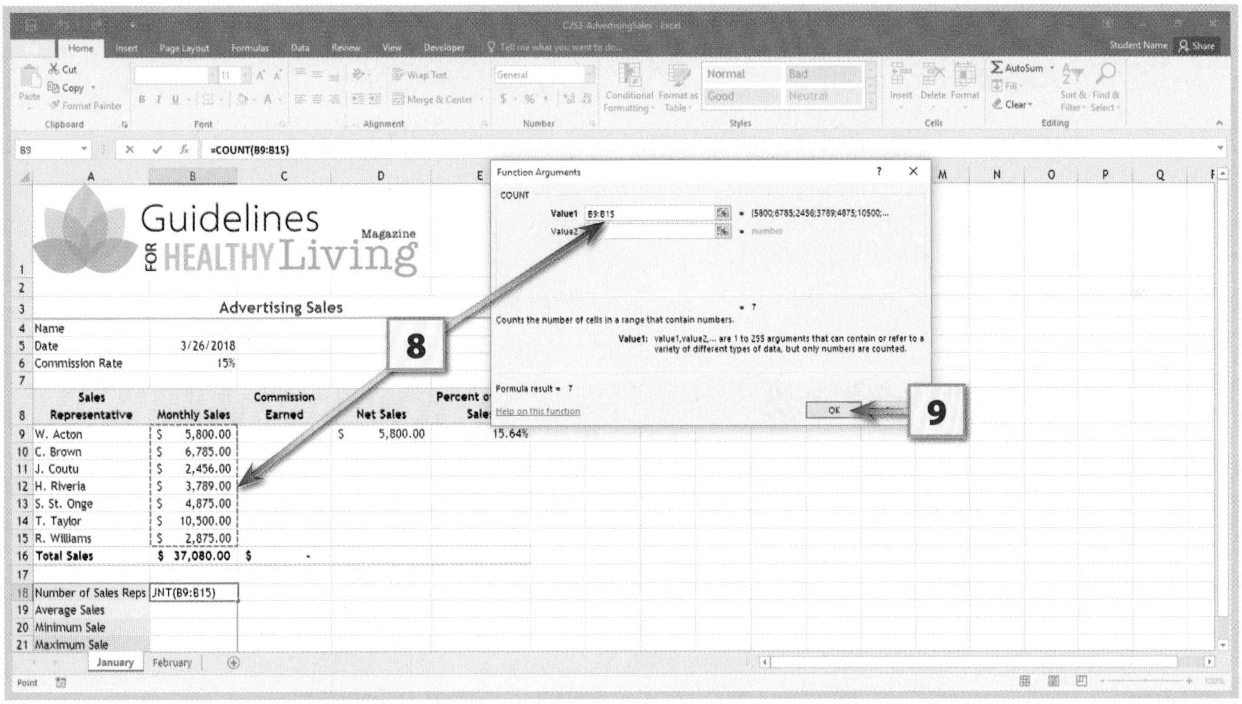

=COUNT(B9:B15)
Function Arguments
COUNT
Value1 B9:B15
Value2
Counts the number of cells in a range that contain numbers.
Value1: value1,value2,... are 1 to 255 arguments that can contain or refer to a variety of different types of data, but only numbers are counted.
Formula result = 7
Help on this function
OK
8
9

More

Use the Formulas Tab

10 Press the Down Arrow key to make B19 active.

11 Click the Formulas tab.

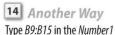

> **Tip** Click a Function button, such as Financial or Logical, in the Function Library group on the Formulas tab to see a list of functions within that category.

12 Click the More Functions button in the Function Library group.

13 Point to *Statistical* in the drop-down list and then click the *AVERAGE* option in the second drop-down list to open the Function Arguments dialog box.

14 Drag over the range B9:B15 in the worksheet to enter it in the *Number1* box in the dialog box.

14 *Another Way*
Type *B9:B15* in the *Number1* box.

15 Click the OK button. The calculated average *$5,297.14* appears in cell B19.

Use the Formula AutoComplete Feature

16 Press the Down Arrow key to make cell B20 active.

17 Type =M.

18 Double-click the *MIN* option in the Formula AutoComplete pop-up list.

19 Drag over the range B9:B15 to enter it in the formula and then type) to close the argument.

20 Press Enter. Cell B20 displays *$2,456.00*, the minimum value found in the range B9:B15.

21 Save the file.

Completed Skill 3

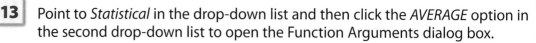

Completed
Skill Preview

Taking It Further •

Inserting Multiple Arguments

More complex functions require multiple arguments. When you are typing in a function and need to include multiple arguments— such as multiple cell or range addresses or other values—add a comma between

arguments. For example, the IF function is used to display one value if a condition is true and another value if the condition is false, and therefore requires multiple arguments, such as =IF(A5>100,1,0).

Excel

Skill 4 **Use AutoSum**

The AutoSum feature provides a quick way to enter commonly used functions in a formula. These functions include SUM, AVERAGE, COUNT, MIN, and MAX. To see the result of an AutoSum function without actually entering the formula in a cell, drag over a range of cells and then check the Status bar.

AutoSum functions are also available by clicking the Quick Analysis button after you have selected a range of cells. In the Quick Analysis gallery, select the TOTALS tab to display AutoSum functions. (The Quick Analysis button was described in the Taking It Further feature for Chapter 1, Skill 2.)

Tutorial

1 If it is not already open, open **C2S3-AdvertisingSales**, the file you saved in the previous skill, and save it as **C2S4-AdvertisingSales**.

2 Click the Home tab.

3 Select the range B9:B15.

4 Observe the *Average*, *Count*, and *Sum* values that appear on the Status bar.

5 Make cell D16 active.

6 Click the AutoSum button in the Editing group.

7 Press Enter to accept the suggested range and insert the formula in cell D16. Cell D16 displays *$5,800.00*, the sum of D9:D15.

8 Scroll down, if necessary, and make cell B21 active.

> **Tip** You can change or add to the functions that appear on the Status bar when you drag over a range. Right-click the Status bar and then click an option, such as *Minimum*, in the pop-up list to add that function to the Status bar.

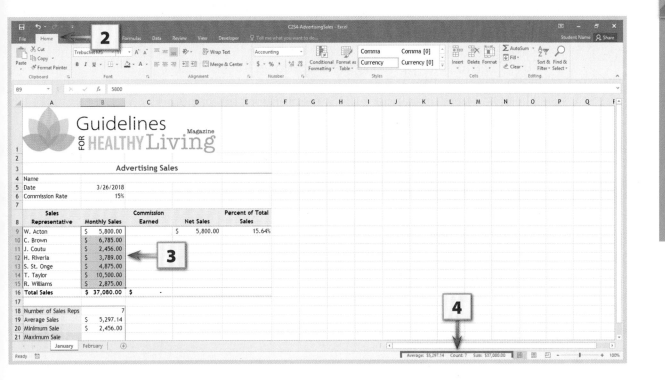

More ►

9 Click the AutoSum arrow.

10 Click the *Max* option in the drop-down list.

11 Drag over the range B9:B15 to enter it in the formula.

12 Press Enter. Cell B21 displays *$10,500.00,* the maximum value found in the specified range.

13 Save the file.

Completed Skill 4

Completed
Skill Preview

Taking It Further ●

Using the IF Function

In addition to MIN, MAX, AVERAGE, SUM, COUNT, and TODAY, you will find several other valuable functions as you begin exploring Excel. The IF function permits you to test a condition and perform different calculations based on the result. The IF function takes the form =IF(logical_test,value_if_true,value_if_false). For example the formula =IF(A10>B2,100,1) displays *100* if the value in cell A10 is greater than the value in cell B2 and displays *1* if the value in cell A10 is not greater than the value in cell B2.

Skill 5   Use Absolute and Relative Cell References

Cell references in formulas can be either relative or absolute. A relative cell reference will change if you copy or move the formula. For example, say you created a worksheet that tracks household expenses by month. In January, you entered the expenses for that month and entered a formula to total them at the bottom of column A. Now it is February. You enter the February expenses in column B, but rather than type the SUM formula again, you copy it from column A and paste it in column B. The column references in the formula automatically adjust by one column, causing the pasted formula to reference the February expenses. For example, =SUM(A3:A10) would change to =SUM(B3:B10) if you copied it one column to the right.

If you don't want a cell reference to change when you are copying a formula, make it an *absolute reference* by placing a dollar sign before the column letter and row number, for example, *A5*. Use an absolute reference when a formula contains a key piece of data, such as an interest rate, that needs to stay the same when a formula is copied.

Use Your Touchscreen
In Step 4, touch keyboard users will need to type the dollar signs before the column letter and the row number.

Tutorial

1. If it is not already open, open **C2S4-AdvertisingSales**, the file you saved in the previous skill, and save it as **C2S5-AdvertisingSales**.

2. Make cell C9 active.

3. Type =B9*B6.

▶**Tip** In Step 4, you make *B6* an absolute reference because cell B6 contains the rate used to calculate the commission for all the sales representatives.

4. Press F4. Excel changes the formula to =B9*B6, making the second cell reference an absolute reference.

5. Press Ctrl + Enter to finish the entry. Notice that the values in cells D9, E9, C16, and D16 recalculate automatically because they contain formulas that reference C9.

6. Make cell E9 active.

7. Double-click the fill handle to Auto Fill the range E10:E15. A number of *#DIV/0!* errors appear in the range because the original formula does not have an absolute reference but needs one. You will learn how to edit the formula to fix this issue in Skill 7.

Use Your Touchscreen
In Step 7, press and hold cell E9 until the Mini toolbar is displayed, tap the AutoFill button on the toolbar, and then drag the button to cell E15.

Completed Skill 5

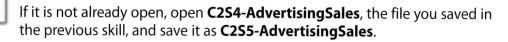

8. *Shortcut*

Undo
Ctrl + Z

8. Click the Undo button on the Quick Access Toolbar.

9. Save the file.

Completed
Skill Preview

Taking It Further

Placing Reference Data

Choosing a good position for key data referenced by formulas on a worksheet can save you trouble later. If you need to change the value in one or more cells referenced in formulas throughout the worksheet, placing that information near the top of the sheet makes it more accessible. Some worksheet designers set up an input range at the top of the sheet to give the worksheet user clear direction about where to enter values. For other types of worksheets, you might want the user to be able to see the results but not the data on which those results are based. In such a case, you would place the input data far down and to the right on the sheet, or even on another worksheet in the workbook file.

Skill 6 Copy and Move Cell Contents

Often, a worksheet or workbook will contain cell content, such as data values and formulas, that repeats. For example, if a workbook contains budget information for two chain store locations, the budget data for each store is likely to use the same column and row headings and the same formulas.

You can save time entering duplicate data by using the Copy and Paste buttons in the Clipboard group on the Home tab. After you copy cells that contain formulas, the relative cell references will adjust automatically when the formula is pasted. Absolute cell references will not adjust automatically; if you want them to change, you will have to adjust them manually.

Similarly, you can use the Cut and Paste buttons in the Clipboard group on the Home tab to move data or formulas to another location on the worksheet. When you move formulas, relative references do not adjust automatically; they act like absolute references and will need to be changed manually if you want to adjust them.

Tutorial

▶**Tip** In Step 3, be sure to click the Copy button, not the Copy arrow.

▶**Tip** The Office Clipboard can store up to 24 items that have been cut or copied. To open the Office Clipboard, click the Clipboard group task pane launcher on the Home tab. You can then choose items to paste.

▶**Tip** In Step 5, be sure to click the Paste button, not the Paste arrow.

▶**Tip** Click the Paste button if you expect to paste copied cells into more than one location. Press Enter to paste the content for a single time or the final time.

Copy and Paste Cell Contents

1 If it is not already open, open **C2S5-AdvertisingSales**, the file you saved in the previous skill, and save it as **C2S6-AdvertisingSales**.

2 Drag to select the range C9:D9.

3 On the Home tab, click the Copy button.

4 Make cell C10 active.

5 Click the Paste button.

6 Look in the Formula bar to see the formula you just pasted in cell C10. Notice that the relative reference B9 has been updated to B10, while the absolute reference B6 has not changed.

7 Make cell C11 active.

8 Press Enter to paste the copied formula again.

9 With the range C11:D11 selected, double-click the fill handle at the lower right corner of cell D11 to use Auto Fill to copy the formulas down through the range C15:D15.

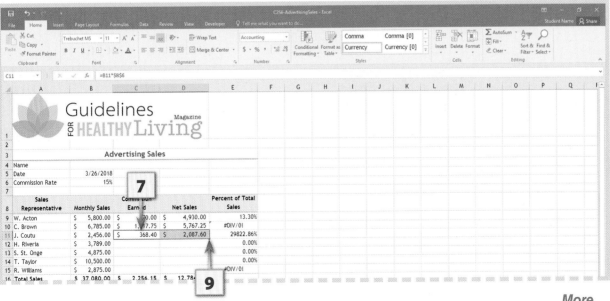

More →

▶**Tip** In Step 11, when you delete row 4, any relative references that reference row 4 or higher adjust automatically. For example, =B10-C10 adjusts to =B9-C9.

Tutorial

13 **Shortcut**
Cut
Ctrl + X

▶**Tip** Pressing Esc clears the scrolling marquee.

15 **Shortcut**
Paste
Ctrl + V

Use Your Touchscreen

In Step 7, press and hold cell E9 to display the Mini toolbar, tap the AutoFill button on the toolbar, and then drag the AutoFill button to cell E15.

Completed Skill Preview

10 Right-click the row 4 row heading.

11 Click the *Delete* option in the drop-down list to delete a row.

Cut and Paste Cell Contents

12 Scroll down, if necessary, and select the range A17:B20.

13 Click the Cut button to cut the range from that location. A scrolling marquee appears around the selected range.

14 Make cell D17 active.

15 Click the Paste button. The moved selection appears in its new location. Notice that the results in cells B17:B20 do not change when you move them to the location E17:E20, even though the cells contain formulas with relative references.

16 Double-click the right border of the column D column heading to AutoFit the width of the column.

17 Save the file.

Completed Skill 6

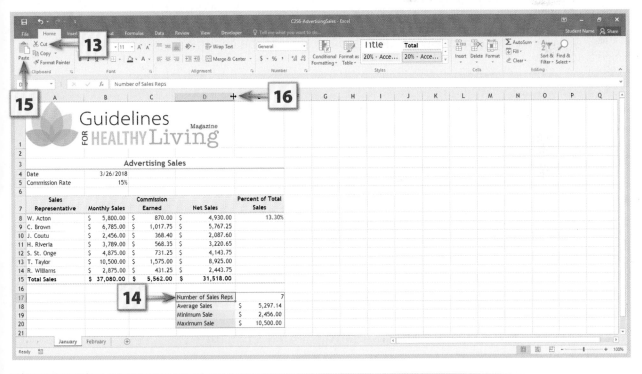

Taking It Further ●

Using Paste Button Options

Clicking the Paste arrow in the Clipboard group on the Home tab displays additional paste options, such as the *Formulas* option for pasting only formulas, the *Transpose* option for transposing (vertical to horizontal and vice versa) the location of the pasted cells, and the *Paste Values* option for pasting data without underlying formulas or formatting. You also can access the Paste options by clicking the Paste Options button that appears at the lower right corner of any pasted cell or range.

Skill 7 Edit Cell Contents

When you want to use different labels for data, update the data to reflect new information, or make corrections to formulas, you have to edit a cell's contents. Excel offers a number of methods for removing or changing cell contents. You can edit a cell's content directly in the cell or in the Formula bar. You can also use the Clear button in the Editing group on the Home tab to edit a cell's contents.

Tutorial

Edit Directly in a Cell or in the Formula Bar

1 If it is not already open, open **C2S6-AdvertisingSales**, the file you saved in the previous skill, and save it as **C2S7-AdvertisingSales**.

2 Make cell B5 active.

3 Type 18 and then press Enter. This number is a new commission rate. Notice that the values in the *Commission Earned* and *Net Sales* columns are automatically recalculated because of the change.

Shortcut
Edit Active Cell
F2

▶ **Tip** Double-clicking in a cell puts Excel in Edit mode and displays *Edit* on the left end of the Status bar.

▶ **Tip** Changing cell contents does not change the formatting. In the Editing group on the Home tab, click the Clear button and then click the *Clear Formats* option to remove cell formatting.

4 Double-click cell A15 to place the insertion point in the cell.

5 Click just to the left of the word *Sales*, type Advertising, press the space bar, and then press Enter.

6 Double-click the divider line between the column A and column B headings to resize column A.

7 Make cell E8 active and then click in the Formula bar. The D8 reference is correct, but the reference to cell B15 needs to be an absolute reference. Click in the B15 cell reference, press F4, and then press Ctrl + Enter.

8 Double-click the fill handle at the lower right corner of cell E8 to copy the formula down the column through cell E14.

Tutorial

Edit Using Copy and Paste and the Clear Button

9 Select the range A3:E20.

10 **Shortcut**
Copy
Ctrl + C

10 On the Home tab, click the Copy button in the Clipboard group.

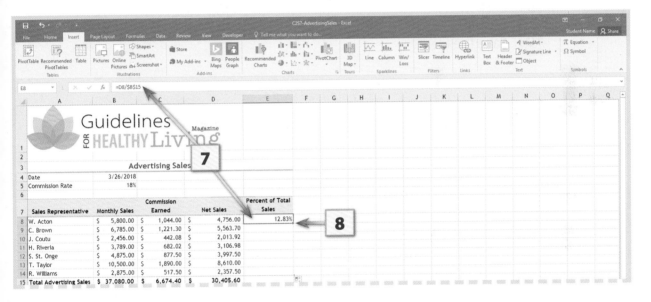

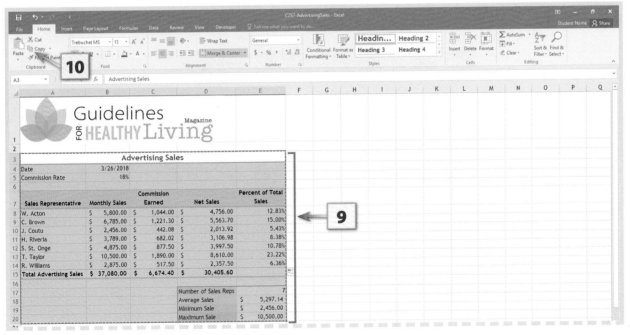

More

11 Click the February sheet tab.

12 Shortcut
Paste
Ctrl + V

12 Make cell A3 active and then click the Paste button to paste the data on the February sheet.

13 Click the Paste Options button that appears at the lower right corner of the pasted range.

14 Click the *Keep Source Column Widths* option in the *Paste* section of the pop-up list.

15 Make cell B4 active and then press Delete.

17,18 Another Way
Right-click the selected range and then click the *Clear Contents* option in the pop-up list or press Delete.

16 Select the range B8:B14.

17 On the Home tab, click the Clear button in the Editing group.

18 Click the *Clear Contents* option in the drop-down list.

19 Save the file.

Completed Skill 7

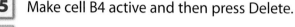

Completed
Skill Preview

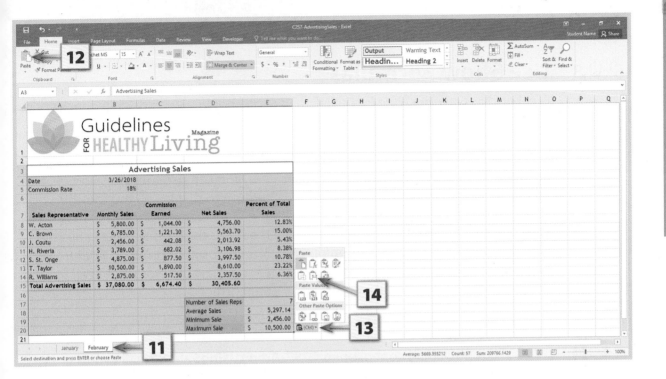

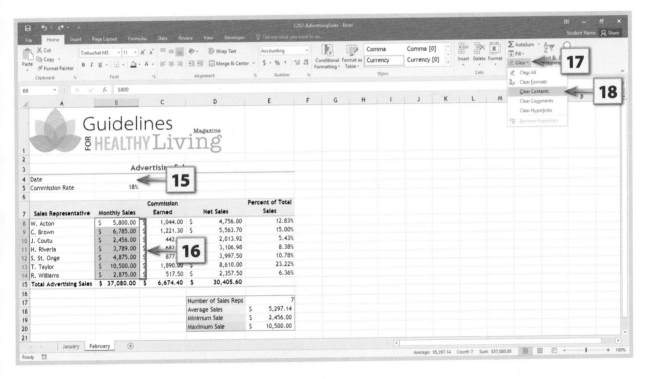

Taking It Further ●

Using the Clear Button Options

The drop-down list for the Clear button in the Editing group on the Home tab offers additional choices so you can specify exactly what to clear from the selected cell or range. For example, you can take separate actions by clicking the *Clear Formats*, *Clear Comments*, or *Clear Hyperlinks* option, or you can use the *Clear All* option to clear the cell contents plus any formatting and comments.

Excel

Skill 8   Use Show Formulas

Excel displays an *error code* in a cell if you have made an error when entering a formula. For example, the error code #DIV/0 means the formula is trying to divide by 0, and the error code #VALUE means the formula is using the wrong type of argument. However, Excel will not catch all errors. For example, if you reference the wrong column of numbers in a SUM function, Excel adds the wrong numbers. Because of this,

you should always double-check your formulas.

Rather than clicking cells one by one to review their formulas in the Formula bar, you can use the *Show Formulas* feature to display all the formulas on the worksheet at once. This makes it easy to thoroughly review all cell references and formula structures to ensure that the worksheet calculations are correct.

Tutorial

1   If it is not already open, open **C2S7-AdvertisingSales**, the file you saved in the previous skill, and save it as **C2S8-AdvertisingSales-Lastname**, but replace *Lastname* with your last name. Be sure to save the file in your Unit 4 working folder on your storage medium.

2   Click the February sheet tab, if it isn't already selected.

3   Make cell A2 active.

4–5   *Shortcut*
Show Formulas
Ctrl + `

▶ **Tip** Click the Show Formulas button again to hide the formulas.

4   Click the Formulas tab.

5   Click the Show Formulas button in the Formula Auditing group to display all formulas on the worksheeet.

6   Save and close the file.

Completed Skill 8

Completed Skill Preview

Taking It Further ●

Printing a Worksheet with Formulas Shown

If you print while formulas are displayed, the formulas print but the cell contents do not. This type of printout can provide a handy reference to how the data in the sheet is constructed. In this situation, review the print preview carefully. You may need to adjust print settings, such as orientation and margins. Printouts are easier to read if gridlines and column and row headings are displayed. To add these options, click the Page Layout tab and then click the *Print Gridlines* and *Print Headings* check boxes in the Sheet Options group to insert a check mark in each box.

Excel Chapter 2 **Tasks Summary**

Task	Ribbon Tab, Group	Button, Option	Shortcut, Alternative
Enter formulas			Press =, type formula, and then press Ctrl + Enter
Insert a function using the Insert Function dialog box	Formulas, Function Library	*fx* Insert Function	Click Insert Function button (*fx*) to left of Formula bar on worksheet
Insert a function using Formula AutoComplete			Type equals sign (=) and first letter or two of function, click function in pop-up list, enter data, and then press Enter
Use AutoSum	Home, Editing *or* Formulas, Function Library	Σ AutoSum	
Make a cell reference an absolute reference when entering or editing it			F4
Copy a cell or selection	Home, Clipboard	Copy	Ctrl + C
Cut a cell or selection	Home, Clipboard	Cut	Ctrl + X
Paste a Clipboard item	Home, Clipboard	Paste	Ctrl + V
Edit active cell			Double-click cell; make cell active and then press F2; or make cell active, and then click in Formula bar
Delete cell contents	Home, Editing	Clear▾	Make cell active, and then press *Delete*; or Right-click selection, and then click *Clear Contents* or press Delete
Show formulas	Formulas, Formula Auditing	Show Formulas	Ctrl + `

Recheck

Recheck your understanding of the skills and features covered in this chapter.

Workbook

Chapter study resources, exercises, and assessments are available in the Workbook ebook.

Chapter 3

Formatting Cells

Precheck

Check your understanding of the skills and features covered in this chapter.

Applying formatting to worksheet cells provides organization and context. Formatting also clarifies the meaning of the data. For example, to specify whether Excel should format a cell value as a date, currency amount, or percentage, you apply a number format. Other formatting tools, such as those that control font and size, determine how labels and values look and align within cells. You can change the column width and row height to ensure entries display completely and correctly.

You can use other tools to group data visually. For example, you can apply a new fill color to cells that contain the column labels in a worksheet, or add a border around a range, or even merge cells. You learn how to use formatting to enhance a worksheet in this chapter.

Skills You Learn

1   Apply number formats

2   Work with other formatting tools

3   Adjust column width and row height

4   Apply conditional formatting

5   Add borders

6   Merge cells

Files You Need

For these skills, you need the following student data file:

C3S1-Budget

If you are a SNAP user, go to your SNAP Assignments page to complete the Precheck, Tutorials, and Recheck.

What You Create

Guidelines for Healthy Living Magazine uses research data to support the content of the articles it publishes. One issue examined in this month's publication is how to eat healthy on a budget, as many readers complain that good-for-you foods tend to be expensive. A staff member has created a worksheet with data showing how it is possible to eat wholesome, nutritious meals without spending a fortune. You have been asked to apply formatting to make this worksheet clear and appealing for the magazine's readers.

Worksheet Illustrating How to Eat Healthy on a Budget

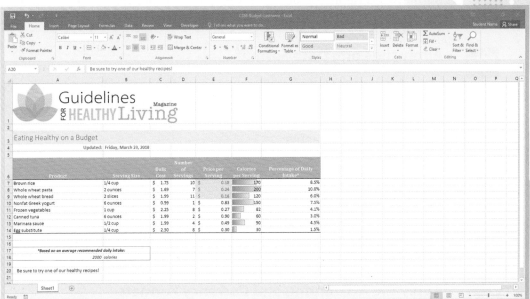

Completed
Skill Preview

Skill 1   Apply Number Formats

When you type an entry into a cell, the data is automatically given the *General format*. When you type a date in a cell, Excel formats it automatically as a date. You can apply formats to add dollar signs, commas, and other characters to the cells. Applying a new format changes the display of an entry.

The *number format* applied to a cell determines how Excel displays numerical data in the cell. For example, applying the *Accounting format* places, by default, a dollar symbol ($) to the left of the cell, adds a thousands separator, adds a decimal point and two places to the right of value for the "cents," and aligns the amount in the cell according to the decimal point. You can apply other formats, such as *Date format*, *Currency format*, and *Percentage format*, and change number formats as needed.

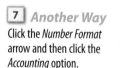

Tutorial

▶ **Tip** When you do not include the year, Excel assumes you want the current year. Dates are stored as sequential serial numbers so they can be used in calculations.

Apply the Long Date Format

1 Open the student data file named **C3S1-Budget** and, if you have not already done so, save it in your Unit 4 working folder on your storage medium.

2 Make cell B4 active.

3 Type the date 3/23 and then press Ctrl + Enter.

4 On the Home tab, click the *Number Format* arrow in the Number group.

5 Click the *Long Date* option in the drop-down list. The width of column B increases automatically to accommodate the longer number format.

Tutorial

▶ **Tip** When you are selecting cells, the mouse pointer displays as a thick white plus sign.

7 *Another Way*
Click the *Number Format* arrow and then click the *Accounting* option.

▶ **Tip** If you type a symbol, such as $ or %, as part of your cell entry, Excel will automatically apply a number format to the cell. For example, if you enter $4.00 in a cell, the *Currency* format will automatically be applied to the cell.

Apply the Accounting and Currency Formats

6 Drag to select the range C7:C14.

7 Click the Accounting Number Format button.

8 Drag to select the range D7:D14.

9 Click the Decrease Decimal button.

Taking It Further •

Accessing More Choices for Number Formatting

Some variations of the number formats are available as styles in the Cell Styles gallery. Click the Home tab and then click the More button in the Styles group to access the gallery. (**Note:** *If you do not see a More button in the Styles* group, click the Cell Styles button.) The *Number Format* section of the gallery lists the number styles you can apply. You also can click the *New Cell Style* option to create a custom cell style to apply to the selected cell or range.

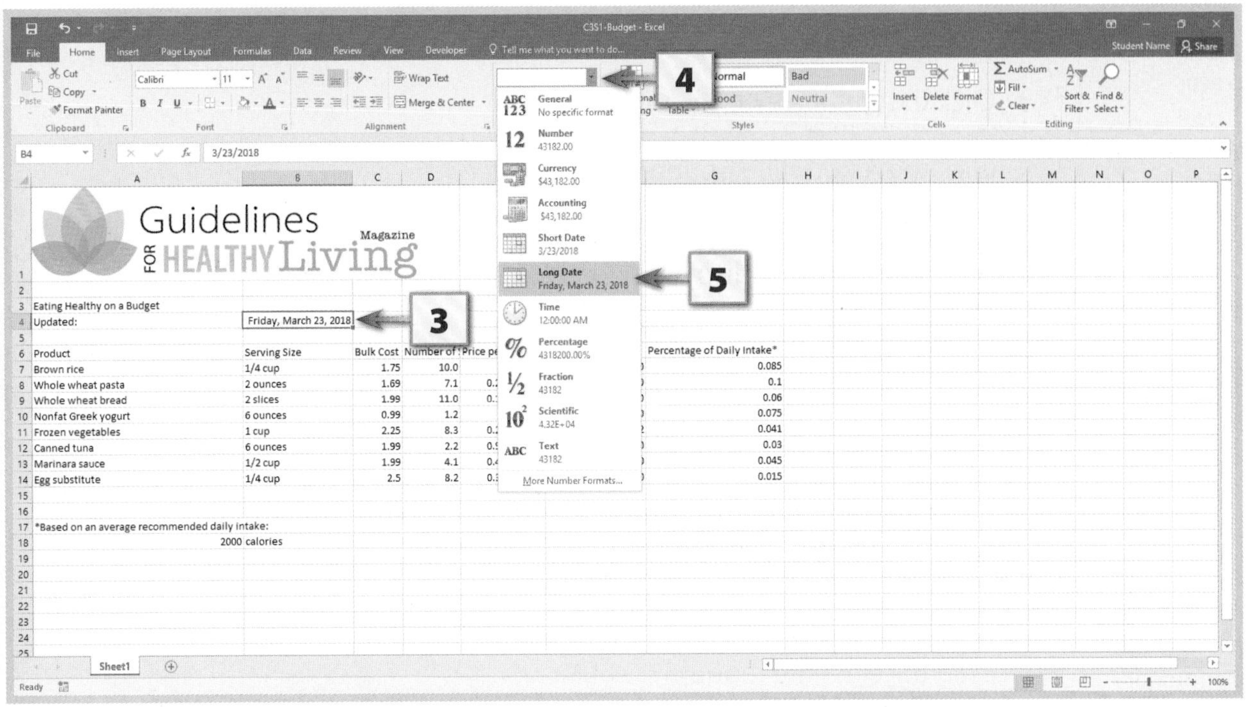

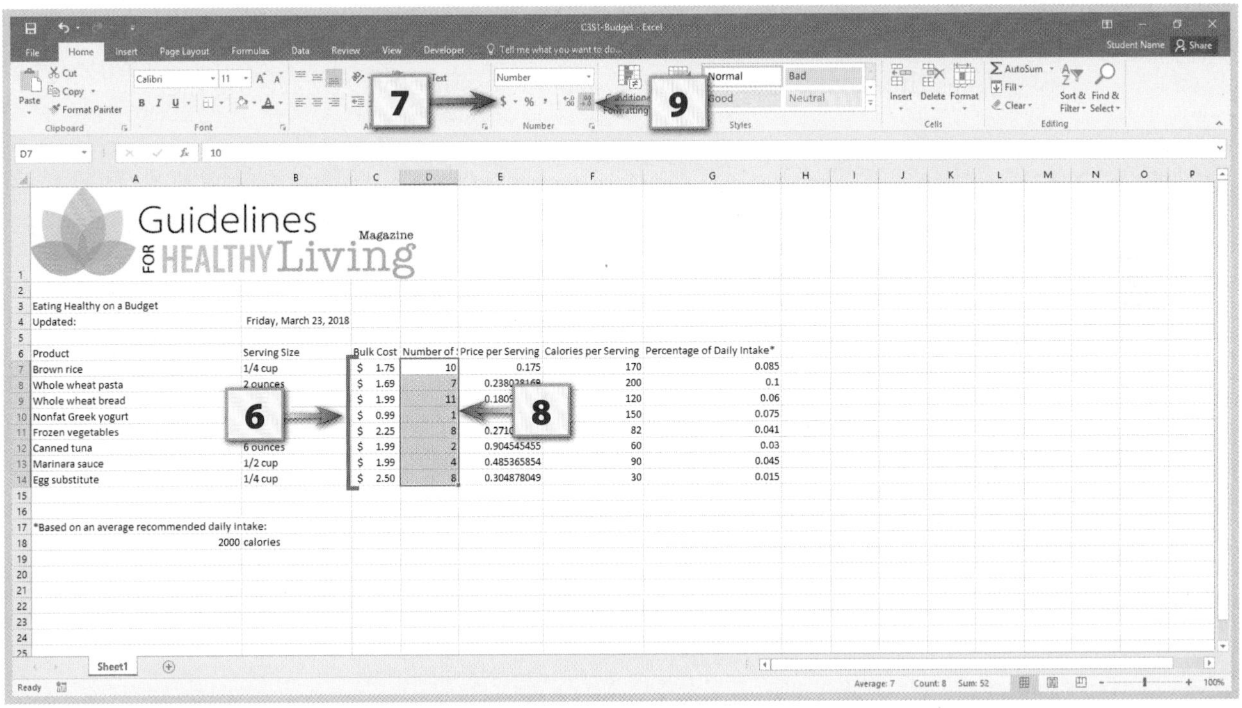

First screenshot — dropdown number format list:

- General — No specific format
- Number — 43182.00
- Currency — $43,182.00
- Accounting — $43,182.00
- Short Date — 3/23/2018
- Long Date — Friday, March 23, 2018
- Time — 12:00:00 AM
- Percentage — 4318200.00%
- Fraction — 43182
- Scientific — 4.32E+04
- Text — 43182
- More Number Formats...

Cell B4: 3/23/2018

	A	B	C	D	...	Percentage of Daily Intake*
3	Eating Healthy on a Budget					
4	Updated:	Friday, March 23, 2018				
6	Product	Serving Size	Bulk Cost	Number of !	Price pe	Percentage of Daily Intake*
7	Brown rice	1/4 cup	1.75	10.0		0.085
8	Whole wheat pasta	2 ounces	1.69	7.1	0.	0.1
9	Whole wheat bread	2 slices	1.99	11.0	0.	0.06
10	Nonfat Greek yogurt	6 ounces	0.99	1.2		0.075
11	Frozen vegetables	1 cup	2.25	8.3	0.	0.041
12	Canned tuna	6 ounces	1.99	2.2	0.	0.03
13	Marinara sauce	1/2 cup	1.99	4.1	0.	0.045
14	Egg substitute	1/4 cup	2.5	8.2	0.	0.015
17	*Based on an average recommended daily intake:					
18		2000 calories				

Second screenshot:

Cell D7: 10

	A	B	C	D	E	F	G
3	Eating Healthy on a Budget						
4	Updated:	Friday, March 23, 2018					
6	Product	Serving Size	Bulk Cost	Number of !	Price per Serving	Calories per Serving	Percentage of Daily Intake*
7	Brown rice	1/4 cup	$ 1.75	10	0.175	170	0.085
8	Whole wheat pasta	2 ounces	$ 1.69	7	0.238028169	200	0.1
9	Whole wheat bread	2 slices	$ 1.99	11	0.1809	120	0.06
10	Nonfat Greek yogurt	6 ounces	$ 0.99	1		150	0.075
11	Frozen vegetables	1 cup	$ 2.25	8	0.2710	82	0.041
12	Canned tuna	6 ounces	$ 1.99	2	0.904545455	60	0.03
13	Marinara sauce	1/2 cup	$ 1.99	4	0.485365854	90	0.045
14	Egg substitute	1/4 cup	$ 2.50	8	0.304878049	30	0.015
17	*Based on an average recommended daily intake:						
18		2000 calories					

Status bar: Average: 7   Count: 8   Sum: 52

More →

Use Your Touchscreen
In Step 10, tap cell E7 and then drag the selection handle to cell E14.

11 Click the *Number Format* arrow.

12 Click the *Accounting* option.

13 Make cell E14 active, type -.30, and then press Ctrl + Enter. Notice the Accounting format displays negative values in parentheses.

14 With cell E14 still selected, click the *Number Format* arrow.

15 Click the *Currency* option. This format displays negative values with a minus sign (-).

16 Click the Undo button on the Quick Access Toolbar two times to restore the original value and Accounting format in cell E14.

Apply the Percentage Format

Tutorial

17 Drag to select the range G7:G14.

18–19 *Another Way*
Click the *Percentage* option in the *Number Format* drop-down list and then click the Increase Decimal button.

18 On the Home tab, click the Percent Style button in the Number group.

19 Click the Increase Decimal button.

▶**Tip** The Percent format displays the number multiplied by 100 with a percent symbol (%) at the right of the number.

20 Click the Save button on the Quick Access Toolbar to save the file.

Completed Skill 1

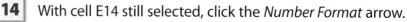

Completed Skill Preview

Excel

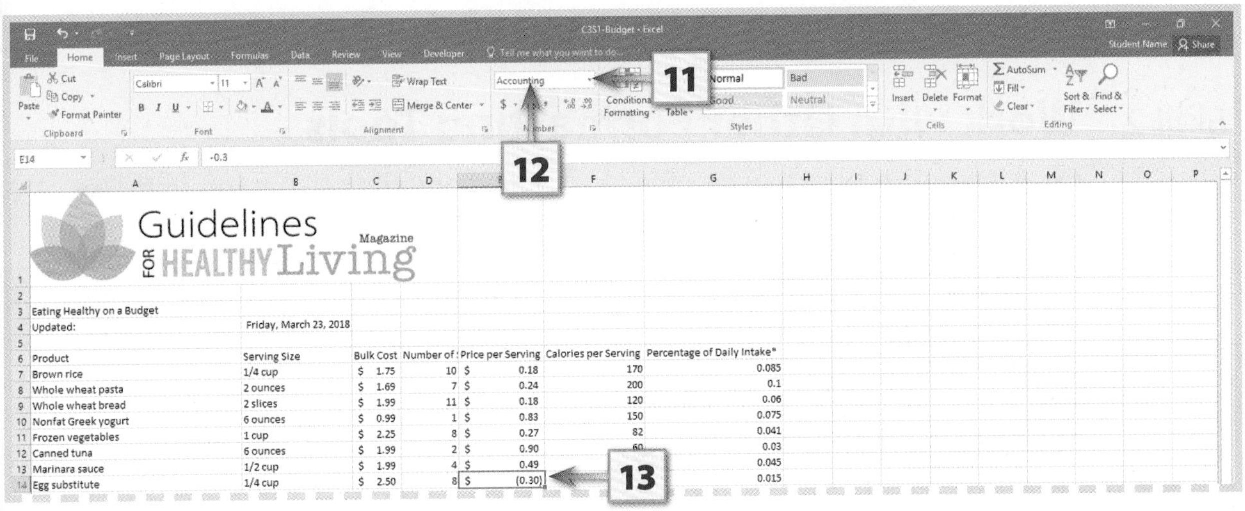
11
12
13
Guidelines
FOR HEALTHY Living
Magazine
Eating Healthy on a Budget
Updated: Friday, March 23, 2018
Product | Serving Size | Bulk Cost | Number of | Price per Serving | Calories per Serving | Percentage of Daily Intake*

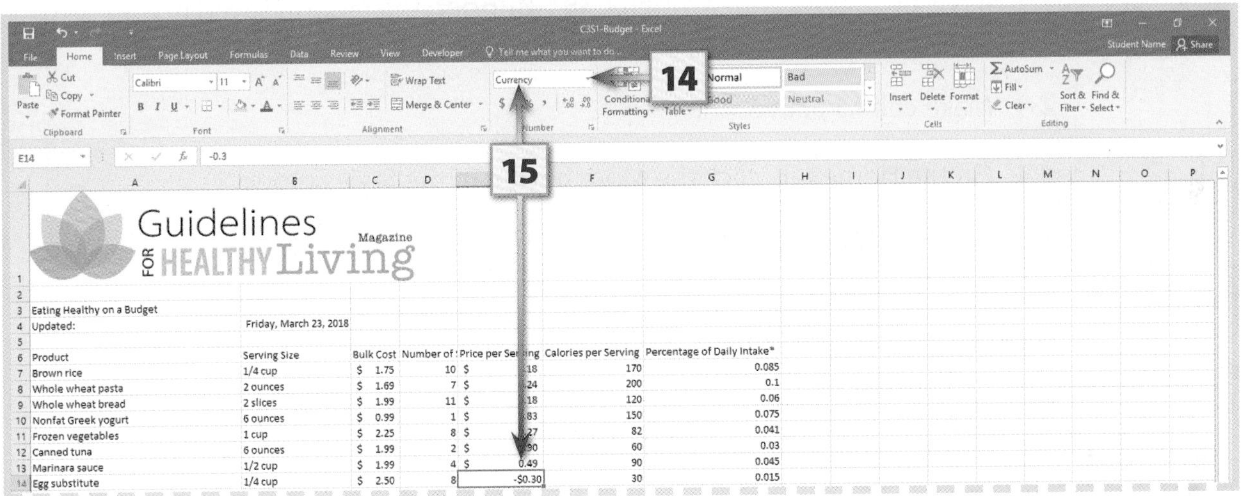
14
15
Guidelines
FOR HEALTHY Living
Magazine
Eating Healthy on a Budget
Updated: Friday, March 23, 2018

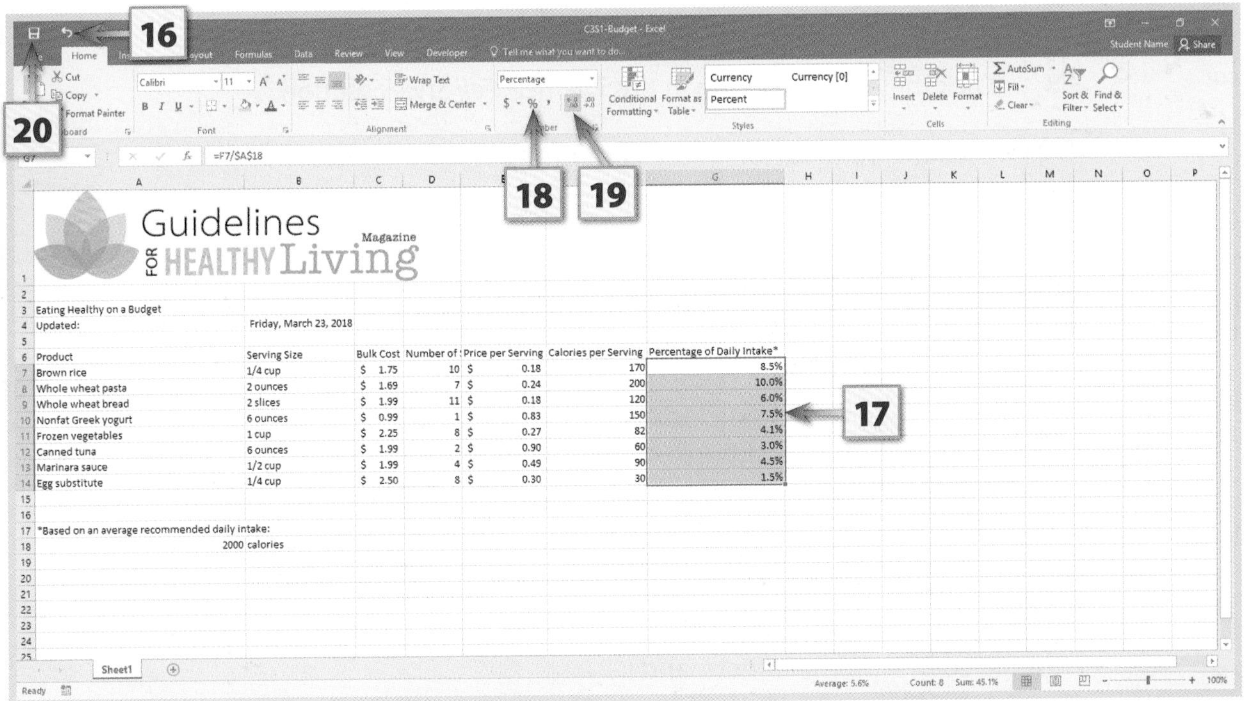
16
17
18
19
20
Guidelines
FOR HEALTHY Living
Magazine
Eating Healthy on a Budget
Updated: Friday, March 23, 2018
*Based on an average recommended daily intake:
2000 calories

Skill 2 Work with Other Formatting Tools

Excel lets you apply a variety of formats to cells to change the basic look of a worksheet. You can use the Increase Font Size and Decrease Font Size buttons to adjust the font size of the contents of selected cells. You can also apply bold, italic, and underlining, as well as change the color of the text and the cell background. Use the alignment tools to change the vertical and horizontal alignment of cell entries. The Cell Styles gallery in the Styles group on the Home tab lets you apply several formatting settings at once.

Tutorial

▶ **Tip** In Step 3, you may see the Cell Styles button instead of the Cell Styles gallery with a More button. If this is the case, click the Cell Styles button to display the Cell Styles gallery.

1 If it is not already open, open **C3S1-Budget**, the file you saved in the previous skill, and save it as **C3S2-Budget**.

2 Make cell A3 active.

3 On the Home tab, click the More button in the Styles group.

4 Click the *Title* option in the *Titles and Headings* section of the drop-down gallery.

5 Drag to select the range A4:B4.

6 Click the More button in the Cell Styles group and then click the *Heading 3* option in the *Titles and Headings* section.

7 Drag to select the range A6:G6.

8 Click the More button in the Cell Styles group.

9 *Shortcut*
Bold
Ctrl + B

9 Click the *Accent6* option in the *Themed Cell Styles* section.

10 Click the Bold button in the Font group.

Taking It Further ● ● ● ● ● ● ● ● ● ● ● ● ●

Changing the Theme

You can change the overall look of the worksheets in a workbook simply by changing the theme. The theme supplies the general formatting settings for the workbook file, including the theme fonts (those used by default for that specific theme), theme colors, theme effects, and cell styles. To choose or change a theme, click the Page Layout tab, click the Themes button in the Themes group, and then click a theme in the drop-down gallery. Pointing to any theme in the gallery displays a live preview of the changes it will apply.

Screenshot 1

C3S2-Budget - Excel

Student Name Share

File Home Insert Page Layout Formulas Data Review View Developer Tell me what you want to do...

Calibri · 11 · A A   Wrap Text   General   Normal   Bad

Paste B I U · · · A ·   Merge & Center · $ · % ·   Conditional Format as Good   Neutral

Clipboard   Font   Alignment   Number   Styles   Cells   Editing

A3   Eating Healthy on a Budget

3

Guidelines
FOR HEALTHY Living Magazine

Eating Healthy on a Budget		**2**
Updated:	Friday, Ma	

Product	Serving Size	Bulk Cost	Number of	Price per Serving	Calories per Serving	Percentage of Daily Intake*
Brown rice	1/4 cup	$ 1.75	10	$ 0.18	170	8.5%
Whole wheat pasta	2 ounces	$ 1.69	7	$ 0.24	200	10.0%
Whole wheat bread	2 slices	$ 1.99	11	$ 0.18	120	6.0%
Nonfat Greek yogurt	6 ounces	$ 0.99	1	$ 0.83	150	7.5%
Frozen vegetables	1 cup	$ 2.25	8	$ 0.27	82	4.1%
Canned tuna	6 ounces	$ 1.99	2	$ 0.90	60	3.0%
Marinara sauce	1/2 cup	$ 1.99	4	$ 0.49	90	4.5%
Egg substitute	1/4 cup	$ 2.50	8	$ 0.30	30	1.5%

Screenshot 2

C3S2-Budget - Excel

Student Name Share

File Home Insert Page Layout Formulas Data Review View Developer Tell me what you want to do...

A4   Updated:

Good, Bad and Neutral

Normal Bad Good Neutral

Data and Model

Calculation Check Cell Explanatory ... Input Linked Cell Note

Output Warning Text

Titles and Headings

Heading 1 Heading 2 Heading 3 Heading 4 Title **4**

Themed Cell Styles

20% - Accent1 20% - Accent2 20% - Accent3 20% - Accent4 20% - Accent5 20% - Accent6

40% - Accent1 40% - Accent2 40% - Accent3 40% - Accent4 40% - Accent5 40% - Accent6

60% - Accent1 60% - Accent2 60% - Accent3 60% - Accent4 60% - Accent5 60% - Accent6

Accent1 Accent2 Accent3 Accent4 Accent5 Accent6

Number Format

Comma Comma [0] **6** Currency [0] Percent

New Cell Style...

Merge Styles...

Guidelines
FOR HEALTHY Living Magazine

Eating Healthy on a Budget	
Updated:	Friday, March 23, 2018 **5**

Product	Serving Size	Bulk Cost	Number of	Price per Serving	Calories per Serving	Percentage
Brown rice	1/4 cup	$ 1.75	10	$ 0.18	170	
Whole wheat pasta	2 ounces	$ 1.69	7	$ 0.24	200	
Whole wheat bread	2 slices	$ 1.99	11	$ 0.18	120	6.0%
Nonfat Greek yogurt	6 ounces	$ 0.99	1	$ 0.83	150	7.5%
Frozen vegetables	1 cup	$ 2.25	8	$ 0.27	82	4.1%
Canned tuna	6 ounces	$ 1.99	2	$ 0.90	60	3.0%
Marinara sauce	1/2 cup	$ 1.99	4	$ 0.49	90	4.5%
Egg substitute	1/4 cup	$ 2.50	8	$ 0.30	30	1.5%

Screenshot 3

C3S2-Budget - Excel

Student Name Share

File Home Insert Page Layout Formulas Data Review View Developer Tell me what you want to do...

10

A6   Product

Good, Bad and Neutral

Normal Bad Good Neutral

Data and Model

Calculation Check Cell Explanatory ... Input Linked Cell Note

Output Warning Text

Titles and Headings

Heading 1 Heading 2 Heading 3 Heading 4 Title Total

Themed Cell Styles

20% - Accent1 20% - Accent2 20% - Accent3 20% - Accent4 20% - Accent5 20% - Accent6

40% - Accent1 40% - Accent2 40% - Accent3 40% - Accent4 40% - Accent5 40% - Accent6

60% - Accent1 60% - Accent2 60% - Accent3 60% - Accent4 60% - Accent5 60% - Accent6

Accent1 Accent2 Accent3 Accent4 Accent5 Accent6

Number Format

Comma Comma [0] Currency Currency [0] Percent

New Cell Style...

Merge Styles...

9

7

Guidelines
FOR HEALTHY Living Magazine

Eating Healthy on a Budget	
Updated:	Friday, March 23, 2018

Product	Serving Size	Bulk Cost	Number of	Price per Serving	Calories per Serving	Percentage
Brown rice	1/4 cup	$ 1.75	10	$ 0.18	170	
Whole wheat pasta	2 ounces	$ 1.69	7	$ 0.24	200	
Whole wheat bread	2 slices	$ 1.99	11	$ 0.18	120	6.0%
Nonfat Greek yogurt	6 ounces	$ 0.99	1	$ 0.83	150	7.5%
Frozen vegetables	1 cup	$ 2.25	8	$ 0.27	82	4.1%
Canned tuna	6 ounces	$ 1.99	2	$ 0.90	60	3.0%
Marinara sauce	1/2 cup	$ 1.99	4	$ 0.49	90	4.5%

More →

11 Click the *Font* arrow in the Font group.

12 Scroll down and then click the *Cambria* option in the drop-down gallery.

13 Click the Wrap Text button in the Alignment group.

14 Click the Center button.

15 Drag to select the range A17:B18.

16 Click the Italic button in the Font group.

17 Click the Decrease Font Size button to change the font size to 10 points.

18 Save the file.

12 *Another Way*

Select the text in the *Font* option box and then type *Cambria.*

13 *Shortcut*

Wrap Lines
Alt + Enter

16 *Shortcut*

Italicize Cell Content
Ctrl + I

17 *Another Way*

Select the number in the *Font Size* box and then type *10,* or click the Font Size arrow and then click *10* in the drop-down gallery.

▶ *Tip* The unit of measurement for font size is the point (pt), which is equal to 1/72nd of an inch.

Completed
Skill Preview

Completed Skill 2

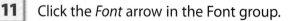

Product	Serving Size	Bulk Cost	Number of Servings	Price per Serving	Calories per Serving	Percentage of Daily Intake*
Brown rice	1/4 cup	$ 1.75	10	$ 0.18	170	8.5%
Whole wheat pasta	2 ounces	$ 1.69	7	$ 0.24	200	10.0%
Whole wheat bread	2 slices	$ 1.99	11	$ 0.18	120	6.0%
Nonfat Greek yogurt	6 ounces	$ 0.99	1	$ 0.83	130	7.5%
Frozen vegetables	1 cup	$ 2.25	8	$ 0.27	82	4.1%
Canned tuna	6 ounces	$ 1.99	2	$ 0.90	60	3.0%
Marinara sauce	1/2 cup	$ 1.99	4	$ 0.49	90	4.5%
Egg substitute	1/4 cup	$ 2.50	8	$ 0.30	30	1.5%

*Based on an average recommended daily intake:
2000 calories

Skill 3 Adjust Column Width and Row Height

When you perform some actions, such as when you change the cell format, Excel automatically widens a column or increases the height of a row. If you make a change and Excel doesn't automatically adjust the column width and row height to accommodate it, you could find that some entries don't fit into their cells. If the cell to the right is empty, the long entry simply runs into it. But if the cell to the right is not empty and the entry is text, Excel only displays as much of the entry as fits in the width of the original cell, hiding the rest. A string of pound signs (#####) is also an indication that the cell is not wide enough to display the entry and you need to resize the column to see the entire number.

You may need to adjust the row height when you wrap text or increase font size. Modifying row height and column width can also help make the worksheet more readable. You can use the *AutoFit* feature to fit the column size or row height to its widest or tallest entry, respectively.

Adjust Column Width

Tutorial

1 If it is not already open, open **C3S2-Budget**, the file you saved in the previous skill, and save the file as **C3S3-Budget**.

2–4 *Another Way*
Right-click the column F heading and then click the *Column Width* option in the pop-up list.

2 Make any cell in column F active.

3 On the Home tab, click the Format button in the Cells group.

4 Click the *Column Width* option in the *Cell Size* section of the drop-down list.

5 Type 15 in the *Column width* box.

6 Click OK.

7 *Another Way*
Click the *AutoFit Column Width* option in the *Cell Size* section of the Format drop-down list to AutoFit the column to its widest entry.

7 Move the mouse pointer over the right border of the column G column heading until the mouse pointer becomes a left-and-right-pointing arrow with a vertical line in the middle and then double-click to allow Excel to AutoFit the column size.

▶**Tip** When text wrapping has been applied to cells in a row, the row height does not adjust automatically to fit the text if you edit it. You have to manually change the row height to fit the modified text.

8 Move the mouse pointer over the right border of the column F column heading until the mouse pointer becomes a left-and-right-pointing arrow with a vertical line in the middle, press and hold the left mouse button, drag to the left until the ScreenTip reads *Width: 12.14 (90 pixels)*, and then release the mouse button.

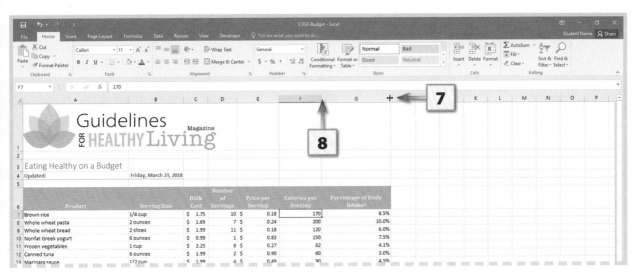

Adjust Row Height

9 Right-click the row 6 row heading and then click the *Row Height* option in the pop-up list.

10 Type 48 in the *Row height* box.

11 Click OK.

12 Make cell A3 active.

13 On the Home tab, click the Format button in the Cells group.

14 Click the *Row Height* option in the *Cell Size* section of the drop-down list.

15 Type 30 in the *Row height* box.

16 Click OK.

17 On the Home tab, click the Middle Align button in the Alignment group.

18 Save the file.

Completed Skill 3

Completed
Skill Preview

Taking It Further •

Changing Column Width Default Settings

With the default Office Theme applied, the default column width is 8.43 characters and the default row height is 15 points. Changing the theme applied to the workbook may change these defaults. You can adjust the default column setting by clicking the Format button in the Cells group on the Home tab and then clicking *Default Width* in the drop-down list. A dialog box displays in which you can enter a new standard column width for the workbook.

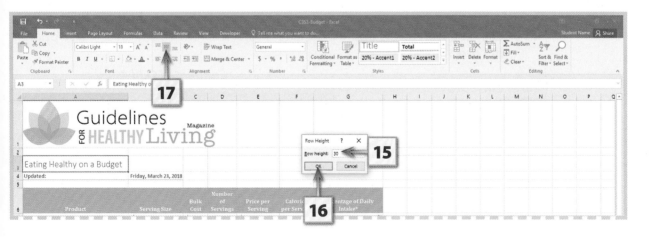

Skill 4 Apply Conditional Formatting

You can use *conditional formatting* to highlight specific values within a worksheet. This formatting lets readers easily spot trends and patterns that may not be clear in a list of numbers.

Conditional formatting can be applied when a specific condition is met, such as a test score over 80. It can also be used to highlight, say, the bottom or top 10 percent values in a selected range, or to highlight values that are above the average value of a selected range. Another type of conditional formatting uses data bars or other visuals to illustrate the value of a cell relative to the other values in a selected range.

Tutorial

1 If it is not already open, open **C3S3-Budget**, the file you saved in the previous skill, and save it as **C3S4-Budget**.

2 Drag to select the range F7:F14.

> **Tip** You can manually fill cells with color by clicking the Fill Color arrow in the Font group on the Home tab and then clicking a color in the drop-down gallery.

3 On the Home tab, click the Conditional Formatting arrow in the Styles group.

4 Point to the *Data Bars* option in the drop-down list.

5 Click the *Light Blue Data Bar* option in the *Gradient Fill* section of the drop-down gallery.

> **Tip** Point to a color option in the *Data Bars* gallery to display a ScreenTip describing the color option.

6 Drag to select the range E7:E14.

7 Click the Conditional Formatting arrow.

8 Point to the *Highlight Cell Rules* option.

9 Click the *Less Than* option.

10 Type .25 in the *Format cells that are LESS THAN* box.

11 Click the *with* arrow and then click the *Green Fill with Dark Green Text* option in the drop-down list.

12 Click OK.

13 Save the file.

Completed Skill 4

Completed Skill Preview

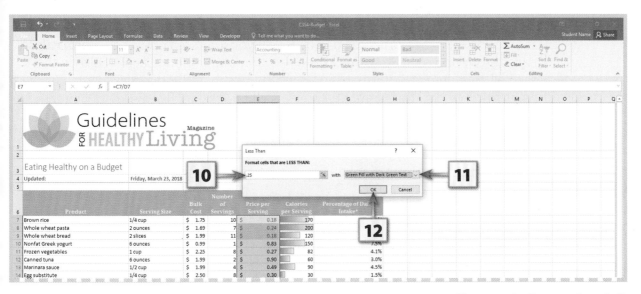

Skill 5   Add Borders

Applying a *border* around a cell or cell range in a worksheet provides another way to group or emphasize the data visually. Borders can be especially useful when you use the default print setting and print a worksheet without cell gridlines. For example, accountants often emphasize a row presenting data totals by placing a single border at the top and a double border at the bottom. You also can use a border to set off a range where the user should type in data for calculations, or to highlight important data or formula results. In addition, you can add borders as purely decorative elements—making sure the border appearance fits with the other formatting you have applied.

Tutorial

▶Tip In Step 3, if a border other than a bottom border appears, click the Borders arrow and then click the *Bottom Border* option.

Use Your Touchscreen

In Step 4, tap cell A7 and then drag the selection handle to cell G14.

1 If it is not already open, open **C3S4-Budget**, the file you saved in the previous skill, and save it as **C3S5-Budget**.

2 Make cell A3 active.

3 On the Home tab, click the Borders button in the Font group. Excel applies a single border to the bottom of the cell.

4 Drag to select the range A7:G14.

5 Click the Borders arrow.

6 Click the *Top and Bottom Border* option in the *Borders* section of the drop-down list.

Taking It Further ●

Using Format Painter

Use the Format Painter to quickly copy formatting, such as borders and cell styles, from one cell to another. Click the cell containing the formatting you want to copy, click the Format Painter button in the Clipboard group on the Home tab, and then either click a cell or drag to select a range of cells to which the formatting will be copied. If you want to copy a cell's formatting to multiple nonadjacent cells on the worksheet, double-click instead of single-clicking the Format Painter button. When you are finished applying the formatting, press the Esc key or click the Format Painter button to turn it off.

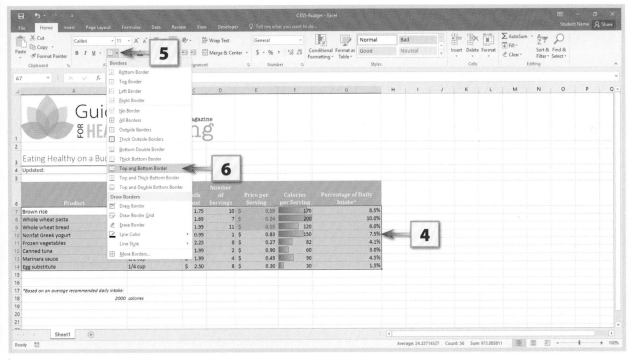

7 Drag to select the range A17:B18.

8 Click the Borders arrow.

9 Click the *More Borders* option.

10 On the Border tab of the Format Cells dialog box, click the *Color* arrow.

11 Click the *Blue* option in the *Standard Colors* section of the palette.

12 Click the Outline button in the *Presets* section.

13 Click OK.

14 Save the file.

Completed Skill 5

Completed
Skill Preview

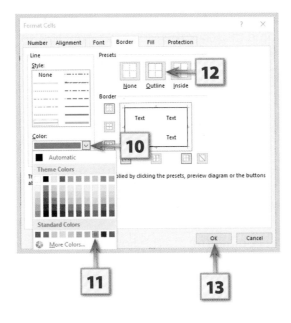

Taking It Further ●

Accessing More Border Options

When you click the Border button in the Font group on the Home tab and then click the *More Borders* option to display the Border tab of the Format Cells dialog box, you will see options in the *Style* list box. These options enable you to choose another border weight or a different border appearance, such as a dashed or dotted line. These border styles are a bit less formal than a plain cell border or outline, so you should use them sparingly, especially in business documents.

Excel

Skill 6 Merge Cells

To enhance the readability of a worksheet, you might choose to center the sheet title across all the columns of data in the sheet. You can use the Merge & Center button in the Alignment group on the Home tab to combine selected cells into a single cell. The combined text is centered in the single cell.

Click the Merge & Center arrow to display three additional formatting options. With these options, you can merge the columns across each selected row without merging the rows themselves (*Merge Across*), merge a range into a single cell (*Merge Cells*), and unmerge a merged cell (*Unmerge Cells*).

Tutorial

1 If it is not already open, open **C3S5-Budget**, the file you saved in the previous skill, and save the file as **C3S6-Budget-Lastname**, but replace *Lastname* with your last name. Be sure to save the file in your Unit 4 working folder on your storage medium.

2 Drag to select the range A17:B17.

3 On the Home tab, click the Merge & Center button in the Alignment group. This action merges and centers a title that is common to the two columns of data.

4 Click the Bold button in the Font group.

5 Drag to select the range A3:G3.

6 Click the Merge & Center arrow in the Alignment group.

7 Click the *Merge Across* option in the drop-down list.

8 Click the Fill Color arrow in the Font group.

9 Click the *Green, Accent6, Lighter 80%* option in the *Theme Colors* section of the drop-down gallery.

▶ **Tip** Be sure to check all formatting when merging and centering. In Step 7, merging across removes the bottom border that you applied to cell A3 in Skill 5. If you want to keep the border across the merged cells, you have to reapply it.

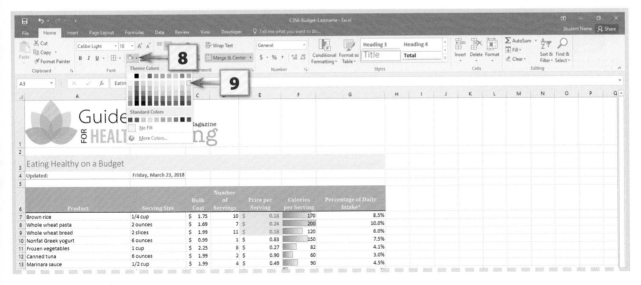

10 Make cell A4 active.

11 Click the Align Right button in the Alignment group.

12 Make cell A20 active.

13 Type Be sure to try one of our healthy recipes! and then press Enter.

14 Drag to select the range A20:G20.

 Tip In Step 15, the cell address listed in the Name box above the upper left corner of the worksheet is the address for the far left cell in the merged range.

15 Click the Merge & Center button.

16 Click the Merge & Center arrow.

17 Click the *Unmerge Cells* option in the drop-down list to unmerge cells A20:G20.

18 Save and close the file.

Completed Skill 6

Completed
Skill Preview

Taking It Further

Designing Worksheets

In this skill, you created a balanced appearance in the completed worksheet by using the same fill color for the top and bottom rows and limiting the number of applied formats. Keeping your design simple and taking advantage of the color palette supplied by the theme helps you to design professional worksheets that highlight the most important data for decision making.

Excel Chapter 3 **Tasks Summary**

Task	Ribbon Tab, Group	Button, Option	Shortcut, Alternative
Apply a number format	Home, Number	General	
Apply Accounting format	Home, Number	$	Click the *Number Format* arrow and then click the *Accounting* option
Apply Percent format	Home, Number	%	Click the *Number Format* arrow and then click the *Percentage* option
Apply a cell style	Home, Styles		Cell Styles
Apply bold	Home, Font	B	Ctrl + B
Apply italic	Home, Font	I	Ctrl + I
Change the font	Home, Font	Calibri	
Increase or decrease the font size	Home, Font	A A	
Change the font size	Home, Font	11	
Wrap cell entries	Home, Alignment	Wrap Text	Press Alt + Enter when making a cell entry to wrap lines manually
Change vertical or horizontal cell alignments	Home, Alignment		
Change column width or row height	Home, Cells	Format, *Column Width* or *Row Height*	Drag the right column border or bottom row border
Apply conditional formatting	Home, Styles	Conditional Formatting	

Task	Ribbon Tab, Group	Button, Option	Shortcut, Alternative
Add borders to a cell or selection	Home, Font		
Merge cells	Home, Alignment	Merge & Center ▾	
Copy cell formatting	Home, Clipboard	Format Painter	
Fill a cell with color	Home, Font		

Recheck

Recheck your understanding of the skills and features covered in this chapter.

Workbook

Chapter study resources, exercises, and assessments are available in the Workbook *ebook.*

Chapter 4

Working with Charts

Precheck

Check your understanding of the skills and features covered in this chapter.

If you have a lot of numbers in a worksheet, a chart can simplify your understanding of the data by showing it in a visual arrangement. When you represent the data in a chart, you can easily show patterns or trends in the data. You can create a variety of chart types in Excel, including pie, bar, and line charts.

A *pie chart* is a circular chart that is divided into parts. Each part represents a piece of the whole pie, or a percentage of the total. The *Website Visitors* pie chart you create in this chapter shows that out of all the visitors to the *Guidelines for Healthy Living Magazine* website, 61 percent are paid subscribers and 39 percent are nonsubscribers.

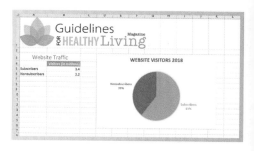

You can use a *bar chart* or a *column chart* to compare differences between values. A bar chart has horizontal bars and a column chart has vertical bars. The *Website Traffic* bar chart compares the total number of visitors to the *Guidelines for Healthy Living Magazine* website by calendar year.

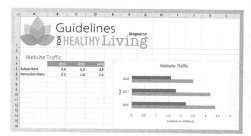

Line charts illustrate changes, or trends, over time. The *Website Traffic* line chart in this chapter illustrates how the number of visitors (both subscribers and nonsubscribers) to the website has steadily increased over the past few years.

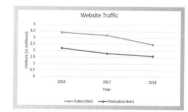

This chapter teaches you how to create a chart from worksheet data and how to modify and format different types of charts.

Skills You Learn

1   Create a line chart

2   Create a column chart

3   Modify chart data

4   Add and edit chart labels

5   Create a pie chart

6   Modify a pie chart

SNAP *If you are a SNAP user, go to your SNAP Assignments page to complete the Precheck, Tutorials, and Recheck.*

Files You Need

For these skills, you need the following student data file:

    C4S1-Comparison

What You Create

Guidelines for Healthy Living Magazine has increased its readership and advertising revenue over the past few years. The publisher of the magazine would like your help preparing graphics that illustrate this success for an upcoming presentation to investors. You have been asked to create a line chart that compares the magazine's advertising revenue with the advertising revenue of similar online magazines—its direct competitors. You will also prepare a column chart and a pie chart to compare reader demographics and readership totals. Finally, you will modify the chart data and change the formatting to enhance the appearance of the charts. You also will add descriptive titles so that the reader can easily understand the data represented in the charts.

Advertising Revenue Comparison Line Chart

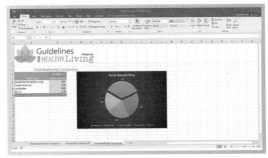

Total Readership Comparison Pie Chart

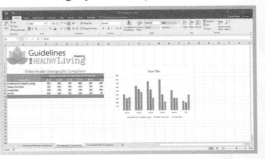

Reader Demographics Comparison Column Chart

Completed
Skill Preview

Excel

Skill 1 Create a Line Chart

Line charts compare differences between values over time. The line chart you create in this skill displays four series of data, with each series representing the advertising revenue of a different magazine over four years. The years are listed along the horizontal axis (bottom) of the chart, and the sales amounts are listed along the vertical axis (left side) of the chart. Each value in a series is a point on the line. Once you create the line chart, you move and size the chart.

Tutorial

Tip If you are not sure which type of chart to use, click the Recommended Charts button in the Charts group on the Insert tab.

Tip In Step 4, hover the mouse pointer over a chart option to display the name of the chart.

Tip To move part of a chart, hover your mouse pointer until you see a four-headed arrow and a ScreenTip for that part of the chart and then drag the part to the new location.

Tip The chart legend tells you which line belongs to which category of data. In this case, the legend tells you, by color, which line belongs to which magazine.

1 Open the student data file named **C4S1-Comparison** and, if you have not already done so, save it in your Unit 4 working folder on your storage medium.

2 In the Advertising Revenue Comparison worksheet, select the range A5:E9.

3 Click the Insert tab and then click the Insert Line or Area Chart button in the Charts group.

4 Click the *Line with Markers* option (the fourth option in the first row of the *2-D Line* section) in the drop-down gallery to insert a line chart in the worksheet.

5 Move the mouse pointer over the chart border so the mouse pointer changes to a four-headed arrow (✥) and the ScreenTip *Chart Area* appears. Press and hold the left mouse button, drag the chart so that its upper left corner is positioned over cell G3, and then release the mouse button.

6 Position the mouse pointer over the lower right corner of the chart border so that the mouse pointer changes to a two-headed diagonal arrow (⤢). Drag down and to the right so that the bottom right corner of the chart covers cell N17. While you drag, the two-headed diagonal arrow displays as a cross. When you release the mouse pointer, the cross turns back into the two-headed diagonal arrow.

7 Click the Save button on the Quick Access Toolbar to save the file.

Completed Skill 1

Completed Skill Preview

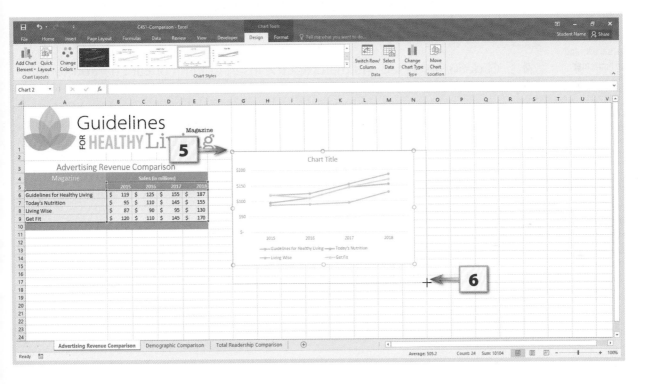

Taking It Further ●

Moving the Chart Location

By default, a chart is placed in the existing worksheet. To move a chart to a new worksheet, select the chart and then on the Chart Tools Design tab, click the Move Chart button in the Location group. In the Move Chart dialog box, click the *New sheet* option and then click OK to move the chart to a new worksheet named *Chart1*. This option automatically adjusts the size of the chart to fill the worksheet page. To move a chart to another sheet in the current workbook, start by selecting the chart. On the Chart Tools Design tab, click the Move Chart button in the Location group. In the Move Chart dialog box, click the Object in drop-down arrow and then click the name of the sheet to move the chart to.

Excel

Skill 2   Create a Column Chart

In this skill, you create a column chart. Column charts compare differences between values. The column chart you create shows how many readers of a certain age there are for each magazine in your comparison. The chart clearly illustrates data such as which magazine is popular with a certain age group.

Tutorial

> **Tip** In Excel, column charts have vertical bars and bar charts have horizontal bars.

4–5 *Shortcut*
Clustered Column chart
Alt + F1

1 If it is not already open, open **C4S1-Comparison**, the file you saved in the previous skill, and save it as **C4S2-Comparison**.

2 Click the Demographic Comparison worksheet tab.

3 Select the range A5:F9.

4 Click the Insert tab and then click the Insert Column or Bar Chart button in the Charts group.

5 Click the *Clustered Column* option (the first option in the *2-D Column* section) in the drop-down gallery to insert the column chart in the worksheet.

6 Move the mouse pointer over the chart so it changes to a four-headed arrow and then drag the chart so that its upper left corner is positioned over cell H3.

7 Position the mouse pointer over the lower right corner of the chart border so that the mouse pointer changes to a two-headed diagonal arrow. Drag down and to the right so that the bottom right corner of the chart covers cell O17.

8 Save the file.

Use Your Touchscreen

In Step 6, press and hold the chart to select it and then drag it so that the upper left corner is positioned over cell H3.

Use Your Touchscreen

In Step 7, tap to select the chart and then drag the lower right corner selection handle so that the bottom right corner of the chart covers cell O17.

Completed Skill 2

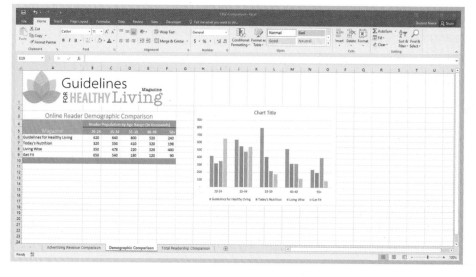

Completed Skill Preview

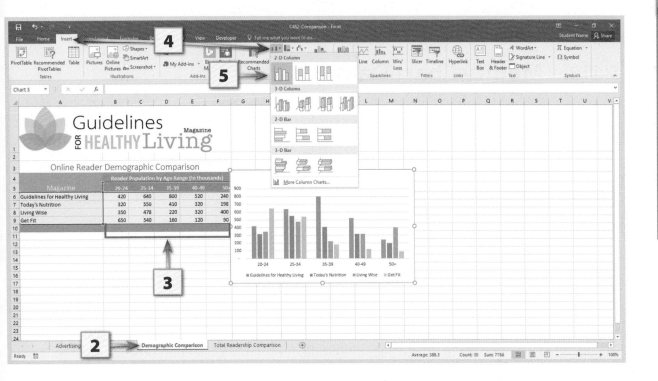

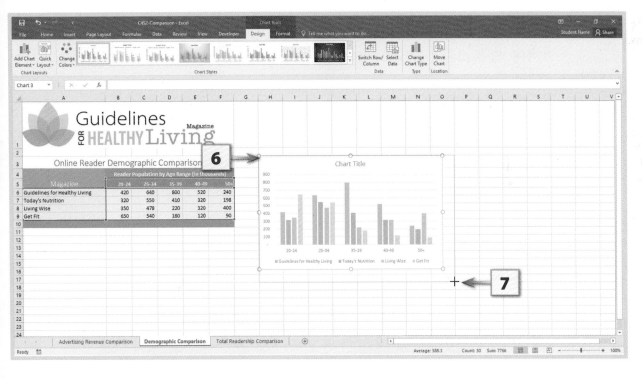

Taking It Further

Changing the Chart Type

Bar charts, like column charts, can clearly show differences in charted values. You can easily change a column chart into a bar chart. To do so, select the chart and then click the Chart Tools Design tab if necessary. Click the Change Chart Type button in the Type group and then click the *Bar* option in the left pane. Click a bar chart option in the right pane and then click OK.

Skill 3   Modify Chart Data

When you select a chart, colored boxes appear around the data that you used to create the chart. Different colored boxes appear around the different types of data. For example, the *data series* used to create the chart has a blue box around it. If you change a number in the data series or add another row to the data series, the chart automatically updates because it is linked to the data. In this skill, you practice editing a chart by change the range, insert a column, and enter new data.

Tutorial

1 If it is not already open, open **C4S2-Comparison**, the file you saved in the previous skill, and save it as **C4S3-Comparison**.

2 With the chart selected in the Demographic Comparison worksheet, drag the lower right selection handle for the blue selection box up until you have changed the range to A5:F8.

3 Right-click the column D column heading.

4 Click the *Insert* option in the pop-up list to insert a new column.

5 Type the following entries in cells D5:D9, pressing the Enter key after each entry.

D5	30-34
D6	750
D7	540
D8	325
D9	200

6 Make cell C5 active, type 25-29, and then press Ctrl + Enter.

7 Save the file.

Completed Skill 3

Completed Skill Preview

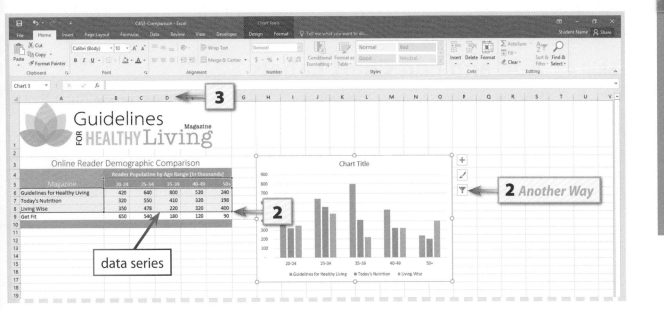

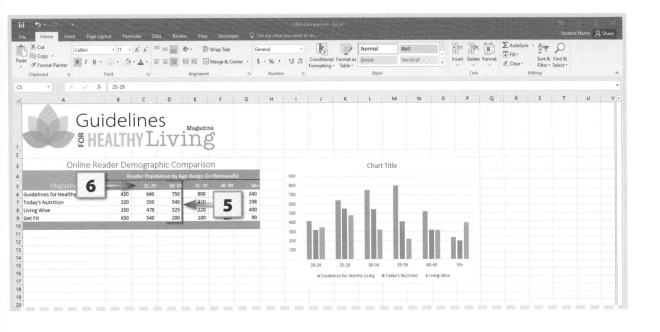

Taking It Further

Editing Chart Data

Sometimes when you create a chart, the data and labels do not appear just the way you would like. You can edit the data and labels by selecting the chart and then clicking the Select Data button in the Data group on the Chart Tools Design tab. This opens a dialog box that shows the current axis labels and legend entries. You can click the Edit button and then select the correct cells in the worksheet to change the labels or the information in the legend. You can also edit chart data by clicking the Chart Filters button ( ) and then checking data you want to show and unchecking data you do not want to display. You might want to save a separate copy of the file you used in Skill 3 and experiment with these editing tools.

Skill 4 Add and Edit Chart Labels

You can use labels to make the elements of a chart easier to understand. When you create a chart, Excel adds some labels automatically, based on the data you selected to create the chart. You can edit these labels and add other labels using options on the Chart Tools Design tab. For example, you can add an individual *data label* to show the quantity that a single column represents. You can also edit the *chart title* to best describe the contents of the chart.

Tutorial

▶ **Tip** To hide a chart element, such as a chart title or legend, click the Chart Elements button (⊞) next to the chart and then click the element check box to remove the check mark. Also use the Chart Elements button to add, delete, or change chart elements.

4 *Another Way*
Right-click the *Chart Title* placeholder and then click the *Edit Text* option in the pop-up list.

▶ **Tip** You can place data labels in various places, such as the outside end of the data point, inside end of the data point, or centered on the data point. For some chart types, you can also use the *Best Fit* option, which places the data labels where Excel determines they fit best in the chart.

1 If it is not already open, open **C4S3-Comparison**, the file you saved in the previous skill, and save it as **C4S4-Comparison**.

2 Click the chart on the Demographic Comparison worksheet if it is not already selected.

3 Click the Chart Title placeholder to select the placeholder.

4 Triple-click anywhere within the *Chart Title* placeholder text to select it.

5 Type Demographic Comparison to edit the title of the chart.

6 Click the Chart Tools Design tab and then click the Add Chart Element button in the Chart Layouts group.

7 Click the *Data Labels* option in the drop-down list.

8 Click the *Outside End* option in the second drop-down list. Notice that this action adds data labels to the outside end of each column in the chart.

9 Enlarge the chart by dragging the lower right corner of the chart border down and to the right so that it covers cell R19.

10 Save the file.

Completed
Skill Preview

Completed Skill 4

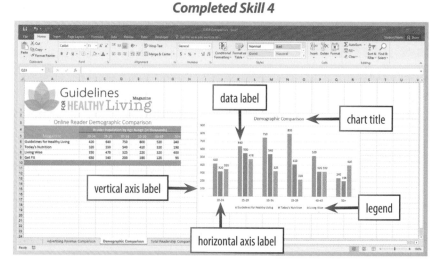

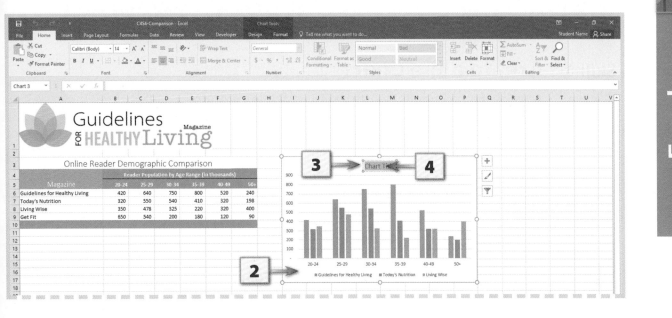

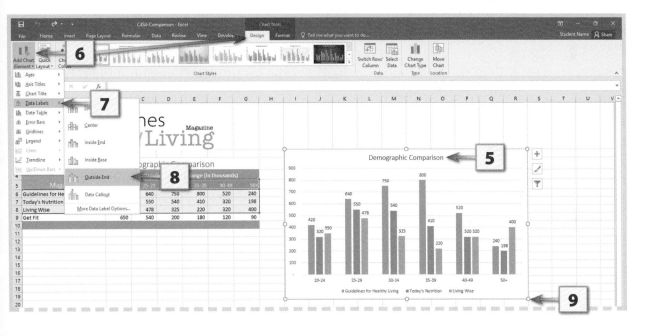

Taking It Further • • • • • • • • • • • • • • • • •

Changing the Chart Legend

The chart *legend* tells you which piece of data each colored column or line represents. You can change the position of the legend by clicking the Add Chart Element button in the Chart Tools Design tab, clicking the *Legend* option in the drop-down list, and then clicking the desired position in the list of options. Click *None* to remove the legend if you think the reader can easily understand the chart without it.

Adding Axis Labels to Column Charts

In a column chart, you may want to use *axis labels* to describe what the numbers and labels along each axis represent. To add labels to the vertical or horizontal axis, select the chart, click the Chart Elements button (looks like a plus sign) to the right of the chart, click the *Axis Titles* option, and then click the right-pointing arrow to see additional options.

Skill 5   Create a Pie Chart

A *pie chart* is a circular chart that is divided into parts. Each part represents a percentage of the total quantity. The pie chart you create in this skill illustrates the total number of readers there are for each of the four magazines. The pie is divided into four parts, with each part representing one of the magazines in your comparison. The size of each piece represents the total readers for that magazine. The pie in its entirety represents all (100%) of the data, which in this case is magazine readers.

Tutorial

▶**Tip** A pie chart can contain only one data series.

1   If it is not already open, open **C4S4-Comparison**, the file you saved in the previous skill, and save it as **C4S5-Comparison**.

2   Click the Total Readership Comparison sheet tab.

3   Select the range A5:B9.

4   Click the Insert tab and then click the Insert Pie or Doughnut Chart button in the Charts group.

5   Click the *Pie* option (the first option in the *2-D Pie* section) in the drop-down gallery to insert the pie chart into the worksheet.

6   Move the mouse pointer over the chart border so that the mouse pointer changes to a four-headed arrow and then drag the chart so that its upper left corner is positioned over cell D4.

7   Position the mouse pointer over the lower right corner of the chart border so that the mouse pointer changes to a two-headed diagonal arrow. Drag down and to the right so that the lower right corner of the chart covers cell L20.

8   Save the file.

Completed Skill 5

Completed Skill Preview

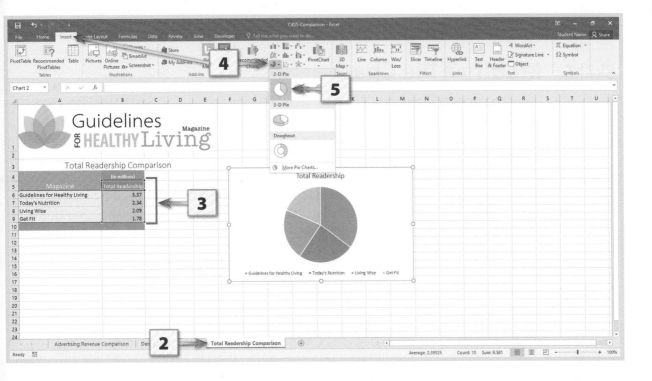

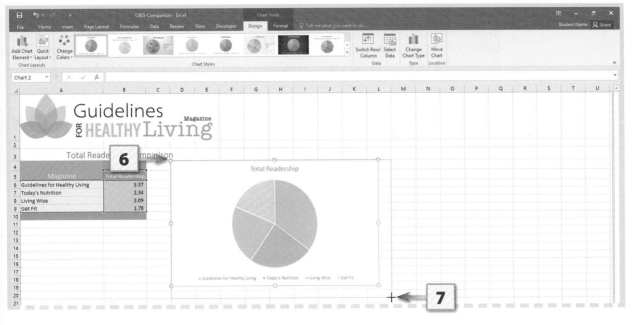

Taking It Further ●

Using Quick Analysis

When you select a range of cells, such as A1:K19, the Quick Analysis button (▦) is displayed to the right of the selected range. You can use this button to create a chart from the selected range of data. Click the Quick Analysis button, click the Charts tab in the drop-down gallery, hover over a chart type option to see how the selected data will appear in the chart, and then click a chart type option to apply the type to your chart.

Formatting	Charts	Totals	Tables	Sparklines
Line	Clustere...	Clustere...	Stacked...	Stacked...	More...

Recommended Charts help you visualize data.

Skill 6 Modify a Pie Chart

You can rotate a pie chart, and you can explode a slice away from the rest of the pie chart. An *exploded slice* sits outside the circle of the pie, to call attention to the content or data it represents. You can add data labels to a chart. By default, these will display as values (numbers) without any special formatting, such as 1011. However, the data labels in pie charts typically display as a percentage, such as 80%. In this skill, you learn to add percentage labels and remove value labels. You also change the position of a chart legend and apply a *chart style* to change the appearance of the chart.

Rotate a Pie Chart and Explode a Slice

Tutorial

1 If it is not already open, open **C4S5-Comparison**, the file you saved in the previous skill, and save it as **C4S6-Comparison-Lastname**, but replace *Lastname* with your last name. Be sure to save the file in your Unit 4 working folder on your storage medium.

2 In the pie chart on the Total Readership Comparison worksheet, double-click the largest slice, the slice that represents the total readership of the *Guidelines for Healthy Living Magazine*. This action opens the Format Data Series pane.

 Another Way
Type *299* in the *Angle of first slice* text box and then press Enter.

3 Drag the *Angle of first slice* slider to the right until the value in the measurement box beside it reads *299°*. The chart is now rotated 299° and the *Guidelines for Healthy Living* slice sits at the top of the pie chart.

4 Click the Close button to close the Format Data Series pane.

5 Drag the *Guidelines for Healthy Living* slice up and away from the rest of the pie.

6 Click a blank area of the chart to deselect the pie slice.

Add Data Labels to a Pie Chart

Tutorial

Tip In Steps 8–10, you are not selecting a position for the data labels. You will do that in Step 13.

7 With the chart selected, click the Chart Elements button.

8 Click the *Data Labels* check box in the drop-down list to insert a check mark.

9 Click the *Data Labels* arrow.

10 Click the *More Options* option in the second drop-down list.

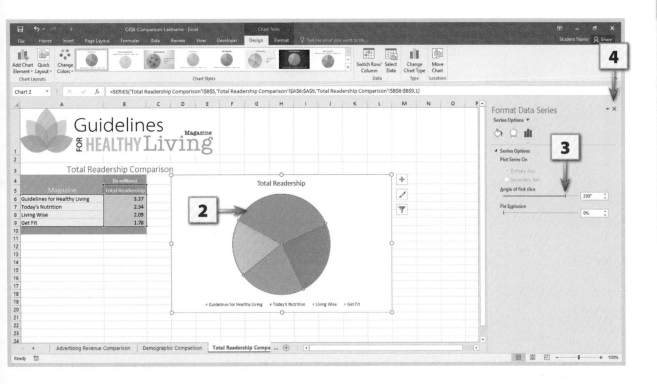

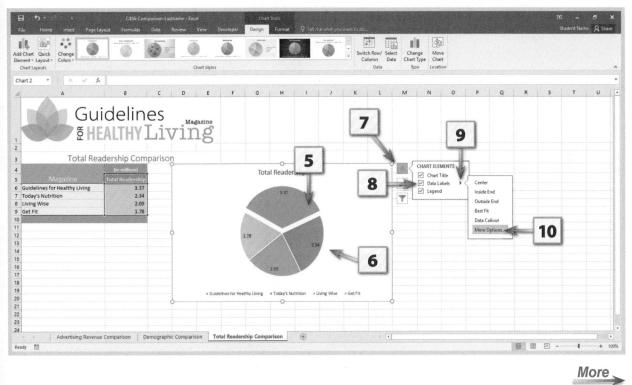

More →

Taking It Further ●

Formatting the Chart Area

You can change the appearance of the chart area by changing the fill color and by adding a border. Right-click the chart area and then click the *Format Chart Area* option in the pop-up list to display the Format Chart Area pane. With the Fill & Line tab selected, click the *Fill* section heading to display fill options, including *Gradient fill*. Click the *Border* section heading to display options for adding a border.

Tip If you do not see the *Percentage* check box in the Format Data labels pane, click the *Label Options* section heading to expand the option list.

11 In the Format Data Labels pane, click the *Percentage* check box in the *Label Contains* section to insert a check mark.

12 Click the *Value* check box to remove the check mark.

13 Click the *Outside End* option in the *Label Position* section to place the data labels outside the slices.

Format a Pie Chart Legend and Apply a Chart Style

Tutorial

14–15 *Another Way*
Right-click the legend in the chart and then click the *Format Legend* option in the pop-up list.

14 In the Format Data Labels pane, click the Label Options arrow.

15 Click the *Legend* option in the drop-down list.

16 Click the *Left* option in the *Legend Position* section.

17 Click the Close button to close the Format Legend pane.

18–19 *Another Way*
Click the More button in the Chart Styles group on the Chart Tools Design tab and then click an option in the drop-down gallery.

18 Click the Chart Styles button.

19 Scroll down and click the *Style 7* option.

20 Save and close the file.

Tip In the Chart Styles list box, the style number displays as a ScreenTip when you point to an option.

Tip Click the Color tab in the Chart Styles box to change the chart colors.

Completed Skill 6

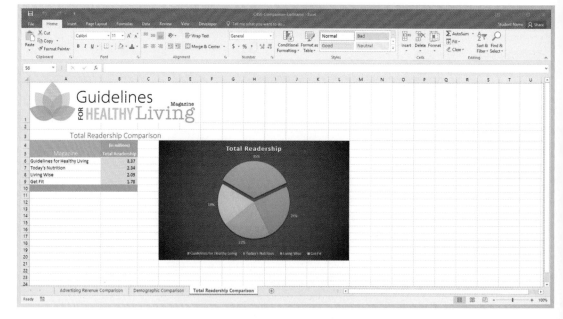

Completed
Skill Preview

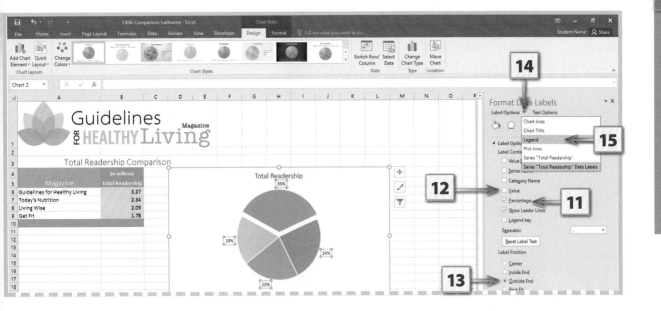

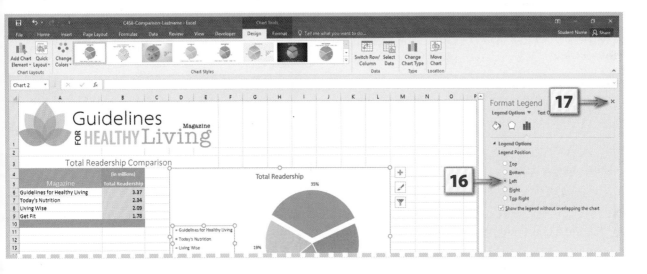

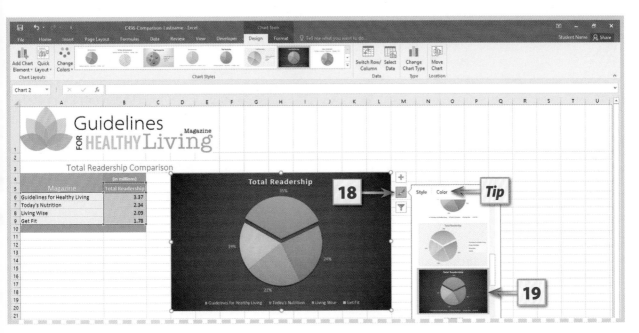

Excel Chapter 4 **Tasks Summary**

Task	Ribbon Tab, Group	Button, Option	Shortcut, Alternative
Insert a line chart on the current worksheet	Insert, Charts	⬚ ▾	
Insert a column or bar chart on the current worksheet	Insert, Charts	⬚ ▾	Alt + F1
Insert a pie chart on the current worksheet	Insert, Charts	⬚ ▾	
Insert another chart type on the current worksheet	Insert, Charts		
Move a chart to a new worksheet	Chart Tools Design, Location	Move Chart	
Modify chart data	Chart Tools Design, Data	Select Data	Add, delete, and edit entries in the data chart; click the Chart Filters button and then click to select categories
Add chart labels	Chart Tools Design, Chart Layouts	Add Chart Element ▾, *Data Labels*	✚ Chart Elements button
Change a chart legend	Chart Tools Design, Chart Layouts	Add Chart Element ▾, *Legend*	✚ Chart Elements button, Right-click a chart legend and then click the *Format Legend* option in the pop-up list
Modify chart style	Chart Tools Design, Chart Styles	▾	✚ Chart Elements button
Change pie chart rotation			Double-click the pie to open Format Data Series pane and then use the *Angle of first slice* slider or measurement box
Explode a pie slice			Double-click the pie slice and then drag the slice away from the pie

Recheck your understanding of the skills and features covered in this chapter.

Recheck

Chapter study resources, exercises, and assessments are available in the Workbook *ebook.*

Workbook

UNIT 5

Access

Student
Data Files

Before beginning the
unit skills, be sure you
have downloaded the
GL16-StudentDataFiles
folder from your ebook
and copied the Unit5-
Access subfolder to
your storage medium.
The copied folder will
become your working
folder for this unit.

Guidelines

for

Understanding Relational Databases and the Best Uses of Access

You may have heard our present time referred to as the *Information Age*. Businesses, schools, and individuals rely on instant access to information and expect to have that information at their fingertips. Computers today enable you to store large amounts of data and to quickly retrieve and organize that data. Much of the information you retrieve from a computer or from a website is stored in a database.

A *database* is an organized collection of related data. A business's employee data, a store's inventory, and an airline's flight listing are all examples of data that is typically stored in a database.

Database Terminology

To understand how databases work, you need to learn some database terminology.

Database applications such as Access use an object called a *table* to enter and organize data. When you open a table in Access, the table displays in a *datasheet*. For example, the Products table below is part of a computer store database for tracking the store's inventory and sales. A table and a datasheet organize the data in rows and columns.

A *field* is an area of a table where a particular type of information is recorded, or a space in the database that is allocated for a particular type of data. The data value for a field is called an *entry*.

Each field has a *field name*, such as *Product ID*, *Model*, *Description*, or *UnitPrice*.

A collection of related fields is called a *record*. In the Products table example below, all the information supplied for one product (ID, model, description, and unit price) makes up a single record.

Access is a *relational database* application, meaning that Access creates files that use a series of related tables to organize data in the database. Each table is usually related to at least one other table by sharing a column of data. For example, assume the Products table and the Inventory table shown below are part of the same Access database. The Products table contains a *ProductID* field but no field to indicate the current inventory level in stock. The *Inventory* field is stored in another table, the Inventory table. But the tables are related because both contain the *ProductID* column of data. This relationship allows you to access all the information for each product, regardless of where it is stored.

field name

record

field

Products				
ProductID	ProductName	Model	Description	UnitPrice
P001	ACC Headphones	AC-2R	Portable Headphones	$16.99
P002	All Purpose Power Adaptor	PA-5K	AC Power Adaptor	$15.00
P003	Expression Pedal	PR-5G	Expression Pedal	$159.99
P004	Acme Keyboard Bench	PR-5A	Folding, Padded Keyboard Bench	$79.00
P005	ACC Foot Switch	PR-7E	Foot Switch	$32.00
P006	Techno Y Cable	PR-5W	Y Cable	$9.99
P007	All Purpose Extension Cord	ZX-2K	Extension Cord	$12.99
*				$0.00

To enter records into a database, you can either enter the data directly into the table or fill in a user-friendly *form* that is designed for data entry. When you enter data in a form, that information is also entered into the corresponding table. A form for entering information about products is shown below.

Once you have entered records into a database, you can use Access to answer queries or questions about the data. For example, you could query the database of a computer store to find out which customers have ordered ACC headphones. The results of this query are shown below.

Alternatively, you could query the database to find out which products have an inventory of 100 items or fewer and may need to be reordered. The results of this query are shown below.

You can also generate printed reports about the stored data. You may want to put query results information in a professional-looking report, such as the one shown below, that you can pass along to the supervisor who makes reordering decisions.

Use Access when you need to organize and store large amounts of data, such as employee or inventory records. By organizing that information in a database, you are able to quickly find the data and answers you need.

If you have a Microsoft account, you can create an *Access app* that can be viewed, edited, and shared on the web. An Access app stores data in the cloud. You can use the Custom web app template that is displayed in the list of available templates when Access is started to create an Access app. Predefined tables can then be added to the app to store data.

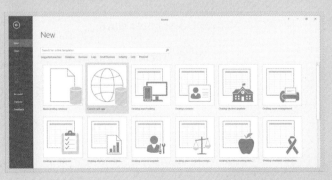

Chapter 1

Working with Databases

Precheck

Check your understanding of the skills and features covered in this chapter.

The Access database application is used to manage large amounts of data, such as the contact information for all the subscribers of the *Guidelines for Healthy Living Magazine*.

In this chapter, you learn to work with the objects in an Access database, including tables, forms, queries, and reports. You use an Access table datasheet to enter and organize data. You can also use an Access form to enter data. Some users prefer to enter records into forms instead of tables because forms allow them to enter and view one record at a time.

Once you have entered data in a database, you can then organize the data by sorting and filtering it. Filtering temporarily displays only those records meeting a certain condition or conditions, such as just those subscribers of the *Guidelines for Healthy Living Magazine* who live in the state of Florida. You can also run a query (ask a question) to locate specific information in a database. For example, you could query the database to find all subscribers whose last name is Brown. Queries can be saved and run at a later time. If you need to print information from a database, you can create a *report* to present the information in a professional-looking format.

In Access, you can create a desktop database, which is saved on a storage medium, or you can create a custom web app, which can be accessed and shared through a web browser. In this chapter, you work with a desktop database, entering data in a table and in a form. You edit, sort, and filter data and format a datasheet. You also run a query and display a report.

Skills You Learn

1   Open and navigate a database

2   Enter data

3   Edit data

4   Sort data

5   Filter data

6   Format a datasheet

7   Use existing queries and reports

If you are a SNAP user, go to your SNAP Assignments page to complete the Precheck, Tutorials, and Recheck.

Files You Need

For these skills, you need the following student data file:

C1-Subscribers

Note: *Before you begin working with the student data files for this chapter, make sure you have downloaded and extracted the GL16-StudentDataFiles zipped file, and have copied the student data files from the Unit5-Access folder to the Unit5-Access-Completed folder on your storage medium. You need to open all database files from your working folder on your storage medium; database files opened directly from a zipped file are read-only, and any changes you make to them will not be saved. Steps for downloading and extracting your student data files and for setting up your working folder are provided in Unit 1, Chapter 2 (pages 9–19).*

What You Create

Guidelines for Healthy Living Magazine publishes enhanced content that subscribers can pay to read on a monthly or annual basis. Subscribers provide personal information, such as their address, which is stored in a database. The CEO and other executives use this data for planning and forecasting. Your role is to update the database and prepare queries and reports for the executive team. In this chapter, you explore the objects in this database. You also add records, sort and filter data, run a query, and display a report.

Magazine Subscribers by State Report

Completed Skill Preview

Skill 1 Open and Navigate a Database

When a database opens, you do not see a document as you do in Word or a workbook as you do in Excel. Instead, you see the *Navigation pane* on the left side of the window that lists the names of the objects that make up the database. This list of objects includes all tables, forms, queries, and reports that are part of the database. To open an object, you double-click the object in the Navigation pane. In this skill, you will open a table and a form object that contain existing records. You will use the *Record Navigation bar*, located at the bottom of a form, to move between records and to create new records.

Tutorial

▶**Tip** Be sure to open the student data files from your working folder, not from the zipped file downloaded from your ebook. Database files within a zipped file are read-only and cannot be changed.

▶**Tip** If the Navigation pane is not open in Step 3, click the Shutter Bar Open/Close button at the top of the Navigation pane.

3 *Another Way*
In the Navigation pane, click *Subscriber Data* in the Tables group and then press Enter.

▶**Tip** You can use the Subscriber Data form to enter records in the Subscriber Data table. The form contains the same fields found in the table.

▶**Tip** You will use the same database file throughout this chapter. If you need to start the chapter again, delete the **C1-Subscribers** file from your Unit 5 working folder and download a new copy of the file to the same folder.

Completed Skill Preview

1 Open the student data file named **C1-Subscribers** from your Unit 5 working folder on your storage medium.

2 If a security warning appears immediately below the ribbon, click the Enable Content button. If a second security warning appears, click the Yes button.

3 Review the objects listed in the Navigation pane and then double-click *Subscriber Data* in the Tables group. The table displays in a datasheet and the first record is selected.

4 On the Record Navigation bar, click the Next record button to select the second record.

5 Click the Last record button to select the last record, numbered 379.

6 Click the Close object button to close the table.

7 In the Navigation pane, double-click *Subscriber Data* in the Forms group. The form displays only one record.

8 On the Record Navigation bar, click the Next record button to display the next record.

9 Click the New (blank) record button to display a new blank record. Do not enter any new data at this time.

10 Click the Close object button to close the Subscriber Data form.

Completed Skill 1

ID	LastName	FirstName	Address	Address2	City	State	Zip	Email
	...ns	David	16 Red Barn Lane		Boston	MA	02135	evansd@ParadigmCollege.net
	...zczewski	Ian	1061 Rue Chinon		Mandeville	LA	70471	roszczewskii@ParadigmCollege.net
	...ous	Nancy	215 E Chestnut Street	#24	Boston	MA	02135	belousn@ParadigmCollege.net
	...lar	Craig	6 Governor's Court		Boston	MA	02118	hollarc@ParadigmCollege.net
353	Stickney	Ada	32 Canal Run		Washington	NC	27889	stickneya@ParadigmCollege.net
354	Brady	Carole	PO Box 1552		Candler	NC	28715	bradyc@ParadigmCollege.net
355	Sassman	Brianne	48 Patton Ave		Boston	MA	02140	sassmanb@ParadigmCollege.net
356	Ball	Diane	90 Turkey Path		Bryson City	TN	28713	balld@ParadigmCollege.net
357	Rimmer	Tom	81 Sunset Lane		Palmyra	PA	17078	rimmert@ParadigmCollege.net
358	Ivey	Curtis	140 Flat Top Mtn Rd		Boston	MA	02135	iveyc@ParadigmCollege.net
359	Avena	Edward	39 Rivendell Road		Boston	MA	02135	avenae@ParadigmCollege.net
360	Cope	Kyle	1 W Pack Square	Ste G-145	Boston	MA	02135	copek@ParadigmCollege.net
361	Ludlow	Kerry	1618 Woodland Ave		Burlington	NC	27215	ludlowk@ParadigmCollege.net
362	Brown	Dorothy	7916 Sherills Ford Road		Sherills Ford	NC	28673	brownd@ParadigmCollege.net
363	Hewitt	Richard	433 Long Shoals Road		Boston	MA	02114	hewittr@ParadigmCollege.net
364	Jones Rafferty	Deborah	4 Wall Street		Boston	MA	02135	jonesd@ParadigmCollege.net
365	Long	Jeannie	PO Box 401		Boston	MA	02135	longj@ParadigmCollege.net
366	McKibrin	Carol	1585 Chatfield Place		Orlando	FL	32814	mckibrinc@ParadigmCollege.net
367	Ellsworth	Jeff	56 Curtis Lane		Boston	MA	02135	ellsworthj@ParadigmCollege.net
368	McAlpine	Michael	230 Elm Bend Road		Boston	MA	02115	mcalpinem@ParadigmCollege.net
369	Allison	Danielle	11 Josie Lane		Boston	MA	02118	allisond@ParadigmCollege.net
370	Postles	Mary	768 Garrren Creek Rd		Boston	MA	02135	postelsm@ParadigmCollege.net
371	Wolfe	Sherif	97 Big Cove Road		Boston	MA	02135	wolfes@ParadigmCollege.net
372	Marino		PO Box 77		Hoosick	NY	12089	marinow@ParadigmCollege.net
373	Dungan		101 Alexander Drive		Johnson City	TN	37604	dunganm@ParadigmCollege.net
	Hasten	...tty	218 Morningside Dr		Mandeville	LA	70448	hastenc@ParadigmCollege.net
	Johnso	...yn	1239 Lindenwood Road		Edwardsville	IL	62025	johnsonc@ParadigmCollege.net
	Bryant	Susan	1325 Middleford Road		Catonsville	MD	21228	bryants@ParadigmCollege.net
	Earwood	Tom	18 N Marley Drive		Boston	MA	02135	earwoodt@ParadigmCollege.net
378	...ndrick	Steve	500 Centerpark Drive		Boston	MA	02135	kendricks@ParadigmCollege.net
379	Ver...	Mary	128 Blaythorne Lane		Statesville	NC	28625	veranim@ParadigmCollege.net

Taking It Further

Opening Multiple Objects

You can have more than one object open at a time in Access. For example, you can open a table and then open a second table or a form. Switch between open objects by clicking the tab at the top of the object. Each tab contains the name of the object and an icon that indicates the object type. For example, notice the Subscriber Data tabs above the table and form in the screenshots on this page. Try opening both the Subscriber Data table and the Subscriber Data form in the **C1-Subscribers** file and then toggling between them using their tabs.

Skill 2 Enter Data

You can enter data in a table or in a form. Entering data in a table is useful for comparing records because you can see multiple records at once. However, this method can be confusing if you are entering a record with a lot of fields and you have to scroll through the fields. A form displays one record at a time. Entering data in a form is less confusing because you usually do not have to scroll to see all the fields in the record, and this can help you avoid errors.

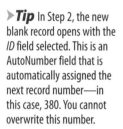

Tutorial

▶**Tip** In Step 2, the new blank record opens with the *ID* field selected. This is an AutoNumber field that is automatically assigned the next record number—in this case, 380. You cannot overwrite this number.

Use Your Touchscreen

In Step 3, you can tap the next field instead of pressing the Tab key.

▶**Tip** Records that you enter in an Access table or form are saved automatically, so you do not have to perform a save before closing in Steps 5 and 9.

1 With **C1-Subscribers** open, double-click *Subscriber Data* in the Tables group in the Navigation pane.

2 On the Record Navigation bar, click the New (blank) record button.

3 Press the Tab key to automatically generate an ID number and move to the *LastName* field.

4 Add the following information to create a new record, pressing the Tab key to move to the next field after each entry:

LastName	FirstName	Address	Address2	City	State	Zip
Marks	Carol	3015 Mossdale Ave	[Tab]	Durham	NC	27707

Email
marksc@ParadigmCollege.net

5 Close the Subscriber Data table.

6 In the Navigation pane, double-click *Subscriber Data* in the Forms group.

7 On the Record Navigation bar, click the New (blank) record button.

8 Press the Tab key and then add the following information to create a new record, pressing Tab to move to the next field after each entry:

LastName	FirstName	Address	Address2	City	State	Zip
Conway	Philip	12 Church Street	Apt A	Boston	MA	02135

Email
conwayp@ParadigmCollege.net

9 Close the Subscriber Data form.

Completed Skill 2

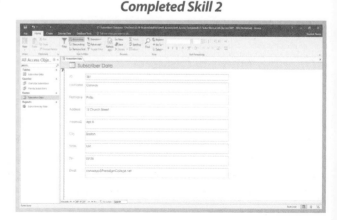

Completed
Skill Preview

Subscriber Data

ID	LastName	FirstName	Address	Address2	City	State	Zip	Email
350	Roszczewski	Ian	1061 Rue Chinon		Mandeville	LA	70471	roszczewskii@ParadigmCollege.net
351	Belous	Nancy	215 E Chestnut Street	#24	Boston	MA	02135	belousn@ParadigmCollege.net
352	Hollar	Craig	6 Governor's Court		Boston	MA	02118	hollarc@ParadigmCollege.net
353	Stickney	Ada	32 Canal Run		Washington	NC	27889	stickneya@ParadigmCollege.net
354	Brady	Carole	PO Box 1552		Candler	NC	28715	bradyc@ParadigmCollege.net
355	Sassman	Brianne	48 Patton Ave		Boston	MA	02140	sassmanb@ParadigmCollege.net
356	Ball	Diane	90 Turkey Path		Bryson City	TN	28713	balld@ParadigmCollege.net
357	Rimmer	Tom	81 Sunset Lane		Palmyra	PA	17078	rimmert@ParadigmCollege.net
358	Ivey	Curtis	140 Flat Top Mtn Rd		Boston	MA	02135	iveyc@ParadigmCollege.net
359	Avena	Edward	39 Rivendell Road		Boston	MA	02135	avenae@ParadigmCollege.net
360	Cope	Kyle	1 W Pack Square	Ste G-145	Boston	MA	02135	copek@ParadigmCollege.net
361	Ludlow	Kerry	1618 Woodland Ave		Burlington	NC	27215	ludlowk@ParadigmCollege.net
362	Brown	Dorothy	7916 Sherills Ford Road		Sherills Ford	NC	28673	brownd@ParadigmCollege.net
363	Hewitt	Richard	433 Long Shoals Road		Boston	MA	02114	hewittr@ParadigmCollege.net
364	Jones Rafferty	Deborah	4 Wall Street		Boston	MA	02135	jonesd@ParadigmCollege.net
365	Long	Jeannie	PO Box 401		Boston	MA	02135	longj@ParadigmCollege.net
366	McKibrin	Carol	1585 Chatfield Place		Orlando	FL	32814	mckibrinc@ParadigmCollege.net
367	Ellsworth	Jeff	56 Curtis Lane		Boston	MA	02135	ellsworth@ParadigmCollege.net
368	McAlpine	Michael	230 Elm Bend Road		Boston	MA	02115	mcalpinem@ParadigmCollege.net
369	Allison	Danielle	11 Josie Lane		Boston	MA	02118	allisond@ParadigmCollege.net
370	Postles	Mary	768 Garrren Creek Rd		Boston	MA	02135	postlesm@ParadigmCollege.net
371	Wolfe	Sherif	97 Big Cove Road		Boston	MA	02135	wolfes@ParadigmCollege.net
372	Marino	Will	PO Box 77		Hoosick	NY	12089	marinow@ParadigmCollege.net
373	Dungan	Mona	101 Alexander Drive		Johnson City	TN	37604	dunganm@ParadigmCollege.net
374	Hasten		218 Morningside Dr		Mandeville	LA	70448	hastenc@ParadigmCollege.net
375	Johnson		1239 Lindenwood Road		Edwardsville	IL	62025	johnsonc@ParadigmCollege.net
376	Bryant		1325 Middleford Road		Catonsville	MD	21228	bryants@ParadigmCollege.net
377	Earwood	Tom	18 N Marley Drive		Boston	MA	02135	earwoodt@ParadigmCollege.net
378	Kendrick	Steve	500 Centerpark Drive		Boston	MA	02135	kendricks@ParadigmCollege.net
379	Verani	Mary	128 Blaythorne Lane		Statesville	NC	28625	veranim@ParadigmCollege.net
380	Marks	Carol	3015 Mossdale Ave		Durham	NC	27707	marksc@ParadigmCollege.net

Subscriber Data

ID	381
LastName	Conway
FirstName	Philip
Address	12 Church Street
Address2	Apt A
City	Boston
State	MA
Zip	02135
Email	conwayp@ParadigmCollege.net

Taking It Further

Checking Spelling

The information that you enter in a database must be correct so that you can run queries and reports successfully and avoid problems in the future. In addition to proofreading, use the spelling checker to check the correctness of your data. To do so, click the Spelling button in the Records group on the Home tab. If Access finds any spelling errors, it displays a dialog box you can use to correct the errors.

Skill 3 Edit Data

A database stores a lot of information, but the information is only useful if the records in the database are kept up-to-date. For example, if a *Guidelines for Healthy Living Magazine* subscriber changes his email address and that information is not updated in the database, the subscriber won't receive emails about subscription renewals or special promotions. In this skill, you learn to edit data in a table.

Tutorial

1 With **C1-Subscribers** open, double-click *Subscriber Data* in the Tables group in the Navigation pane.

2 In record 2, double-click *Dasha* in the *FirstName* column.

3 *Another Way*
Type *Darla* and then press the Right Arrow key or Enter.

3 Type Darla and then press the Tab key.

4 Close the Subscriber Data table.

5 In the Navigation pane, double-click *Subscriber Data* in the Forms group.

Use Your Touchscreen
In Step 5, in the Navigation pane, tap *Subscriber Data* two times in the Forms group.

6 In the first record, double-click *Allen* in the *FirstName* field.

7 Type Ellen and then press the Tab key.

8 Close the Subscriber Data form.

Completed Skill 3

Completed Skill Preview

Taking It Further

Deleting a Record

If a member does not renew his subscription, you need to delete the record. To do this, locate the record in the table and then click the *record selector bar*, which is the gray box to the left of the record's first field. Click the Home tab, and then click the Delete arrow in the Records group. Click the *Delete Record* option in the drop-down list and then click the Yes button to confirm the deletion.

Access

Skill 4 Sort Data

It is good practice to enter database records in the order in which you receive them. For example, you might enter the data for a new *Guidelines for Healthy Living Magazine* subscriber on the day you receive it. However, when you are looking for specific information, such as a subscribers by state, you may find it helpful to sort a table by a particular column, such as *LastName*, rather than by date entered. You may also want to sort a column in a particular order. For example, you can sort the *LastName* column in *ascending* order—that is, from *A* to *Z*. In this skill, you learn to sort the data in a table.

Tutorial

1 With **C1-Subscribers** open, double-click *Subscriber Data* in the Tables group in the Navigation pane.

2 In the first record, click *Mills* in the *LastName* column.

3 *Another Way*
Click the *LastName* arrow and then click the *Sort A to Z* option in the drop-down list.

3 On the Home tab, click the Ascending button in the Sort & Filter group.

4 Click the Remove Sort button. The records are no longer sorted by the *LastName* column.

5 In the first record, click *Charlotte* in the *City* column.

6 Click the Ascending button.

7 Click the Remove Sort button.

8 Close the Subscriber Data table.

9 Click the No button in the dialog box that appears.

Completed Skill 4

Completed Skill Preview

Taking It Further

Sorting a Form

When you sort records in a table, the sort affects only that table. It does not affect the order of records displayed in the related forms. For example, if you sort the Subscriber Data table by the *LastName* column and then open the Subscriber Data form, the records in the Subscriber Data form will not be sorted by last name.

However, you can sort the records in forms the same way you sort them in tables. For example, you can sort the open Subscriber Data form by opening any of the records, clicking the *Lastname* field, and then clicking the Ascending button in the Sort & Filter group on the Home tab.

Skill 5 Filter Data

If you are looking for specific records, such as the records of all subscribers who live in the city of Charlotte, North Carolina, you can *filter* the records based on data in a specific field. When you apply a filter, records that do not meet the condition you specify are temporarily hidden from view. When you remove the filter, those records that have been "hidden" in the table redisplay.

Tutorial

▶ **Tip** In Step 2, you can click any entry in the column to indicate you are filtering the data in that field.

 Another Way
Click the down-pointing arrow in the *City* column heading.

1 With **C1-Subscribers** open, double-click *Subscriber Data* in the Tables group in the Navigation pane.

2 In the first record, click *Charlotte* in the *City* column.

3 On the Home tab, click the Filter button in the Sort & Filter group.

4 Click the *(Select All)* check box to remove all the check marks from the check boxes in the drop-down list.

5 Scroll down the list and click the *Charlotte* check box to insert a check mark.

6 Click the OK button. Only three records display, and all the displayed records have the entry *Charlotte* in the *City* column.

7 Click the Toggle Filter button to redisplay all records in the table.

8 Close the Subscriber Data table and click the No button in the dialog box that appears.

Completed Skill 5

Completed
Skill Preview

Taking It Further

Learning More about Filtering Data

You can filter records based on more than one piece of information in a particular field. For example, you can filter records to find subscribers who live in Charlotte and those who live in Boston. To do so, click on any entry in the *City* field and then select both city names in the Filter drop-down list. You can also filter by more than one column. For example, if you apply a filter that displays just those subscribers living in Charlotte, you can then click in the *LastName* column and apply a second filter to display only those subscribers having the last name Mills who also live in Charlotte.

Skill 6 Format a Datasheet

When you open a table, it displays in a datasheet. A datasheet organizes the data in rows and columns. You may want to apply formatting, such as bold and italic, or change the font size to make the datasheet easier to read. You can also align the data in a column and adjust the width of a column so that all the data in the fields display.

Tutorial

▶**Tip** By default, numeric data is right aligned and text is left aligned.

1 With **C1-Subscribers** open, double-click *Subscriber Data* in the Tables group in the Navigation pane.

2 Click the first record in the *State* column.

3 On the Home tab, click the Align Left button in the Text Formatting group. The formatting is applied to all the records in the *State* column.

4 Click the Font Size arrow.

5 Click *14* in the drop-down list. The font size changes for the entire table. Notice that the *Address* column and *Zip* column are not wide enough to display all their data.

6 Hover the mouse pointer over the right border of the *Zip* column heading. When the pointer changes to a left-and-right-pointing arrow with a vertical line in the middle (✛), double-click to AutoFit the data in the column.

7 Hover the mouse pointer over the right border of the first *Address* column heading. When the pointer changes to a left-and-right-pointing arrow with a vertical line in the middle, double-click to AutoFit the data in the column.

8 Hover the mouse pointer over the right border of the first *Email* column heading. When the pointer changes to a left-and-right-pointing arrow with a vertical line in the middle, double-click to AutoFit the data in the column.

▶**Tip** Format changes are saved automatically when you close a database object. To save format changes without closing a database object, click the Save button in the Quick Access Toolbar.

9 Close the Subscriber Data table and click the Yes button to save the changes to the table. The changes are permanent and will appear the next time you open the table.

Completed Skill 6

Completed
Skill Preview

Taking It Further

Learning More about Formatting a Datasheet

By default, every other row in a datasheet has a different background color. You can change the background color of every second row by clicking the Alternate Row Color arrow in the Text Formatting group on the Home tab and selecting a different color. Also by default, the horizontal and vertical gridlines display. Visible gridlines help you to clearly see the borders of each cell in the datasheet. You can change the gridlines that are displayed by clicking the Gridlines button in the Text Formatting group on the Home tab.

Skill 7 Use Existing Queries and Reports

In previous skills in this chapter, you learned to use existing table and form objects to enter and edit data. In this skill, you work with two other objects: queries and reports. A *query* is a database object that, based on specified criteria, pulls data from one or more tables. You create a query to find records that meet a certain condition. The records are pulled from one or more tables. You also run two queries that have been created for you. Lastly, you display a report that has been saved in the database. A *report* presents data from a combination of one or more tables and queries.

Tutorial

▶Tip In Chapter 3, you will learn how to create a query. Creating a query differs from simply filtering records. Because a query is an Access object, it is saved with the database. As a result, once you create a query, you can run it over and over again.

1 With **C1-Subscribers** open, double-click *Charlotte Subscribers* in the Queries group in the Navigation pane to display records for all subscribers living in Charlotte, North Carolina.

2 Close the Charlotte Subscribers query.

3 In the Navigation pane, double-click *Florida Subscribers* in the Queries group to display records for all subscribers living in the state of Florida.

4 Close the Florida Subscribers query.

5 In the Navigation pane, double-click *Subscribers by State* in the Reports group to display records of subscribers grouped by the state they live in.

6 Close the Subscriber by State report.

7 Close the database.

Completed Skill 7, Subscribers by State Report

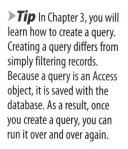

Completed Skill Preview

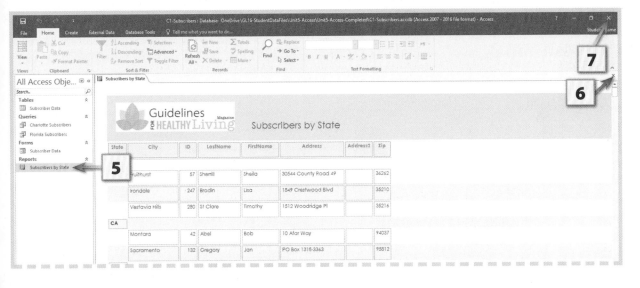

Taking It Further

Printing an Object

You can print any open objects, including tables, forms, queries, and reports. To print an active object, click the File tab and then click the *Print* option to open the Print backstage area. You then have three print options to choose from. You should always click *Print Preview*, the third option, to view the object before you print it. You can then use commands on the Print Preview tab to adjust settings, such as the page size or page orientation (portrait or landscape), before clicking the Print button in the Print group to print the object.

Access Chapter 1 **Tasks Summary**

Task	Ribbon Tab, Group	Button, Option	Shortcut, Alternative
Collapse or expand the Navigation pane		«	
Open an object	Navigation pane		Double-click object in Navigation pane; select object in Navigation pane and press Enter
Close a database object		×	
Display the next record	Record Navigation bar	▶	
Display the last record	Record Navigation bar	▶⏸	
Display a new (blank) record	Record Navigation bar	▶⏸	
Navigate in a database object			Tab key, Arrow keys
Check spelling	Home, Records	ABC✔ Spelling	
Delete a record	Home, Records	✕ Delete	
Sort data	Home, Sort & Filter	A↓Z Ascending	
Remove sort	Home, Sort & Filter	A↓Z Remove Sort	
Filter data	Home, Sort & Filter	▽ Filter	
Remove a filter	Home, Sort & Filter	▽ Toggle Filter	

Task	Ribbon Tab, Group	Button, Option	Shortcut, Alternative
Left align text in a field	Home, Text Formatting	≡	
Change the font size	Home, Text Formatting	14 ▾	
AutoFit a column			Double-click the right border of column heading
Format the background color of every second row in a datasheet	Home, Text Formatting	⊞ ▾	
Format gridlines in a datasheet	Home, Text Formatting	▨ ▾	

Recheck

Recheck your understanding of the skills and features covered in this chapter.

Workbook

Chapter study resources, exercises, and assessments are available in the Workbook *ebook.*

Chapter 2

Creating Forms and Tables

Check your understanding of the skills and features covered in this chapter.

Precheck

In this chapter, you learn to create a table and a form. When you create a table, you need to give each field a name and also assign it a data type. The data type tells Access which type of data you will be storing in that field. You can choose a number of field types, including these:

- *AutoNumber* field—automatically stores a number that is one greater than the last number used

- *Short Text* field—stores characters and numbers that do not require calculations, such as names and zip codes

- *Number* field—stores numbers only

- *Date/Time* field—stores dates and times

- *Currency* field—stores dollar amounts

Access has several views that you use to perform different tasks. When you enter records in a table, you do so in Datasheet view. When you create a table in this chapter, you create it in Design view. To switch views, you use the View arrow on the Home tab.

A form provides a user-friendly interface to enter data to be stored in a table. When you enter a record using a form, that record is added to the corresponding table just as if you added the record directly into the table in Datasheet view. When you use the Form button to create a form, the form initially displays in *Layout view*. You can edit the form in either Design or Layout view. You then must switch to Form view to add records to the underlying table.

In this chapter, you learn how to create a table and a form and you also enter data in a table and a form.

Skills You Learn

1   Create a table

2   Enter data in a table

3   Create a form

4   Enter data in a form

If you are a SNAP user, go to your SNAP Assignments page to complete the Precheck, Tutorials, and Recheck.

Files You Need

For these skills, you need the following student data files:

> C2-Subscribers
> C2-Logo

Note: *Before you begin working with the student data files for this chapter, make sure you have downloaded and extracted the GL16-StudentDataFiles zipped file, and have copied the student data files from the Unit5-Access folder to the Unit5-Access-Completed folder on your storage medium. You need to open all database files from your working folder on your storage medium; database files opened directly from a zipped file are read-only, and any changes you make to them will not be saved. Steps for downloading and extracting your student data files and for setting up your working folder are provided in Unit 1, Chapter 2 (pages 9–19).*

What You Create

Guidelines for Healthy Living Magazine offers subscribers three payment options to access enhanced website content. New subscribers may purchase an annual subscription for $50.00. For this year, the magazine ran a promotion offering customers who renewed their subscriptions a reduced annual rate of $35.88 ($2.99 a month). Subscribers can also access content on a one-time basis for $0.99. In this chapter, you create a table that stores data on the annual subscriber revenue. You also create a form so that you can easily enter records in the table.

Subscriber Revenue Table

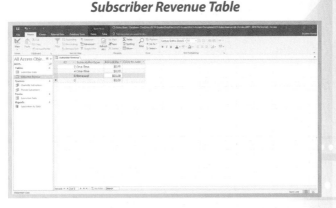

Subscriber Revenue Form Record

Completed
Skill Preview

Skill 1　Create a Table

In Chapter 1, you opened a table, added a record to the table, and edited data in the table. In this skill, you add a new table to the database. This new table will store revenue data for each of the magazine's subscribers. You create the table in *Design view*. This view is used to define the structure of the table.

You will need to name each field and select a data type for each field in the table. You will use the *Lookup Wizard* data type to create a *Lookup* field to

specify that only certain values can be entered in that field and to simplify data entry. The *Lookup field* then displays a list of values from which the user can choose.

You will also specify a primary key for the table. A *primary key* is assigned to a field in a table, such as the subscriber ID number, to simplify retrieval of a specific record and to make sure no two records in a table are the same. The primary key column cannot contain duplicate entries.

Tutorial

Create a Simple Table

1 Open the student data file named **C2-Subscribers** from your storage medium.

2 If a security warning appears immediately below the ribbon, click the Enable Content button. If a second security warning appears, click the Yes button.

3 Click the Create tab.

4 Click the Table Design button in the Tables group to open the table in Design view.

5 With the insertion point in the first cell of the *Field Name* column, type ID and then press the Tab key.

6 Click the *Data Type* arrow and then click the *Number* option in the drop-down list.

6 *Another Way*
Start typing *Number* in the *Data Type* box. Stop typing when *Number* appears in the box, and then press the Tab key.

▶ *Tip* You could also include an entry in the *Description* column, to the right of the *Data Type* column. This entry would be used to describe the contents of the field.

▶ *Tip* To open Access, type *access* in the search box on the Windows taskbar and then click *Access 2016 Desktop app* in the search results list.

Taking It Further

Using Templates

In this unit, you open existing desktop databases and then start working in Access. To create a new database, open Access and then in the backstage area, select one of the available templates. You will see templates for both desktop and web apps. For example, if you want to start with a blank database for

use on your desktop, select the Blank desktop database template, or if you want to create a database that you can share online, select the *Custom web app template*. When you select the Custom web app template, you will also be able to add table templates to the online database.

More →

Taking It Further •

Changing Field Size

Some field data types have a specified *field size* or a maximum size. For example, Short Text fields can store up to 255 characters. In some situations, you might want to limit a Short Text field to fewer characters—for instance, you might want to limit fields for phone numbers or zip codes to help reduce data entry errors. To do this, you replace the *Field Size* value of *255* with another value. Change this setting in the *Field Properties* section of the Design view window. A field size cannot be set for Long Text, Date/Time, Currency, or Hyperlink fields.

7 Click the record selector bar to the left of the *ID* field name.

Tip The Subscriber Revenue table is designed to contain one entry per subscriber. Setting the *ID* field as the primary key ensures duplicate entries cannot be entered.

8 Click the Primary Key button in the Tools group.

9 Click the Save button on the Quick Access Toolbar.

10 In the Save As dialog box, type Subscriber Revenue in the *Table Name* box.

11 Click the OK button.

Tutorial

Specify Field Values Using the Lookup Wizard

12 Click the second cell in the *Field Name* column, type SubscriptionType, and then press the Tab key.

Tip The data type of a *Lookup* field is either Text or Number, depending on the values you specify. The *Lookup* field you create in Steps 12–15 has the data type Text.

13 Click the *Data Type* arrow and then click the *Lookup Wizard* option in the drop-down list.

14 Click *I will type in the values that I want* to select that option and then click the Next button.

15 Click the blank cell under the *Col1* heading and then type the following entries, pressing the Down Arrow key after each entry:
One-Time
Renewal
Annual

Use Your Touchscreen
In Step 15, tap the first blank cell under the *Col1* heading, type an entry, and then tap the next blank cell to begin the next entry.

16 Click the Finish button.

17 Click the third cell in the *Field Name* column, type AnnualRevenue, and then press the Tab key.

18 Click the *Data Type* arrow and then click the *Currency* option in the drop-down list.

19 *Shortcut*
Save
Ctrl + S

19 Click the Save button on the Quick Access Toolbar.

20 Click the Close object button to close the Subscriber Revenue table.

Completed Skill 1

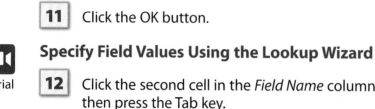

Completed
Skill Preview

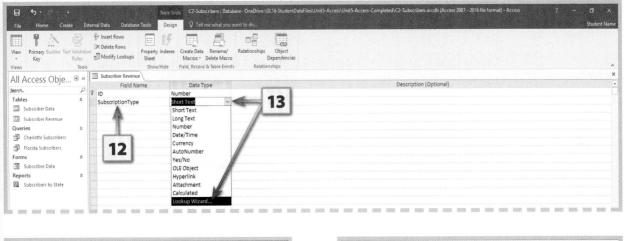

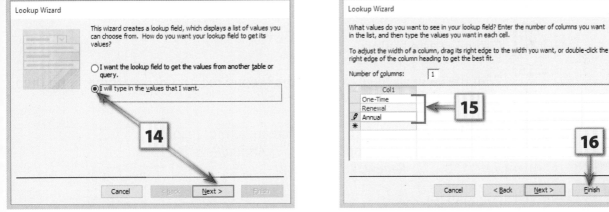

Skill 2 | Enter Data in a Table

In the previous skill, you created a new table. The new table is an object in the database. In this skill, you add records to the table. You add records to a table in *Datasheet view*. Typing records is one way to enter data in a table.

You can also copy and paste data from other programs or databases, which saves time and also prevents data entry errors. Adding records is sometimes referred to as *populating the database*.

Tutorial

▶**Tip** To verify the view in Step 2, click the View arrow in the Views group on the Home tab.

▶**Tip** The *ID* field in the Subscriber Revenue table matches the *ID* field in the Subscriber Data table.

▶**Tip** The *AnnualRevenue* entries are automatically formatted as currency to match the field type.

 Shortcut
Copy
Ctrl + C

 Shortcut
Paste
Ctrl + V

▶**Tip** You can copy and paste an entire record to save time when a new record is almost identical to an existing record. After pasting, you change only the part of the record that differs. In this case, all the data for the second record is the same as for the first record, except the value in the *ID* field.

1 With **C2-Subscribers** open, double-click *Subscriber Revenue* in the Tables group in the Navigation pane.

2 Verify that you are in Datasheet view and then add the following information to create a new record, pressing the Tab key after each entry and clicking the *SubscriptionType* arrow to select the subscription type:

ID	SubscriptionType	AnnualRevenue
2	One-Time	0.99

3 Click the record selector bar to the left of the first record to select all the fields in that record.

4 On the Home tab, click the Copy button in the Clipboard group.

5 Click the record selector bar to the left of the second record.

6 Click the Paste button.

7 With the value in the *ID* field for the second record selected, type 4 and then press Tab three times.

8 Add the following information to create a third record:

ID	SubscriptionType	AnnualRevenue
8	Renewal	35.88

9 Double-click the right border of the *SubscriptionType* column heading to AutoFit the data in the column.

10 Save and then close the Subscriber Revenue table.

Completed Skill 2

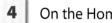

**Completed
Skill Preview**

Taking It Further ●

Copying and Pasting Data

Another way to populate a table is to copy existing data from a Word or Excel file into an Access table. To copy all the data from a Word source, first separate the data by tabs or copy it from a table. Whether you copy the data from Word or Excel, the field names, data types, and data have to match the fields in the Access table. In the Access table, click the record selector bar for the next blank record before pasting the data. Note that you may copy and paste multiple records. Unit 7 provides more information about data sharing between Office applications.

Skill 3 Create a Form

A form is a database object used for entering records in a table. You can also use a form to view existing records. Most forms show only one record at a time, which provides a simple interface for entering data and helps you avoid data entry mistakes. A new form can be based on one or more database objects. The form you create in this skill is based on a table. When you first create a new form using the Form button in the Forms group on the Create tab, it displays in Layout view. Both Layout view and Design view can then be used to format a form.

Tutorial

> **Tip** In Step 1, you single-click to make the table active so that you can create a form for the table. You would double-click to open the table.

3 *Another Way*
You can use the Form Design button in the Forms group to create a form and display it in Design view instead of in Layout view.

> **Tip** You can add the date and time to a form header by clicking the Date and Time button in the Header/Footer group on the Form Layout Tools Design tab.

1 With **C2-Subscribers** open, click *Subscriber Revenue* in the Tables group in the Navigation pane.

2 Click the Create tab.

3 Click the Form button in the Forms group to create a form based on the Subscriber Revenue table and display it in Layout view.

4 On the Form Layout Tools Design tab, click the Logo button in the Header/Footer group.

5 Navigate to the student data file named **C2-Logo** in your Unit 5 working folder on your storage medium, click the file to select it, and then click the OK button.

6 Double-click the bottom right corner of the logo to AutoFit the logo.

7 Click the View arrow in the Views group and then click the *Design View* option in the drop-down list to display the form in Design view.

Taking It Further

Changing Form Formatting and Views

When you create a form, the Form Layout Tools tabs are displayed on the ribbon. You can use commands on the Form Layout Tools Format tab to change the font, font size, and font style. You can use options on the Form Layout Tools Arrange tab to insert fields or alter the order of the fields. You can use options on the Form Layout Tools Design tab to add an image to the form or to change the theme of the form. However, you cannot enter records in the form until you switch to Form view. To do so, click the View arrow in the Views group on the Form Layout Tools Design tab or the Home tab, and then click the *Form View* option in the drop-down list.

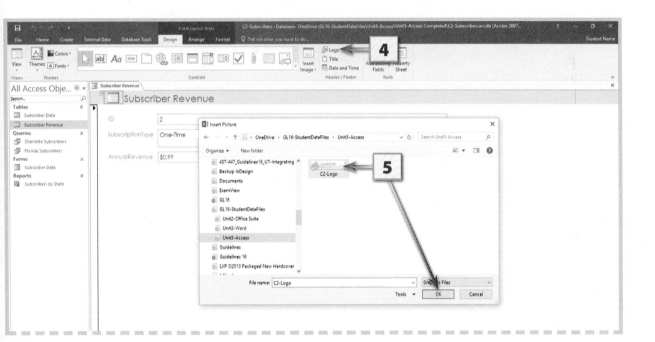

More ➤

8 Click the *ID* field.

▶**Tip** Changing the width of the *ID* field also changes the width of all the other fields on the form.

9 Hover over the right border of the *ID* field until the mouse pointer becomes a left-and-right-pointing arrow and then drag the right border to the 6-inch mark on the ruler.

10 On the Form Layout Tools Design tab, click the View arrow in the Views group.

11 Click the *Layout View* option in the drop-down list to display the form in Layout view.

12 Click the Save button on the Quick Access Toolbar.

▶**Tip** Once the form is saved, it appears as an object in the Forms group in the Navigation pane.

13 Click the OK button to accept the form name *Subscriber Revenue*.

14 Close the Subscriber Revenue form.

Completed Skill 3

Completed
Skill Preview

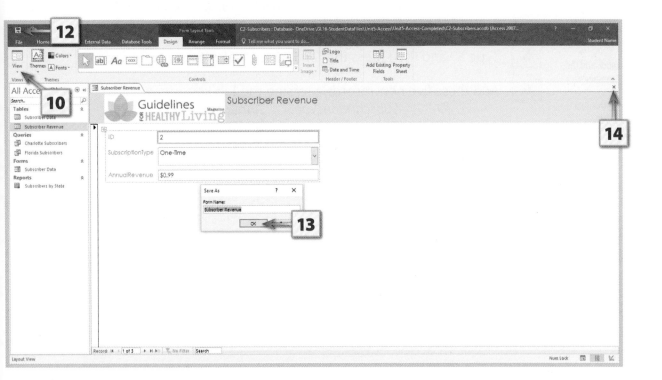

Skill 4 Enter Data in a Form

When you open a form from the Navigation pane, it displays in Form view. You use this view to enter data in a form. The Record Navigation bar displays at the bottom of the form. You can add a new record by clicking the New (blank) record button on the Record Navigation bar. Use the Tab key to move between fields as you enter data in a record. If you press the Tab key after you enter data in the last field, a new blank form displays.

Tutorial

▶ **Tip** In Step 1, if the form does not display in the Navigation pane, click the down-pointing arrow in the Navigation pane header and then click the *All Access Objects* option in the drop-down list.

4 *Another Way*

Start typing *Annual*, and the field will AutoComplete.

▶ **Tip** In Step 5, the data type for the *AnnualRevenue* field is Currency and this format is automatically applied to the entry when the Tab key is pressed.

1 With **C2-Subscribers** open, double-click *Subscriber Revenue* in the Forms group in the Navigation pane.

2 Verify that you are in Form view and then click the New (blank) record button on the Record Navigation bar.

3 Type 12 and then press the Tab key.

4 Click the *SubscriptionType* arrow, click the *Annual* option in the drop-down list, and then press the Tab key.

5 Type 50 and then press the Tab key to display a new blank record.

6 Add these five new records, pressing the Tab key after each entry:

ID	SubscriptionType	AnnualRevenue
48	Renewal	35.88
17	Renewal	35.88
5	One-Time	0.99
37	One-Time	0.99
25	Annual	50

7 Close the Subscriber Revenue form.

8 Close the database.

Completed Skill 4, Subscriber Revenue Form, Record 9

Completed
Skill Preview

Taking It Further ●

Using the Record Navigation Bar Counter

The Record Navigation bar indicates which record is currently displayed and how many records are available for viewing—for example, 1 of 381. If you have not filtered the table or form, the second number indicates the total number of records in the object.

If you have filtered the object, the second number indicates the number of records that match your request and the Filtered icon (▼) is highlighted in the Record Navigation bar.

Access Chapter 2 **Tasks Summary**

Task	Ribbon Tab, Group	Button, Option	Shortcut, Alternative
Create a table	Create, Tables	Table	
Create a Primary Key	Table Tools Design, Tools	Primary Key	
Save a table	Quick Access Toolbar	💾	Ctrl + S
Switch or verify view	Form Layout Tools Design, Views	View	View button in Views group on Home tab
Select a record	Record selector bar	☐	
Copy a record	Home, Clipboard	Copy	Ctrl + C
Paste a record	Home, Clipboard	Paste	Ctrl + V
Create a form	Create, Form	Form	Form Design button in Forms group on Create tab
Add a logo to a form	Form Layout Tools Design, Header/Footer	Logo	
Add the date and time to a form header	Form Layout Tools Design, Header/Footer	Date and Time	

Recheck

Recheck your understanding of the skills and features covered in this chapter.

Workbook

Chapter study resources, exercises, and assessments are available in the Workbook ebook.

Chapter 3

Working with Queries and Reports

Precheck

Check your understanding of the skills and features covered in this chapter.

A database may contain hundreds of records that are divided among many related tables. An easy way to find the information you are looking for is to create and run a query.

A query asks the database a question, such as "How many subscribers purchased an annual subscription to *Guidelines for Healthy Living Magazine*?" or "Which subscribers live in the state of Florida?" A query shows only the data you want to view at any given time. You can look at a limited number of fields from a single table or at selected fields from multiple tables. You can even sort or filter the query results to display only a subset of the data, arranged in the order you prefer.

You can use the information in a table or in a query to create a professional-looking report. Then you can distribute the report in printed or electronic form. When preparing a report, you have several options. You might sort or group the report data, or format the report by changing the font or by applying a theme.

In this chapter, you learn how to create queries to find the information you are looking for within an Access database. You also learn how to create, preview, and print a report.

Skills You Learn

1   Use the Query Wizard

2   Create a query in Design view

3   Use more than one table in a query

4   Use the Report Wizard

5   Create and preview a report

Files You Need

For these skills, you need the following student data file:

C3-Subscribers

 SNAP   *If you are a SNAP user, go to your SNAP Assignments page to complete the Precheck, Tutorials, and Recheck.*

Note: *Before you begin working with the student data files for this chapter, make sure you have downloaded and extracted the GL16-StudentDataFiles zipped file, and have copied the student data files from the Unit5-Access folder to the Unit5-Access-Completed folder on your storage medium. You need to open all database files from your working folder on your storage medium; database files opened directly from a zipped file are read-only, and any changes you make to them will not be saved. Steps for downloading and extracting your student data files and for setting up your working folder are provided in Unit 1, Chapter 2 (pages 9–19).*

What You Create

You create three queries in this chapter. One query displays certain fields from the Subscriber Data table in the *Guidelines for Healthy Living Magazine* database. Another query finds all subscribers whose last names start with the letter *K* and who live in a specific zip code. The last query finds subscribers whose annual subscription costs were greater than $30. You then use the queries to create two reports. In one report, you group and sort the data. In the other report, you apply formatting and adjust the print settings.

Subscriber Last Name and Zip Query   *K Subscribers 02114 Query*

Annual Revenue > $30 Query

Subscriber Last Name and Zip Report   *Annual Revenue > $30 Report*

Completed
Skill Preview

Skill 1 Use the Query Wizard

Once you have entered information into a database, you can query the database to find data that meet certain *criteria*, or conditions. A query pulls data from one or more tables. In this skill, you use the *Query Wizard* to create a select query from fields that you pick. The simple query you create in this skill displays the *LastName* and *Zip* fields from the Subscriber Data table.

Tutorial

1 Open the student data file named **C3-Subscribers** from your storage medium.

2 If a security warning appears immediately below the ribbon, click the Enable Content button. If a second security warning appears, click the Yes button.

3 In the Navigation pane, click *Subscriber Data* in the Tables group.

4 Click the Create tab.

5 Click the Query Wizard button in the Queries group.

6 In the New Query dialog box, click the *Simple Query Wizard* option, if it is not already highlighted, and then click the OK button.

7–8 *Another Way*
Double-click the *LastName* option.

▶**Tip** In Steps 7 and 9, if you accidentally select a field you do not want, click the field name in the *Selected Fields* box and then click the single left arrow button (<) to deselect the field.

7 In the Simple Query Wizard dialog box, click the *LastName* option in the *Available Fields* box.

8 Click the single right arrow button (>) to add the field to the query.

9 Click the *Zip* option in the *Available Fields* box.

10 Click the single right arrow button to add the field to the query.

11 Click the Next button.

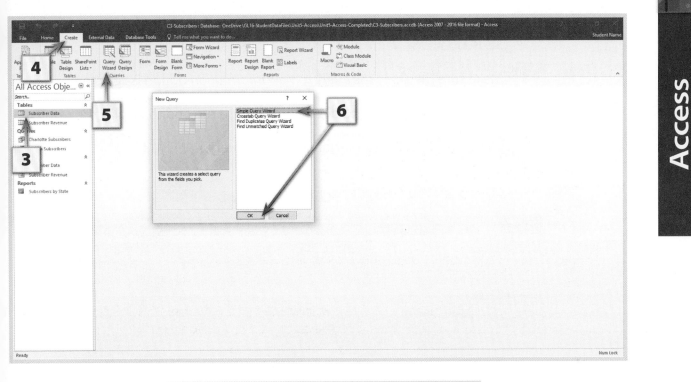

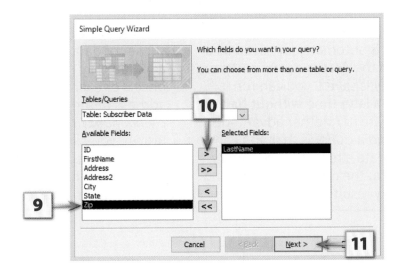

More

12 Select the text in the *What title do you want for your query?* box and then type Subscriber Last Name and Zip.

 13 Make sure the *Open the query to view information* option is selected.

 14 Click the Finish button to direct the query to run and to display the results.

15 Close the Subscriber Last Name and Zip query.

▶ *Tip* At the end of Step 14, the Subscriber Last Name and Zip query appears in the Queries group in the Navigation pane.

Completed Skill 1

Completed Skill Preview

Taking It Further ●

Deciding Whether to Query or to Filter

There are important differences between running a query and simply filtering data. When you create a query, it is automatically saved as an object in the Access database. Because the query is saved, you can run it again at a later time without having to re-create it. Another advantage of running a query is that you can easily create a report from a query, giving you the option of presenting the query results in a professional format. In contrast, filtering displays the results temporarily. Filtering is useful when you need to see a subset of data in datasheet format, and you only need to see that subset once. For example, if you need the address of the *Guidelines for Healthy Living Magazine* subscriber Cara Brown, you can filter the *LastName* column to display all subscribers with the last name *Brown* and locate this information quickly.

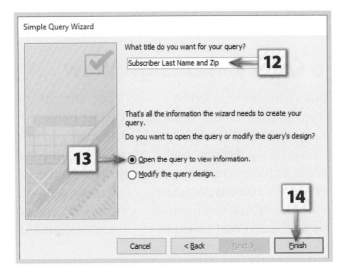

Skill 2 Create a Query in Design View

In the previous skill, you learned to create a query using the Query Wizard. You can also create a query in Design view by using the *query design grid*. When you create a query in Design view, you have more options and more control than you do with the Query Wizard. In this skill, you create a query to find all the subscribers who live in a specific zip code. You sort the query by last name and then further narrow the query to find subscribers in the specific zip code whose last names start with the letter K. You do this by using a wildcard character (*) to represent any combination of letters, numbers, and special symbols.

Tutorial

1 With **C3-Subscribers** open, click the Create tab, if necessary, to select it.

2 Click the Query Design button in the Queries group.

3 On the Tables tab of the Show Table dialog box, click the *Subscriber Data* option, if necessary, to select it.

4 Click the Add button.

5 Click the Close button to close the Show Table dialog box.

> **Tip** In Step 6, double-click carefully, choosing only the fields needed for the query and choosing them in the order listed. You may need to scroll to see the *Zip* field.

6 In the Subscriber Data table field box, double-click the *LastName*, *FirstName*, and *Zip* options, in that order, to add those fields to the query design grid.

7 In the query design grid, click the *Sort* cell for the *LastName* field and then click the *Sort* arrow.

8 Click the *Ascending* option in the drop-down list.

9 Click the *Criteria* cell for the *Zip* field and then type 02114.

10 *Another Way*
You can also run the query by clicking the View button. When you click the View button, you switch from Design view to Datasheet view and the query results display.

10 On the Query Tools Design tab, click the Run button in the Results group to display the query results in a datasheet.

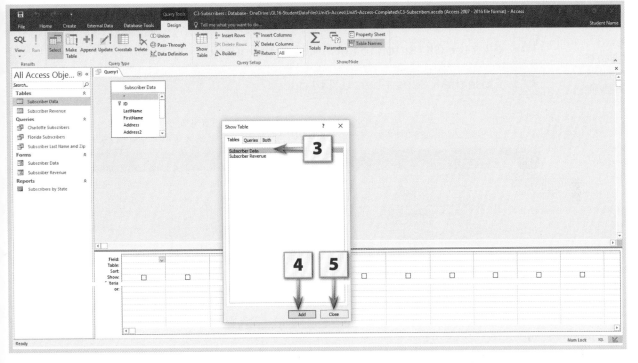

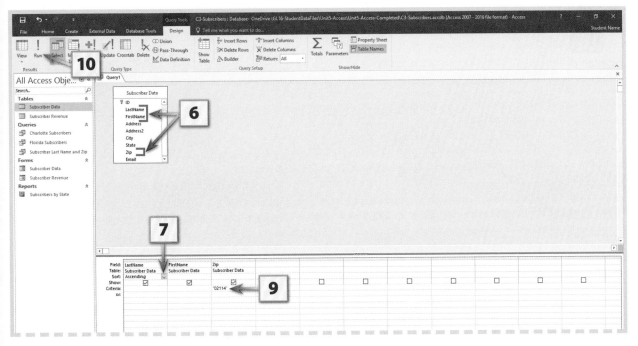

More →

11 On the Home tab, click the View arrow, and then click the *Design View* option in the drop-down list.

 12 Click the *Criteria* cell for the *LastName* field and then type K*.

13 On the Query Tools Design tab, click the Run button in the Results group to display the query results in a datasheet.

14 Click the Save button on the Quick Access Toolbar.

15 In the Save As dialog box, type K Subscribers 02114 in the *Query Name* box.

▶**Tip** At the end of Step 16, the K Subscribers 02114 query appears in the Queries group in the Navigation pane.

16 Click the OK button to finish saving the query.

17 Close the K Subscribers 02114 query.

Completed Skill 2

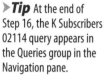

Completed
Skill Preview

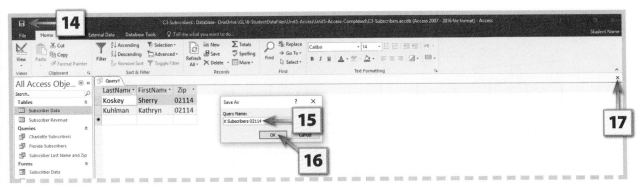

Skill 3 Use More Than One Table in a Query

Tables in a database can be related through a common field of data. For example, the Subscriber Data table and the Subscriber Revenue table are related through the *ID* field, which assigns a unique number to each magazine subscriber. Such database design features are helpful because they keep the tables from containing a lot of duplicate data and, as a result, enable the database to operate more efficiently. When Access tables are related, you can pull data from more than one table to create a query. In this skill, you create a query that pulls data from both the Subscriber Data table and the Subscriber Revenue table.

Tutorial

1 With **C3-Subscribers** open, click the Create tab.

2 Click the Query Design button in the Queries group.

3 On the Tables tab of the Show Table dialog box, make sure the *Subscriber Data* option is selected and then click the Add button.

4 Click the *Subscriber Revenue* option and then click the Add button.

5 Click the Close button to close the Show Table dialog box.

6 In the Subscriber Data table field box, double-click the *ID*, *LastName*, and *FirstName* options, in that order.

7 In the Subscriber Revenue table field box, double-click the *SubscriptionType* and *AnnualRevenue* options, in that order.

8 In the query design grid, click the *Sort* cell for the *LastName* field and then click the *Sort* arrow.

9 Click the *Ascending* option in the drop-down list.

10 Click the *Criteria* cell for the *AnnualRevenue* field and then type >30.

11 On the Query Tools Design tab, click the Run button in the Results group to display the query results in a datasheet.

> **Tip** In Step 4, a join line appears between the *ID* fields. Joins are to queries what relationships are to tables: an indication of how data in two objects can be combined based on data values they have in common.

Use Your Touchscreen
In Step 6 and 7, double-tap fields to add them to the query design grid.

> **Tip** Relational operators are used to specify search criteria. Relational operators include > (greater than), > = (greater than or equal to), < (less than), < = (less than or equal to), = (equal to), and < > (not equal to).

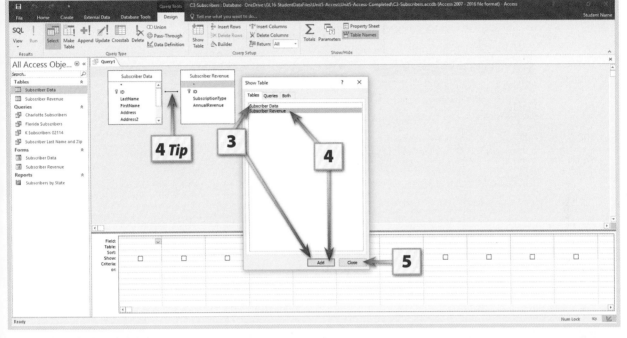

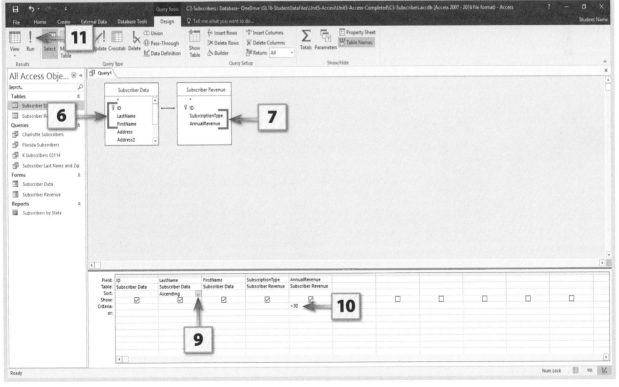

More →

Access

Click the Save button on the Quick Access Toolbar.

 In the Save As dialog box, type Annual Revenue > $30 to replace the selected text in the *Query Name* box.

14 Click the OK button.

 Close the Annual Revenue > $30 query.

Completed Skill 3

Completed
Skill Preview

Taking It Further

Creating Table Relationships

Most Access databases contain multiple tables that share data. An effective database designer avoids *data redundancy* (the duplication of data) by creating relationships between tables for the data fields that they share. You can define a relationship by clicking the Relationships button in the Relationships group on the Database Tools tab, adding tables to the design grid, and then dragging a common data field from one table to another table. To view existing table relationships, click the Relationships button and then click the All Relationships button.

Skill 4 Use the Report Wizard

Reports present Access data in an attractive, easy-to-print format. A report is based on multiple related tables or queries. When you create a report, Access links the report to the objects (queries and/or tables) you used to create it. Because the report is linked to the objects, it always displays current data. You can create a report in several ways. In this skill, you use the Report Wizard to create a report based on the Subscriber Last Name and Zip query. The *Report Wizard* displays a series of dialog boxes to help you select the objects and fields to include in a report, add grouping levels, assign a sort order for detail records, and lay out the report. A *grouping level* combines like data from a specified field.

Tutorial

1 With **C3-Subscribers** open, click *Subscriber Last Name and Zip* in the Queries group in the Navigation pane.

2 Click the Create tab.

3 Click the Report Wizard button in the Reports group.

4 In the Report Wizard dialog box, click the double right arrow button (>>) to select all available fields.

5 Click the Next button.

> **Tip** Adding the *Zip* field as a grouping level in Step 6 means your report will group together subscribers who live in the same zip code.

6 Click the *Zip* option in the box on the left and then click the single right arrow button (>) to add this field as a grouping level.

7 Click the Next button.

8 Click the field 1 arrow and then click the *LastName* option in the drop-down list.

9 Click the Next button to accept your changes to the sort order.

10 Click the Next button to accept the default settings for the report layout.

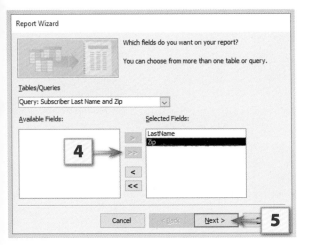

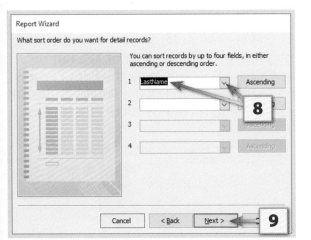

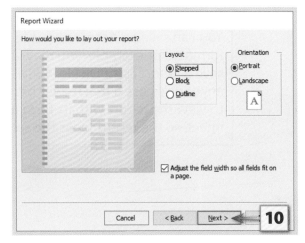

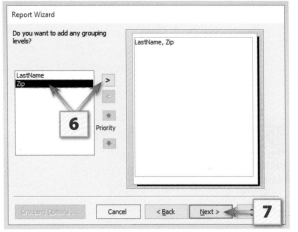

More →

▶Tip In Step 11, notice that the report is grouped by zip code, and within each zip code the data is sorted by last name.

▶Tip Print Preview view displays the report as it will appear on a printed page.

11 Click the Finish button to accept the *Subscriber Last Name and Zip* report name and to view the report in Print Preview view.

12 On the Print Preview tab, click the Print button in the Print group.

13 In the Print dialog box, click the OK button if your instructor asks you to print the report. If not, click the Cancel button.

14 Close the Subscriber Last Name and Zip report.

Completed Skill 4

Completed Skill Preview

Taking It Further ●

Saving a Report as a PDF File

You can save an Access report in other formats. For example, you may want to save a report as a PDF file. A PDF allows anybody to use a free reader program to view the report with its formatting intact, so the report looks the same on every computer. To save a report as a PDF file, click the PDF or XPS button in the Data group on the Print Preview tab and then click the Publish button in the Publish as PDF or XPS dialog box.

Report Wizard

What title do you want for your report?

Subscriber Last Name and Zip

That's all the information the wizard needs to create your report.

Do you want to preview the report or modify the report's design?

● Preview the report.
○ Modify the report's design.

Cancel   < Back   Next >   Finish   **11**

Subscriber Last Name and Zip

Zip	LastName
02114	
	Anzeluo
	Bulluck
	Cogburn Jr.
	Hewitt
	Jeffries
	Koskey
	Kuhlman
	Pinkston
	Reed
	Sarti
02115	
	Ecoff
	Fore
	McAlpine
02118	
	Allison

Skill 5 Create and Preview a Report

In this skill, you use the Report button to create a report based on the Annual Revenue > $30 query. When you use the Report button to create a report, the report is displayed in Layout view, where you can then format it. Before printing, it is good practice to use the Print Preview feature to view what the printed copy will look like and adjust the print settings, if necessary. The Print Preview tab contains print and layout options.

Tutorial

Create and Format a Report Based on a Query

1 With **C3-Subscribers** open, click *Annual Revenue > $30* in the Queries group in the Navigation pane.

2 Click the Create tab.

3 Click the Report button in the Reports group to display the report in Layout view.

4 On the Report Layout Tools Design tab, click the Themes button in the Themes group.

5 Click the *Integral* option in the drop-down gallery to apply the Integral theme to the report.

6 Click the Group & Sort button in the Grouping & Totals group.

7 In the Group, Sort, and Total pane, click the Add a sort button.

8 Click the *LastName* option in the *Sort by* pop-up list.

9 Close the Group, Sort, and Total pane.

10 Click the *AnnualRevenue Total* cell to make it active.

11 Hover over the border of the cell until the mouse pointer becomes a left-and-right-pointing arrow and then double-click the cell border to AutoFit the cell.

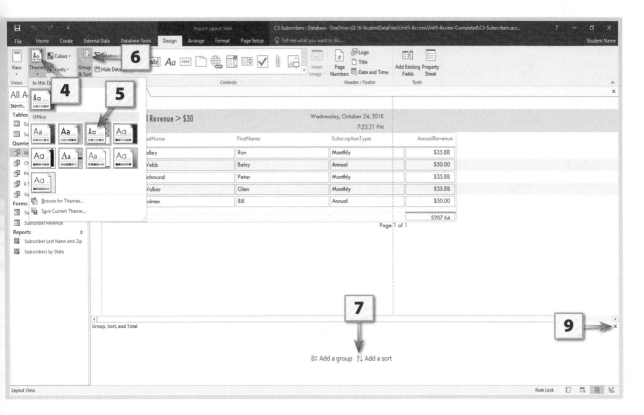

Access

More

Tip The Report Layout Tools Page Setup tab contains options for formatting the page size and page layout.

Tip In Step 13, the dashed lines you see in the report indicate where the page margins will be when the document is printed.

Tip The Report Layout Tools Arrange tab contains options for inserting rows and columns and altering the report layout.

12 Click the Report Layout Tools Page Setup tab.

13 Click the Landscape button in the Page Layout group.

14 Click the *SubscriptionType* column heading.

15 Click the Report Layout Tools Arrange tab, and then click the Select Column button in the Rows & Columns group.

16 Press the Delete key.

17 Click the Save button on the Quick Access Toolbar.

18 Click the OK button to accept the *Annual Revenue > $30* report name.

Tutorial

Tip The Report Layout Tools Design tab contains options for formatting the report.

Tip To adjust the report margins, click the Margins button in the Page Layout group on the Print Preview tab.

Preview and Print a Report

19 Click the Report Layout Tools Design tab and then click the View arrow in the Views group.

20 Click the *Print Preview* option in the drop-down list.

21 On the Print Preview tab, click the Print button in the Print group.

22 In the Print dialog box, click the OK button if your instructor asks you to print the report. If not, click the Cancel button.

23 Close the Annual Revenue > $30 report.

24 Close the database.

Completed Skill 5

Completed
Skill Preview

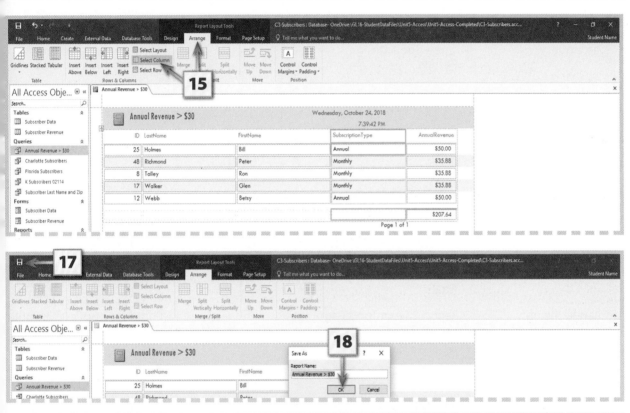

Access Chapter 3 **Tasks Summary**

Task	Ribbon Tab, Group	Button, Option	Shortcut, Alternative
Create a query using the Query Wizard	Create, Queries	Query Wizard	
Create a query in Design view	Create, Queries	Query Design	
Run a query	Query Tools Design, Results	Run	Click the View button to switch to Datasheet view
Create a report using the Report Wizard	Create, Reports	Report Wizard	
Create a report in Layout view	Create, Reports	Report	
Apply a theme to a report	Report Layout Tools Design, Themes	Themes	
Display the Group, Sort, and Total pane	Report Layout Tools Design, Grouping & Totals	Group & Sort	
Change the print orientation to landscape	Report Layout Tools Page Layout, Page Setup	Landscape	Print Preview, Page Layout
Select a column	Report Layout Tools Arrange, Rows & Columns	Select Column	
View a report in Print Preview layout	Report Layout Tools Design, Views	Print Preview	Click the View button to cycle through available views
Print a report	Print Preview, Print	Print	
Create a PDF copy of the report	Print Preview, Data	PDF or XPS	

Recheck your understanding of the skills and features covered in this chapter.

Recheck

Chapter study resources, exercises, and assessments are available in the Workbook ebook.

Workbook

PowerPoint

Student
Data Files

Before beginning this unit, be sure you have downloaded the GL16-StudentDataFiles folder from your ebook and copied the Unit6-PowerPoint subfolder to your storage medium. The copied folder will become your working folder for this unit.

Guidelines
for
Creating a PowerPoint Presentation

PowerPoint is an easy-to-use presentation program for creating a *slide show* that can be run in front of an audience to reinforce the creator's key points.

Slides may include text, graphics, animation, videos, and sound. PowerPoint provides different slide layouts that you can use for different purposes. For example, use a Title Slide layout for the first slide in your show.

Title Slide Layout

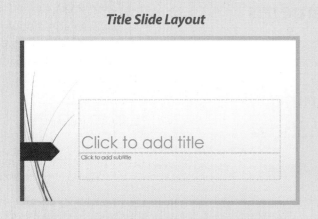

Use Content layouts such as Title and Content, Two Content, and Content with Caption to present concise bullet points or to insert graphics, videos, or photos for visual interest and richer communication.

Title and Content Layout

It is generally best to include no more than six bullet points per slide, and to keep the bullet points brief—fitting on a single line when possible. Bullet points guide the audience through the presentation and don't need to spell out every detail. The speaker's words are the focus and should provide the full story.

While you don't want to crowd your slides with information, you also don't want to overuse multimedia elements and animations. These features, used sparingly, can provide interest and entertain. But if overdone, they can distract viewers from your message (and greatly increase file size).

You can keep the look of your slides consistent by using a built-in design. The example slides on this page use the Wisp design. If you modify the design, a good tip is to avoid using more than two fonts on a single slide and two or three fonts in the entire presentation. Similarly, color can be used to help the audience focus on a word or point, but too many colors can be distracting.

Before you begin to create a PowerPoint presentation, you should choose a focused topic, define a clear purpose, and identify your audience. Ask yourself how much your audience members are likely to know about your topic, what they might do with the information, and whether they would appreciate humor, for example.

A well-organized slide show helps you lead your audience to the goal of your presentation. That goal may be to get them to take an action, such as joining a group or buying a new car, or it may be to give them the information they need to do their job, achieve a goal, or accomplish a task.

A PowerPoint presentation can be run manually with a person advancing the slides one at a time, or it can be set up to *run* automatically with each slide advancing itself after a set amount of time. A recorded narration can be included when there is no speaker present. Options in the Set Up Show dialog box can be used to set up your slide show.

Set Up Show Dialog Box

You can also present a PowerPoint presentation online, or publish a PowerPoint slide show to the web where anybody who accesses it can run the presentation at their convenience.

When a slide show is presented by a speaker, it is usually run in *Slide Show view*. In this view, slides are displayed in full-screen mode. Presentation tools are displayed in the Slide Show control bar in the lower left corner of the slide and can be

used to highlight points on a slide and control the order slides are presented.

When presenting a slide show using this method, it is important to rehearse your show to help avoid technical problems and to make sure the show runs within your allotted time slot, allowing time for audience questions.

You may also want to add *speaker notes* to your slides. Speaker notes are not visible to the audience when the presentation is run, but can be viewed by the presenter if the presentation is run in *Presenter view*.

Speaker notes can also be viewed and printed in *Notes Page view*.

Presenter View

Slide Show View

Notes Page View

Chapter 1

Creating a Presentation

Precheck

Check your understanding of the skills and features covered in this chapter.

In this chapter, you begin to build a simple slide show. Once you have created slide content, you reorganize the slides and apply different layouts and designs to enhance their visual impact.

PowerPoint offers several views for accomplishing these tasks, including Normal, Outline, Slide Sorter, Notes Page, and Reading. Most of your work building a slide show is done using *Normal view*, which splits the screen into three main sections, or panes. The *slide pane* includes a large view of an individual slide, the smaller *notes pane* is below the slide pane and provides an area for entering speaker notes, and the left side panel is called the *slide thumbnails pane*. You can click a slide thumbnail and view the corresponding slide in the larger slide pane.

slide thumbnails pane

slide pane

notes pane

In this chapter, you work with Normal view and Slide Sorter view. Slide Sorter view is the best view to use for organizing your presentation. You will also learn to run a slide show.

 **SNAP**   *If you are a SNAP user, go to your SNAP Assignments page to complete the Precheck, Tutorials, and Recheck.*

Skills You Learn

1. Open PowerPoint and insert a slide

2. Enter text on slides

3. Add notes

4. Apply a layout and run a slide show

5. Apply a theme

6. Organize slides using the Slide Sorter feature

Files You Need

For these skills, you do not need any student data files.

What You Create

The writers for *Guidelines for Healthy Living Magazine* present their article ideas to the editors before they begin writing. This team approach allows for the discussion of key points that should be in an article and also helps ensure the article will be appropriate for the upcoming magazine issue.

In this chapter, you create a simple PowerPoint presentation for an article about foods everyone should include in their diet. You create slides; enter text; add notes; and use layouts, themes, and color variants to add visual appeal. When the slides are completed, you use the Slide Sorter feature to rearrange them in a logical order.

"Foods You Should Eat" Presentation

Completed
Skill Preview

PowerPoint

Skill 1 Open PowerPoint and Insert a Slide

When you open PowerPoint, you can create a blank presentation or select a presentation template. A blank presentation contains a single title slide and is displayed in Normal view. Most slides contain placeholders. A *placeholder* is an element into which you can enter text or objects. A title slide contains a title placeholder, with the text *Click to add title*, and a subtitle placeholder, with the text *Click to add subtitle*. When you insert a new slide to follow the title slide, by default it has the Title and Content layout, which includes a title placeholder and a content placeholder. The content placeholder contains a bullet symbol and the words *Click to add text,* as well as buttons that can be clicked to add other objects, such as charts or videos, to the slide. When you insert additional new slides, each new slide has the same layout as the current slide.

Tutorial

▶**Tip** To open PowerPoint, type *powerpoint* in the search box on the Windows taskbar and then click *PowerPoint 2016 Desktop app* in the search results list.

7 *Shortcut*

Insert New Slide
Ctrl + M

7 *Another Way*

Right-click a slide in the slide thumbnails pane and then click the *New Slide* option in the pop-up list.

▶**Tip** To apply a different layout when you insert a new slide, click the New Slide arrow and then click the desired option in the drop-down list.

10 *Shortcut*

Save
Ctrl + S

Completed
Skill Preview

1 Open PowerPoint.

2 Click *Blank Presentation* to open a new, blank presentation in Normal view. The presentation contains one slide with the Title Slide layout.

3 Click the File tab and then click the *Save* option.

4 Click the *Browse* option.

5 In the Save As dialog box, navigate to the Unit 6 working folder you created on your storage medium.

6 Type C1S1-Food in the *File name* box and then click the Save button.

7 On the Home tab, click the New Slide button in the Slides group to insert a new slide with the Title and Content layout.

8 Click the New Slide button to insert another slide with the Title and Content layout.

9 Repeat Step 6 to insert two more slides with the Title and Content layout. The presentation now contains a total of five slides.

Completed Skill 1

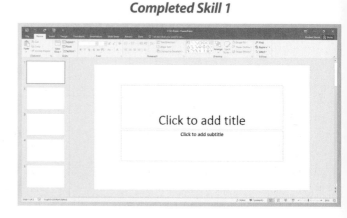

10 Click the Save button on the Quick Access Toolbar to save the file.

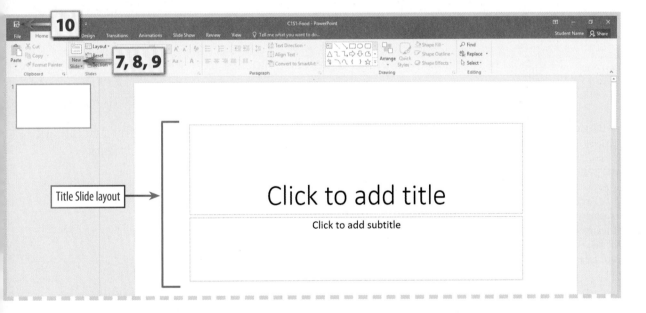

Taking It Further

Using a Template

When you open PowerPoint, you see the backstage area. Here you can select from a variety of templates that are preformatted, allowing you to quickly create a professional-looking presentation. If you do not see a template you want to use, you can type search criteria in the seach box. Links to suggested search criteria, such as <u>Business</u> and <u>Orientation</u>, are listed under the search box to help you find what you are looking for.

Skill 2 Enter Text on Slides

No matter how many graphics, videos, or animations you include in a slide show, the heart of your presentation is often the text. Text that you enter on slides helps reinforce the ideas presented, helps viewers focus on the key points of the presentation, and helps the speaker stay on track throughout the presentation. In this skill, you add text on slides in Normal view.

Tutorial

1 If it is not already open, open **C1S1-Food**, the file you saved in the previous skill, and save it as **C1S2-Food** in your Unit 6 working folder on your storage medium.

2 If the first slide does not already appear in the slide pane, click the first thumbnail in the slide thumbnails pane.

> **Tip** If you do not see the slide thumbnails pane in your presentation, click the View tab and then click the Normal button in the Presentation Views group.

3 In the slide pane, click the title placeholder (with the text *Click to add title*) and then type Foods You Should Eat.

4 Click the subtitle placeholder (with the text *Click to add subtitle*) and then type Guidelines for Healthy Living Magazine.

5 In the slide thumbnails pane, click Slide 2.

6 In the slide pane, click the title placeholder and then type Blueberries.

> **Tip** You press Enter to start a new bullet point in a content placeholder, but there is no need to press Enter in other types of placeholders. PowerPoint automatically wraps text to fit within the placeholder width, expanding the height of the placeholder as needed.

7 Click the content placeholder (formatted as a bulleted list by default) and then type the following text, pressing the Enter key as indicated:
High in antioxidants [Enter]
Help prevent heart disease [Enter]
Help with memory loss [Enter]
Recommended serving: 1/2 cup daily

8 In the slide thumbnails pane, click Slide 3.

9 In the slide pane, click the title placeholder and then type Garlic.

> **Tip** In PowerPoint, when you type two numbers with a forward slash between them (such as 1/2), PowerPoint automatically formats them as a fraction (½).

10 Click the content placeholder and then type the following text, pressing the Enter key as indicated:
Improves cholesterol levels [Enter]
Can boost your immune system [Enter]
Can lower blood pressure [Enter]
Recommended serving: 1 clove daily

> **Tip** If you accidentally press Enter after typing the last bullet point, press Ctrl + Z or Backspace to undo the action.

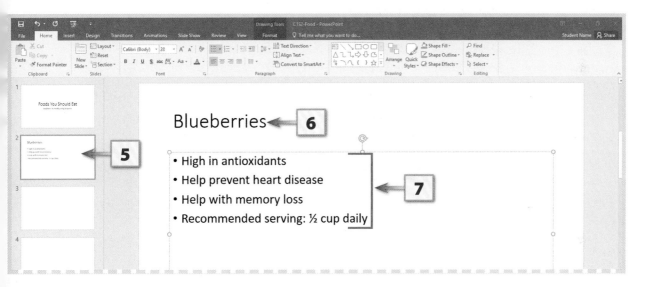

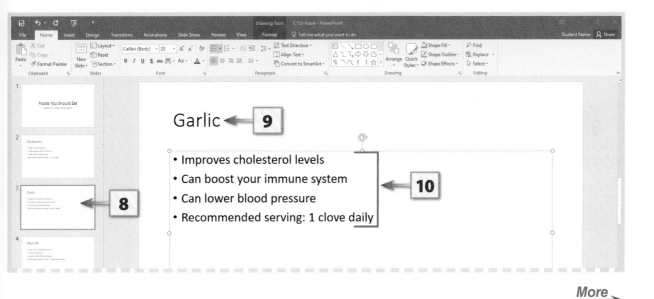

11 In the slide thumbnails pane, click Slide 4.

12 In the slide pane, click the title placeholder and then type Olive Oil.

▶**Tip** To edit text on a slide, select the text you need to change and then type the replacement text. You can also place the insertion point and use the Backspace and Delete keys to make edits as needed.

13 Click the content placeholder and then type the following text, pressing the Enter key after each line as indicated:
Improves cholesterol levels [Enter]
Rich in vitamin E [Enter]
Lowers risk of heart disease [Enter]
Recommended serving: 1 tablespoon daily

14 In the slide thumbnails pane, click Slide 5.

15 In the slide pane, click the title placeholder and then type Yogurt.

16 Click the content placeholder and then type the following text, pressing the Enter key as indicated:
Source of calcium [Enter]
Contains probiotics to help with digestion [Enter]
Source of protein [Enter]
Recommended serving: 3/4 cup daily

17 Click the Save button on the Quick Access Toolbar to save the file.

Completed Skill 2

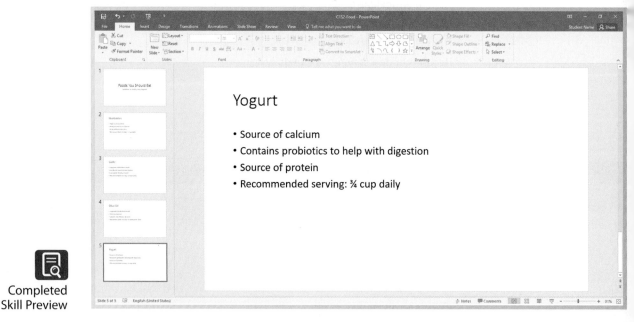

Completed
Skill Preview

Taking It Further ●●●●●●●●●●●●●●●●●●●●●●●●●●

Exploring Views

You can look at your PowerPoint slides in a number of different views. Normal view is the default view and is typically where a presentation is created. Slide Sorter view displays all the slides in the presentation on one screen as thumbnails. This view is often used to rearrange the order of slides. Notes Page view displays the current slide with any added notes below it. *Reading view* displays the slides in full-screen view and is often used to review a presentation. You can change views using buttons on the View tab. You can also change to Normal, Slide Sorter, Reading, or Slide Show view by using the following buttons in the view area of the Status bar: ▦ ▦ ▦ ▽ . If you do not see these buttons, right-click the Status bar and then click the *View Shortcuts* option to insert a check mark beside it.

PowerPoint

Skill 3 Add Notes

The text you type on a slide should consist of key points and serve as an outline for your presentation. If you need additional notes to remind you of everything you want to say during your presentation, you can enter speaker notes in the notes pane of each slide in Normal view. You can then switch to Notes Page view to view and print your speaker notes. If you deliver the slide show in Presenter view, the speaker notes will not be visible to the audience but will be visible to you. You will learn to deliver a presentation in Presenter view in Chapter 4.

Tutorial

1 If it is not already open, open **C1S2-Food**, the file you saved in the previous skill, and save it as **C1S3-Food**.

2 In the slide thumbnails pane, click Slide 2.

3 Click the View tab.

4 Click the Notes button in the Show group to display the notes pane at the bottom of the active slide.

> **Tip** If the notes pane is already displayed, skip Step 4.

> **4** *Another Way*
Click the Notes button (Notes) in the view area of the Status bar.

5 Click the notes placeholder (with the text *Click to add notes*) and then type Blueberries rank the highest of any fruit for antioxidants.

> **Tip** Enlarge the notes pane when in Normal view by dragging the line dividing it from the slide pane upward.

6 In the slide thumbnails pane, click Slide 5.

7 Click the notes placeholder and then type Yogurt is also a source of potassium, zinc, and vitamin B5.

8 Click the Notes Page button in the Presentation Views group to display Slide 5 along with the associated note.

> **9** *Another Way*
Click the Normal button ( ) in the view area of the Status bar.

9 Click the Normal button in the Presentation View group to return to Normal view.

10 Save the file.

Completed Skill 3

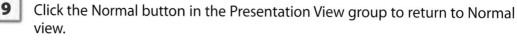

Completed
Skill Preview

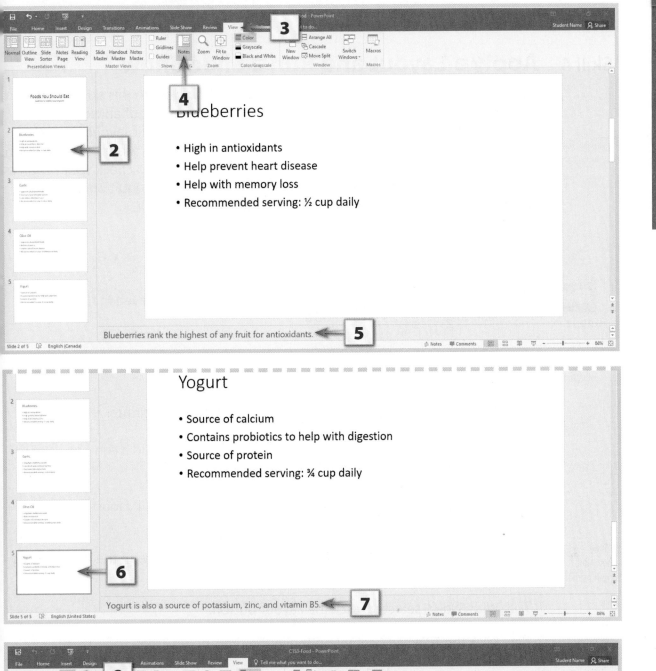

Taking It Further

Formatting Speaker Notes

The default font and size for notes is Calibri 12 points. To change the font or font size to make your notes easier to read, click the notes box in Notes Page view. A solid border appears around the notes text frame. You can then click the Font arrow or Font Size arrow in the Font group on the Home tab and click a different font or size in the drop-down list.

Skill 4 Apply a Layout and Run a Slide Show

The way placeholders are arranged on a slide is known as a *layout*. You can apply an existing layout to a new slide or design your own layout for the content you wish to present. Layouts can include titles, subtitles, one or two content placeholders, or captions. They can even be blank, with no placeholders. In this skill, you will change the layout of an existing slide and apply a specific layout to a new slide. You will also run the slide show in Slide Show view to check your progress and view the presentation as the audience will see it.

Tutorial

1 If it is not already open, open **C1S3-Food**, the file you saved in the previous skill, and save it as **C1S4-Food**.

2 With your presentation displaying in Normal view, click Slide 5 in the slide thumbnails pane, if it is not already selected.

3 On the Home tab, click the Layout button in the Slides group.

4 Click the *Two Content* option in the drop-down list to add a content placeholder to the right side of Slide 5.

5 Click the right content placeholder and then type Not all yogurt is made equal, so be sure to check the label.

6 Click the New Slide button to insert a new slide (Slide 6) with the Two Content layout.

7 With Slide 6 selected, click the Layout button.

8 Click the *Title and Content* option in the drop-down list to apply that layout to Slide 6.

9 Click the title placeholder and then type Cinnamon.

10 Click the content placeholder and then type the following text, pressing the Enter key as indicated:
Contains antioxidants [Enter]
Has anti-inflammatory properties [Enter]
Helps fight bacterial infections [Enter]
Recommended serving: ½ teaspoon daily

11 Save the file.

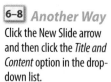
> **Tip** The New Slide button inserts a new slide with the same layout as the previous slide.

6–8 *Another Way*
Click the New Slide arrow and then click the *Title and Content* option in the drop-down list.

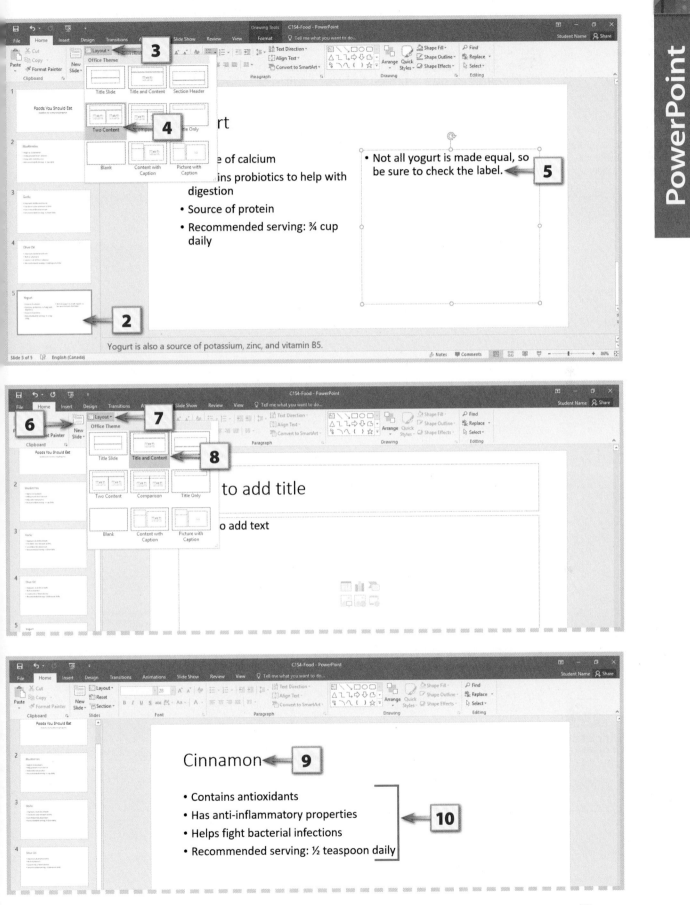

Tip Running a slide show is covered in further detail in Chapter 4.

13 *Shortcut*
Start Slide Show from Beginning
F5

14 *Shortcut*
Advance to Next Slide
Page Down
Down Arrow
Right Arrow
Enter

 Use Your Touchscreen
To advance to the next slide, swipe to the left.

15 *Shortcut*
End Slide Show
Esc

12 Click the Slide Show tab.

13 Click the From Beginning button in the Start Slide Show group to start the slide show and display Slide 1 full-size on your screen.

14 Click anywhere on the screen to advance to Slide 2.

15 Click to advance through the remaining slides. When you reach the screen that reads *End of slide show, click to exit,* click to return to Normal view.

Completed Skill 4

Foods You Should Eat
Guidelines for Healthy Living Magazine

Blueberries
- High in antioxidants
- Help prevent heart disease
- Help with memory loss
- Recommended serving: ½ cup daily

Garlic
- Improves cholesterol levels
- Can boost your immune system
- Can lower blood pressure
- Recommended serving: 1 clove daily

Olive Oil
- Improves cholesterol levels
- Rich in vitamin E
- Lowers risk of heart disease
- Recommended serving: 1 tablespoon daily

Yogurt
- Source of calcium
- Contains probiotics to help with digestion
- Source of protein
- Recommended serving: ¾ cup daily

- Not all yogurt is made equal, so be sure to check the label.

Cinnamon
- Contains antioxidants
- Has anti-inflammatory properties
- Helps fight bacterial infections
- Recommended serving: ½ teaspoon daily

Completed
Skill Preview

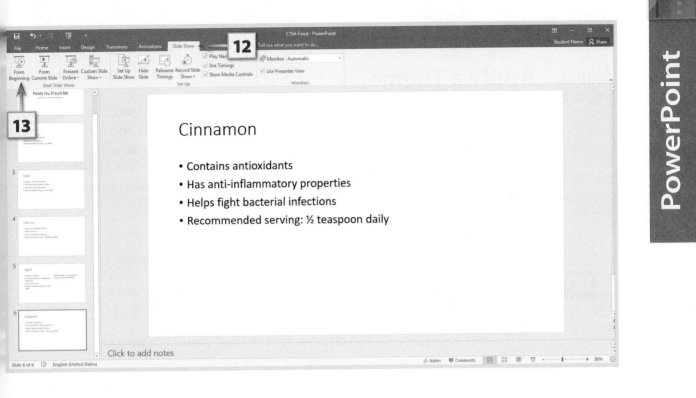

Taking It Further ●

Working with Placeholders

The predefined layouts in PowerPoint contain a variety of placeholders, such as title, content, and caption. If you can't find a predefined layout that works for your slide, you can modify a layout by inserting text boxes to create placeholders. A *text box* is a text container. To insert a text box, click the Text Box button in the Text group on the Insert tab, click a blank area of the slide, and then drag to create the text box. You can then add content and drag the placeholder to an appropriate location on the slide. You can also delete a placeholder from a slide; however, blank placeholders are not visible during the viewing of a presentation.

Skill 5 Apply a Theme

Just as the Layout feature controls the type and number of placeholders on slides, the Themes feature controls the color scheme, fonts, and effects on slides. You can apply a theme to a presentation to give it a professional appearance. A theme is a quick way to format a presentation, as it applies coordinating colors and fonts along with a matching background to all the slides in the presentation in one step. A *color variant* can be applied to give the theme a variety of looks.

Tutorial

▶ **Tip** You can search for additional PowerPoint themes in the New backstage area.

▶ **Tip** In Step 4, hover your mouse pointer over each theme to display a ScreenTip with the name of the theme.

1 If it is not already open, open **C1S4-Food**, the file you saved in the previous skill, and save it as **C1S5-Food**.

2 With your presentation displaying in Normal view, click the Design tab.

3 Click the More button in the Themes group.

4 Click the *Wisp* theme in the drop-down gallery to apply that theme to all slides in the presentation.

5 Click the third color variation of the Wisp design theme in the Variants group.

6 Save the file.

Completed Skill 5

Completed
Skill Preview

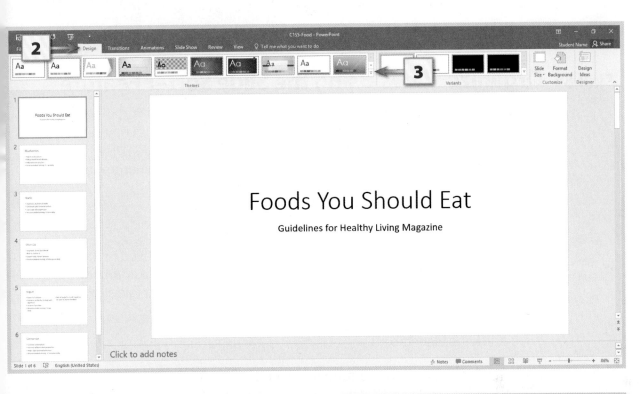

Taking It Further

Changing Slide Size

The default slide size in PowerPoint 2016 is widescreen (16:9). You can resize your slides by clicking the Slide Size button in the Customize group on the Design tab and then clicking the *Standard (4:3)* option or the *Customize Slide Size* option in the drop-down list.

Skill 6 **Organize Slides Using the Slide Sorter Feature**

The best view for reorganizing slides is *Slide Sorter view*. This view presents thumbnail images of your slides in rows and columns so you can view several at once and think about your options for organizing them. You can drag slides from one position to another in the Slide Sorter view and determine the best arrangement for your presentation.

Tutorial

1 If it is not already open, open **C1S5-Food**, the file you saved in the previous skill, and save it as **C1S6-Food-Lastname**, but replace *Lastname* with your last name. Be sure to save the file in your Unit 6 working folder on your storage medium.

2–3 *Another Way*
Click the Slide Sorter button ( ) on the Status bar.

2 Click the View tab.

3 Click the Slide Sorter button in the Presentation Views group.

4 Point to Slide 2 (titled *Blueberries*), press and hold the left mouse button, and then drag the slide to the space between Slide 3 and Slide 4.

5 Release the mouse button to place the slide in the new position. Notice that the slides renumber.

6 Click Slide 5 (titled *Yogurt*), press and hold down the Shift key, and then click Slide 6 (titled *Cinnamon*). Notice that both Slides 5 and 6 are now selected.

▶ **Tip** If you need to move more than one slide, use the Shift key to select multiple contiguous slides. Use the Ctrl key to select multiple noncontiguous slides.

7 Point to Slide 5 or 6, press and hold the left mouse button, drag the slides to the space between Slide 1 (titled *Foods You Should Eat*), and Slide 2 (titled *Garlic*), and then release the mouse button.

8 Save and close the file.

Completed Skill 6

Completed
Skill Preview

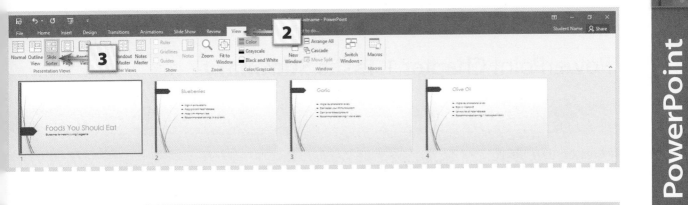

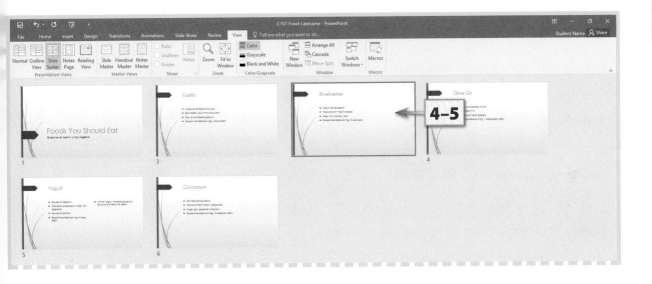

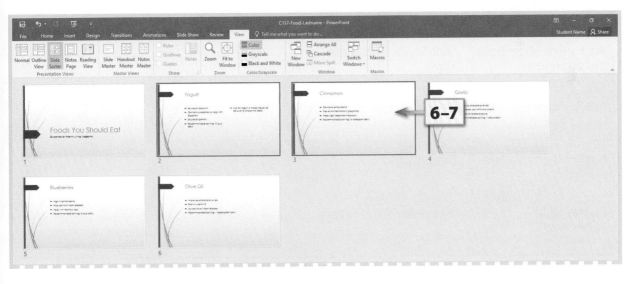

Taking It Further ●

Deleting, Inserting, and Duplicating Slides in Slide Sorter View

You can delete a slide or add a new slide while in Slide Sorter view. Right-click a slide and then click the *Delete Slide* or *New Slide* option in the pop-up list. You can also duplicate a slide in Slide Sorter view by right-clicking the slide you want to duplicate and then clicking the *Duplicate Slide* option.

PowerPoint Chapter 1 **Tasks Summary**

Task	Ribbon Tab, Group	Button, Option	Shortcut, Alternative
Create a new, blank presentation	File, New	Blank Presentation	Ctrl + N
Insert a new slide	Home, Slides	New Slide	Ctrl + M
Display Normal view	View, Presentation Views	Normal	on Status bar
Save a presentation	File, Save		Ctrl + S; on Quick Access Toolbar
Display notes pane	View, Show	Notes	Notes on Status bar
Display Notes Page view	View, Presentation Views	Notes Page	
Apply a layout	Home, Slides	Layout	
Start a slide show from the beginning	Slide Show, Start Slide Show	From Beginning	F5; on Status bar
Apply a theme	Design, Themes		
Apply a theme variant	Design, Variants		
Display Slide Sorter view	View, Presentation Views	Slide Sorter	on Status bar

Recheck

Recheck your understanding of the skills and features covered in this chapter.

Workbook

Chapter study resources, exercises, and assessments are available in the Workbook ebook.

Chapter 2

Customizing a Slide Show

Precheck

Check your understanding of the skills and features covered in this chapter.

A presentation contains at least one slide master. The *slide master* stores details about the presentation's design theme, including its slide layout and formatting. When you make a change to the slide master, that change is automatically applied to every slide in your presentation. For example, if you change the font color on the slide master, the font color will automatically change on all the slides in your presentation. This can save you a lot of work because you only have to make the change on one slide as opposed to every slide in the presentation.

If you create a blank presentation, the Office Theme will be applied to the presentation's slide master. The Office Theme contains no background or graphics but does assign font formatting and layouts to all placeholders in the slide presentation. If you apply a different design theme, like you did in Chapter 1, the slide master will contain the formatting and layout associated with the selected theme.

In this chapter, you will use *Slide Master view* to change the formatting of the slide master and insert a logo. You will change the formatting for a particular type of placeholder on all slides and hide background graphics on individual slides. You will also switch to Normal view and insert a footer to identify the slides in your presentation.

This chapter shows you how to customize your presentation using Slide Master view. Knowing how to work with slide masters will come in handy when you can't find a theme that is quite right or when you want to design a customized presentation.

Skills You Learn

1   Change formatting in Slide Master view

2   Insert a picture in Slide Master view

3   Hide and modify slide master elements on a slide

4   Change the color scheme in Slide Master view

5   Add a footer

If you are a SNAP user, go to your SNAP Assignments page to complete the Precheck, Tutorials, and Recheck.

Files You Need
For these skills, you need the following student data file:

C2S1-Food

What You Create
In this chapter, you continue to develop the "Foods You Should Eat" article presentation that you started in Chapter 1. You change the formatting and insert a graphic in Slide Master view. You then hide the background graphics on a slide that appears cluttered and format the background gradient color. You also change the color scheme to go with the color palette that has been chosen for this issue of the magazine. Finally, in Normal view, you add a footer to your slides.

"Foods You Should Eat" Presentation

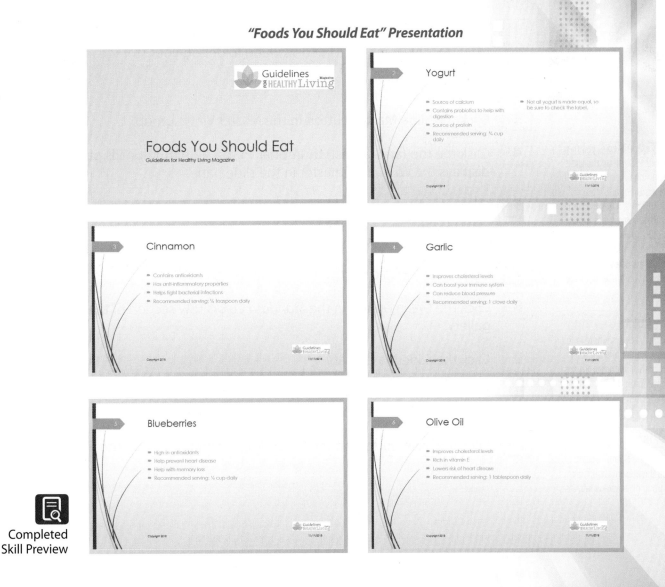

Completed
Skill Preview

Skill 1

Change Formatting in Slide Master View

In Chapter 1, you applied the Wisp theme to your presentation. You like the way the theme presents the slide content, but you would like the content text to display in a green font instead of a black font. This font color change will coordinate better with the magazine logo. It would be time-consuming to format the content of every slide individually. An alternative is to change the formatting of the content placeholder in the slide master and this change will apply to the content placeholder of every slide that uses that slide master. In Slide Master view, the slide master is the top and largest thumbnail in the slide thumbnails pane. The smaller thumbnails are slide masters for the different slide layouts and allow you to make changes to all the slides with a specific layout, such as the Title and Content layout.

Tutorial

1 Open the student data file named **C2S1-Food** and, if you have not already done so, save it in your Unit 6 working folder on your storage medium.

2 Click the View tab.

3 Click the Slide Master button in the Master Views group.

4 Click the top (and largest) thumbnail in the slide thumbnails pane. This action displays the Wisp slide master in the slide pane.

▶**Tip** In Step 4, you may need to scroll up the slide thumbnails pane to find the top thumbnail.

▶**Tip** Hover your mouse pointer over a thumbnail to display the name of the slide layout and find out which slides use that slide master.

5 Click anywhere in the content placeholder text *Edit Master text styles*.

6 Click the Home tab.

7 Click the Font Color arrow in the Font group.

8 Click the *Green* option in the *Standard Colors* row section of the drop-down gallery.

5–8 *Another Way* Right-click anywhere in the placeholder text and then click the *Font* option in the pop-up list. Make changes to the font in the Font dialog box.

9 Click the Slide Master tab.

10 Click the Close Master View button in the Close group to return to the previous view—in this case, Normal view.

9–10 *Another Way* Click the Normal button in the Presentation Views group on the View tab.

11 Click the Save button on the Quick Access Toolbar to save the file.

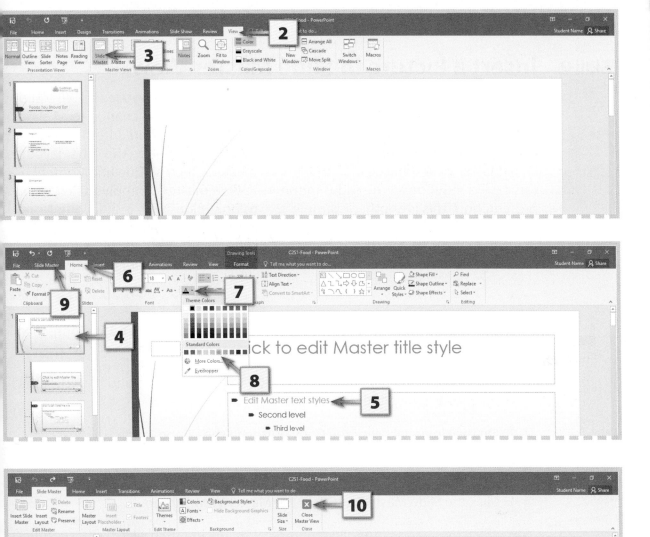

Completed Skill 1

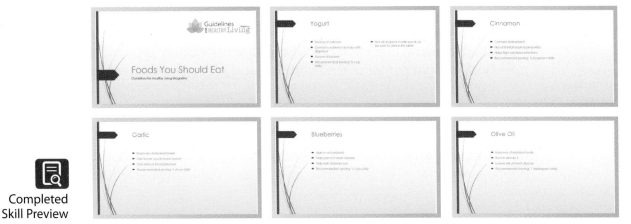

Completed
Skill Preview

Skill 2 **Insert a Picture in Slide Master View**

In Chapter 2, you used the Wisp Theme Slide Master to change the font color of the content text on all slides in a single action. In this skill, you will use Slide Master view to place a picture (in this case, a logo) on all the slides in the presentation. This is another example of how Slide Master view can save you time and help you avoid having to modify every slide in a presentation.

Skills 1 and 2 both use the Wisp Slide Master to make a change to all slides in the presentation. Alternatively, you could select one of the other layout masters, such as Title and Content Layout master, to apply the change to only slides with that layout. *Note: See Chapter 3 for information about using pictures, videos, and other graphic objects in PowerPoint presentations.*

Tutorial

1 If it is not already open, open the student data file named **C2S1-Food**, the file you saved in the previous skill, and save it as **C2S2-Food**.

2 In Normal view, click Slide 1 in the slide thumbnails pane and then click the magazine logo in the slide pane.

3 *Shortcut*
Copy
Ctrl + C

3 On the Home tab, click the Copy button in the Clipboard group.

4 Click the View tab.

5 Click the Slide Master button in the Master Views group.

6 Scroll to the top of the slide thumbnails pane and then click the Wisp slide master.

7 Click the Home tab.

8 *Shortcut*
Paste
Ctrl + V

8 Click the Paste button in the Clipboard group to paste the copied logo into the slide master.

9 Click the Picture Tools Format tab.

10 *Another Way*
Click the decrement arrow on the *Width* box.

10 Click in the *Width* box in the Size group, type 2, and then press the Enter key.

11 *Another Way*
Click the object to select it and then use the arrow keys to move the selected object on the slide.

11 Hover your mouse pointer over the logo until the pointer becomes a four-headed arrow, press and hold the left mouse button, drag the logo to the bottom right corner of the content placeholder, and then release the mouse button.

12 Click the View tab.

13 Click the Normal button in the Presentation Views group. Notice that the logo appears in the bottom right corner of all slides in the presentation.

14 Save the file.

Completed Skill 2

Completed
Skill Preview

PowerPoint

Skill 3 Hide and Modify Slide Master Elements on a Slide

In Skill 2, you used Slide Master view to insert the magazine logo on all the slides in the presentation. When you preview the presentation, you notice that adding the logo makes one slide look too crowded and that the logo now appears twice on the title slide. Images added in Slide Master view cannot be deleted or modified on individual slides, but you are able to hide background graphics you added in Slide Master view on individual slides. Changes made on individual slides override slide master settings.

In this skill, you hide the magazine logo on Slide 1 and then modify elements of the Wisp theme on that slide. You also format the appearance of the background gradient fill. A *gradient fill* creates a three-dimensional look by gradually changing from one color to another.

Tutorial

1 If it is not already open, open the student data file named **C2S2-Food**, the file you saved in the previous skill, and save it as **C2S3-Food**.

2 In Normal view, click Slide 1 in the slide thumbnails pane.

3 Click the Design tab.

4 Click the Format Background button in the Customize group.

▶**Tip** Hiding background graphics hides all graphics on the slide master for the current slide. If you have more than one graphic in the slide master, you cannot hide each individually.

5 In the Format Background pane, click the *Hide background graphics* check box to insert a check mark. The magazine logo from the slide master and the Wisp theme graphic both disappear.

6 Click the *Type* arrow and then click the *Radial* option in the drop-down list to change the background gradient on the Title slide from a straight progression to a circular progression.

7 Click the *Brightness* increment (up) arrow until the measurement box displays *25%* to adjust the background color level brightness on the Title slide.

8 Close the Format Background pane.

9 Save the file.

Completed Skill 3

Completed
Skill Preview

Guidelines
HEALTHY Living

Foods You Should Eat

Guidelines for Healthy Living Magazine

PowerPoint

Skill 4 · Change the Color Scheme in Slide Master View

The colors used for text, slide backgrounds, and graphical elements are preset by the theme and variant you apply. However, once you have applied a theme, you can change its color palette to enhance your presentation or adjust it for clearer viewing. The background color drop-down gallery enables you to preview color schemes on your slide before you choose one. Changing the color palette on the slide master is a quick way to update your entire presentation with a coordinated, predesigned color scheme.

1 If it is not already open, open the student data file named **C2S3-Food**, the file you saved in the previous skill, and save it as **C2S4-Food**.

2 In Normal view, click the View tab.

3 Click the Slide Master button in the Master Views group.

4 Scroll to the top of the slide thumbnail pane, and then click the top (and largest) thumbnail.

▶**Tip** To view the name of the currently applied color scheme, hover your mouse pointer over the Colors button. The current theme name is listed in the *Theme Colors* information box that appears.

5 Click the Colors button in the Background group.

6 Scroll down and click the *Aspect* option in the drop-down gallery.

7 Click the Close Master View button in the Close group to return to Normal view.

▶**Tip** To create a custom color scheme, click *Customize Colors* in the Colors drop-down gallery.

8 Save the file.

Completed Skill 4

Completed
Skill Preview

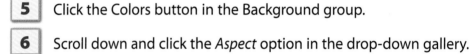

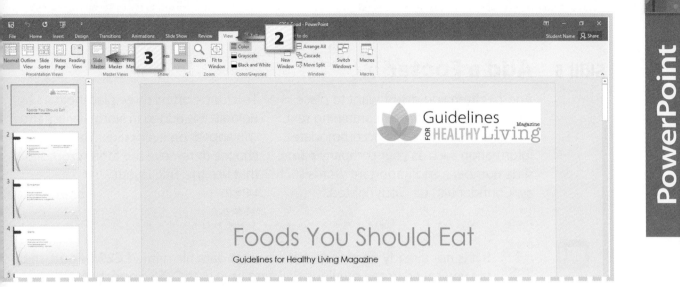

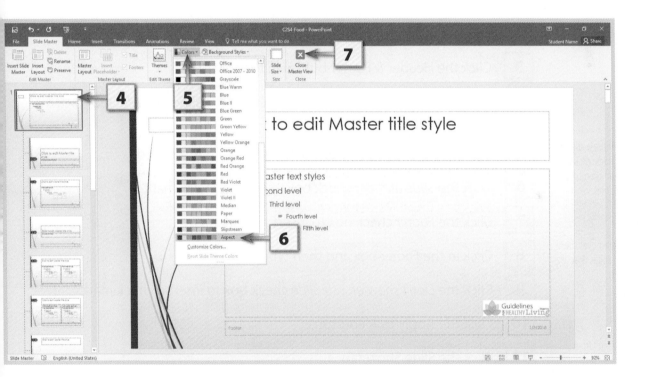

Taking It Further

Customizing in Slide Master View

Along with changing the color scheme in Slide Master view, you can also change the fonts used in the presentation by clicking the Font button in the Background group on the Slide Master tab and selecting a font option. Similarly, you can click the Effects button in the Background group to choose from a variety of built-in effects, with features including shadows, reflections, lines, and fills.

Skill 5 **Add a Footer**

Another item you might want to place on every slide is a footer containing text. Footer placeholders can accommodate information such as your company name, slide numbers, and important words such as "Confidential" or "Copyrighted."

The footer offers three placeholders by default. It is added in Normal view and will appear on every slide. You can choose to remove the footer from slides that use the Title layout.

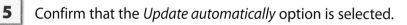

Tutorial

1 If it is not already open, open the student data file named **C2S4-Food**, the file you saved in the previous skill, and save it as **C2S5-Food**, but replace *Lastname* with your last name. Be sure to save the file in your Unit 6 working folder on your storage medium.

2 In Normal view, click the Insert tab.

3 Click the Header & Footer button in the Text group.

4 In the Header and Footer dialog box with the Slide tab selected, click the *Date and time* check box to insert a check mark.

> **Tip** If you want a specific date on your slides, click the *Fixed* option and then type the date in the box.

5 Confirm that the *Update automatically* option is selected.

6 Click the *Slide number* check box to insert a check mark.

7 Click the *Footer* check box to insert a check mark.

> **Tip** Step 9 removes the footer from all slides that use the Title layout.

8 Click in the *Footer* box and then type Copyright 2018.

9 Click the *Don't show on title slide* check box to insert a check mark.

10 Click the Apply to All button.

11 Click the Slide Show tab.

> **Tip** To navigate from slide to slide in Step 12, click the left mouse button or press the Page Down, Right Arrow, Down Arrow, or Enter key.

12 Click the From Beginning button in the Start Slide Show group and then navigate through the slide show to view the changes you have made in this chapter. Click at the end of the slide show to return to Normal view.

Taking It Further

Customizing Slide Footers

You can apply a different footer to individual slide by selecting the slide, choosing options in the Header and Footer dialog box, and then clicking the Apply button. If only a few slides require a different footer, you can save time by applying a global footer to all slides and then making footer changes on the few individual slides one by one.

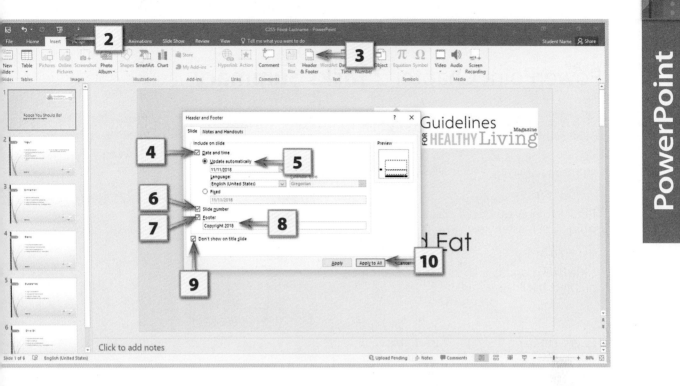

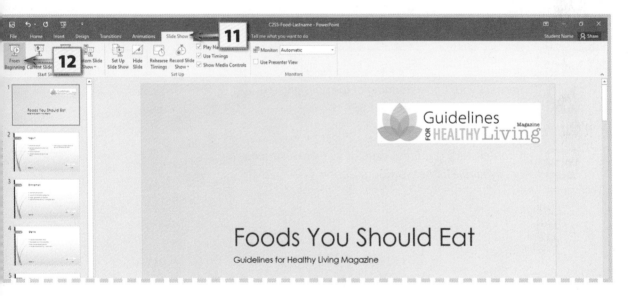

Completed Skill 5

Completed
Skill Preview

PowerPoint Chapter 2 **Tasks Summary**

Task	Ribbon Tab, Group	Button, Option	Shortcut, Alternative
Open Slide Master view	View, Master Views	Slide Master	
Return to previous view from Slide Master view	Slide Master, Close	Close Master View	
Hide background graphics in slide masters	Design, Customize	Format Background, *Hide background graphics*	
Insert a footer	Insert, Text	Header & Footer	
Change the color scheme in Slide Master view	View, Background	Colors	

Recheck

Recheck your understanding of the skills and features covered in this chapter.

Workbook

Chapter study resources, exercises, and assessments are available in the Workbook ebook.

Adding Media Elements and Effects

Precheck

Check your understanding of the skills and features covered in this chapter.

PowerPoint slides typically use words to communicate the ideas in your presentation, but visuals and other media can help reinforce those ideas and make your slides more attractive. Media elements and effects may include photos or illustrations, transition effects for moving from one slide to another, sounds, animated sequences, and video clips. When you combine these elements in your presentation, you get your message across and keep your audience engaged and entertained.

Skills You Learn

1. Insert and position a picture
2. Format a picture
3. Insert a video
4. Add transitions
5. Add sound
6. Add animations
7. Choose animation effects
8. Format individual slides

Files You Need

For these skills, you need the following student data files:

  C3S1-Food

  C3S1-Logo

  C3S3-FoodLabels

 If you are a SNAP user, go to your SNAP Assignments page to complete the Precheck, Tutorials, and Recheck.

What You Create

In Chapters 1 and 2 of this unit, you created a PowerPoint presentation to outline ideas for an article about foods everyone should include in their diet to the editors at *Guidelines for Healthy Living Magazine*. In this chapter, you enhance the presentation to include visual and other media elements, including images, a video, transitions, sound effects, and animations. You learn how to work with visual objects in slides and apply basic formatting to those objects. You use effects to transition between slides and add animations that put slide objects in motion. You also add sound effects to transitions in your presentation and format individual slides.

"Foods You Should Eat" Presentation with Media

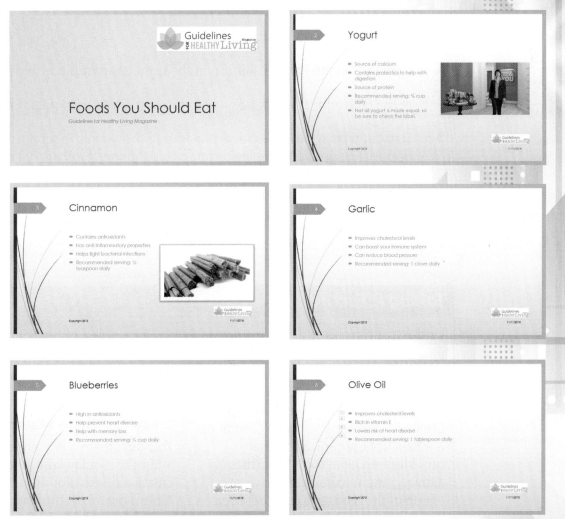

Completed
Skill Preview

Skill 1   Insert and Position a Picture

Adding a picture to a slide can make the content more interesting and engaging. Pictures also provide visuals to help the audience understand the slide content. You can insert a picture file from your computer or search for online pictures. The content placeholder on a slide contains placeholder buttons that can be used to insert various objects including pictures and online pictures. For example, clicking the Online Picture button displays a dialog box with an option to use the Bing search engine to search for pictures. Alternatively, you can use buttons on the Insert tab to insert pictures.

Tutorial

Insert an Online Picture

1   Open the student data file named **C3S1-Food** and, if you have not already done so, save it in your Unit 6 working folder on your storage medium.

2   In the slide thumbnails pane, click Slide 3.

 Another Way
Click the Online Pictures button in the Images group on the Insert tab.

3   Click the Online Pictures button in the right content placeholder.

4   In the *Bing Image Search* box, type cinnamon, and then press Enter.

5   Scroll and then click the cinnamon image shown in the screenshot on the opposite page. *Note: Online pictures may change. If you are not able to find the image shown here, select a similar image.*

6   Click the Insert button.

Taking It Further ● ● ● ● ● ● ● ● ● ● ● ● ●

Understanding Creative Commons

When searching for pictures using the Bing Image search feature, the images displayed in the search results are images that are licensed under Creative Commons. *Creative Commons* is a nonprofit organization that provides free legal tools for artists, allowing them to select from a set of copyright licenses to protect their creative works. Creative Commons has a large collection of content, including songs, videos, pictures, and academic material, that are free and legal to use.

Be sure to review the license details for any item you use and comply with the requirements.

Creating a Photo Album

You can create a PowerPoint photo album to display your photographs. To create a photo album, click the Photo Album button in the Images group on the Insert tab and then click *New Photo Album*. You can then navigate to the appropriate location to insert your pictures.

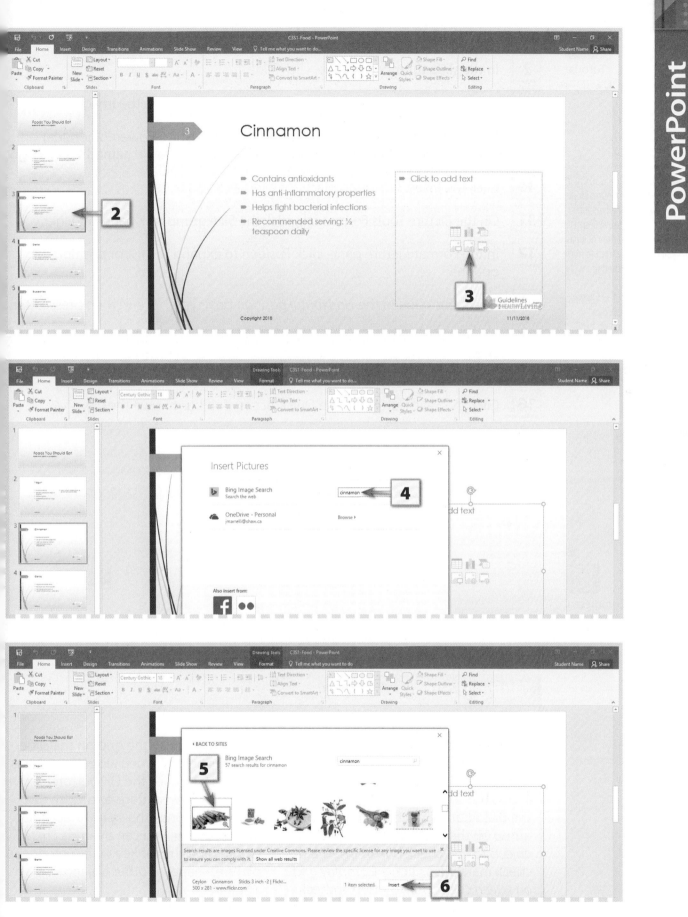

More ➤

Chapter 3 Adding Media Elements and Effects   409

Tutorial

Insert and Position a Picture File

7 In the slide thumbnails pane, click Slide 1.

8 Click the Insert tab and then click the Pictures button in the Images group.

9 In the Insert Picture dialog box, navigate to the Unit6-PowerPoint folder on your storage medium and then click the student data file named **C3S1-Logo**.

▶**Tip** If you are working in Office 365, the Design Ideas pane will open when you insert the picture in Step 10, presenting a variety of ideas you can choose from to make your slide look better.

10 Click the Insert button to place the picture on Slide 1.

11 On the Picture Tools Format tab, click the Size group task pane launcher.

12 In the Format Picture pane, click *Position* to expand the list of position options.

▶**Tip** Steps 11–15 show how to place an object in an exact location on a slide. You can place objects in approximate locations by dragging them.

13 Select the value in the *Horizontal position* box, type 7.6, and then press Enter.

14 Select the value in the *Vertical position* box, type 0.6, and then press Enter.

15 Close the Format Picture pane.

16 Click the Save button on the Quick Access Toolbar to save the file.

Completed Skill 1, Slides 1 and 3

Completed
Skill Preview

Taking It Further ●

Snapping Pictures and Objects to a Grid

You can use the *Snap* feature to align pictures, shapes, and other objects to a specific location on a slide. You access the snap-to options by clicking the dialog box launcher in the Show group on the View tab. Click the *Snap objects to grid* check box to insert a check mark. Also click the *Display grid on screen* check box to insert a check mark and display the grid on the slide, which is helpful when aligning pictures and objects. Click the OK button to apply the new settings and close the dialog box. Once the snap-to options are turned on, you can override them by pressing the Alt key while you drag a picture, shape, or other object.

Skill 2 Format a Picture

PowerPoint provides several tools for formatting pictures, including the ability to set a frame around a picture, add shadows or a glowing effect to a border, add artistic effects, modify photo colors and brightness, and crop or resize an image. You can take advantage of these tools to give your picture a unique appearance.

1 If it is not already open, open **C3S1-Food**, the file you saved in the previous skill, and save it as **C3S2-Food**.

2 In the slide thumbnails pane, click Slide 3.

3–11 *Another Way*
Right-click the image and then click the *Format Picture* option in the pop-up list. In the Format Picture pane, click the Effects button and then click options to make the changes listed in Steps 4–12.

3 In the slide pane, click the cinnamon image.

4 Click the Picture Tools Format tab.

5 Click the More button in the Picture Styles group.

6 Click the *Moderate Frame, White* option in the drop-down gallery to select it.

7 Click the Picture Effects button.

8 Click the *Glow* option in the drop-down list.

9 Click the *Dark Green, 8 pt glow, Accent color 4* option in the *Glow Variations* section.

▶**Tip** If you want to change the color of the image itself, click the Color button in the Adjust group and then click an option in the *Recolor* section of the drop-down gallery.

10 Click the Artistic Effects button in the Adjust group.

11 Click the *Texturizer* option in the drop-down gallery.

12 Save the file.

Completed Skill 2, Slide 3

Completed Skill Preview

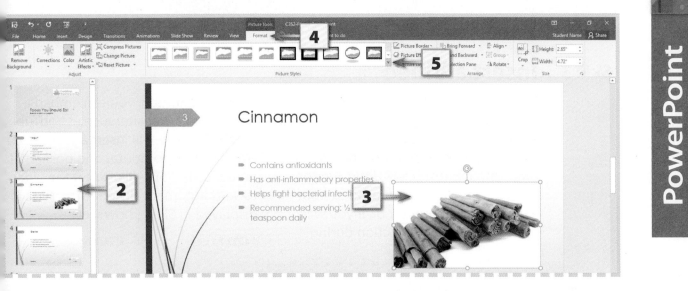

Skill 3 Insert a Video

PowerPoint allows you to insert a video on a slide and play the video during your presentation. Adding a video can make your presentation more engaging and interesting to the audience. You can insert a video from a file on your computer or, if you will have an Internet connection during your presentation, you can embed a video from a website, such as YouTube. In this skill, you will insert a video from a file on your computer and position it on the slide. You will also set the video to start automatically once the slide is displayed in Slide Show view.

Tutorial

1 If it is not already open, open **C3S2-Food**, the file you saved in the previous skill, and save it as **C3S3-Food**.

2 In the slide thumbnails pane, click Slide 2.

3–4 *Another Way*

Click the Video button in the Media group on the Insert tab and then click the *Video on My PC* option in the drop-down list.

3 Click the Insert Video button in the right content placeholder.

4 In the Insert Video dialog box, click the *From a file* Browse button.

5 In the Insert Video dialog box, navigate to the Unit6-PowerPoint folder on your storage medium and then click the student data file named **C3S3-FoodLabels**.

6 Click the Insert button.

7 Click the Video Tools Playback tab.

8 Click the Start arrow in the Video options group, and then click the *Automatically* option in the drop-down list.

▶ **Tip** The Video Tools Playback tab contains options for playing the video, such as playing it full screen and specifying a video starting point.

9 Click the Play button in the Preview group.

10 Save the file.

Completed Skill 3, Slide 2

**Completed
Skill Preview**

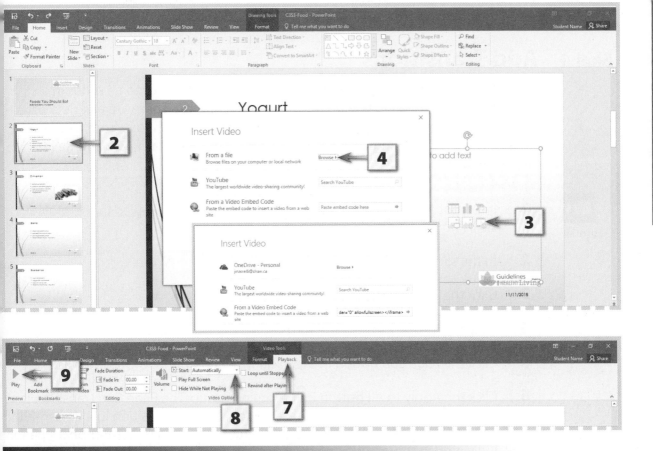

Taking It Further

Embedding a Video

Embedding a video involves inserting code that creates a video object and links the object to the source video so you can play it in your presentation. To embed a YouTube video in a PowerPoint slide, click the slide, click the Video button in the Media group on the Insert tab, and then click the *Online Video* option in the drop-down list. In the Insert Video dialog box, click in the *Search YouTube* box, type the name of the video (if you know it) or a keyword, and then press the Enter key. Click the video link in the search results and then click the Insert button.

Alternatively, you can open your Internet browser, go to www.youtube.com, click in the search box, type the name of the video or a keyword, click the video link to open the video,

right-click the video, and then click the *Get embed code* option in the pop-up list. You can then switch to PowerPoint, click the slide you want to insert the video on, click the Online Video button in the Media group on the Insert tab, click in the *From a Video Embed Code* box, and then click the Paste button in the Clipboard group on the Home tab.

Be aware that when you embed a video, you are actually inserting a link to the video, not the video file itself, and you will rely on a live Internet connection to play the video during a presentation. During your presentation, you may run into problems such as a content filter blocking the video or a weak Internet connection slowing or interrupting the video.

Copyright and Video

Before you use a video in a presentation, make sure you are not violating any copyright laws. If the video is posted on a website, you need to read the website policy (usually a link at the bottom of the website home page) to determine

if you are able to use the video. If the video is from a government site, such as the video in this skill, you are usually able use it without having to obtain permission unless otherwise noted.

PowerPoint

Skill 4   Add Transitions

Slide transitions are visual effects that occur when you move from slide to slide in Slide Show view. You can apply transition effects to a single slide, to multiple slides, or to all slides in a presentation. There are a variety of transitions to choose from, such as Blinds Horizontal, Push, and Reveal.

Tutorial

1 If it is not already open, open **C3S3-Food**, the file you saved in the previous skill, and save it as **C3S4-Food**.

2 In the slide thumbnails pane, click Slide 1.

3 Click the Transitions tab.

4 Click the More button in the Transition to This Slide group.

5 Click the *Page Curl* option in the *Exciting* section of the drop-down list.

6 Click the Apply to All button in the Timing group. The Page Curl transition is applied to all the slides in the presentation. A small transition icon (resembling a sliding star) appears below each slide number in the slide thumbnails pane, indicating that the transition has been applied to each slide.

7 Save the file.

8 Click the Slide Show tab.

9 Click the From Beginning button in the Start Slide Show group.

10 Navigate through the slide show to view the transition effects you applied. Click at the end of the slide show to return to Normal view.

▶ *Tip* To navigate from slide to slide in Step 10, click the left mouse button or press the Page Down, Right Arrow, Down Arrow, or Enter key.

Completed Skill 4

Completed Skill Preview

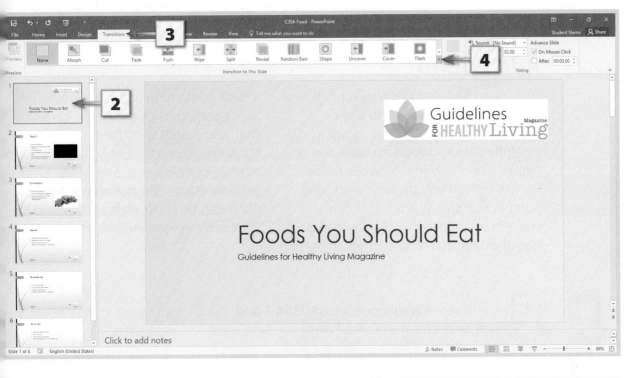

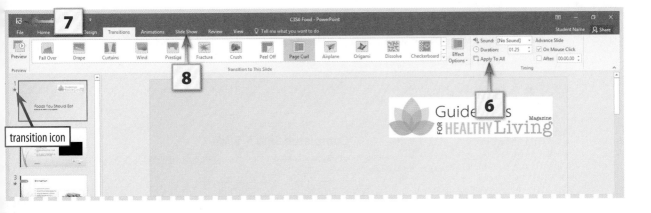

Taking It Further •••••••••••••••••••••

Removing Transitions

Using too many transitions in a single presentation can be distracting for your audience. If you decide that you have too many transitions, you can remove some of them. To remove a transition from one or more slides, select the slide or slides in the slide thumbnails pane and then click the Transitions tab. Click the Transition to This Slide More button and then click the *None* option in the *Subtle* section of the drop-down gallery.

Skill 5 Add Sound

The *Sound* feature in PowerPoint allows a sound file to be added to a slide transition. It is usually best to use a carefully chosen sound for only one or two transitions within a presentation. For example, if you display great sales numbers for the quarter, you might add a brief sound of applause to the transition for that slide or if you display a slide containing a photo, you might add a camera click sound. Be careful that you do not overuse sounds. Playing a sound for every transition can annoy your audience and detract from your message. The duration a sound plays can be controlled and should be set to an appropriate length.

Tutorial

1 If it is not already open, open **C3S4-Food**, the file you saved in the previous skill, and save it as **C3S5-Food**.

2 In the slide thumbnails pane, click Slide 1.

3 Click the Transitions tab if it is not already selected.

4 Click the *Sound* arrow in the Timing group.

5 Click *Drum Roll* option in the drop-down list to apply this sound to the selected slide.

 6 *Another Way*
Click in the *Duration* box and then type 1.75.

6 Click the the Duration increment (up) arrow two times to change the time to *01.75*.

7 Click the Preview button in the Preview group to preview the transition and the sound.

8 Save the file.

Completed Skill Preview

Completed Skill 5, Slide 1

Guidelines for HEALTHY Living Magazine

Foods You Should Eat
Guidelines for Healthy Living Magazine

The drum roll sound automatically runs for 1.75 seconds when this slide displays.

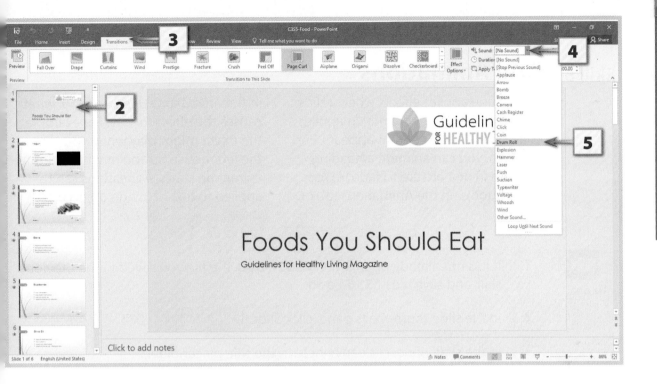

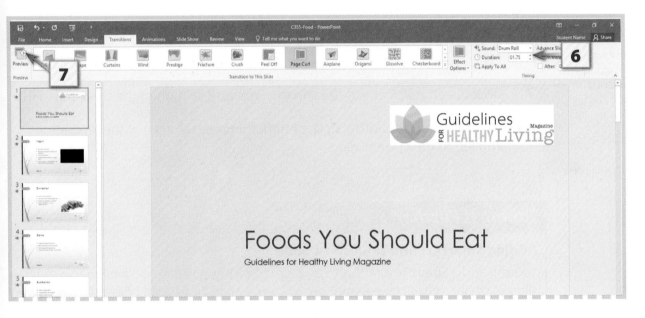

Taking It Further

Using Your Own Audio in a Presentation

The *Audio* feature enables you to use any audio file that you have created or downloaded in your PowerPoint presentation. Select the slide in the slide thumbnails pane, click the Insert tab, click the Audio button in the Media group, and then click the *Audio on My PC* option in the drop-down list. Browse to locate the audio file on your computer or storage medium and insert it. A small speaker icon appears on your slide during the slide show. Point to the icon to display the Play button and then click the button to play the audio.

Skill 6 Add Animations

A transition applies effects when a slide appears, whereas an *animation* applies effects when slide content appears. For example, you can animate a heading to zoom in or a picture to fade in. You can use tools on the Animations tab or in the *Animation Pane* to control what causes the effect to play. For example, the effect might play when you click the left mouse button or when another animation starts. Animations can be applied to text or image objects.

Tutorial

1 If it is not already open, open **C3S5-Food**, the file you saved in the previous skill, and save it as **C3S6-Food**.

2 In the slide thumbnails pane, click Slide 1.

3 In the slide pane, click anywhere in the title placeholder.

4 Click the Animations tab.

5 Click the *Float In* option in the Animation group.

▶**Tip** The Add Animation button is used to add an additional animation to an already animated object.

6 Click the Add Animation button in the Advanced Animation group.

7 Click the *Complementary Color* in the *Emphasis* section of the drop-down list.

8 Click the Preview button on the Animations tab to preview the animations applied to the current slide.

Taking It Further

Adding SmartArt and Tables to a Slide

You can add a SmartArt graphic to a slide to create a visual representation of information or instructions. To create a SmartArt graphic, click the Insert a SmartArt Graphic icon in the slide placeholder, choose a SmartArt layout, and then add the appropriate text.

Similarly, you can add a table to a slide. In a slide, tables can be used to organize data to make it easier to understand. To create a table, click the Insert Table icon in the slide placeholder, specify the number of rows and columns, and then add data to the table.

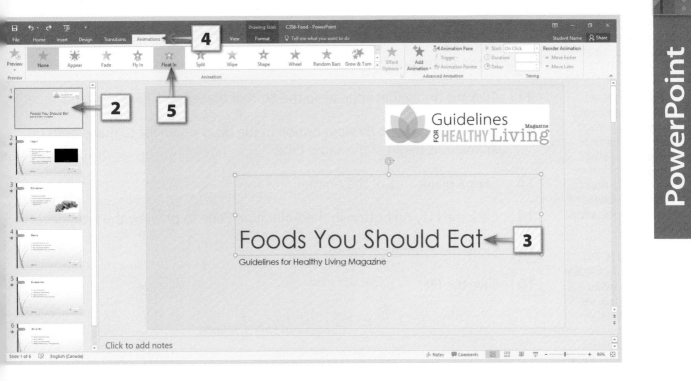

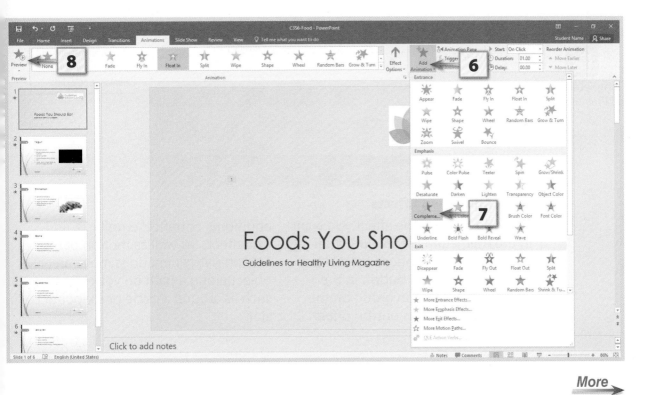

More →

▶ **Tip** The Animation Pane displays a summary of the animations you have added to a slide.

▶ **Tip** Items that are animated are numbered in order in the Animation Pane. You can reorder an animation by selecting it in the Animation Pane and then clicking the Move Earlier or Move Later button in the Timing group on the Animations tab.

▶ **Tip** In Step 14, if the Play button in the Animation Pane says *Play Selected*, repeat Step 13 to be sure you have deselected all animations in the Animation Pane. When there are no animations selected, the button will read *Play All*.

Completed
Skill Preview

9 Click the Animation Pane button in the Advanced Animation group.

10 In the Animation Pane, click the *2 Title 1: Foods…* item.

11 Click the arrow that appears to the right of the *2 Title 1: Foods…* item.

12 Click the *Start With Previous* option in the drop-down list to make both title animations begin at the same time.

13 Click a blank area of the Animation Pane.

14 Click the Play All button in the Animation Pane to preview the timing.

15 Close the Animation Pane.

16 Save the file.

Completed Skill 5, Slide 6

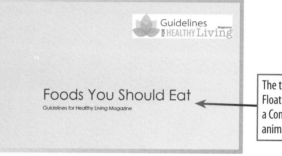

The title enters with Float In animation and a Complementary Color animation on a click.

Taking It Further •

More Animation Effects

If you do not find the effect you want in the Animation list, explore additional animation options by clicking the Add Animation button in the Advanced Animation group on the Animations tab. This button offers additional entrance, emphasis, and exit effects, as well as motion paths. Motion path animations move an object along a path on your slide, such as around a circle or six-pointed star.

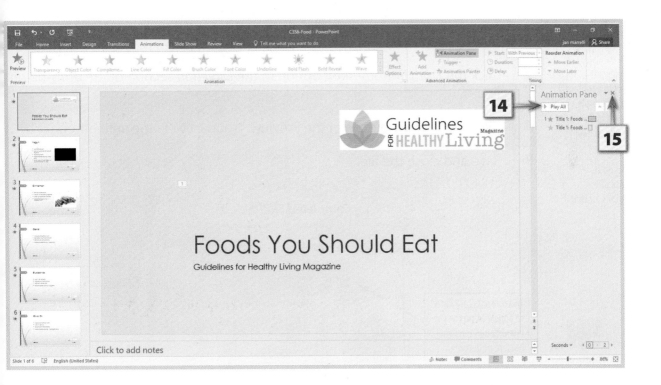

Skill 7 ## Choose Animation Effects

You can refine an *animation effect* in a variety of ways. For example, if you animate text so that it flies in, you can also choose the direction from which the text enters. The ways you can refine an animation effect depend on the effect you choose. In this skill, you experiment with adding and refining two animation effects.

Tutorial

1 If it is not already open, open **C3S6-Food**, the file you saved in the previous skill, and save it as **C3S7-Food**.

2 In the slide thumbnails pane, click Slide 6.

3 Click anywhere in the content placeholder.

4 Click the Animations tab if necessary to select it.

5 Click the *Fly In* effect in the Animation group.

6 Click the Effect Options button.

7 Click the *From Bottom-Right* option in the *Direction* section of the drop-down list.

8 Click the Preview button in the Preview group to view the animation.

9 Save and close the file.

▶**Tip** If the *Fly In* effect is not visible in Step 5, click the More button in the Animation group.

▶**Tip** If you apply an animation effect to a content placeholder with multiple bullet points, each bullet point is animated separately in sequential order.

▶**Tip** Note that each effect you choose offers appropriate options for that effect.

**Completed
Skill Preview**

Completed Skill 7, Slide 6

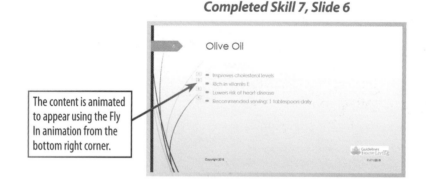

The content is animated to appear using the Fly In animation from the bottom right corner.

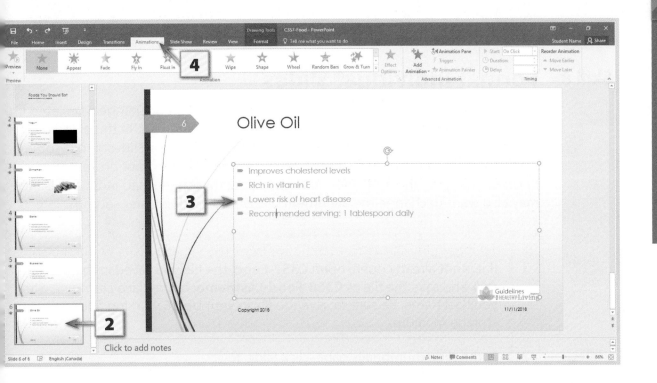

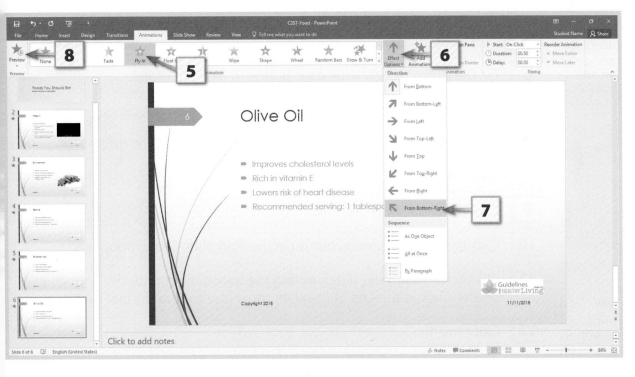

Taking It Further

Timing Animations

You can change the timing of animations with the *Duration* and *Delay* options measurement boxes in the Timing group on the Animations tab. Select an object with an animation applied and use the *Duration* measurement box to set the length of time the animation should play. Use the *Delay* measurement box to set the length of delay between two animations.

Skill 8 Format Individual Slides

When putting the final touches on a presentation, you may want to format individual slides. For example you may want to emphasize text by putting it in italics or changing the font color. You may also want to change the alignment of certain text or change a bulleted list to a numbered list. In this skill, you will format individual slides to put some final touches on your presentation. Note that changes to individual slides override slide master settings.

1 If it is not already open, open **C3S7-Food**, the file you saved in the previous skill, and save the file as **C3S8-Food-Lastname**, but replace *Lastname* with your last name. Be sure to save the file in your Unit 6 working folder on your storage medium.

2 In the slide thumbnails pane, click Slide 1.

3 Click anywhere in the subtitle placeholder.

> **▶Tip** Once a placeholder is selected (displaying a solid border), any formatting will apply to all the text in the placeholder.

4 Click the dotted border around the subtitle to change it to a solid line border.

5 On the Home tab, click the Italic button in the Font group.

6 Click the Font Color arrow.

7 Click the *Blue* option in the Standard Colors section of the drop-down palette.

8 Save the file.

9 Click the Slide Show tab.

10 Click the From Beginning button in the Start Slide Show group.

11 Advance through the slides, noting the transition, sound, and animation effects. Click at the end of the slide show to return to Normal view.

12 Close the file.

> **Use Your Touchscreen**
> Swipe to the left to advance to the next slide. Swipe to the right to display the previous slide.

Completed Skill 8, Slide 1

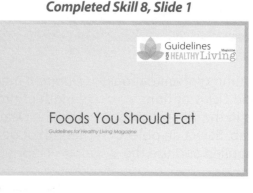

Guidelines
HEALTHY Living

Foods You Should Eat

Guidelines for Healthy Living Magazine

Completed
Skill Preview

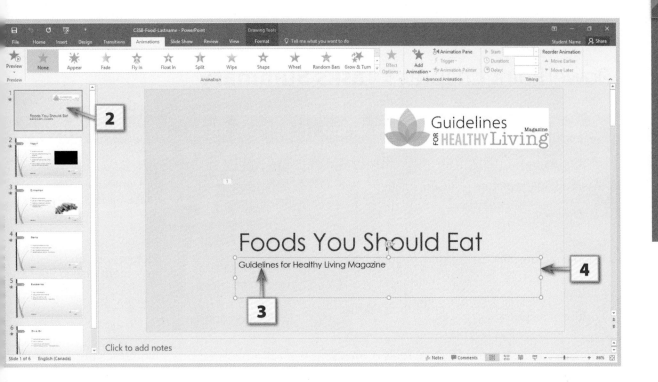

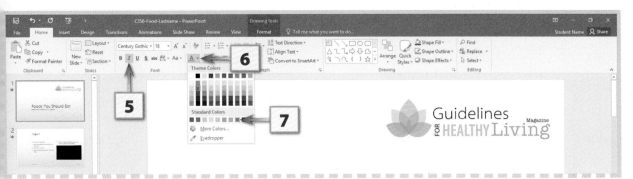

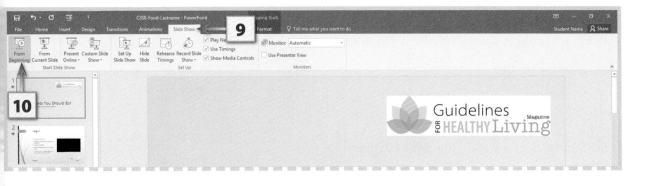

Taking It Further

Increasing and Decreasing Bullet List Levels

You may want to create an indented (subordinate) list within a bulleted list. To increase the left indent of the paragraph, click the Increase List Level button ( ) in the Paragraph Group on the Home tab. To move a paragraph back an indent level, click the Decrease List Level button ( ) in the Paragraph Group on the Home tab.

PowerPoint Chapter 3 **Tasks Summary**

Task	Ribbon Tab, Group	Button, Option	Shortcut, Alternative
Insert an online picture	Insert, Images		( ) Online pictures button in content placeholder
Insert a picture file	Insert, Images	Pictures	Pictures button ( ) in content placeholder
Position a picture	Picture Tools Format, Size	, *Position* options	
Format a picture	Picture Tools Format, Picture Styles		Right-click the image, click the *Format Picture* option in the pop-up list
Snap picture to a grid	View, Show	*Snap objects to grid* check box	
Insert a video	Insert, Media	Video	Video button ( ) in content placeholder
Add a transition	Transitions, Transition to This Slide		
Add a transition to all slides in the presentation	Transitions, Timing	Apply To All	
Remove a transition	Transitions, Transition to This Slide		
Add a sound to a transition	Transitions, Timing	Sound: [No Sound]	
Set transition sound duration	Transitions, Timing	Duration: 02.00	
Preview a transition and sound, or an animation	Transitions or Animations, Preview	Preview	
Add an audio file	Insert, Media	Audio	

Task	Ribbon Tab, Group	Button, Option	Shortcut, Alternative
Add an animation to a single object	Animations, Animation	⏷	
Add additional animations to an object	Animations, Advanced Animation	Add Animation ▾	
Open the Animation Pane	Animations, Advanced Animation	Animation Pane	
Insert a SmartArt graphic	Insert, Illustrations	SmartArt	SmartArt button ( ) in content placeholder
Insert a Table	Insert, Tables	Table ▾	Table button ( ) in content placeholder
Choose animation effects	Animations, Animation	Effect Options ▾	
Change animation timing	Animations, Timing		
Increase or decrease the indent level of a bulleted list	Home, Paragraph	⮕ ⬅	Tab, Shift Tab

Recheck your understanding of the skills and features covered in this chapter.

Recheck

Chapter study resources, exercises, and assessments are available in the Workbook *ebook.*

Workbook

Chapter 4

Completing, Running, and Sharing Your Show

Check your understanding of the skills and features covered in this chapter.

Precheck

After you have finished adding content to your presentation, you should perform a spelling check to make sure that no embarrassing errors lurk in your text. You must also specify settings for how your slide show should run. These settings control how your show moves from slide to slide, either manually with a click or key press or automatically using recorded slide timings. You can also set up a show to loop continuously so that it plays over and over again.

You might want to print a copy of your slides for your own reference, print handouts for your audience, or print speaker notes to use while presenting or for reference later on. You can also use the powerful tools in PowerPoint to broadcast your presentation online, where it can be viewed by others as you navigate through the slides.

Skills You Learn

1 Check spelling

2 Run a show for an audience

3 Rehearse timings

4 Set up a show to run using timings

5 Print speaker notes with a header

6 Present online

Files You Need
For these skills, you use the following student data file:

C4S1-Food

 If you are a SNAP user, go to your SNAP Assignments page to complete the Precheck, Tutorials, and Recheck.

What You Create

You are finally ready to deliver your "Foods You Should Eat" article presentation to the editorial team at *Guidelines for Healthy Living Magazine*. Members of the team are located in various offices across the country, so you need to set up your presentation to be run in different ways. In this chapter, you learn to finalize and share your presentation efficiently. You start by ensuring that the slide content uses proper spelling. Then you customize the presentation to hide a slide, specify the show's playback settings, and set timings for how long each slide is displayed. You also print speaker notes for yourself and handouts for the team. Finally, you learn how to broadcast the presentation online.

"Foods You Should Eat" Presentation with Timings

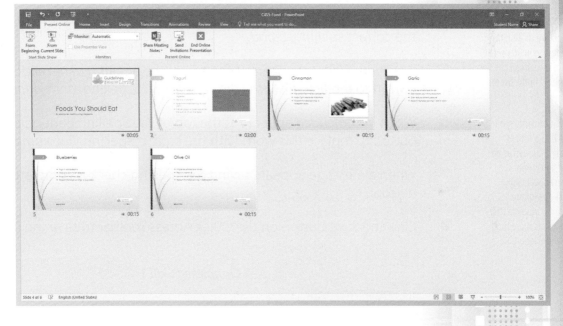

Completed
Skill Preview

PowerPoint

Skill 1 Check Spelling

If the content of your presentation is spelled correctly, your audience is more likely to take your message seriously. PowerPoint's built-in spelling checker can help you find spelling errors and make suggestions for correcting them, but you need to decide what to do with those recommendations.

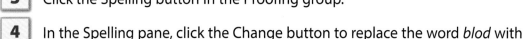

Tutorial

1 Open the student data file named **C4S1-Food** and, if you have not already done so, save it in your Unit 6 working folder on your storage medium.

2 Click the Review tab.

3 *Shortcut*
Spelling Check
F7

3 Click the Spelling button in the Proofing group.

4 In the Spelling pane, click the Change button to replace the word *blod* with the correct spelling, *blood*.

▶**Tip** Before clicking the Change button in Steps 4–6, make sure the correct spelling is highlighted in the list of choices.

5 When *antixidants* appears at the top of the Spelling pane, click the Change button to replace this word with the correct spelling, *antioxidants*.

▶**Tip** If a correctly spelled word, such as a proper name, is highlighted as an error and you are certain that word appears only once, click the Ignore button. If it is possible that a word appears more than once, click the Ignore All button.

6 When *Recomended* appears at the top of the Spelling pane, click the Change button to replace this word with the correct spelling, *Recommended*.

7 When a message appears saying the spelling check is complete, click the OK button.

8 Click the Save button on the Quick Access Toolbar to save the file.

Completed Skill 1

Completed Skill Preview

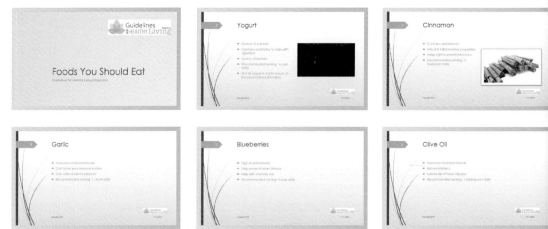

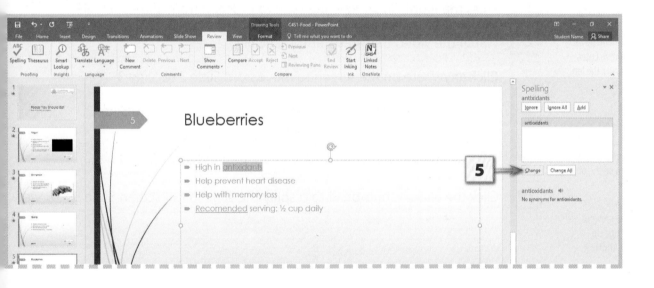

Taking It Further ● ● ● ● ● ● ● ● ● ● ● ● ● ● ● ● ● ● ●

Adding Words to the Spelling Check Dictionary

Any word not found in the dictionary is questioned during the spelling check. If you frequently use a word that the spelling check questions, such as your company name or your last name, you can add that word to the spelling check dictionary—just click the Add button in the Spelling pane when that word is questioned during a spelling check. Once you add a word to the dictionary, it no longer appears as an error in the Spelling pane. If you later need to remove a word from the dictionary, click the File tab, click the *Options* option, click the *Proofing* option, and then click the Custom Dictionaries button.

PowerPoint

Skill 2 Run a Show for an Audience

In previous chapters in this unit, you learned to run a slide show to preview your presentation. In this chapter, you will learn about Slide Show view features you can use when delivering a presentation to an audience, such as setting up timing so your slides advance automatically. In this skill, you learn to navigate a show that is set up to advance manually.

Tutorial

1 If it is not already open, open **C4S1-Food**, the file you saved in the previous skill. You will not be making changes to this file in this skill.

2 Click the Slide Show tab.

3 *Shortcut*

Start slide show from beginning
F5

3 Click the From Beginning button in the Start Slide Show group.

5 *Another Way*

To advance to the next slide, press N, Page Down, Down Arrow, Right Arrow, Enter, or spacebar, or click the left mouse button.

4 Press the space bar to display the title animation on Slide 1.

5 Press the Right Arrow key one time to proceed from Slide 1 to Slide 2.

6 Watch the video that starts automatically.

> **Tip** To play the video again at the end of Step 6, move the pointer over the video object and then click the Play button on the object.

7 Click anywhere on the screen to move from Slide 2 to Slide 3.

8 Press the Backspace key one time to move from Slide 3 to Slide 2.

8 *Another Way*

To return to the previous slide, press P, Page Up, Up Arrow, Left Arrow, or Backspace.

9 Right-click anywhere on the screen and then click the *See All Slides* option in the pop-up list.

10 Click the Slide 4 thumbnail to display the slide in full-screen Slide Show view.

Taking It Further

Delivering a Presentation

There are a few things you can do to make sure you deliver an effective presentation to an audience. Be sure to show up early and test your equipment, especially if you are using a different computer or using a projector. Check to make sure your font size is readable from all areas of the room and check your colors as colors can project differently than they appear on your monitor. Do not read your presentation, look at the audience as you speak, speak in a clear voice, and monitor the audience's attention and behavior. If they seem distracted, adjust your presentation accordingly. Be sure to stay on time, too.

11 Hover your mouse pointer over the lower left corner of the slide to reveal the buttons in the slide show toolbar. Click the Previous button (⬱) to navigate from Slide 4 to Slide 3.

12 Click the Magnifying Glass button (🔍) in the slide show toolbar and then click the word *antioxidants* in the slide to zoom in on that word.

13 Right-click anywhere on the screen to zoom back out.

14 Click the See All Slides button (▦) in the slide show toolbar.

15 Click the Slide 5 thumbnail to display the slide in Slide Show view.

16 Click the Pen button (✏) in the slide show toolbar.

17 Click the *Laser Pointer* option in the pop-up list.

18 Use the laser pointer to point to the first bullet point on Slide 5.

19 *Another Way*
Right-click the current slide and then click the *End Show* option in the pop-up list.

19 Press the Esc key to end the slide show and return the presentation to Normal view.

Taking It Further ●

Using Presenter View

Another way to view your PowerPoint slides is in *Presenter view*. If you have the necessary hardware, Presenter view lets you see your notes while you are delivering your presentation. (The audience sees just the presentation, not your notes.) To access Presenter view, click the *Use Presenter View* check box in the Monitors group on the Slide Show tab to insert a check mark and then run the presentation. In Presenter view, you have access to the slide show toolbar, which allows you to navigate your presentation, see all your slides as thumbnails (making it easy to jump to a particular slide), zoom in on slides, and use digital tools, such as a pen, to highlight information on a slide.

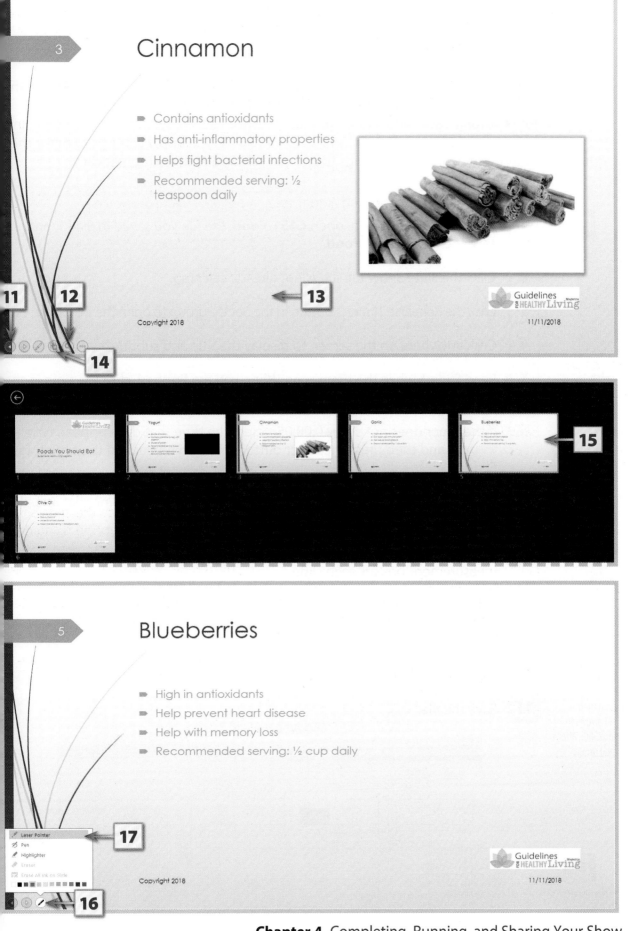

Skill 3 Rehearse Timings

If no speaker will be present to run a slide show, you need to record timings for how long each slide should display before advancing to the next slide. PowerPoint uses those timings to automatically advance the show. In this skill, you learn how to rehearse and save specific timings for each slide. In Skill 4, you apply settings to make the show advance automatically.

Tutorial

1 If it is not already open, open **C4S1-Food**, the file you saved in Skill 1, and save the file as **C4S3-Food**.

2 Click the Slide Show tab if it is not already selected.

3 Click the Rehearse Timings button in the Set Up group to open the Recording box.

4 Click anywhere on the screen to display the title and subtitle.

5 Read Slide 1 while the timer runs. When you are finished, click the time in the timing measurement box to make the timer stop running.

5 Shortcut
Stop Timer
Enter

6 If the timer does not show 0:00:05, select the time that does appear, type 0:00:05, and then press the Enter button to begin rehearsing the timing for Slide 2.

▶**Tip** In Steps 6–8, the idea is to provide an appropriate amount of time for each slide to display, depending on the amount of information on the slide. For example, additional time is allotted to play the video on Slide 2.

7 Click in the timing measurement box for Slide 2, select the time that appears in the box, type 0:03:00, and then press the Enter key.

8 Repeat Step 6 for Slides 3 through 6, typing 0:00:15 in the timing measurement box for each slide.

▶**Tip** In Step 8, if you are not happy with the timings you recorded, click the No button in the warning box and they will not be saved.

9 In the message box indicating that the total time was 0:04:05, click the Yes button to open the presentation in Normal view.

10 Click the View tab and then click the Slide Sorter button in the Presentation Views group. View the assigned times for each slide in the presentation.

▶**Tip** To modify the saved timing for a slide, click the slide thumbnail, click the Transitions tab, and then use the increment arrows to adjust the Advance Slide After value in the Timing group.

11 Save the file.

Completed Skill 3

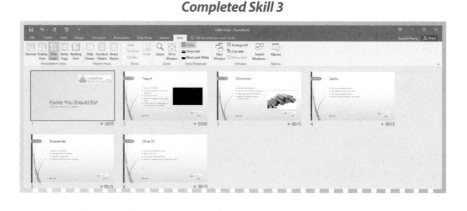

**Completed
Skill Preview**

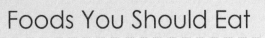

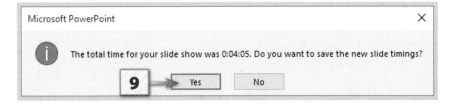

Taking It Further ●

Recording a Slide Show

A *narration* is a recorded audio track saved with a PowerPoint presentation. If you have a sound card, microphone, and speakers, you can record your presentation and capture your voice narrations, slide timings, and pointer gestures. To record an open slide show, click the Record Slide Show button in the Setup group on the Slide Show tab and then click the *Start Recording from Beginning* option. You can then select recording options in the Record Slide Show dialog box and click the Start Recording button to start recording the presentation. To stop recording, click the Pause button or press the Esc key.

Skill 4 Set Up a Show to Run Using Timings

PowerPoint provides three different playback options. One option is for a live speaker to give the presentation. With this choice, the speaker presents information and manually advances each slide when he or she is ready to go to the next topic. Another option is to allow the show to be run by a viewer using onscreen controls. The final option is to have the show run on its own, continuously looping through the slides. The final option is the one you will use to set up the show in this skill. When you set up a show to run on its own, the timings you have saved determine when the show advances from one slide to another. You can customize the presentation by hiding slides.

Tutorial

1 If it is not already open, open **C4S3-Food**, the file you saved in the previous skill, and save it as **C4S4-Food**.

2 In Slide Sorter view, on the Slide Show tab, click the Set Up Slide Show button in the Set Up group.

▶**Tip** When you select the *Browsed at a kiosk (full screen)* option in the Set Up Show dialog box, viewers cannot control the show.

3 In the Set Up Show dialog box, click the *Browsed at a kiosk (full screen)* option in the *Show type* section to select the option.

4 Confirm that the *Using timings, if present* option is selected in the *Advance slides* section.

5 Click the OK button.

6 Click the Slide 2 thumbnail.

▶**Tip** To unhide a slide, select the slide thumbnail and then click the Hide Slide button to turn off the option.

7 Click the Hide Slide button in the Setup group. Slide 2 remains part of the presentation file but will not be viewed when the slide show is run.

8 Save the file.

9 Run the show and watch it advance slide by slide. Press Esc to end the show and return to Slide Sorter view.

Completed Skill 4

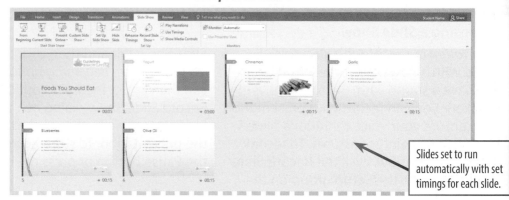

Slides set to run automatically with set timings for each slide.

Completed Skill Preview

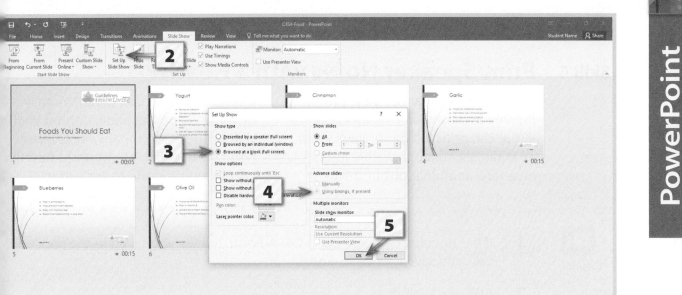

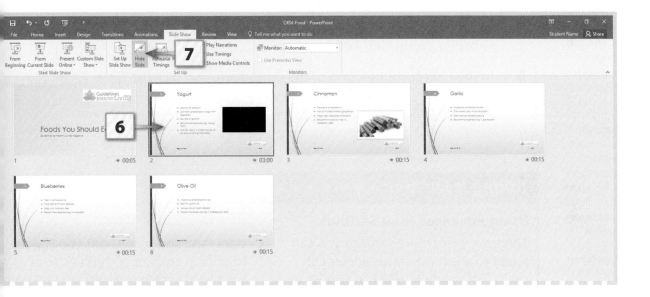

Taking It Further

Creating a Custom Show

In this skill, you learned to customize a slide show presentation by hiding a single slide. An alternative way to customize a slide show presentation is to click the Custom Slide Show button in the Start Slide Show group on the Slide Show tab. The *Custom Slide Show* feature lets you name and save your customized show so that you can use it at a later date and select which slides you would like to include in the presentation.

Skill 5 Print Speaker Notes with a Header

Once you have finalized your presentation you may want to print copies of it. You can print full-page slides, print an audience *handout* that includes any of several combinations of single or multiple slides oriented horizontally or vertically on the page, or print each slide with its accompanying speaker notes. In this skill, you perform the third option: printing the Notes pages.

Tutorial

2–3 *Shortcut*
Print
Ctrl + P

▶ **Tip** In Step 4, the option box displays the last option selected for this presentation. The default setting is *Full Page Slides*, which prints one slide per page.

▶ **Tip** When you click the *Full Page Slides* arrow in Step 4, the drop-down list also gives you options for printing handouts with various layouts, framing the slides, scaling the printout to fit the paper, and producing high-quality printouts.

▶ **Tip** If you want to print a subset of slides, click the *Print All Slides* arrow in the *Settings* category and then choose to print the currently active slide or click the *Custom Range* option and enter a range of slides to print.

1 If it is not already open, open **C4S4-Food**, the file you saved in the previous skill, and save it as **C4S5-Food**.

2 Click the File tab.

3 Click the *Print* option.

4 In the Print backstage area, click the *Full Page Slides* arrow in the *Settings* category of the *Print* panel.

5 In the *Print Layout* section of the drop-down list, click the *Notes Pages* option.

6 Click the Edit Header & Footer link.

Taking It Further

Using Advanced Print Settings

There are a few more settings you can select to affect how your document prints. For example, you can choose to collate copies so that multiple copies print as sets (rather than printing three page 1s in a stack, three page 2s in a stack, and so on). You can also choose to print in color or on both sides of the paper (which may require that you turn over the paper in your printer after printing the first side). All these options are available in the Print backstage area

Using Smart Printing

You can make some smart choices when printing in order to save on paper and printing costs. In PowerPoint, there are a number of options in the Setting category, such as printing multiple slides on a page, printing on both sides of the paper, and printing in pure black and white or grayscale as opposed to color.

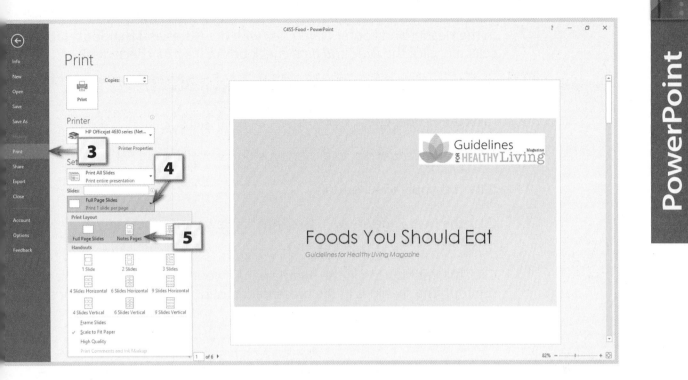

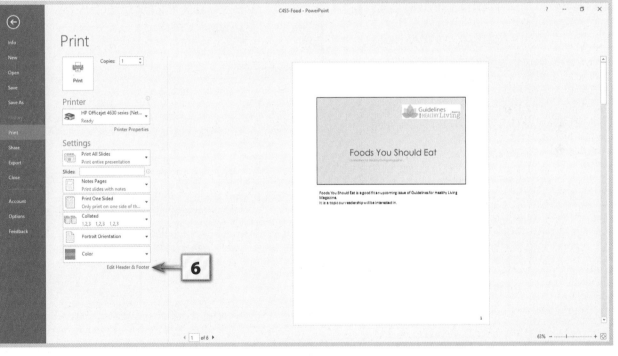

More →

PowerPoint

7 In the Header and Footer dialog box with the Notes and Handouts tab selected, click the *Date and time* check box to insert a check mark.

8 Click the *Update automatically* option if it is not already selected.

9 Click the *Header* check box to insert a check mark.

10 Click in the *Header* box and then type Foods You Should Eat.

11 Click the Apply to All button.

12 Click the Next Page arrow in the Print Preview pane repeatedly to view all six Notes pages.

13 Click the Print button in the middle pane if your instructor would like a printout. The six slides in the presentation print in a format useful for speaker notes, using your default printer.

Completed Skill 5

Completed
Skill Preview

Taking It Further ●

Printing Handouts

It is sometimes helpful for the audience to have copies of your slides to refer to as you are delivering the presentation. Handouts also save the audience from having to write extensive notes or record the presentation for future reference. To print handouts, click the File tab and then click the *Print* option. Click the *Full Page Slides* arrow in the *Settings* category of the *Print* panel and then select an appropriate option from the *Handout* category. The *3 Slides* option is a good option for handouts because it contains lines beside each slide for notes.

Skill 6 Present Online

PowerPoint provides a powerful feature for presenting your presentation online in real time. This feature, called *Present Online*, is free and uses the Office Presentation Service, so you don't even need your own website to present online. However, you are required to have a Microsoft account. You can use the same Microsoft account that you used to create a OneDrive account in the Introduction (Your Digital Toolkit), Chapter 2.

Tutorial

2–5 *Another Way*
Click the Slide Show tab, click the Present Online button in the Start Slide Show group, and then click the CONNECT button in the Present Online dialog box.

▶ *Tip* In Step 5, if you want remote users to be able to download the presentation to their computers after viewing the online presentation, click the *Enable remote viewers to download the presentation* check box in the *Present Online* category, to insert a check mark.

1 If it is not already open, open **C4S5-Food**, the file you saved in the previous skill. You will not be making changes to this file.

2 Click the File tab.

3 Click the *Share* option.

4 Click the *Present Online* option in the *Share* category.

5 Click the Present Online button in the *Present Online* category. If you are already signed in to your Microsoft account, you will skip Steps 6–9.

6 In the Sign in dialog box, type the email address associated with your Microsoft account in the text box and then click the Next button.

7 Type your user ID in the *User ID* box.

8 Type your password in the *Password* box.

9 Click the Sign in button.

Share

C4S5-Food
F: » Guidelines

Share

- Share with People
- Email
- **Present Online**
- Publish Slides

3

4

Present Online

Present through Office Presentation Service
- No setup required
- A link is created to share with people
- Anyone using the link can see the slide show while you are presenting online
- The presentation will be made available for download

You will need a Microsoft account to start the online presentation.

By clicking Present Online, you agree to the following terms:
Service Agreement

☐ Enable remote viewers to download the presentation ← **5 Tip**

Present Online ← **5**

Sign in

Call us overprotective, but we need to verify your account again

Type your email address or phone number ← **6**

Next

When you sign in, your documents and settings are online

Learn more | Privacy statement

Sign In

User ID:

← **7**

Password:

← **8**

☐ Keep me signed in

Sign in ← **9**

Can't access your account?

More →

Tip You can provide the link in Step 10 to as many people as you would like to view the presentation. Don't forget to provide a presentation starting time when you pass along the URL to your attendees! They need to know when you will be running the presentation.

 In the Present Online dialog box, click *Send in Email...* and then send the link to yourself.

 Click the START PRESENTATION button to begin the live presentation. Individuals who have received a link to the online presentation and have clicked that link can watch the presentation as you run it. The slides advance automatically according to the timings set in the slide show. The show continues to loop from Slide 6 back to Slide 1. (*Note that the presentation skips Slide 2 because it is still hidden.*)

 Press the Esc key when you are done watching the slide show.

13 Click the End Online Presentation button in the Present Online group on the Present Online tab.

14 At the warning box indicating that all remote viewers will be disconnected if you continue, click the End Online Presentation button.

15 Save and then Close the file.

Completed Skill 6

Completed Skill Preview

Taking It Further ●

Sharing a Presentation Using OneDrive

You can also share a presentation by first saving it to your OneDrive account. To save an open presentation to your OneDrive account, click the File tab, click the *Save As* option, click your OneDrive account in the *Save As* category, and then click the Save button in the Save As dialog box. You can then share the presentation with other people by clicking the File tab, clicking the *Share* option, and then clicking the *Share with People* option in the *Share* category.

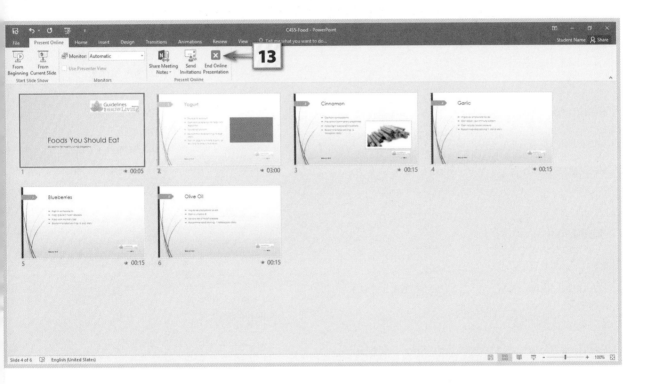

PowerPoint Chapter 4 **Tasks Summary**

Task	Ribbon Tab, Group	Button, Option	Shortcut, Alternative
Check spelling	Review, Proofing	Spelling	F7
Add words to spelling dictionary	Review, Proofing	Spelling, Add	
Start a show from the beginning	Slide Show, Start Slide Show	From Beginning	F5
Advance to Next Slide			N Page Down Down Arrow Enter
Return to Previous Slide			P Page Up Up Arrow
Rehearse timings	Slide Show, Set Up	Rehearse Timings	
Stop Timer			Enter
Record a slide show	Slide Show, Set Up	Record Slide Show	
Set up a show	Slide Show, Set Up	Set Up Slide Show	
Set up a custom show	Slide Show, Start Slide Show	Custom Slide Show	
Print a presentation, notes, or handouts	File, *Print*	Print	Ctrl + P
Present a presentation online	File, *Share* *or* Slide Show, Start Slide Show	Present Online	

Recheck

Recheck your understanding of the skills and features covered in this chapter.

Workbook

Chapter study resources, exercises, and assessments are available in the Workbook ebook.

UNIT 7

Integrating Office Applications

Student Data Files

Precheck

Check your understanding of the skills and features covered in this unit.

The files you create in an Office application, such as Word, can be integrated into other Office applications, such as PowerPoint. This capability allows you to create a file with the application that is best suited to the task and then transfer that data to another application. For example, you can create a line chart in Excel and then use that line chart in a PowerPoint presentation or a Word document.

Skills You Learn

1. Export a Word outline to PowerPoint

2. Insert an Excel chart in Word

3. Create an Access table from Excel data

Files You Need
For these skills, you need the following student data files:

> S1-Technology
> S2-Charity
> S2-Fundraising
> S3-Donors
> S3-Fundraising

What You Create
In this unit, you export a Word outline of an article presentation into PowerPoint to create a new presentation. You then enhance a media release by inserting an Excel chart into a Word document. You also copy fund-raising data from an Excel worksheet into an Access table.

Media Release

Article Presentation

Fund-raising Database

Completed
Skill Preview

Before beginning this unit, be sure you have downloaded the GL16-StudentDataFiles folder from your ebook and copied the Unit7-Integrating subfolder to your storage medium. The copied folder will become your working folder for this unit.

SNAP

If you are a SNAP user, go to your SNAP Assignments page to complete the Precheck, Tutorials, and Recheck.

Guidelines

for
Integrating Content between Programs

A key advantage in using the Office 2016 suite is that you can integrate data between the application programs. *Integrating* means bringing together two or more application files. First you create a file in the Office application that best suits the data. That application is called the *source program*. Then you copy that file or *export* its data to one of the other applications, called the *destination program*. For example, you might create an inventory chart for a flower shop using Excel.

Source Program: Excel

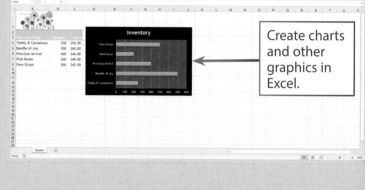

Create charts and other graphics in Excel.

Destination Program: Word

You could then insert the Excel chart in a Word document to help the store manager order stock.

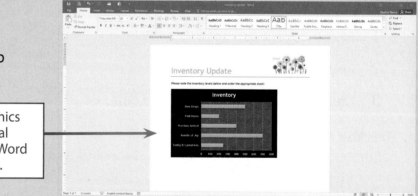

Insert graphics to add visual interest to Word documents.

You could also copy the Excel chart data into an Access table to create new database records that can be updated by the store manager.

Destination Program: Access

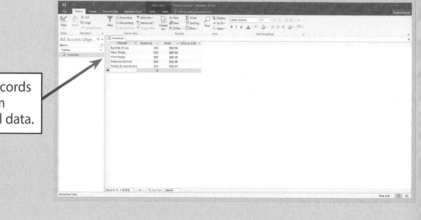

Database records created from copied Excel data.

As another example, if you need to create a PowerPoint presentation and you already have the information for the slide show typed as an outline in a Word document, you don't need to retype the text into PowerPoint. Instead, you simply export, or copy, the Word outline into a blank PowerPoint presentation as shown below.

Source Program: Word

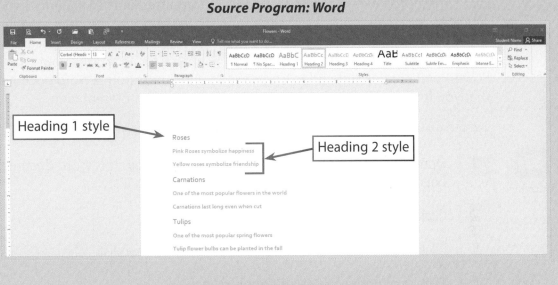

Destination Program: PowerPoint

When you integrate data or objects from one application into another, you can choose between two methods: (1) copying and pasting or (2) embedding or linking. Copying and pasting works well for single-use situations, such as the above example of copying the Word outline into PowerPoint. Embedding or linking works well for situations in which you might continue to use the source and destination files separately as well as together.

Embedding and linking are notably different. When you *embed* an object in a file, the source object and embedded object are independent. For example, if you embed an Excel chart in a Word document, any changes you make to the source chart in the Excel workbook will not affect the embedded chart in the Word document.

In contrast, if you *link* an object in a file, the source object and linked object are dependent. If you link an Excel chart in a Word document, any changes you make to the source chart in the Excel workbook will also appear in the linked chart in the Word document. The embed option and the link option both have an advantage over copying and pasting, because you can edit an embedded or a linked object using the tools of the source program.

Skill 1 Export a Word Outline to PowerPoint

Some people prefer to plan their PowerPoint presentations by creating an outline in Word and then exporting that content to PowerPoint to work on slide design. PowerPoint creates new slides based on the heading styles that you used in the Word outline. PowerPoint creates slide titles from text that you formatted with the Heading 1 style. Paragraphs you formatted in the Heading 2 style become the first-level bulleted text. Paragraphs you formatted in the Heading 3 style become the second-level bulleted text and so on. In this skill, you export an outline for an article about technology and fitness from a Word document into PowerPoint presentation.

Tutorial

1 Open the student data file named **S1-Technology**. This Word document has been formatted with the Heading 1 and Heading 2 styles.

2 Click the Customize Quick Access Toolbar button.

3 Click the *More Commands* option in the drop-down list.

4 Click the *Choose commands from* arrow.

5 Click the *All Commands* option in the list box.

6 *Another Way*
Scroll through the list box, click the command, and then click the Add button.

6 Scroll through the *All Commands* list box and then double-click the *Send to Microsoft PowerPoint* option.

7 Click the OK button.

8 Click the Send to Microsoft PowerPoint button on the Quick Access Toolbar. PowerPoint opens and displays the presentation in Normal view.

▶**Tip** The *All Commands* options are listed in alphabetical order.

▶**Tip** Your Quick Access Toolbar may have different buttons than the ones shown in the image on the opposite page. If you are unsure which button to use, hover the mouse pointer over each button until you locate the one with the ScreenTip that reads *Send to Microsoft PowerPoint*.

Taking It Further • • • • • • • • • • • • • • • • •

Exporting a PowerPoint Presentation to Word

You can also export a PowerPoint presentation to Word. You may want to do this so that you can use Word features to customize your handout formatting. Another reason might be to use the contents of your presentation as the basis for a report or other document. To send presentation data to Word, click the File tab, click the *Export* option, click the *Create Handouts* option and then click the *Create Handouts* option. In the Send To Microsoft Word dialog box, click a layout option and then click the OK button.

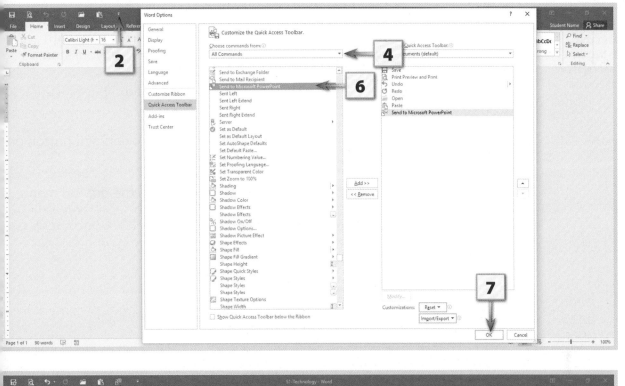

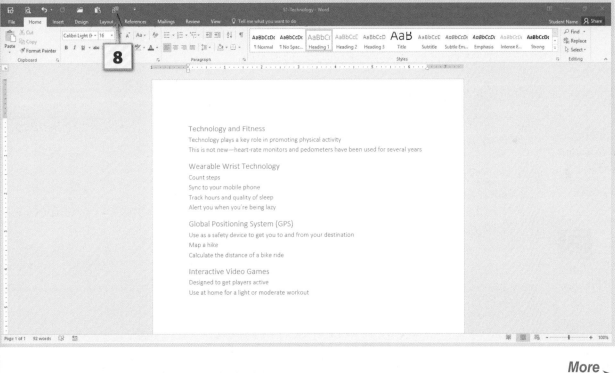

More →

Taking It Further ●

Import a Word Outline into PowerPoint

When you *import* data, the file is converted for use by the destination application. To import a saved Word outline into an open PowerPoint presentation, click the New Slide arrow in the Slides group on the Home tab, and then click the *Slides from Outline* option in the drop-down list. In the Insert Outline dialog box, navigate to a saved Word document, click the file to select it, and then click the Open button.

▶**Tip** When you save the file in PowerPoint in Step 9, notice that it has a .pptx extension, even though the initial data came from a Word file, with a .docx extension.

9 Click the Save button on the Quick Access Toolbar. Save the PowerPoint presentation as **S1-Technology-Lastname**, but replace *Lastname* with your last name. Save the file in your Unit 7 working folder on your storage medium.

10 Close PowerPoint.

11 In the Word window, right-click the Send to Microsoft PowerPoint button on the Quick Access Toolbar.

12 Click the *Remove from Quick Access Toolbar* command in the pop-up menu.

13 Close Word without saving the document.

Completed Skill 1

Technology and Fitness

- Technology plays a key role in promoting physical activity
- This is not new—heart-rate monitors and pedometers have been used for several years

Wearable Wrist Technology

- Count steps
- Sync to your mobile phone
- Track hours and quality of sleep
- Alert you when you're being lazy

Global Positioning System (GPS)

- Use as a safety device to get you to and from your destination
- Map a hike
- Calculate the distance of a bike ride

Interactive Video Games

- Designed to get players active
- Use at home for a light or moderate workout

Completed
Skill Preview

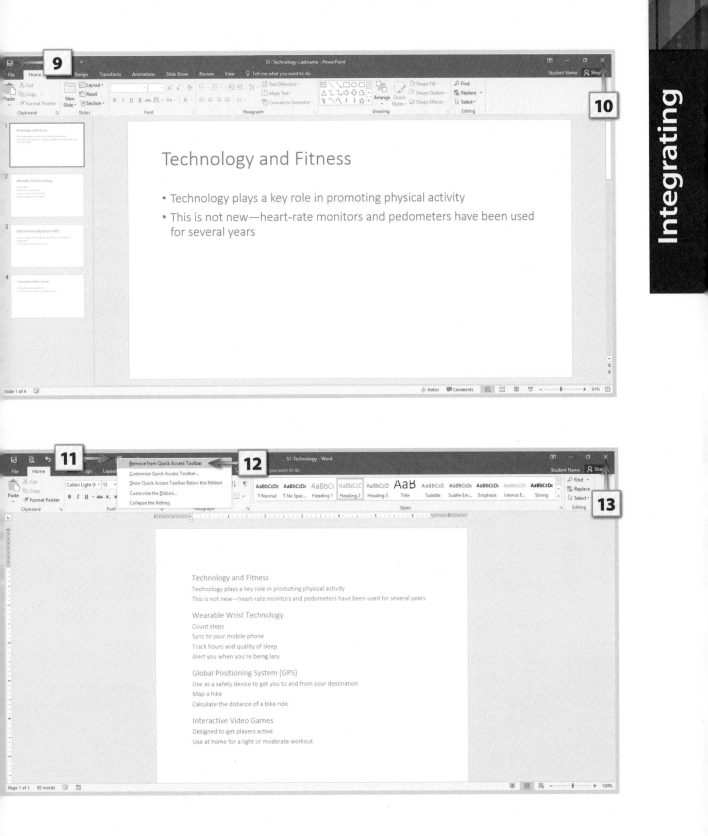

Skill 2 Insert an Excel Chart in Word

You can copy an Excel chart to a Word document. When you do so, you have the option to link the chart. When you link the chart, you will be able to edit the object in Excel (called the *source program*) even though the chart is in a Word document. If you change the chart in Excel, the chart will also be updated in Word (called the *destination program*) if the Word file is open on the same computer when the Excel file is edited. In other words, if you edit a linked chart with both the source and destination files open on the same computer at the same time, you will always have an up-to-date chart. ***Note:*** *If you edit data in Excel, you may need to click the Refresh Data button in the Data group on the Chart Tools Design tab for the edits to appear in the linked Word chart. In this skill, you insert a chart displaying fund-raising data from an Excel spreadsheet into a Word document, linking the chart so that you can later update it in both the spreadsheet and document at the same time.*

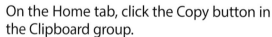

Tutorial

1 Open the student data file, a Word document named **S2-Charity**, and save it as **S2-Charity-Lastname**, but replace *Lastname* with your last name. Be sure to save the file in your Unit 7 working folder on your storage medium.

Use Your Touchscreen
In Step 2, tap at the end of the document.

2 Press Ctrl + End to move the insertion point to the end of the document. ***Note:*** *This step ensures that the chart from Excel will be inserted in the correct position in the Word document.*

3 Open the student data file, an Excel file named **S2-Fundraising**, and, if you have not already done so, save the file to your Unit 7 working folder.

4 Click a blank area of the chart to select the chart.

5 On the Home tab, click the Copy button in the Clipboard group.

▶ **Tip** You can see the linked object (chart) in the Word document, but the object itself is located in its original Excel file.

6 On the Windows taskbar, click the Word button to redisplay the Word document.

7 On the Home tab, click the Paste arrow in the Clipboard group.

▶ **Tip** Click the Destination Theme & Link Data button to link the chart and change the chart formatting to match the formatting in the Word document.

8 Click the *Keep Source Formatting & Link Data* option in the drop-down gallery (the fourth option in the *Paste Options* section).

9 Save the Word document.

Completed Skill Preview

10 Close Word and Excel.

Completed Skill 2

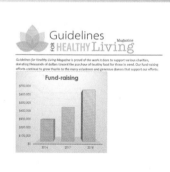

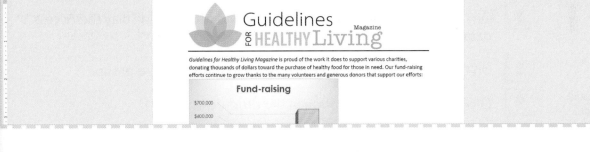

Taking It Further ●

Editing and Formatting a Linked Chart in Word

In Word, click a linked chart to display the Chart Tools Design tab and Chart Tools Format tab. You can use options on these tabs to edit and format the linked chart without having to leave Word. For example, to edit the chart data, click the Chart Tools Design tab and then click the Edit Data button. To change the chart style, click the Chart Tools Design tab and then select a chart style from the Chart Styles gallery. The Chart Tools Format tab includes options for changing shape styles and position the chart. You can also use the Layout Options, Chart Elements, Chart Styles, and Chart Filters buttons that appear next to a selected chart to format and edit a linked chart.

Skill 3 Create an Access Table from Excel Data

Add, or *append*, new records to an Access table by directly typing them in or by copying the information from a Word file or an Excel file. In this skill, you add records to an Access table by copying them from an existing Excel file. Copying existing data can help you avoid mistakes that can sometimes occur when retyping data. In this skill, you copy and paste donor data from an Excel spreadsheet into an Access database.

Tutorial

1 Open the student data file, an Access file, named **S3-Fundraising** from your Unit 7 working folder on your storage medium.

2 If a security warning appears immediately below the ribbon, click the Enable Content button. If a second security warning appears, click the Yes button.

3 Open the Donors table. Notice that the table currently does not contain any records.

4 Open the student data file, an Excel workbook, named **S3-Donors**. The worksheet provides a list of people who have donated money.

5 Select cells A1:C18.

6 On the Home tab, click the Copy button in the Clipboard group.

7 On the Windows taskbar, click the Access button to redisplay the Access database.

8 On the Home tab, click the Paste arrow in the Clipboard group.

> **Tip** In Step 9, you click the *Paste Append* option because you are adding (appending) records to an existing table.

9 Click the *Paste Append* option in the drop-down list.

10 In the warning box asking if you are sure you want to paste the 17 records, click the Yes button.

11 Print the Donors table or submit the Access file as directed by your instructor.

Completed Skill 3

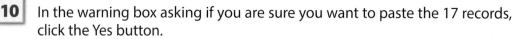

12 Close Access and then close Excel without saving the file.

Completed Skill Preview

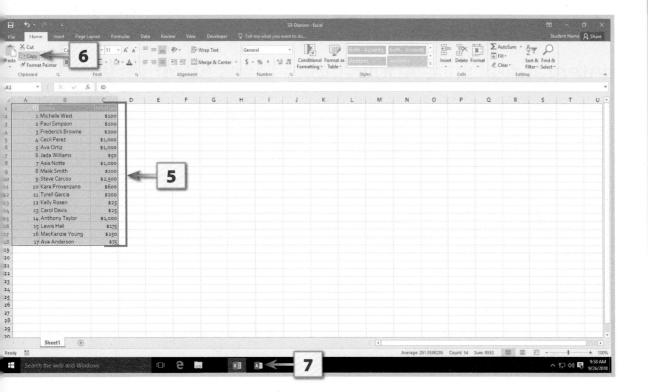

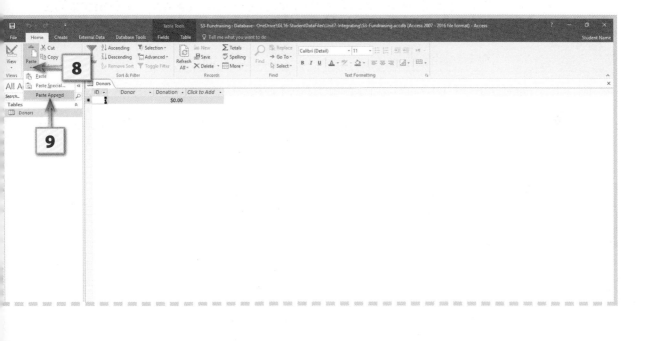

Taking It Further ●

Importing Data from Excel into Access

Another way to enter data into an Access table is to import the data from an existing Excel file. To import an Excel file into an Access database, start with both files open. In the Access database, click the External Data tab and then click the Excel button in the Import & Link group. You can then select the Excel file and specify other import options in the Import Spreadsheet Wizard dialog box.

Integrating Office Applications **Tasks Summary**

Task	Ribbon Tab, Group	Button, Option	Shortcut, Alternative
Customize Quick Access Toolbar	Quick Access Toolbar	, *More Commands*	
Send a Word outline to PowerPoint	Quick Access Toolbar		
Export a PowerPoint presentation to Word	File	*Export*	
Remove the Send to Microsoft PowerPoint button	Quick Access Toolbar	Right-click , *Remove from Quick Access Toolbar*	
Link data	Home, Clipboard	, *Keep Source Formatting & Link Data*	
Add file to an existing Access table	Home, Clipboard	, *Paste Append*	

Recheck your understanding of the skills and features covered in this chapter.

Recheck

Chapter study resources and assessments are available in the Workbook *ebook.*

Workbook

Glossary/Index

(pound signs)

deleting series of, 211

indication Excel cell is too narrow, 274

> (not equal to) operator, 356

(less than) operator, 356

(equal to) operator, 356

(greater than) operator, 356

= (greater than or equal) to operator, 356

(dollar sign) creating, 250

bsolute reference a cell reference in which the row and column letter do not change when you fill or copy the formula; a dollar sign precedes the column letter and row number (A1), 250

using, 250–251

CCDB the file format for an Access 2016 document, 48

ccept a Word feature that allows you to accept some or all changes made by reviewers, 3.43

ccess the Microsoft Office database application, 310–311

adding date and time to header, 338

adjusting margin, 366

automatic alignment of numbers, 324

automatic alignment of text, 324

AutoNumber, 330

background color, 325

changing field size, 333

checking spelling, 317

copying and pasting entire record in, 336

copying and pasting from Word or Excel file into, 337

creating and formatting report based on query, 364–367

creating Lookup field, 334

creating report using Report Wizard, 360–363

creating table, 332–335

creating table from Excel data, 462–463

criteria, 348

currency, 330

deleting record, 319

displaying record when filtering, 322

editing data, 318–319

entering data, 311, 316–317, 336–337, 342–343

filtering data, 322–323

importing data from Excel into, 463

making table active, 338

moving between fields, 342

opening and navigating databases, 314–315

opening multiple objects, 315

opening object, 332

previewing and printing report, 366–367

printing object, 327

pulling data from multiple tables to create query, 356–359

saving as, 46

saving report as PDF, 362

sorting data, 320–321

sorting records in table, 321

Text Formatting tools, 66

updating database files, 309

using touchscreen to add field to query design grid, 356

zipped files, 314

Access app an Access database that is viewed, edited, and shared on the web and stored in the cloud, 311

creating with template, 311

Accounting format in Excel, a number format that displays the value in a cell by placing the dollar symbol ($) or another currency symbol at the left edge of the cell, using a thousands separator, including two decimal places and aligning cell amounts by decimal point; places negative numbers in parentheses, 266

active cell in a worksheet, the cell that the user has selected by clicking it or navigating to it using another method, such as the keyboard; also known as the *current cell*, 200

editing shortcut, 256

finishing entry and staying in same cell, 212

making, shortcut, 202

moving down one cell, 208

Address bar the location in Windows 10, Internet Explorer, and Chrome browser windows where you type a web address, 15

Adobe Acrobat a document-sharing software program used to view and make edits to PDF files, 192

Adobe Reader free software used to view PDF files, 48, 192, 193

obtaining, 192

align to set text in one of four ways relative to the left and right margins of the document; alignment options are left, right, center, and justify, 122

automatic in Access, 324

default in Excel, 208

setting in Word, 122–123

shortcuts, 122

All Commands options, 456

All Markup a Track Changes setting in Word that shows all changes to formatting as well as all content deletions and additions to a document, 179

animation a sequence of visual effects that influences how content appears on the currently displayed slide in PowerPoint; can be applied to text or graphical objects, 420

adding, 420–423

finding more effects, 422

animation effect a movement effect, such as flying in or spinning, that you can apply to an animation in PowerPoint, 424

choosing, 424–425

timing, 425

Animation Pane the pane you display using a button on the Animations tab in PowerPoint; allows you to locate, apply, and control animations, 420, 422

APA (American Psychological Association) a professional style used for citations, detailed in the *Publication Manual of the American Psychological Association* and one of the built-in styles you can apply to references in Word, 136

inserting citations, 136–139

publications using, 141

465

App a small application that is available for a variety of computing devices such as smartphones and tablets; typically written to perform a specific single task, 7

append in Access, to add records to an existing table, 462

applications software the group of programs you use to complete computer-based projects; includes spreadsheet programs to perform calculations, word processors to create text-based documents, games, and drawing programs, among others, 6–7

closing shortcut, 50

opening, 42–43

appointment an activity you schedule in an electronic calendar (such as the one in Outlook) with starting and ending times, 26

creating new shortcut, 26

scheduling on Calendar, 26–27

searching, 34–35

argument a value used by a function when performing a calculation; functions can have required or optional arguments; arguments include numeric values, dates, text, and cell references and ranges, 240

inserting multiple, 245

arithmetic control unit (ALU) the part of the CPU that performs arithmetic and logic operations, 3

arrows, using in Word, 146

ascending a sort order that sorts data alphabetically from A to Z or from the smallest value to the largest value, 320

audience

Excel worksheet creation, 197

running PowerPoint presentation for, 384–385, 434–437

running PowerPoint presentation for, using timings, 440–441

Word document creation, 79

Audio a PowerPoint feature used to insert an audio file in a presentation, 419

AutoComplete list an Excel feature that displays a pop-up list of functions as you start to type a formula, 242

AutoCorrect, using in Excel, 217

Auto Fill an Excel feature used to copy an entry or fill a series across a row or down a column, 212

using, 212–215

AutoFit behavior, 150

AutoFit in Excel, a feature in the Convert Text to Table process that creates a flexible column width for each column in the table, based on the contents of each column, 274

using, 274

AutoFit to contents, 150

AutoNumber in Access, a data type that automatically stores a number that is one greater than the last number used, 330

AutoSum an Excel feature that provides a quick way to insert commonly used functions into a formula; functions that can be inserted include SUM, AVERAGE, COUNT, MIN, and MAX, 246

using, 246–249

AVERAGE function, 240

axis labels an Excel feature that describes what the numbers and labels along a chart axis represent, 299

B

Backspace key, 84

backstage area an interface element in all Microsoft Office programs; contains a variety of options and commands that allow you to manage your files and perform tasks such as saving and printing, 42

displaying, 44

bar chart a chart that is used to compare differences between values; has horizontal bars in Excel, 290

Best Fit option in Excel, 298

blank pages, finding in Word, 87

Bluetooth technology used to communicate over short distances without wires, 5

blue wavy underlines, interpreting in Word, 85

bold a font effect used to add emphasis by making text appear darker and heavier than the text around it, 118

applying, in Word, 118

shortcut, 66, 270

border an outline around a certain area, such as a cell or cell range in an Excel worksheet; used to group or emphasize data, 280

accessing more options, 283

adding, 280–283

adding with Format Painter, 280

bulleted list a list format used for items without a set order or sequence, 126

applying custom, 128–129

creating, 126–129

creating, with multiple levels, 129

increasing and decreasing in PowerPoint, 427

styles, 126

bullet points

maximum per PowerPoint slide, 370

C

calculations

entering formula for, in Excel, 240–241

performing in table, in Word, 160

Calendar an Outlook scheduling tool that can keep track of appointments, create reminders about events, and schedule meetings, 20

adding city to Weather, 24

customizing, 24

displaying, 24–25

displaying shortcut, 24

organizing, 27

scheduling appointment, 26–27

scheduling meeting, 28–31

searching in, 34–35

searching shortcut, 34

cell the intersection of a row and a column in a worksheet; a location for entering data, 200

adding borders around, in Excel using Format Painter, 280

applying number format to, 266–269

copying and pasting contents, 252–254

cutting and pasting contents, 254–255

deleting entry from, 208

deleting series of pound signs (###), 211

displaying entire contents, 204

editing Active cell shortcut, 256

editing contents, 256–259

filling with color manually, 278

increasing width, 211

jumping to, 202

making, active shortcut, 202

merging, 284–287

mouse point appearance when selecting, 266

moving, using touchscreen, 268

moving from one to another in table, 149

positioning input, in worksheet, 197

removing entry from single, after using Auto Fill, 214

selecting range, 202

selecting range with touchscreen, 266

selecting scattered multiple, 282

using Quick Analysis button, 164

visually separating, 160

ell address in a worksheet, a combination of a column heading letter and a row heading number, such as A1; uniquely identifies a cell location; also known as a cell name or cell reference, 204

after cell merge, 286

entering in formula, 236

using, 204–207

using absolute and relative, 250–251

ell name. *See cell address*

ell reference. *See cell address*

ell Styles gallery, 270

enter aligned an alignment that places the document text at the middle point between the left and right margins, 122

shortcut, 122

entral processing unit (CPU) the part of the computer that performs mathematical operations and coordinates the functions of the computer system; typically a microprocessor located on the motherboard, 2, 3

hart

adding and editing labels, 297–299

automatic updating, 296

changing type, 295

choosing type, 292

editing and formatting linked, in Word, 461

modifying data, 296–297

moving to new worksheet, 293

hart Elements button, 298

hart Filters button, 297

hart title a chart element that describes the contents of the chart, 298

hicago *(The Chicago Manual of Style)*, 141

citation notes that give credit to a source of information used in a document, 136

inserting, 136–139

Clear button options in Excel, 259

Clipboard a holding area for cut/ copied text or objects; items in the Clipboard are available to be pasted into a file, 91

using in Excel, 252

using in Word, 91

Close button used to close an open file or application, 41

Cloud-based subscription software, 7

cloud storage a type of storage that allows you to access your data from any device with an active Internet connection, 3

Clustered Column chart, shortcut for creating, 294

color

background, in Access of rows, 325

changing, of picture in PowerPoint, 412

changing scheme in PowerPoint in Slide Master view, 400–401

changing with Font color button, 67

creating custom in PowerPoint, 400

filling cell manually in Excel, 278

options in Excel, 278

color variant an option that applies a different set of colors; color variants can be applied to give a theme a variety of looks, 386

column a vertical section of text; Word allows you to divide portions of a document or other file into one or more columns, 130

adjusting, in table to fit text in Word, 150

adjusting width in Excel, 274–275

adjusting width in Word, 150

changing default width settings in Excel, 276

creating, of unequal widths in Word, 131

formatting text in Word, 130–131

inserting and deleting in Excel, 218, 220–221

inserting and deleting in table in Word, 154–157

inserting using Insert Controls in Word, 154

merging in table in Word, 158–159

column chart a chart that is used to compare differences between values; has vertical bars in Excel, 290

adding axis labels, 299

creating, 294–295

column heading a capital letter at the top of a worksheet that identifies the column below it, 200

Comments a reviewing feature in Word that you can use to suggest changes rather than making them directly in the text, 180

adding, 180–183

automatic deletion, 184

deleting, 184

Compare a Word feature that shows the differences between two documents, 183

conditional formatting in Excel, a type of formatting in Excel that highlights specific values within a worksheet, 278

applying, 278–279

control unit (CU) the part of the CPU that directs the operations of the processor, 3

copy to place a duplicate of a selected portion of text or a selected object on the Clipboard so that the duplicated item can be pasted into other locations, 88

COUNT function, 240

CPM, 210

Creative Commons a non-profit organization that provides free legal tools for artists, allowing them to select from a set of copyright licenses to protect their creative works, 408

criteria in Access, one or more conditions that must be met for data to be selected in a query, 348

Currency in Excel, a number format that displays the value in a cell by placing the dollar symbol ($; or other currency symbol) next to the left-most number, using a thousands separator, including two decimal places, and aligning cell amounts by decimal point; offers options for how negative numbers are displayed; in Access, a data type used to store amounts using a dollar sign, comma separator, and two decimal places, 266, 330

current cell. *See active cell*

Custom Slide Show a feature that allows you to define a subset of slides in a PowerPoint file for running as a variation on the longer slide show, 441

Custom web app in Access, a template that can be used to create an online database, 332

accessing and sharing, 312

cut to remove a selected portion of text or a selected object from its current location and place it on the Clipboard so that it can be pasted into a different location, 88

shortcut, 58, 254

D

data

copying and pasting from Word or Excel file into Access table, 337

editing in Access, 318–319

entering in Access, 316–317, 336–337, 342–343

filtering in Access, 322–323

importing, from Excel into Access, 463

pulling, from multiple tables to create query, 356–359

sorting in Access, 320–321

using Excel, to create Access table, 462–463

database in Access

adding records, 336

described, 310

opening and navigating, 314–315

terminology, 310–311

zipped files, 314

data label a chart element that tells the exact value or percentage that each pie slice, bar, or line represents, 298

editing, 297–299

data redundancy the duplication of data; data redundancy should be avoided, 359

data series data used to create a chart, 296

in pie chart, 300

datasheet in Access, a table that organizes data in rows and columns, 310, 324

formatting, 324–325

Datasheet view the view used to enter records in a table in Access, 330

date

entering in Excel, 208

inserting in Word, 82, 96

without year in Excel, 266

Date format in Excel, a format that stores a date as a serial number so that calculations using dates can be performed; Date format options include Short Date (1/7/2018) and Long Date (Sunday, January 7, 2018), 208

Date & Time button in Word, 82, 108

Date/Time in Access, a data type that stores dates and/or times; dates are stored as sequential numbers and can be used to do date-based arithmetic, such as finding the number of days between two dates, 330

Decrease Font Size button a button in the Font group on the Home tab of the ribbon in Microsoft Office applications; you click it to decrease the text size, 67

Decrease List Level button, 427

decrement arrow in Word, 146

definition of word, finding, using Smart Lookup, 54

Delete key, 84

Design Ideas pane in PowerPoint, 410

Design tab in Word, 114

Design view in Access, the view used to design a table; field name, data type, and other properties are specified in Design view, 332

creating query in, 352–355

destination program to insert an object in a file so that the source object and embedded object are independent; any changes you make to the source object in the source program will not affect the embedded object in the destination program, 454, 460

dictionary, adding words, 95

documents

building by formatting with tables, 159

checking spelling and grammar, 92–95

comparing, 183

counting words in, 183

copying current and opening copy in new window, 63

creating, based on template, 96–99

creating PDFs, 192–193

entering and editing text, 82–85

formatting marks, 86–87

inserting properties in header and footer, 111

online sharing space, 189, 190–191

planning, 78–79

saving, 90

sending by email, 188–189

sending to more than one person by email, 190

working with multiple, 63

DOCX the file format for a Word 2016 document, 48

dollar sign ($), creating, 250

E

email

adding picture, 33

opening attachments, 188

sending Word documents and files by, 188–189

sending Word documents and files to more than one person by, 190

separating addresses, 30

embed to insert an object in a file so that the source object and embedded object are independent; any changes you make to the source object in the source program will not affect the embedded object in the destination program, 455

video in PowerPoint, 415

endnote a type of note used in reports and research papers to document or cite the source of information or to add additional information or comments; placed at the end of a document, 134

navigating, 135

Enter key, using, 82

entry the data value for a cell in Excel or a field in Access, 200, 310

equal to (=) operator, 356

error code a code, such as #DIV/0, that displays in a cell when you make an error while entering a formula in Excel, 260

Excel the Microsoft Office spreadsheet application, 40

accessing more border options, 283

adding and editing labels in chart, 297–299

adding axis labels to column chart, 299

adding borders, 280–283

adding borders around cell using Format Painter, 280

adding worksheets, 222

adjusting column width, 274–275

expansion slot a socket in a computer, used to insert expansion cards into your motherboard to add capabilities such as increased processing power and enhanced video and audio, 4

exploded slice to move a pie slice away from the rest of the pie chart to draw attention to that particular slice, 302

export the process of copying a file or data from a source program into a destination application, 454

extract a process in which a compressed file or folder is decompressed; in Access, the process of pulling data from one or more tables, 10

F

field an area of an Access table where a particular type of information is recorded, or a space in an Access database that is allocated for a particular type of data, 310 changing size, 333

moving between, 342

name, 310

using touchscreen to add, to query design grid, 356

field size in Access, the maximum number of characters you can enter in a field, 333

file

closing, 48, 49

creating new, 42–43

creating new shortcut, 42

database zipped in Access, 314

frequency of saving Word, 84

naming, 46

navigating within, 52–53

opening, 46–47

opening shortcut, 46

printing, 68–71

saving, 48–49

saving as, in Access, 46

saving as, in Excel, 46–48

saving in alternative formats, 48

sending by email, 188–189

sending to more than one person by email, 190

shortcut for printing, 68

syncing with OneDrive, 11

updating Access, 309

using File Explorer to access, 16–19

File Explorer

navigating in, 15

using Details view, 16

using Preview view, 16

using to access files and folders, 16–19

Filtered icon, 343

filtering in Access or Excel, a process used to temporarily display only those records or cells that meet a certain condition or conditions, 322

using query versus, 350

Find a Microsoft Office feature that allows you to search for specific characters or formatting, 54

narrowing limits, 57

shortcut, 54

Find and Replace a Microsoft Office feature that allows you to search for specific characters or formatting and replace them with other characters or formatting, 54

shortcuts, 54

using, 54–57

Flash Fill an Excel feature that looks for patterns in data and then automatically enters the rest of the data based on the pattern, 212

using, 215

folders

navigating through, 10–11

setting up working, 12–15

using File Explorer to access, 16–19

font a combination of a typeface (such as Calibri) and other characteristics, including size and style, that defines the appearance of text, 116

default, 66

font effects a command used to add emphasis or set text apart; bold, italic, underlining, and color are common font effects, 118

applying, in Word, 118–119

font family a group of fonts that all share the same name, such as Arial, and come in several variations, such as Arial Bold and Arial Narrow, 116

Font group, 66–67

font size the vertical measurement of a font that is usually measured in a point (pt) size, 116

in inches, 272

selecting, in Word, 116, 117

footer the area at the bottom of a page, slide, or worksheet that you can use to insert text or graphics, such as the date or a company logo, that are to appear on every page, slide, or worksheet in the file, 108

adding, in PowerPoint, 402–403

customizing, in PowerPoint, 402

going to, in Word, 110

inserting, in Excel, 226–227

inserting, in Word, 108–111

inserting document properties in, 111

inserting shortcut, 110

footnote a type of note used in reports and research papers to document or cite the source of information or to add additional information or comments; placed at the bottom of the page, 134

inserting, 134–135

inserting shortcut, 134

navigating, 135

form a database object that provides access to data; usually allows you to view or edit only one record at a time, 311

building by formatting with tables, 159

changing formatting and views, 338

creating in Access, 338–341

entering data in Access, 311, 316–317, 342–343

sorting in Access, 321

format the way a document, presentation, text, or an object appears, 66

using tools, 66–67

Format Painter a Word tool that allows you to copy formatting from one set of text to another, 114, 132

adding borders around cells in Excel, 280

copying formatting with, 132–133

shortcut for copying formatting with, 133

using, multiple times, 133

formatting in Access

changing form, 338

datasheet, 324–325

report based on query, 364–367

formatting in Excel, 270–273

adding borders, 280–283

applying number formats, 266–269

chart area, 303

currency, 210

merging cells, 284–287

pie chart legend, 304–305

using Quick Analysis button, 266

formatting in PowerPoint

individual slides, 426–427

numbers, 376

pictures, 412–413

in Slide Master view, 394–395

speakers notes, 381

formatting in Word, 114

aligning text, 122–123

aligning text with tabs, 123

applying styles, 120–121

applying themes, 121

bolding, 118

changes due to upgrading, 98

copying, using Format Painter, 132–133

copying shortcut using Format Painter, 133

font, 116–117

fractions, 149

italicizing, 118

paragraph and line spacing, 124–125

PDF to Word conversion, after, 193

showing/hiding marks, 86–87

tables, 160

tables using Quick Tables, 149

templates for, 96

text in columns, 130–131

using Quick Analysis button, 164

using tables to build forms and documents, 159

visual media, 172–173

formula text entered in a cell to perform a calculation; always begins with an equals sign (=) and can include cell references, values, and functions, 200, 236

automatic adjustment, 234

entering, 236–239

entering functions in, using *Formula AutoComplete,* 244–245

entering functions in, using Formula Tab, 244–245

entering functions in, using Function button, 242–243

printing worksheet showing, 261

using Show Formulas, 260–261

formula bar the area immediately above the column headings in an Excel worksheet; used to view and edit the contents of the active cell, 200

form view the view used to add or edit a record using a form object in Access, 338, 342

fractions, typing, in Word, 149

freeware, 7

function a predefined calculation that can be inserted into a formula in Excel, 240

changing or adding on Status bar, 246

entering, 240–241

using *Formula AutoComplete,* 244, 245

using Formula Tab, 244, 245

using Function button, 242–243

G

General format default format for a cell entry in Excel, 266

gradient fill used to fill an area such as a slide background and create a three-dimensional look by gradually changing from one color to another, 398

grammar

checking in PowerPoint, 64–65

checking in Word, 64–65, 92–95

greater than (>) operator, 356

greater than or equal to (>=) operator, 356

gridlines intersecting vertical and horizontal guidelines you can display to help you see how objects and text are aligned on a worksheet, page, or slide, 228

in Access, 325

displaying in Word, 100

snapping pictures and objects in PowerPoint, 410

group a way to organize an Access report by causing specified fields with the same value to be grouped together, 314

grouping level in Access, a design option for a report that combines like data from a specified field, 360

H

handle a small box at the corner or side of a selected objects that you can drag to resize the object, 165

using, in Word, 165, 170

using rotation, in Word, 172

handout a printed version of a PowerPoint presentation, 442

printing, 445

hard copy a printout, 228

hard return a command that moves the insertion point to the next line and at the same time creates a new paragraph, 82

hardware the physical parts of a computer, 2

types, 3

header the area at the top of a page, slide, or worksheet that you can use to insert text, such as the document title, or graphics that are to appear on every page, slide, or worksheet in the file, 108

adding date and time to, in Access, 338

automatic updating in Excel, 226

inserting, in Excel, 226–227

inserting, in Word, 108–111

inserting document properties in, 111

inserting shortcut, 110

printing speaker notes in PowerPoint with, 442–445

Help a Microsoft Office feature that allows you to search and browse for information about Office application features, 71

shortcut, 72

using, 72–73

History feature, using, 42

Home tabs

tools in Excel, 66

tools in PowerPoint, 66

tools in Word, 66, 114

horizontal axis the axis along the bottom of a bar, column, or line chart; runs between the left and right areas of the chart, 292

I

IF function, 249

Ignore versus Ignore All, 92, 432

import the process of converting data for use by the destination application, 457

Increase Font Size button a button in the Font group on the Home tab of the ribbon in Microsoft Office applications; you click it to decrease the text size, 67

Increase Indent button, 100

Increase List Level button, 427

increment arrow in Word, 146

indented lists, creating, 427

indent to move text a certain amount of space from the left or right margin; indent settings can be applied to the first line in a paragraph or to an entire paragraph or document, 100

using ruler to, 100–103

information processing cycle hardware and software working together to turn data into information; the four parts of the information processing cycle are input, process, output, and storage, 2

input device a device, such as a mouse, keyboard, microphone, webcam, or touchscreen, that allows you to communicate commands and enter data into your computer, 2, 3

Insert Controls, 154

integrating bringing together two or more application files by copying, pasting, embedding, or linking data or objects, 454

italic a font effect used to add emphasis by slanting the characters evenly toward the right; widely used for book and movie titles, 118

applying, 67

applying, in Word, 118

shortcut, 272

J

justified alignment an alignment that spreads the document text across the line from the left margin to the right, resulting in an even right margin, 122

shortcut, 122

K

keyboard commands. *See* shortcuts

KeyTip a letter displayed with a command on the ribbon of a Microsoft Office application when the Alt key is pressed; KeyTips letters can be pressed in place of clicking a command, 50

L

landscape the page orientation that turns the page sideways so that it is wider than it is tall, 152

LAN (local area network), 5

Layout Options button, 171

layout the arrangement of placeholder elements in a slide, 382

applying, in PowerPoint, 382–383

using Slide Master view to apply changes, 396–397

Layout view in Access, the view used to apply formatting to a form, 330

legend a chart element that describes what each pie slice, bar, or line represents, 292

changing, 299

formatting pie chart, 304–305

less than (<) operator, 356

less than or equal to (<=) operator, 356

licensing agreements, 168

line chart a chart that is used to illustrate changes or trends over time, 290

creating in Excel, 292–293

displaying name, 292

moving part, 292

link to insert an object in a file so that the source object and embedded object are dependent; any changes you make to the source object in the source program will also appear in the embedded object in the destination program, 455

lists

creating bulleted, in Word, 126–129

creating indented, in PowerPoint, 427

creating numbered, in Word, 126–129

logo and worksheet appearance, 197

Long date a date that displays in a spelled-out format such as Sunday, January 8, 2015, 266

Lookup field in Access, displays a list of values from which the user can choose, 332

creating, 334

M

margin an area of white space at the top, bottom, left, or right of a document, 104

adjusting in Access, 366

creating custom in Word, 105

setting in Word, 104–105

Margins button, 105

Match case, 57

MAX function, 240

media

aligning and formatting, in Word, 172–173

inserting, in Word document, 168–169

resizing, in Word, 170–171

meeting request an appointment that is sent to other people in Outlook; can include the meeting location and associated information, such as the meeting topic and goals, 28

memory a device that stores programs and data currently in use; may be permanent (as with read-only memory, or ROM) or temporary (as with random access memory, or RAM), 4

Merge Cells button, 158

merge the process of combining multiple table cells into a single cell, 158

cells, 284–287

microprocessor a central processing unit (CPU), also called a processor; contains an integrated circuit and is located on the motherboard; processes your requests, 3, 4

MIN function, 240

MLA (Modern Language Association a professional style used for citations detailed in the *MLA Handbook for Writers of Research Papers* and one of the built-in styles you can apply to references in Word, 136

publications using, 141

mobile computer a portable compute such as a smartphone, tablet, laptop, e-reader, or gaming device, 2

modem the hardware that sends and receives data to or from a transmissio source, such as a phone or cable line; types of modems include cable, DSL, and satellite, 5

motherboard the main circuit board in the computer; composed of a thin sheet of fiberglass or other material with electrical pathways that connect key components of hardware, including the microprocessor/CPU, memory, and expansion slots, 4

motion path animations in PowerPoint, 422

move a technique used on a touchscreen in which the user presses an image or text area and drags it from one part of the screen to another; also to cut a selection or object from its current location and then paste it in a different destination location, 8, 88

N

Name box a worksheet element that displays the cell address of the active cell; used to navigate to a specific cell or cell range, 200, 204

naming

customized slide show, 441

file, 46

narration a recorded audio track saved with a PowerPoint presentation; can replace a live speaker in a setting where the presentation is run without a speaker present, 439

recording, 439

Navigation bar a grouping located at the bottom of the Outlook window; contains buttons used to switch between Outlook views, 22

customizing, 22